GRASSROOTS
with Readings

As part of Houghton Mifflin's ongoing commitment to the environment, this text has been printed on recycled paper.

GRASSROOTS
with Readings

THE WRITER'S WORKBOOK

Fifth Edition

Susan Fawcett

Alvin Sandberg

HOUGHTON MIFFLIN COMPANY   Boston   Toronto

Geneva, Illinois   Palo Alto   Princeton, New Jersey

Cover design by Len Massiglia.

Cover image by Gabor Perdi, *The Big Wetland, I*, 1983. Oil on canvas, 60" × 80". Collection of the Metropolitan Museum of Art, New York, New York.

Sponsoring Editor: Mary Jo Southern
Senior Basic Book Editor: Martha Bustin
Senior Project Editor: Cathy Labresh Brooks
Production/Design Coordinator: Sarah Ambrose
Manufacturing Coordinator: Priscilla Bailey
Marketing Manager: George Kane

Acknowledgments appear on p. 505.

Copyright © 1994 by Houghton Mifflin Company. All rights reserved.

No part of this work may be reproduced or transmitted in any form or by any means, electronic or mechanical, including photocopying and recording, or by any information storage or retrieval system without the prior written permission of Houghton Mifflin Company unless such copying is expressly permitted by federal copyright law. Address inquiries to College Permissions, Houghton Mifflin Company, 222 Berkeley Street, Boston, MA 02116-3764.

Printed in the U.S.A.

Student's Edition ISBN: 0-395-66109-9

Instructor's Annotated Edition ISBN: 0-395-66851-4

4 5 6 7 8 9-WC-97 96

Contents

Preface   *xiii*

UNIT 1   The Process of Writing Paragraphs   *1*

1   Getting Started   *3*

Part A   Freewriting   *4*
Part B   Brainstorming   *6*
Part C   Clustering   *7*
Part D   Keeping a Journal   *9*
Chapter Highlights   *10*

2   Writing Effective Paragraphs   *11*

Part A   Defining the Paragraph and the Topic Sentence   *11*
Part B   Limiting the Topic and Writing the Topic Sentence   *14*
Part C   Developing Ideas for the Body   *18*
Part D   Selecting and Dropping Ideas   *21*
Part E   Grouping Ideas in a Plan   *22*
Part F   Writing and Revising the Paragraph   *23*
Part G   Writing the Final Draft   *28*
Chapter Highlights   *32*

3   Improving the Paragraph   *33*

Part A   More Work on Developing the Body: Examples   *33*
Part B   More Work on Grouping Ideas: Coherence   *36*
Part C   Turning Assignments into Paragraphs   *41*
Chapter Highlights   *43*

Unit 1   Writing Assignments   *44*
Unit 1   Review   *45*

UNIT 2   The Complete Sentence   *49*

4   Subjects and Verbs   *51*

Part A   Defining and Spotting Subjects   *51*
Part B   Spotting Singular and Plural Subjects   *54*
Part C   Spotting Prepositional Phrases   *56*
Part D   Defining and Spotting Action Verbs   *58*
Part E   Defining and Spotting Linking Verbs   *60*
Part F   Spotting Verbs of More Than One Word   *61*
Chapter Highlights   *64*
Chapter Review   *64*

5 Avoiding Sentence Fragments 66

 Part A Writing Sentences with Subjects and Verbs 66
 Part B Writing Sentences with Complete Verbs 68
 Part C Completing the Thought 72
 Chapter Highlights 76
 Chapter Review 76

Unit 2 Writing Assignments 78
Unit 2 Review 79

UNIT 3 Verbs *81*

6 Present Tense (Agreement) 83

 Part A Defining Agreement 83
 Part B Troublesome Verb in the Present Tense: TO BE 86
 Part C Troublesome Verb in the Present Tense: TO HAVE 88
 Part D Troublesome Verb in the Present Tense: TO DO (+ NOT) 90
 Part E Changing Subjects to Pronouns 93
 Part F Practice in Agreement 95
 Part G Special Problems in Agreement 99
 Chapter Highlights 108
 Chapter Review 108

7 Past Tense 110

 Part A Regular Verbs in the Past Tense 110
 Part B Irregular Verbs in the Past Tense 114
 Part C Troublesome Verb in the Past Tense: TO BE 118
 Part D Review 120
 Chapter Highlights 122
 Chapter Review 122

8 The Past Participle in Action 124

 Part A Defining the Past Participle 124
 Part B Past Participles of Regular Verbs 125
 Part C Past Participles of Irregular Verbs 128
 Part D Using the Present Perfect Tense 136
 Part E Using the Past Perfect Tense 138
 Part F Using the Passive Voice 140
 Part G Using Past Participles as Adjectives 144
 Chapter Highlights 149
 Chapter Review 150

9 Progressive Tenses (TO BE + -ING Verb Form) 151

 Part A Defining and Writing the Present Progressive Tense 151
 Part B Defining and Writing the Past Progressive Tense 154

Contents **vii**

    Part C Using the Progressive Tenses *156*
    Part D Avoiding Incomplete Progressives *158*
    Chapter Highlights *159*
    Chapter Review *160*

10 Fixed-Form Helping Verbs and Verb Problems *161*

    Part A Defining and Spotting the Fixed-Form Helping Verbs *161*
    Part B Using the Fixed-Form Helping Verbs *162*
    Part C Using CAN and COULD *164*
    Part D Using WILL and WOULD *166*
    Part E Writing Infinitives *167*
    Part F Revising Double Negatives *170*
    Chapter Highlights *172*
    Chapter Review *172*

Unit 3 **Writing Assignments** *174*
Unit 3 **Review** *175*

UNIT 4 Joining Ideas Together *179*

11 Coordination *181*

    Chapter Highlights *186*
    Chapter Review *186*

12 Subordination *187*

    Part A Defining and Using Subordinating Conjunctions *187*
    Part B Punctuating Subordinating Conjunctions *191*
    Chapter Highlights *195*
    Chapter Review *196*

13 Avoiding Run-ons and Comma Splices *197*

    Chapter Highlights *202*
    Chapter Review *202*

14 Semicolons *206*

    Chapter Highlights *209*
    Chapter Review *210*

15 Conjunctive Adverbs *211*

    Part A Defining and Using Conjunctive Adverbs *211*
    Part B Punctuating Conjunctive Adverbs *214*
    Chapter Highlights *217*
    Chapter Review *217*

16 Relative Pronouns 218

Part A   Defining and Using Relative Pronouns   218
Part B   Punctuating Ideas Introduced by WHO, WHICH, or THAT   221
Chapter Highlights   224
Chapter Review   224

17 -ING Modifiers 226

Part A   Using -ING Modifiers   226
Part B   Avoiding Confusing Modifiers   228
Chapter Highlights   230
Chapter Review   230

Unit 4   Writing Assignments   232
Unit 4   Review   233

UNIT 5   Nouns, Pronouns, Adjectives, Adverbs, and Prepositions 239

18 Nouns 241

Part A   Defining Singular and Plural   241
Part B   Signal Words: Singular and Plural   244
Part C   Signal Words with OF   246
Chapter Highlights   248
Chapter Review   248

19 Pronouns 250

Part A   Defining Pronouns and Antecedents   250
Part B   Referring to Indefinite Pronouns   253
Part C   Referring to Collective Nouns   256
Part D   Referring to Special Singular Constructions   259
Part E   Avoiding Vague and Repetitious Pronouns   261
Part F   Using Pronouns as Subjects, Objects, and Possessives   263
Part G   Choosing the Correct Case after AND or OR   266
Part H   Choosing the Correct Case in Comparisons   268
Part I   Using Pronouns with -SELF and -SELVES   271
Chapter Highlights   273
Chapter Review   273

20 Adjectives and Adverbs 275

Part A   Defining and Writing Adjectives and Adverbs   275
Part B   A Troublesome Pair: GOOD/WELL   279
Part C   Writing Comparatives   280
Part D   Writing Superlatives   283

Contents ix

      Part E   Troublesome Comparatives and Superlatives   *285*
      Part F   Demonstrative Adjectives: THIS/THAT and THESE/THOSE   *286*
      Chapter Highlights   *288*
      Chapter Review   *288*

21 Prepositions *290*

      Part A   Defining Prepositions   *290*
      Part B   Troublesome Prepositions   *292*
      Part C   Words Requiring Certain Prepositions   *294*
      Chapter Highlights   *298*
      Chapter Review   *298*

Unit 5 Writing Assignments *300*
Unit 5 Review *301*

UNIT 6 Consistency and Parallelism *305*

22 Consistent Tense *307*

      Chapter Highlights   *309*
      Chapter Review   *309*

23 Consistent Person *312*

      Chapter Highlights   *314*
      Chapter Review   *314*

24 Parallelism *316*

      Part A   Defining and Writing Parallels   *316*
      Part B   Using Parallelism for Special Writing Effects   *321*
      Chapter Highlights   *322*
      Chapter Review   *323*

Unit 6 Writing Assignments *324*
Unit 6 Review *325*

UNIT 7 Mechanics *327*

25 Beginning and Ending Sentences *329*

      Chapter Highlights   *331*
      Chapter Review   *331*

26 Capitalization *332*

Chapter Highlights   336
Chapter Review   336

27 Commas *339*

Part A Commas after Items in a Series   340
Part B Commas after Introductory Phrases   341
Part C Commas for Direct Address   343
Part D Commas to Set Off Appositives   344
Part E Commas for Parenthetical Expressions   345
Part F Commas for Dates   346
Part G Commas for Addresses   347
Part H Commas for Coordination and Subordination   349

Chapter Highlights   351
Chapter Review   351

28 Apostrophes *353*

Part A Using the Apostrophe for Contractions   353
Part B Defining the Possessive   355
Part C Using the Apostrophe to Show Possession (in Words That Do Not Already End in -S)   355
Part D Using the Apostrophe to Show Possession (in Words That Already End in -S)   357

Chapter Highlights   360
Chapter Review   361

29 Direct and Indirect Quotations *362*

Part A Defining Direct and Indirect Quotations   362
Part B Punctuating Simple Direct Quotations   363
Part C Punctuating Split Quotations   364
Part D Ending Direct Quotations   366

Chapter Highlights   368
Chapter Review   368

Unit 7 Writing Assignments   370
Unit 7 Review   371

UNIT 8 Improving Spelling *373*

30 Spelling *375*

Part A Suggestions for Improving Your Spelling   375
Part B Spotting Vowels and Consonants   376

        Part C   Doubling the Final Consonant (in Words of One Syllable)   *377*
        Part D   Doubling the Final Consonant (in Words of More Than One Syllable)   *379*
        Part E   Dropping or Keeping the Final *E*   *381*
        Part F   Changing or Keeping the Final *Y*   *382*
        Part G   Adding *-S* or *-ES*   *384*
        Part H   Choosing *IE* or *EI*   *385*
        Part I   Review   *387*
    Chapter Highlights   *389*
    Chapter Review   *389*
    Personal Spelling Lists   *390*

31 Look-alikes/Sound-alikes   *392*

    Chapter Highlights   *424*
    Chapter Review   *425*

Unit 8 Writing Assignments   *428*
Unit 8 Review   *429*

Appendix: Parts of Speech Review   *431*

UNIT 9 Reading Selections and Quotation Bank   *435*

Reading Selections   *437*

Introduction*   *Effective Reading: Strategies for the Writer*   *437

Ellen Goodman, "Women Are Missing from Newspaper Pages" [with sample student annotations]   *438*
Malcolm X, "A Homemade Education"   *441*
Maya Angelou, "Mrs. Flowers"   *444*
Leo Buscaglia, "Papa, the Teacher"   *448*
Anna Quindlen, "Homeless"   *452*
Joseph T. Martorano/John P. Kildahl, "Say Yes to Yourself"   *454*
Julia Alvarez, "Yolanda"   *458*
Peter Gzowski, "People and Their Machines and Vice Versa"   *460*
Courtland Milloy, "The Gift"   *462*
Langston Hughes, "Salvation"   *465*
Francine Klagsbrun, "Forever"   *468*
Dave Barry, "Sports Nuts"   *471*
Tim Giago, "I Hope the Redskins Lose"   *474*
Edward Abbey, "Desert Kin"   *477*
Barbara Garson, "Perfume"   *481*
Ann Lovejoy, "Friends of Dirt, Unite!"   *484*

Sherwood Anderson, "Discovery of a Father" 486
Amy Tan, "Four Directions" 491
Ana Veciana-Suarez, "For a Parent, There's No Language Dilemma" 494

Quotation Bank *499*

Acknowledgments *505*
Index *506*
Index to the Readings *510*

Preface

Grassroots with Readings combines in one book the new Fifth Edition of our widely used basic writing text *Grassroots* with eighteen high-interest reading selections. *Grassroots*, which grew out of our classroom experience at Bronx Community College of the City University of New York, is designed for students who have not yet mastered the basic writing skills necessary for success in college and in many careers. Through clear, paced lessons and a variety of engaging practices and writing assignments, *Grassroots* has helped hundreds of thousands of students to write better.

Now instructors who wish to incorporate reading in their basic writing classes may choose from a diverse group of readings, selected with an eye to engaging subject matter, stylistic excellence, and racial and gender balance. Authors include Amy Tan, Malcolm X, Julia Alvarez, Maya Angelou, Sherwood Anderson, Anna Quindlen, Dave Barry, Tim Giago, and others. Each selection is accompanied by a headnote, vocabulary glosses, comprehension questions, and writing assignments.

We are proud of this Fifth Edition, which has been further strengthened by the addition of several new features.

Features of the Fifth Edition

- **Eighteen Reading Selections.** These essays, articles, and two fictional pieces range in length from one to four pages. They represent a variety of authors, subjects, and styles. An introduction contains tips for effective reading and a sample essay with student annotations; each reading selection is followed by four reading comprehension questions and three writing assignments.

- **New Continuous Discourses, Paragraphs, and Essays for Proofreading.** We have replaced a number of practice sets, adding more of the high-interest continuous discourses (sequential sentences developing one topic), paragraphs, and essays so popular in the fourth edition. New topics include celebrity addiction and recovery, black filmmakers, pilot Beryl Markham, psychic crime solvers, rap music, hurricanes, and Revolutionary War soldier Deborah Sampson. These exercises, multicultural in range, sustain interest as students apply the concepts learned in each part, chapter, and unit.

- **New Practices in Key Problem Areas.** Paragraph-length practices have been added to lessons on special problems such as verb agreement and sentence fragments.

- **Newly Organized Unit 1, The Process of Writing Paragraphs.** This unit now combines all writing instruction at the beginning of the text, thus emphasizing writing as the context for grammar work. The idea that the topic sentence controls the content of a paragraph is explained in greater detail.

- **Expanded Prewriting Material.** Clustering has been added to the prewriting techniques in Chapter 1, "Getting Started," and the section on keeping a journal now includes many specific suggestions and writing ideas.
- **Quotation Bank.** This new feature consists of witty, wise, and provocative quotations from a wide range of authors. These quotations on topics such as writing, learning, work and success, love, and wisdom for living, can inspire or support students' writing, stimulate class discussions, or simply provide enjoyable reading.

Organization of the Text

The range of materials and flexible format of *Grassroots with Readings* make this worktext adaptable to almost any teaching/learning situation: classroom, laboratory, or self-teaching. Each chapter is a self-contained lesson. A student needing work in just three or four areas can go straight to the chapters tailored to his or her needs, or instructors may teach the chapters in any sequence that fits their course designs. Since most instructors find that they cannot cover all the material in the text in one term, they assign only those chapters that their classes need.

Acknowledgments

We wish to thank the following people whose thoughtful comments and suggestions helped us develop the Fifth Edition: Chandler Clifton, Edmonds Community College, Lynwood, WA; Genetha Hollingsworth, Indiana Vocational Technical College, Gary, IN; Kathleen Jacquette, SUNY Farmingdale, NY; Diane Janowiak, Prairie State College, Park Forest, IL; Kamal Kapur, Grassmont College, San Diego, CA; Sandra Kelley-Daniel, Kapiolani Community College, Kailua, HI; Mary Ann Merz, Oklahoma City Community College, Norman, OK; Linda Whisnant, Guilford Technical Community College, MA.

Susan Fawcett thanks her husband, Richard Donovan, for loving her even when she is wedded to her computer, for making her laugh every day, and for his example of life-long dedication to students: his own and, through the Urban Partnership Program, students all over the country who make up in hard work for what they may lack in privilege.

Alvin Sandberg is especially grateful to Marilyn Weissman, whose writing, editing, and proofreading skills added much to this fine revision. Special thanks to Beth and Miriam for their love and support.

Most of all, the two of us thank our students, who inspired us to write this book.

Susan Fawcett and Alvin Sandberg

GRASSROOTS
with Readings

UNIT 1

The Process of Writing Paragraphs

Chapter 1

Getting Started

PART A Freewriting
PART B Brainstorming
PART C Clustering
PART D Keeping a Journal

One of the authors of this book used to teach ice skating. On the first day of class, the students practiced falling down. Once they knew how to fall without fear, they were free to learn to skate.

Writing is much like ice skating: The more you practice, the better you get. If you are free to make mistakes, you'll want to practice, and you'll look forward to new writing challenges.

The problem is that many people avoid writing. Faced with an English composition or a report at work, they put it off and then scribble something at the last minute. Or they sit staring at that blank page—writing a sentence, crossing it out, unable to get started.

Grassroots will guide you step by step through the basics of good writing—the writing process, grammar, punctuation, and spelling. But this chapter will cover what for many people is the hardest part, just getting started. Four techniques to help you loosen up and get started are *freewriting, brainstorming, clustering,* and *keeping a journal.*

Unit 1 The Process of Writing Paragraphs

PART A Freewriting

Freewriting is a method many writers use to warm up and get ideas onto paper. Here are the guidelines: For five or ten full minutes, write without stopping about anything that comes into your head. Don't worry about grammar or about writing complete sentences; just set a timer and go. If you get stuck, repeat or rhyme the last word you wrote, but *keep writing nonstop until the timer sounds.*

Afterward, read what you have written, and underline any parts you like.

Here is one student's first freewriting, with her underlinings:

> Freewrite free without stopping hopping popping pills and Mark in trouble <u>the more he messes up, the harder I work</u>, explain that. Go to school, work nights, study late, no privacy, no sleep, no fun fun fun. This is fast alright and I'm getting lost cost coasting on my pen I never wrote before without bending my brain for hours first this doesn't feel like writing it feels like flying or a fast car at night, no—like something quick and quiet except for the sound of all these pens maybe 30 pens on paper what a weird noise scratch scratch hiss hiss and sleeves, <u>left handed sleeves dragging in the ink</u> sink pink skies and blue sounds. <u>Fast ink is a blue sound, the sea is a blue sound.</u>

- This example has the vital energy of many freewritings.
- Why do you think the student underlined what she did?
- Would you have underlined any other words or phrases? Why?

_____

_____

Freewriting is a wonderful way to let ideas pour onto paper *without getting stuck* by worrying too soon about correctness or "good writing." Sometimes freewriting produces nonsense, but often it provides interesting ideas for further thinking and writing.

Practice 1

1. Set a timer for ten minutes, or have someone time you. Freewrite without stopping for the full ten minutes. Repeat or rhyme words if you get stuck, but *keep writing!* Don't let your pen or pencil leave the page.

2. When you finish, write down one or two words that describe how you felt while freewriting. _____

3. Now read your freewriting. Underline any words or lines you like—anything that strikes you as powerful, moving, funny, or important. If nothing strikes you, that's okay.

Practice 2 Try two more freewritings at home, each one ten minutes long. Do them at different times of the day when you have a few quiet moments. If possible, use a timer; set it for ten minutes, and then write fast until it rings. Later, read your freewritings, and underline any striking lines or ideas.

Focused Freewriting

In *focused freewriting,* just try to focus your thoughts on one subject as you freewrite. The subject can be one assigned by your instructor, one you choose, or one you have discovered in unfocused freewriting.

Here is one student's focused freewriting on the topic *someone who strongly influenced you.*

> Queen, queen of the feathery sofa where we are not allowed to sit, so clean, the gleaming Tiffany lamp, the elegance, the smoke that chokes me. Puff puff, red nails, puffing away at her eternal cigarette she calls herself the master of the house and threatens me without a word. I sit on a bridge chair afraid to look her way. Her seersucker robe is exactly like mine her hair is like mine and her eyes are as blue but she weighs 10 pounds less she fits into jeans I threw away and loves it loves. We are so alike, Amy, she says popping grapes into her mouth and drinking wine. Laurel leaves of success should have been on her head but instead I have found them on mine.
>
> AMY ADLER, STUDENT

- This student later used her freewriting as the basis for an excellent paragraph.
- Underline any words or lines that you find especially striking or powerful. Be prepared to discuss your choices.
- Can you guess the relationship between the writer and the woman she describes?

Practice 1 Read over your earlier freewritings, and notice your underlinings. Do you find any words or ideas that you would like to write more about? List two or three of them here:

_____

_____

Practice 2 Now choose one word or idea. Focus your thoughts on it, and do a ten-minute focused freewriting. Try to stick to the topic, but don't worry too much about it. Just keep writing! When you finish, read and underline as usual.

To inspire you, consider these words and ideas:

1. someone who strongly influenced you
2. your experiences with writing
3. blue
4. illness
5. winning
6. beach
7. child
8. a dream

PART B Brainstorming

Brainstorming means freely jotting ideas about a topic. As in freewriting, the purpose of brainstorming is to get as many ideas as possible onto paper, so you will have something to work with later. Just write down everything that comes to mind about a topic—words and phrases, ideas, details, examples, little stories. Once you have brainstormed, read over your list, underlining any ideas you might want to develop further.

Here is one student's brainstorming list on *an interesting job*:

> midtown messenger
>
> frustrating but free
>
> I know the city backwards and forwards
>
> good bike needed
>
> fast, ever-changing, dangerous
>
> drivers hate messengers—we dart in and out of traffic
>
> old clothes don't get respect
>
> I wear the best Descent racing gear, a Giro helmet
>
> people respect you more
>
> I got tipped $100 for carrying a crystal vase from the showroom to Wall Street in 15 minutes
>
> other times I get stiffed
>
> lessons I've learned—controlling my temper
>
> having dignity
>
> staying calm no matter what—insane drivers, deadlines, rudeness
>
> weirdly, I like my job

As he brainstormed, this writer produced many interesting facts and details about his job as a bicycle messenger, all in just a few minutes. He might want to underline the ideas that most interest him—perhaps the time he was tipped $100—and then brainstorm again for more details.

Practice Choose one of the following topics that interests you, and write it at the top of your paper. Then brainstorm! Write anything that comes into your head about the topic. Let your ideas flow.

1. the best/worst class I've had
2. making a difference
3. a place to which I never want to return
4. computers
5. the future
6. an interesting job

Once you fill a page with your list, read it over, underlining the most interesting ideas. Draw arrows to connect related ideas. Do you find one idea that might be the subject of a paper?

PART C Clustering

Some writers find *clustering* or *mapping* an effective way to get ideas on paper. To begin clustering, write one idea or topic—usually one word—in the center of your paper. Then let your mind make associations, and write these ideas down, branching out from the center, like this:

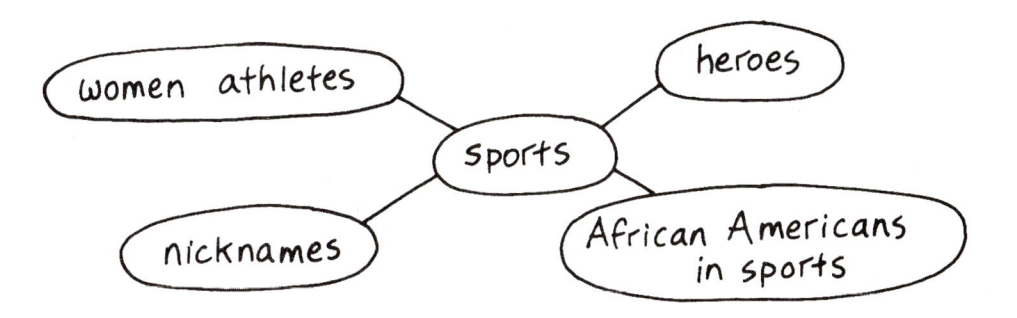

```
   women athletes              heroes
              \               /
               sports
              /               \
       nicknames        African Americans
                            in sports
```

When one idea suggests other ideas, details, or examples, jot these around it in a cluster. Once you finish, pick the cluster that most interests you, and write further. You might want to freewrite for more ideas.

Unit 1 The Process of Writing Paragraphs

- **Sports**
  - **women athletes**
    - taken more seriously now
      - track, tennis
  - **heroes**
    - What is a hero?
      - big $? skill? admirable values?
    - Magic Johnson
      - Do heroes make mistakes?
        - drugs
  - **African Americans in sports**
    - baseball
      - Jackie Robinson, first in majors
        - Larry Doby, first in American League
          - progress
            - more managers and coaches needed
  - **nicknames**
    - Refrigerator
    - Clyde the Glide Drexler
    - Lady Magic
    - way names relate to qualities, skills, body type
      - audience loves names, fun to shout
      - Neon Deion Sanders, blazing with gold jewelry
      - Carl Malone, the Mailman. He always delivers
        - Xavier McDaniel, the Xman

Practice Choose one of these topics or another topic that interests you. Write it in the center of a piece of paper and then try clustering. Keep writing down associations until you have filled most of the page.

1. sports
2. a villain
3. a lesson
4. my hometown
5. self-esteem
6. the good student

PART D Keeping a Journal

Keeping a journal is an excellent way to practice your writing skills, and a journal can be a gold mine of writing ideas. Set aside a section of your notebook, or get yourself a special book with $8\frac{1}{2}$-by-11-inch lined paper. Every night, or several times a week, write for at least ten minutes in your journal.

What you write about will be limited only by your imagination. Here are some ideas:

- Write in detail about things that matter to you—family relationships, falling in (or out) of love, an experience at school or work, something important you just learned, something you did well.

- List your personal goals, and brainstorm possible steps toward achieving them.

- Write about problems you are having, and "think on paper" about ways to solve them.

- Comment on classroom instruction or assignments, and evaluate your learning progress. What needs work? What questions do you need to ask? Write out a study plan for yourself and refer to it regularly.

- Write down your responses to your reading—class assignments, newspaper items, magazine articles that impress or anger you.

- Read through the quotations in the back of the book until you come to one that strikes you. Copy it into your journal, think about it, and write your thoughts and responses.

- Be alert to interesting writing topics all around you. If possible, carry a notebook during the day for "fast sketches." Jot down moving or funny moments, people or things that catch your attention—a homeless person in your neighborhood, a scene at the day-care center where you leave your child, a man trying to persuade an officer not to give him a parking ticket.

You will soon find that writing ideas will occur to you all day long. Before they slip away, capture them in words.

And don't forget to reread what you have written. Do this once a week or so, underlining interesting topics and good writing, putting a check beside ideas you might like to write more about.

Practice Get an $8\frac{1}{2}$-by-11-inch looseleaf notebook for your journal. Write in it for at least ten minutes three times a week.

At the end of each week, read what you have written. Underline striking passages, and put a check beside interesting topics and ideas that you would like to write more about.

As you complete the exercises in this book and work on the writing assignments, try all four techniques—freewriting, brainstorming, clustering, and keeping a journal—and see which ones work best for you.

Chapter Highlights

To get started and to discover your ideas, try these techniques.

- **Freewriting:** writing for five or ten minutes about anything that comes into your head

- **Focused freewriting:** freewriting for five or ten minutes about one topic

- **Brainstorming:** freely jotting many ideas about a topic

- **Clustering:** making word associations on paper

- **Keeping a journal:** writing regularly about things that interest and move you

Chapter 2

Writing Effective Paragraphs

PART A   Defining the Paragraph and the Topic Sentence
PART B   Limiting the Topic and Writing the Topic Sentence
PART C   Developing Ideas for the Body
PART D   Selecting and Dropping Ideas
PART E   Grouping Ideas in a Plan
PART F   Writing and Revising the Paragraph
PART G   Writing the Final Draft

The paragraph is the basic unit of writing. This chapter will guide you through the process of writing paragraphs.

PART A   Defining the Paragraph and the Topic Sentence

A *paragraph* is a group of related sentences that develops one main idea.
    Although a paragraph has no definite length, it is often four to eight sentences long. A paragraph usually occurs with other paragraphs as

part of a longer piece of writing—an essay or a letter, for example. A paragraph looks like the following example.

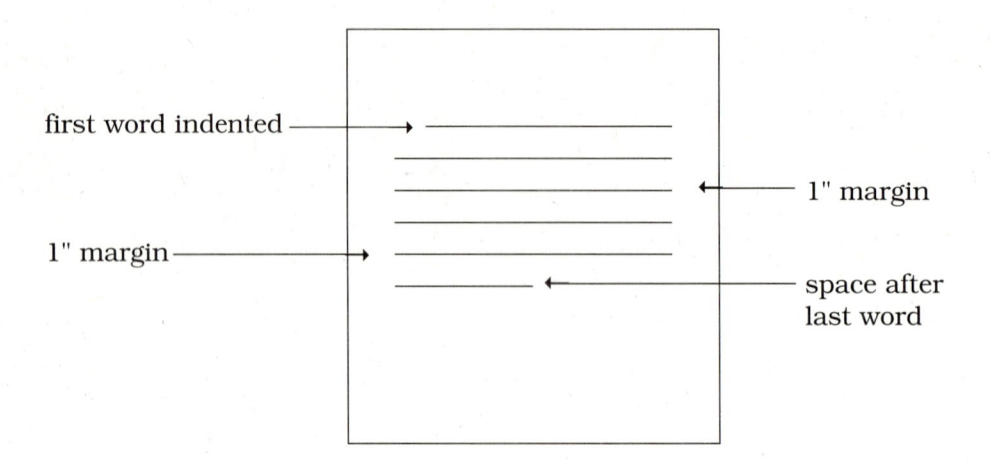

- first word indented
- 1" margin
- 1" margin
- space after last word

- Clearly *indent* the first word of every paragraph about one-half inch or five spaces on the keyboard.
- Extend every line of a paragraph to the right-hand margin.
- However, if the last word of the paragraph comes before the end of the line, leave the rest of the line blank.

Topic Sentence and Body

Most paragraphs contain one main idea to which all the sentences relate. The *topic sentence* states this main idea. The body explains this main idea with specific details, facts, and examples.

> When I was growing up, my older brother Joe was the greatest person in my world. If anyone teased me about my braces or buckteeth, he fiercely defended me. When one boy insisted on calling me "Fang," Joe threatened to knock his teeth out. It worked—no more teasing. My brother always chose me to play on his baseball teams though I was a terrible hitter. Even after he got his driver's license, he didn't abandon me. Instead, every Sunday, the two of us went for a drive. We might stop for cheeseburgers, go to a computer showroom, drive past some girl's house, or just laugh and talk. It was one of childhood's mysteries that such a wonderful brother loved me.

- The first sentence of this paragraph is the *topic sentence.* It states in a general way the main idea of the paragraph: that *Joe was the greatest person in my world.* Although the topic sentence can appear anywhere in the paragraph, it is usually the first sentence.

- The rest of the paragraph, the *body,* fully explains this statement with details about braces and buckteeth, baseball teams, Sunday drives, cheeseburgers, and so forth.

Practice Each group of sentences below can be arranged and written as a paragraph. Circle the letter of the sentence that would be the best topic sentence. REMEMBER: The topic sentence states the main idea of the entire paragraph and includes all the other ideas.

Example: a. Exercise is part of my daily routine.

(b.) Staying healthy and fit is important to me.

c. I get a good night's sleep.

d. I eat as many fresh fruits and vegetables as possible.

(Sentence [b] is more general than the other sentences; it would be the best topic sentence.)

1. a. My father looks handsome in his old-fashioned top hat and tails.

   b. My mother is seated before him wearing a lacy gown.

   c. I will always treasure this wedding picture of my parents.

   d. In the background are velvet drapes and a spiral staircase.

2. a. Many old toys and household objects are now collectors' items.

   b. A Barbie or Madame Alexander doll from the 1950s can bring more than $1,000.

   c. Old baseball cards are worth money to collectors.

   d. Fiesta china, made in the 1930s, has become popular again.

3. a. I made my husband an oak desk with space for his computer.

   b. My son's toy chest was my first project.

   c. For ten years, I have been building furniture as a hobby.

   d. I will soon finish a new living room coffee table.

4. a. Shut off the current.

   b. Connect the new switch to the wires in the wall.

   c. Replacing a wall switch is not difficult.

   d. Unscrew the switch plate.

   e. Pull the old switch from the wall.

5. a. Horses are available for day trips.

   b. There are many scenic hiking trails.

   c. The Sierra Nevada mountains are a challenge to rock climbers.

   d. Yosemite National Park offers a variety of activities to the visitor.

   e. Those who like to fish can cast for trout in Yosemite's lakes and rivers.

PART B Limiting the Topic and Writing the Topic Sentence

The rest of this chapter will guide you through the process of writing paragraphs of your own. Here are the steps we will discuss:

1. Limiting the topic and writing the topic sentence
2. Developing ideas for the body
3. Selecting and dropping ideas
4. Grouping ideas in a plan
5. Writing and revising the paragraph
6. Writing the final draft

Limiting the Topic

Often your first step as a writer will be *limiting* a broad topic—one assigned by your instructor, one you have thought of yourself, or one suggested by a particular writing task, like a letter. That is, you must cut the topic down to size and choose one aspect that interests you.

Assume, for example, that you are asked to write a paragraph describing a person you know. The trick is to choose someone you would *like* to write about, someone who interests you and would probably also interest your readers.

At this point, many writers find it helpful to think on paper by *brainstorming, freewriting* or *clustering.** As you jot or freely write ideas, ask yourself questions. Whom do I love, hate, or admire? Who is the funniest or most unusual person I know? Is there a family member about whom others might like to read?

Suppose you choose to write about your friend Beverly. Beverly is too broad a topic for one paragraph. Therefore, you should limit your topic further, choosing just one of her qualities or acts. What is unusual about her? What might interest others? Perhaps what stands out in your mind is that Beverly is a determined person who doesn't let difficulties defeat her. You have now *limited* your broad topic to just *Beverly's determination.*

Writing the Topic Sentence

The topic sentence states your complete and limited topic in sentence form. It establishes the point that the rest of your paragraph supports and explains. The topic sentence can be quite simple (*Beverly is a determined person*) or, better yet, it can convey your attitude or idea about your topic (*Beverly inspires admiration because she is so determined*). In either case, the topic sentence determines the direction and content of your paragraph.

As the second sentence about Beverly shows, a good topic sentence does more than just announce the topic; it answers the question, "So what?" It tells why the topic is significant. Good topic sentences assert an interesting opinion or idea about the topic. They make an engaging point that is neither too broad nor too narrow to be conveniently supported in a paragraph. As a rule, the more *specific* and well defined the topic sentence, the better the paragraph. Which of these topic sentences do you think will produce the better paragraph?

> (1) My recent trip to Colorado was really bad.
>
> (2) My recent trip to Colorado was disappointing because the weather ruined my camping plans.

- Topic sentence (1) is so broad that the paragraph could include almost anything.
- Topic sentence (2), on the other hand, is specific enough to provide the main idea for a good paragraph: how terrible weather ruined the writer's camping plans.

At this point, it is best and safest to place your topic sentence at the beginning of the paragraph. When it is placed first, the topic sentence clearly establishes—for both you and your reader—the paragraph's focus. Placed first, the topic sentence helps to keep the paragraph organized and unified. All that follows it in the rest of the paragraph will develop and support that initial topic sentence. (If necessary, you can later revise

---

*Brainstorming is discussed further in Part C. Also see Chapter 1 for more information about brainstorming, freewriting, and clustering.

your topic sentence so that it accurately matches the body of the paragraph you have written.) With the topic sentence first, the reader knows immediately what you intend to say.

After you have mastered this pattern, you can try variations. Sometimes the topic sentence appears last, for example. Wherever it appears, the topic sentence controls what goes into the paragraph. All other sentences must relate to it and support it with specific facts, details, examples, arguments, and explanations.

In forming your topic sentence, do not begin, *This paragraph will be about . . .* or *I am going to write about . . .* These extra words say the obvious and contribute nothing. Instead, state your topic directly. Make every word in your topic sentence count.

Practice 1 Put a checkmark beside each topic sentence that is specific enough to write a good paragraph about. If you think a topic sentence is too broad, limit the topic according to your own interests, and then write a new, specific topic sentence.

Examples: ___✓___ Owning a computer has improved my writing in three ways.

Rewrite: _____

_____ I am going to write about my family.

Rewrite: *My mother finds gardening a creative and financially rewarding hobby.*

1. _____ Working as a mechanic was the best job I ever had.

    Rewrite: _____

    _____

2. _____ Children are really something.

    Rewrite: _____

    _____

3. _____ Living in a one-room apartment forces a person to be organized.

    Rewrite: _____

    _____

4. _____ This paragraph will discuss music.

    Rewrite: _____

    _____

5. _____ Some things about college have been great.

Rewrite: _____

_____

6. _____ It is hard to change many of the attitudes about food that we learn as children.

Rewrite: _____

_____

7. _____ Lana's tendency to spend too much time on the phone is a problem in the office.

Rewrite: _____

_____

8. _____ Single parents have a hard time.

Rewrite: _____

_____

Practice 2 Here is a list of broad topics. Choose *three* that interest you; then narrow each topic and write a specific topic sentence.

aging	your first impression of college
a person you like (or dislike)	an ideal vacation
learning a new skill	writing
overcoming fears	marriage
an ideal job	the value of humor

1. Topic: _____

   Limited topic: _____

   Topic sentence: _____

   _____

2. Topic: _____

   Limited topic: _____

   Topic sentence: _____

   _____

3. Topic: _____

　　Limited topic: _____

　　Topic sentence: _____

　　_____

PART C　Developing Ideas for the Body

Which of these paragraphs is clearer and more interesting?

> A. Every Saturday morning, Fourteenth Street is alive with activity. Vendors sell many different things on the street, and storekeepers try to get customers inside their stores. There are all kinds of people on the street.

> B. Every Saturday morning, Fourteenth Street is alive with activity. Vendors line the sidewalks, selling everything from cassette tapes to wigs. Trying to lure customers inside, the shops blast pop music into the street or hang brightly colored banners announcing "Grand Opening Sale" or "Everything Must Go." Shoppers jam the sidewalks, both serious bargain hunters and families just out for a stroll, munching chili dogs as they survey the merchandise. Here and there, drunks and panhandlers hustle for handouts, taking advantage of the Saturday crowd.

- Paragraph A contains vague and general statements, so the reader gets no clear picture of the activity on Fourteenth Street.
- Paragraph B, however, includes many specific *details* that clearly explain the topic sentence: *vendors selling everything from cassette tapes to wigs, shops blasting pop music, brightly colored banners.*

- What other details in paragraph B help you see just how Fourteenth Street is alive with activity?

___

___

___

___

Brainstorming

One good way to develop the body of a paragraph is by *brainstorming*, or freely jotting down ideas. This important step may take just a few minutes, but it gets your ideas on paper and may pull ideas out of you that you didn't even know you had!

Freely jot down anything that might relate to your topic—details, examples, little stories. Don't worry at this point if some ideas seem not to belong. For now, just keep jotting.

Here is a possible brainstorming list for the topic sentence *Beverly inspires admiration because she is so determined.*

1. saved enough money for college
2. worked days, went to school nights
3. has beautiful brown eyes
4. nervous about learning to drive but didn't give up
5. failed road test twice—passed eventually
6. her favorite color—wine red
7. received degree in accounting
8. she is really admirable
9. with lots of will power, quit smoking
10. used to be a heavy smoker
11. married to Virgil
12. I like Virgil too
13. now a good driver
14. never got a ticket
15. hasn't touched another cigarette

As you saw in Part B, some writers also brainstorm *before* they write the topic sentence. Do what works best for you. Brainstorming and other prewriting techniques are presented in Chapter 1.

Practice 1   Here are three topic sentences. For each one, brainstorm, freewrite, or cluster for several specific details that you might use to develop an interesting paragraph.

1. That car looks ready for the junk heap.

   _____
   _____
   _____

2. Bailey gave a wonderful party.

   _____
   _____
   _____

3. The best job I ever had was _____.

   _____
   _____
   _____

Practice 2   Now choose the topic from Part B, Practice 2, that most interests you. Write that topic and your topic sentence here.

Topic: _____

Topic sentence: _____

   Next brainstorm. Write anything that comes to you about your topic sentence. Just let your ideas pour onto paper!

1. _____
2. _____
3. _____
4. _____
5. _____
6. _____
7. _____

8. _____

9. _____

10. _____

11. _____

12. _____

13. _____

14. _____

15. _____

and more . . .

PART D Selecting and Dropping Ideas

This may be the easiest step in paragraph writing because all you have to do is to select those ideas that relate to your topic sentence and drop those that do not. Also drop ideas that just *repeat* the topic sentence but add nothing new to the paragraph.

Here is the brainstorming list for the topic sentence *Beverly inspires admiration because she is so determined*. Which ideas would you drop? Why?

1. saved enough money for college
2. worked days, went to school nights
3. has beautiful brown eyes
4. nervous about learning to drive but didn't give up
5. failed road test twice—passed eventually
6. her favorite color—wine red
7. received degree in accounting
8. she is really admirable
9. with lots of will power, quit smoking
10. used to be a heavy smoker
11. married to Virgil
12. I like Virgil too
13. now a good driver

14. never got a ticket
15. hasn't touched another cigarette

You probably dropped ideas 3, 6, 11, and 12 because they do not relate to the topic. You also should have dropped idea 8 because it merely repeats the topic sentence.

Practice Now read through your own brainstorming list in Part C, Practice 2. Select the ideas that relate to your topic sentence, and cross out those that are not related to it. In addition, drop ideas that repeat the topic sentence. You should be able to give good reasons for keeping or dropping each idea in the list.

PART E Grouping Ideas in a Plan

Now choose an *order* in which to arrange your ideas. First, group together ideas that have something in common, that are related or alike in some way. Then decide which ideas should come first, which second, and so on. Many writers do this by numbering the ideas on their list.

Here are the ideas for a paragraph about Beverly grouped together in one possible way.

worked days, went to school nights
saved enough money for college
received degree in accounting

nervous about learning to drive but didn't give up
failed road test twice—passed eventually
now a good driver
never got a ticket

used to be a heavy smoker
with lots of will power, quit smoking
hasn't touched another cigarette

- How are the ideas in each group related? _____

_____

- Does it make sense to discuss college first, driving second, and smoking last? Why? _____

_____

Keep in mind that there is more than one way to group ideas. As you group your own brainstorming list, think of what you want to say; then group ideas accordingly.*

---
*For more work on choosing an order, see Chapter 3, Part B.

Practice   On a separate sheet of paper, group the ideas from your brainstorming list into a plan. First, group together related ideas. Then decide which ideas will come first, which second, and so on.

PART F   Writing and Revising the Paragraph

Writing the First Draft

By now, you should have a clear plan from which to write the first draft of your paragraph. The *first draft* should contain all the ideas you have decided to use in the order you have chosen to present them. Writing on every other line will leave room for later corrections.

Explain your ideas fully, including details that will interest or amuse your reader. If you are unsure about something, put a check in the margin and come back to it later, but avoid getting stuck on any one word, sentence, or idea. If possible, set the paper aside for several hours or even for several days.

Practice   On a separate sheet of paper, write a first draft of the paragraph you have been working on.

Revising

Whether you are a beginning writer or a professional, you must *revise*—that is, rewrite what you have written in order to improve it. You may cross out and rewrite words or entire sentences. You may add, drop, or rearrange details.

As you revise, keep the reader in mind. Ask yourself these questions:

- Are my ideas clear?
- Will this paragraph keep the reader interested?
- Is the body fully developed, or are more details needed?
- Is the order of ideas logical?

In addition, revise your paragraph for *unity, exact language,* and *concise language.*

Revising for Unity

While writing, you may sometimes drift away from your topic and include information that does not belong in the paragraph. It is important, therefore, to revise your paragraph for *unity;* that is, drop any ideas or sentences that do not relate to the topic sentence.

This paragraph lacks unity:

> (1) Franklin Mars, a Minnesota candy maker, created many popular candy snacks. (2) Milky Way, his first bar, was an instant hit. (3) Snickers, which he introduced in 1930, also sold very well. (4) Milton Hershey developed the very first candy bar in 1894. (5) M&Ms were a later Mars creation, supposedly designed so that soldiers could enjoy a sugar boost without getting sticky trigger fingers.

- What is the topic sentence in this paragraph? _____

- Which sentence does *not* relate to the topic sentence? _____

- Sentence (4) has nothing to do with the main idea, that *Franklin Mars created many popular candy snacks.* Therefore, sentence (4) should be dropped.

Practice Check the following paragraphs for unity. If a paragraph is unified, write *U* in the blank. If not, write the number of the sentence that does not belong in the paragraph.

1. _____ (1) My favorite shop, the Soap Opera, attractively displays bath items. (2) On the left wall, homemade soaps are stacked by color and scent: almond, lavender, honeysuckle, and musk. (3) In rows on the right are bath oils and bath salts in every possible fragrance. (4) On a table in the center of the shop stand large and small gift baskets containing soaps, oils, dried flowers, and tiny natural sponges from Greece. (5) My grandmother was born in Greece and made her own soap.

2. _____ (1) Swimming is great exercise. (2) The motions of swimming, such as reaching out in the crawl, stretch the muscles in a healthy, natural way. (3) Unlike jogging and many other sports, swimming does not jolt the bones and muscles with sudden pressure. (4) Some swimmers wear goggles to keep the chlorine or salt out of their eyes. (5) Finally, swimming vigorously for just twelve minutes provides aerobic benefits to the heart.

3. _____ (1) Owning a van has both advantages and disadvantages. (2) Because a van has so much storage space, it can transport even large, heavy items. (3) At vacation time, when most cars seem too small, a van makes packing easy. (4) On the other hand, parking a van in the city can be difficult because parking spaces are scarce and private lots can be expensive. (5) Another disadvantage is the high cost of gas. (6) Some vans have double tanks and don't get many miles to the gallon. (7) Knowing the pros and cons, consumers can decide whether or not a van is for them.

Revising for Exact Language

Good writers do not always settle for the first words that come to them; instead, they *revise* what they have written, replacing vague words and phrases with *vivid* and *exact language.*

Which sentence in each of the following pairs contains the more vivid and exact language?

> (1) The office was noisy.
>
> (2) In the office, phones jangled and typewriters clattered loudly.
>
> (3) What my tutor said made me feel good.
>
> (4) When my tutor whispered, "Fine job," I felt like singing.

- Sentence (2) is more exact than sentence (1) because *phones jangled and typewriters clattered loudly* provides more vivid information than the general word *noisy.*

- What exact words does sentence (4) use to replace the general words *said* and *made me feel good?* _____

You do not need a large vocabulary to write exactly and well, but you do need to work at finding the right words to fit each sentence.

Practice These sentences contain vague language. Revise each one, using vivid and exact language wherever possible.

Example: A man went through the crowd.

Revise: <u>A man in a blue leather jacket pushed through the crowd.</u>

1. An automobile went down the street.

    Revise: _____

2. The child played with the toy.

    Revise: _____

3. When Alison comes home, her pet greets her.

    Revise: _____

4. The moon made everything look pretty.

   Revise: _____

   _____

5. The expression on his face made me more comfortable.

   Revise: _____

   _____

6. My work is interesting.

   Revise: _____

   _____

7. There was a big storm here last week.

   Revise: _____

   _____

8. Hobbies can be nice.

   Revise: _____

   _____

9. The emergency room has a lot of people in it.

   Revise: _____

   _____

10. After classes, I need to take a break.

    Revise: _____

    _____

Revising for Concise Language

Concise writing never uses five or six words when two or three will do. It avoids repetitious and unnecessary words that add nothing to the meaning of a sentence. As you revise your writing, cross out unnecessary words and phrases.

Which sentence in each of the following pairs is more concise?

> (1) Because of the fact that Agnes owns an antique shop, she is always poking around in dusty attics.
>
> (2) Because Agnes owns an antique shop, she is always poking around in dusty attics.
>
> (3) Mr. Tibbs entered a large, dark blue room at the end of the hallway.
>
> (4) Mr. Tibbs entered a room that was large in size and dark blue in color at the end of the hallway.

- Sentence (2) and (3) are concise; sentences (1) and (4) are wordy.
- In sentence (1), *because of the fact that* is a wordy way of saying *because*.
- In sentence (4), *in size* and *in color* just repeats which ideas?

_____

Of course, conciseness does not mean writing short, choppy sentences. It does mean dropping unnecessary words and phrases.

Practice The following sentences are wordy. Make them more concise by deleting unnecessary words. Write each revised sentence on the lines provided.

Example: We celebrate Halloween on October 31 in the autumn.

Revise: We celebrate Halloween on October 31.

1. For a great many thousands of years, people have celebrated the holiday of Halloween.

   Revise: _____
   _____

2. The Celts of ancient Britain in their opinion believed that Samhain, the God of Death, held a meeting on October 31.

   Revise: _____
   _____

3. He gathered together at a gathering the evil and bad souls that had died during the year.

   Revise: _____
   _____

4. The reason that the Celts lit candles was because they hoped the candlelight would scare away these evil spirits.

   Revise: _____

   _____

5. Children also dressed in costumes that were ugly in looks to scare away these spirits.

   Revise: _____

   _____

6. By coincidence, the Romans also held an autumn festival in the fall of the year on October 31.

   Revise: _____

   _____

7. Their autumn festival honored Pomona, a goddess who was the goddess of fruits and produce.

   Revise: _____

   _____

8. Our Halloween seems to combine together in one both the Celt and Roman festivals.

   Revise: _____

   _____

9. Children dress up in frightening costumes that scare people, put candles into pumpkins, and eat fruits and other treats.

   Revise: _____

   _____

PART G Writing the Final Draft

When you are satisfied with your revisions, recopy your paper. If you are writing in class, this second draft will often be your final one. Be sure to include all your corrections, and write neatly and legibly—a carelessly scribbled paper seems to say that you don't care about your work.

The first draft of the paragraph about Beverly and the revised, final draft follow. Compare them.

> **First Draft:** (1) Beverly inspires admiration because she is so determined. (2) Although she could not afford to attend college right after high school, she worked to save money. (3) It took a long time, but she got her degree. (4) She is now a good driver. (5) At first, she was very nervous about getting behind the wheel and even failed the road test twice, but she didn't quit. (6) She passed eventually. (7) Her husband, Virgil, loves to drive; he races cars on the weekend. (8) Anyway, Beverly has never gotten a ticket. (9) A year ago, Beverly quit smoking. (10) For a while she had a rough time, but she hasn't touched a cigarette. (11) Now she says that the urge to smoke has faded away. (12) She doesn't let difficulties defeat her.

> **Final Draft:** (1) Beverly inspires admiration because she is so determined. (2) Although she could not afford to attend college right after high school, she worked as a cashier to save money for tuition. (3) It took her five years working days and going to school nights, but she recently received a B.S. in accounting. (4) Thanks to this same determination, Beverly is now a good driver. (5) At first, she was very nervous about getting behind the wheel and even failed the road test twice, but she didn't give up. (6) The third time she passed, and she has never gotten a ticket. (7) A year ago, Beverly quit smoking. (8) For a month or more, she chewed her nails and endless packs of gum, but she hasn't touched a cigarette. (9) Now she says that the urge to smoke has faded away. (10) When Beverly sets a goal for herself, she doesn't let difficulties defeat her.

- The writer has made sentences (2) and (3) more specific by adding *as a cashier; for tuition; five years working days and going to school nights;* and *recently received a B.S. in accounting.*

- What other revisions did the writer make? How do these revisions improve the paragraph? _____

  _____

  _____

  _____

  _____

- Note that the last sentence in the final draft provides a brief *conclusion* so that the paragraph feels finished.

Proofreading for Omitted Words

Finally, proofread your paper for spelling and grammatical errors, consulting your dictionary and this book as necessary. Proofread also for omitted words. In the rush to hand in a paper or an assignment, it is easy to leave out words—especially little ones like *and, at, of, on,* and so on.

Some students find it helpful to point to each word and say it softly; in this manner they are able to catch the omitted words that are often hard to spot when they are proofread silently.

In which of the following sentences have words been omitted?

> (1) Despite its faulty landing gear, the 747 managed land safely.
>
> (2) Plans for the new gym were on display the library.
>
> (3) Mr. Sampson smiled at his reflection in the bathroom mirror.

- Sentences (1) and (2) are missing words.

- Sentence (1) requires *to* before *land*.

- What word is omitted in sentence (2)? _____

- Where should this word be placed? _____

Practice Proofread these sentences for omitted words. Add the necessary words above the lines. Some sentences may already be correct.

Example: People were not always able ^to^ tell time accurately.

1. People used to guess the time day by watching the sun move across the sky.

2. Sunrise and sunset were easy recognize.

3. Recognizing noon easy, too.

4. However, telling time by the position of sun was very difficult at other times.

5. People noticed that shadows lengthened during the day.

6. They found it easier to tell time by looking at the shadows than by looking the sun.

7. People stuck poles into the ground to time by the length of the shadows.

8. These the first shadow clocks, or sundials.

9. In 300 B.C., Chaldean astronomer invented a more accurate, bowl-shaped sundial.

10. Today, most sundials decorative, but they can still be used to tell time.

Writing Paragraphs

The assignments that follow will give you practice in writing basic paragraphs. In each assignment, aim for (1) a clear topic sentence and (2) a body that fully explains and develops the topic sentence. As you write, refer to the checklist in the Chapter Highlights.

Paragraph 1: Describe a public place. Reread paragraph B on page 18. Then choose a place in your neighborhood that is "alive with activity"—a park, street, restaurant, or club. In your topic sentence, name the place and say when it is most active. For example, "Every Saturday night, the Hard Rock Cafe is alive with activity." Begin by freewriting or by jotting as many details about the scene as possible. Then describe the scene, choosing lively and interesting details that will help the reader to see the place as clearly as you do. Arrange your observations in a logical order. Revise for concise language.

Paragraph 2: Choose your time of day. Many people have a favorite time of day—the freshness of early morning, 5 p.m. when work ends, late at night when the children are asleep. In your topic sentence, name your favorite time of day. Then develop the paragraph by explaining why you look forward to this time and exactly how you spend it. Remember to conclude the paragraph; don't just stop.

Paragraph 3: Describe a person. Choose someone you strongly do (or do not) admire. In your topic sentence, focus on just *one* of the person's qualities. For example, "I admire Tony's courage (athletic ability, unusual sense of humor, and so on)." Then discuss two or three incidents or actions that clearly show this quality. Freewrite, brainstorm, or cluster for details and examples. Revise for unity; make sure that every sentence supports your topic sentence. Check your final draft for omitted words.

Paragraph 4: Create a holiday. Holidays honor important people, events, or ideas. If you could create a new holiday for your town or state, or for the country, what would that holiday be? In your topic sentence, name the holiday and tell exactly what it honors. Then explain why this holiday is important, and discuss how it should be celebrated. Take a humorous approach if you wish. For instance, you might invent a national holiday in honor of the first time you got an A in English composition. Revise for exact language. Check for omitted words.

Chapter Highlights

Checklist for Writing an Effective Paragraph

☐ 1. Limit the topic: Cut the topic down to one aspect that interests you and will probably interest your readers.

☐ 2. Write the topic sentence. (You may wish to brainstorm or freewrite first.)

☐ 3. Brainstorm, freewrite, or cluster ideas for the body: Write down anything and everything that might relate to your topic.

☐ 4. Select and drop ideas: Select those ideas that relate to your topic and drop those that do not.

☐ 5. Group together ideas that have something in common; then arrange the ideas in a plan.

☐ 6. Write your first draft.

☐ 7. Read what you have written, making any necessary corrections and additions. Revise for unity, exact language, and concise language.

☐ 8. Write the final draft of your paragraph neatly and legibly, making sure to indent the first word.

☐ 9. Proofread for grammar, punctuation, spelling, and omitted words. Make your corrections neatly and legibly.

Chapter 3

Improving the Paragraph

PART A More Work on Developing the Body: Examples
PART B More Work on Grouping Ideas: Coherence
PART C Turning Assignments into Paragraphs

In Chapter 2, you practiced the steps of the paragraph-writing process. Once you have gained confidence in writing basic paragraphs, you may wish to go on to this chapter, which discusses in more detail three skills that can greatly improve your writing: using examples to develop paragraphs, making sure your paragraphs are coherent, and finally, turning assignments into paragraphs.

PART A More Work on Developing the Body: Examples

One effective way to make your writing specific is to use *examples*. Someone might write: "That store carries unusual gifts for the very rich. For instance, last week there was a sale on gold-handled back scratchers." The first sentence makes a general statement about the store's *unusual gifts for the very rich.* The second sentence gives a specific example of such an item: *gold-handled back scratchers.*

Use one, two, or three well-chosen examples to develop a paragraph.

> In a number of ways, my supervisor tries to make working in her office a pleasant experience. For example, she allows those of us who are students to leave early, so we can get to classes on time. Of course, we later make up this time by coming in early or taking short lunch hours. In addition, she never assigns overtime without first finding out who wants extra hours; then she divides the work as fairly as possible. Finally, when any one of us is ill, she phones or sends a get-well card. When I become a supervisor, I will model myself after her.

- The writer begins this paragraph with a topic sentence praising her supervisor.

- What three examples does the writer then use to explain the topic sentence? _____

_____

_____

The simplest way to tell your reader that an example will follow is to say so: *For example, she allows . . .* Other transitional phrases that introduce examples are *for instance, to illustrate,* or *an illustration of this.*

Practice 1

Each example in a paragraph must clearly relate to and explain the topic sentence. Each topic sentence below is followed by several examples. Circle the letter of any example that does not clearly illustrate the topic sentence. Be prepared to explain your choices.

Example: Some animals camouflage themselves in interesting ways.

a. Snowshoe rabbits turn from brown to white in order to blend into the snow.

b. Pretending to be seaweed, a certain kind of eel can surprise its prey.

(c.) Bighorn sheep may soon be extinct.

d. The Kallima butterfly hangs for hours on a branch, looking like a dead leaf.

(Bighorn sheep are not an example of animals that camouflage themselves.)

1. Efforts are being made to save the whale from extinction.

   a. Since 1979, whale hunting has been prohibited in the Indian Ocean.

   b. Whales are the largest animals on earth.

   c. Under the Marine Protection Act of 1972, the United States banned both whaling and the sale of products obtained from whales.

   d. A five-year, worldwide ban on commercial whaling went into effect in 1986.

2. Jazz musicians are often known by colorful nicknames.

   a. John Birks Gillespie's friends called him "Dizzy."

   b. The French love American jazz.

   c. Louis Armstrong is best known as "Satchmo."

   d. Band leaders often introduced the famous blues singer Billie Holiday as "Lady Day."

3. English borrows words from many other languages.

   a. The Spanish *la reata* gives us *lariat,* "a rope."

   b. The expression *gung ho* comes from the Chinese *keng ho,* which literally means "more fire."

   c. Westerners find Asian languages difficult to learn.

   d. *Kimono* is the Japanese word for "thing for wearing."

4. Cinnamon had many unusual uses in the ancient world.

   a. In Biblical times, cinnamon was burned as incense during religious ceremonies.

   b. Wealthy Romans perfumed their bath water with cinnamon.

   c. Cinnamon is especially tasty when sprinkled on whipped cream.

   d. Egyptians used cinnamon to embalm the dead.

Practice 2 The secret of good illustration lies in well-chosen and well-written examples. Think of one example that illustrates each of the following general statements. Write out the example in sentence form—one to three sentences—as clearly and exactly as possible.

1. Dennis has a different sweater for each mood.

   Example: _____

   _____

2. Roberta's hot temper gets her into trouble.

   Example: _____

   _____

   _____

3. Dan is always buying strange gadgets.

   Example: _____

   _____

   _____

4. Grace understands less about cooking than anyone I know.

   Example: _____

   _____

5. Children often say the unexpected.

   Example: _____

   _____

PART B More Work on Grouping Ideas: Coherence

Every paragraph should have *coherence*. A paragraph *coheres*—holds together—when its ideas are arranged in a clear and logical order.

Sometimes, the order of ideas will flow logically from your topic. However, three basic ways to organize ideas are *time order, space order,* and *order of importance*.

Time Order

Time order means arranging ideas chronologically, from present to past or from past to present. Careful use of time order helps to avoid such confusing writing as *Oops, I forgot to mention before that . . .*

Most instructions, histories, and stories follow the logical order of time.

> The life of Grandma Moses proves that a person is never too old to develop her talents. As a child, Anna Robertson Moses loved to draw; she often made pictures with berry juice when paint was scarce. When Anna eventually married and had a large family, she found little time to paint. Years later, with her children grown, she began to knit pictures with yarn, but her fingers ached, and she returned to her first love, painting. She was seventy years old! An art dealer saw her pictures in a local drugstore and bought them. Grandma Moses, as she was called, soon became famous, with her paintings of simple country life exhibited throughout the world. She continued to paint until her death at age 101.

- The paragraph moves in time from Grandma Moses's childhood to her fame as an elderly artist.

- Note how these transitional expressions—*as a child, when Anna . . . married,* and *years later*—show time and connect the events in the paragraph.

Practice

Arrange each set of sentences in time order, numbering them 1, 2, 3, and so on. Be prepared to explain your choices.

1. In 1862, two British scientists decided to go up in a gas balloon to test the air above sea level.

    _____ At about 30,000 feet, he passed out completely.

    _____ Because of oxygen deprivation, however, one of the scientists began to lose his vision at 25,000 feet.

    _____ As they began to rise, they collected air samples and measured the air temperature.

    _____ As the gas escaped, the balloon started down, and both men survived to tell about the oxygen experiment that they had not planned to conduct.

    _____ The other scientist, gasping for air, finally managed to use his teeth to open the gas valve.

2. Meatless lasagna is an easy dish to prepare.

    _____ Put ricotta, Parmesan, and mozzarella cheese over the lasagna and tomato sauce.

    _____ Bake in a 300° oven for forty minutes.

    _____ Boil the lasagna noodles.

    _____ Place a layer of the noodles on the bottom of a baking dish.

    _____ Pour tomato sauce over the strips of lasagna.

    _____ Repeat the layering process two more times.

3. Mark Twain sometimes invested foolishly.

_____ Paige told Twain he had invented an automatic typesetter.

_____ In the late nineteenth century, Twain met James Paige, an inventor.

_____ Unfortunately, the typesetter never worked.

_____ By 1895, this useless contraption had bankrupted Twain.

_____ Twain invested heavily in the machine.

Space Order

Space order means describing a person, a thing, or a place from top to bottom, from left to right, from foreground to background, and so on.

Space order is most often used in descriptions because it moves from detail to detail, like a camera's eye.

> As usual, Sid had put his room in order before leaving. On the left wall, the shiny oak bookcase was neatly arranged, magazines in stacks and books in rows. The brass bed was against the far wall, its striped sheet carefully turned down over a red wool blanket. Two striped pillows were piled against the headboard. To the right stood a round oak table with two chairs facing each other, as if waiting for Sid and a friend to return.

- The objects in this paragraph are arranged in space order: from left, to center, to right.

- Note how transitional expressions indicating space—*on the left wall, against the far wall, to the right*—help connect the details in the paragraph.

Practice Arrange each set of details according to space order, numbering them 1, 2, 3, and so on. Be prepared to explain your choices.

1. The last woman to board the bus had to stand until the last stop.

_____ bright blue high-heeled shoes

_____ heavy leather purse dangling from left hand

_____ grinding teeth

_____ hat slipping over eyes

_____ tensed shoulders

2. After the party, the living room was a complete mess.

   _____ overflowing ashtrays on the coffee table

   _____ empty soda cans on the floor

   _____ crepe-paper streamers on the ceiling light

   _____ pictures hanging at odd angles on the wall

3. We took in the sights of Fifth Avenue.

   _____ soaring glass towers of office buildings

   _____ lunch-hour crowds on the sidewalks

   _____ pigeons sitting on top of the streetlights

   _____ an airplane passing in the blue sky

Order of Importance

Order of importance means starting your paragraph with the most important idea (or the largest, most expensive, most surprising).

> State legislators should provide more money to community colleges. Most important, more teachers are needed. Faculty size has not kept pace with the great increase in community college students. Therefore, classes keep getting larger, and students get less personal attention. In addition, colleges need better learning facilities. Many community colleges occupy old buildings. Classrooms are small and in poor condition. These schools often lack well-equipped science labs and computer centers for language learning. Community colleges also need more parking lots. Currently, students spend so much time looking for parking spaces that they are frequently late to class.

- The three reasons in this paragraph are discussed from the most important reason to the least important.
- Note that the words *most important, in addition,* and *also* help the reader move from one reason to another.

Sometimes you may wish to begin with the least important idea and build toward a climax at the end of the paragraph. Paragraphs arranged in this way can have dramatic power:

> It was graduation day at the college, and faces beamed with pride. Teachers vigorously shook hands with their students, delighted that so many had successfully completed the program. Even prouder were relatives of the graduates. They had encouraged wives, husbands, sons, and daughters who, tired and discouraged, had threatened to leave college. Proudest of all were the graduates. Many had returned to school after years in the world of work. They had toiled at their jobs, gone to school at night, and cared for their families. This day made all the sacrifices worthwhile.

- The three groups of people in this paragraph are discussed from the *least* to the *most proud.*
- Note how the words *prouder* and *proudest* help the reader move from one group to another.

Practice Arrange the ideas that develop each topic sentence in order of importance, numbering them 1, 2, and 3. Begin with the most important idea (largest, most expensive, and so on). Or reverse the order if you think that a paragraph would be more effective if it began with the least important idea. Be prepared to explain your choices. Then on a separate sheet of paper, write the ideas in a paragraph.

1. Jay has finally decided to move to Indianapolis.

    _____ His old apartment didn't get enough sun.

    _____ He was tired of living in the same city for so long.

    _____ He was offered a big promotion and raise if he went to Indianapolis as district sales manager.

2. Dissatisfied with his appearance, Daniel decided to make some changes and give himself a new look.

    _____ He replaced his old black frames with contact lenses.

    _____ He lost forty pounds on a strict diet.

    _____ He bought a pair of bright red socks.

3. The Ruizes made three purchases for their home last year.

    _____ The rocking chair made a perfect addition to the living room.

    _____ The new light switch panel replaced the old cracked one.

    _____ Everybody loved the new VCR with stereo sound.

PART C Turning Assignments into Paragraphs

In Chapter 2, Part B, you learned how to narrow down a broad topic and write a specific topic sentence. Sometimes, however, your assignment may take the form of a specific question, and your job may be to answer the question in one paragraph.

For example, this question asks you to take a stand on—for or against—a particular issue.

> Are professional athletes overpaid?

You can often turn this kind of question into a topic sentence:

> (1) Professional athletes are overpaid.
>
> (2) Professional athletes are not overpaid.
>
> (3) Professional athletes are sometimes overpaid.

- These three topic sentences take different points of view.
- The words *are, are not,* and *sometimes* make each writer's opinion clear.

Sometimes you will be asked to agree or disagree with a statement:

> (4) Salary is the most important factor in job satisfaction. Agree or disagree.

- This is really a question in disguise: *Is salary the most important factor in job satisfaction?*

In the topic sentence, make your opinion clear, and repeat key words.

> (5) Salary is the most important factor in job satisfaction.
>
> (6) Salary is not the most important factor in job satisfaction.
>
> (7) Salary is only one among several important factors in job satisfaction.

- The words *is, is not,* and *is only one among several* make each writer's opinion clear.
- Note how the topic sentences repeat the key words from the statement—*salary, important factor, job satisfaction.*

Once you have written the topic sentence, follow the steps described in Chapter 2—brainstorming or clustering, selecting, grouping—and then write your paragraph. Be sure that all ideas in the paragraph support the opinion you have stated in the topic sentence.

Practice 1 Here are four questions. Write one topic sentence to answer each of them. REMEMBER: Make your opinion clear in the topic sentence, and repeat key words from the question.

1. Is it necessary for everyone to be able to operate a computer?

   Topic sentence: _____

   _____

2. Do you pay more attention to what you eat now than you did a few years ago?

   Topic sentence: _____

   _____

3. Is there too much bad news on television news programs?

   Topic sentence: _____

   _____

4. How has your neighborhood changed in the last ten years?

   Topic sentence: _____

   _____

Practice 2 Choose the question that most interests you in Practice 1, and write a paragraph answering that question.

Practice 3 Here are four statements. Agree or disagree, and write a topic sentence for each.

1. Parents should forbid a child to see friends they disapprove of. Agree or disagree.

   Topic sentence: _____

   _____

2. All higher education should be free. Agree or disagree.

   Topic sentence: _____

   _____

3. Silence is golden. Agree or disagree.

   Topic sentence: _____

   _____

4. Marriage seems to be back in style. Agree or disagree.

   Topic sentence: _____

   _____

Practice 4 Choose the statement that most interests you in Practice 3. Then write a paragraph in which you agree or disagree.

Chapter Highlights

To improve your writing, try these techniques:

- Use well-chosen examples to develop a paragraph.
- Organize your ideas by time order.
- Organize your ideas by space order.
- Organize your ideas by order of importance, either from the most important to the least or from the least important to the most.
- Turn assignment questions into topic sentences.

UNIT 1

Writing Assignments

Writing Assignment 1: *Describe a person.* Choose someone whose looks interest you—a relative, a friend, or a person in your neighborhood whom you see often. In your topic sentence, give an overall impression of this person: "Cynthia's outfits always make me happy." "Herbert usually looks like an unmade bed." Brainstorm or cluster to get as many specific details as possible. Then using space order, describe the person, choosing details of his or her appearance to make the reader see him or her as clearly as you do.

Writing Assignment 2: *Discuss a goal.* Complete this topic sentence: "An important goal in my life is to _____." You might wish to finish school, learn word processing, start a family, or stop smoking, for example. Begin by jotting various reasons for having this goal. Then choose the three most important reasons and arrange them in order of importance—either from least to most important, or the reverse. Explain each reason, making clear to the reader why you feel as strongly as you do.

Writing Assignment 3: *Interview a classmate about an achievement.* Write about a time your classmate achieved something important, like winning a sales prize at work, losing thirty pounds, or helping a friend through a bad time. To gather interesting facts and details, ask your classmate questions like these, and take notes: *Is there one accomplishment of which you are very proud? Why was this achievement so important? Did it change the way you feel about yourself?* Keep asking questions until you feel you can give your reader a vivid sense of your classmate's triumph.

In your first sentence, state the person's achievement—for instance, *Getting her first A in English was a turning point in Jessica's life.* Then explain specifically why the achievement was so meaningful.

Writing Assignment 4: *Describe an annoying trait.* Choose someone you like or love, and describe his or her most annoying habit or trait. In your topic sentence, name the trait. For instance, you might say, "My husband's most annoying trait is carelessness." Then give one to three examples explaining the topic sentence. Make your examples as specific as possible; be sure they support the topic sentence.

Writing Assignment 5: *Develop a paragraph with examples.* Below are topic sentences for possible paragraphs. Pick the topic sentence that most interests you, and write a paragraph using one to three examples to explain the topic sentence.

a. A sense of humor can make difficult times easier to bear.
b. Mistakes can be great teachers.
c. Television commercials often insult my intelligence.
d. Adolescents are less respectful today than they were in the past.
e. Some people perform well under pressure.

UNIT 1

Review

Choosing a Topic Sentence

Each group of sentences could be unscrambled and written as a paragraph. Circle the letter of the sentence that would be the best topic sentence.

1. a. A flock of sandpipers raced back and forth at the water's edge.

    b. On the beach lay heaps of turtle grass, a large starfish, and many shells.

    c. The scene at Pine Beach was relaxing but fascinating.

    d. In the distance, a white cruise ship slowly churned.

    e. Windsurfers sailed back and forth, moving their transparent sails like fantastic insects or sea-going angels.

2. a. One man suggested that if a giant triangle in the Siberian forest were cleared and then planted with wheat, astronauts from outer space might come to investigate.

    b. Another tried to raise money for a huge mirror that would reflect sunbeam flashes to Mars.

    c. A woman wanted to dig vast ditches in the Sahara Desert, fill them with fuel, and light them on a clear night so that extraterrestrials might see the fire and reply.

    d. In recent years, many people have come up with imaginative ways to contact beings from outer space.

Selecting Ideas

Below is a topic sentence and a brainstormed list of possible ideas for a paragraph. Check "keep" for ideas that best support the topic sentence and "drop" for ideas that do not.

Topic sentence: Probably the greatest female athlete of all time was Texan Babe Didrikson.

45

Keep	Drop	
_____	_____	1. during the 1940s, she won every women's golf title at least once
_____	_____	2. in 1932, won eight out of ten track and field events in the Amateur Athletic Union's national championships
_____	_____	3. married George Zaharias in 1939
_____	_____	4. in photos, an attractive, dark-haired woman
_____	_____	5. after 1932 Olympics, she became a professional athlete, excelling in basketball, baseball, swimming, diving, and billiards!
_____	_____	6. Babe was the daughter of Norwegian immigrants
_____	_____	7. a woman of many talents in our time is Oprah Winfrey
_____	_____	8. Oprah overcame many obstacles on her way to the top
_____	_____	9. at 1932 Olympics, Didrikson broke world records in the javelin throw and 80-meter hurdles
_____	_____	10. also broke world high jump record, but Olympic judges disqualified her for using what they called the "Texas roll"

Examining a Paragraph

Read this paragraph and answer the questions.

(1) Students at some American colleges are learning a lot from trash by studying "garbology." (2) Wearing rubber gloves, they might sift through the local dump, counting and collecting treasures that they examine back at the laboratory. (3) First, they learn to look closely and to interpret what they see, thus reading the stories that trash tells. (4) More important, they learn the truth about what Americans buy, what they eat, and how they live. (5) Students at the University of Arizona, for instance, were surprised to find that low-income families in certain areas buy more educational toys for their children than nearby middle-income families. (6) Most important, students say that garbology courses can motivate them to be better citizens of planet Earth. (7) One young woman, for example, after seeing from hard evidence in her town's landfill how many people really recycled their glass, cans, and newspapers and how many cheated, organized an annual recycling awareness day.

1. Write the number of the topic sentence in the paragraph. _____

2. What kind of order does this writer use? _____

3. Students learn three things in garbology courses. (a) Write the numbers of the sentences stating these. (b) Which two ideas are supported by examples? (a) _____

    (b) _____

UNIT 2

The Complete Sentence

Chapter 4

Subjects and Verbs

PART A Defining and Spotting Subjects
PART B Spotting Singular and Plural Subjects
PART C Spotting Prepositional Phrases
PART D Defining and Spotting Action Verbs
PART E Defining and Spotting Linking Verbs
PART F Spotting Verbs of More Than One Word

PART A Defining and Spotting Subjects

The sentence is the basic unit of all writing. To write well, you need to know how to write correct and effective sentences. A *sentence* is a group of words that expresses a complete thought about something or someone. It contains a subject and a verb.

(1) _____ jumped over the black Buick, scaled the building, and finally reached the roof.

(2) _____ needs a new coat of paint.

These sentences might be interesting, but they are incomplete.

- In sentence (1), *who* jumped, scaled, and reached? Batman, Whitney Houston, the English teacher?
- Depending on *who* performed the action—jumping, scaling, or reaching—the sentence can be exciting, surprising, or strange.
- What is missing is the *who* word—the *subject.*
- In sentence (2), *what* needs a new coat of paint? The house, the car, the old rocking chair?
- What is missing is the *what* word—the *subject.*

For a sentence to be complete, it must contain a *who* or *what* word—a subject. The subject tells you *who* or *what* does something or exists in a certain way.

The subject is often a *noun,* a word that names a person, place, or thing (such as *Whitney Houston, English teacher,* or *house*). However, a *pronoun* (*I, you, he, she, it, we,* or *they*) also can be the subject.*

Practice 1 In each of these sentences, the subject (the *who* or *what* word) is missing. Fill in your own subject to make the sentence complete.

Example: A(n) ____fox____ dashed across the road.

1. The _____ skidded across the ice.

2. A(n) _____ hung from the ceiling.

3. That slinky black _____ looks wonderful on Sheila.

4. Because of the publicity, _____ left by the back door.

5. For years, _____ piled up in the back of the closet.

6. A(n) _____ knocked on our door one afternoon.

7. _____ and _____ were scattered all over the doctor's desk.

8. The _____ believed that his _____ would return someday.

9. Watching the sunrise, the _____ felt tired and happy.

10. The _____ was in bad shape. The _____ was falling in, and the _____ were all broken.

---

*For more on pronoun subjects, see Chapter 19, Part F.

Chapter 4 Subjects and Verbs 53

As you may have noticed, the subject can be a noun only, but it can also include *words that describe the noun* (such as *the, slinky,* or *black*).

The noun or pronoun alone is called the *simple subject;* the noun or pronoun plus the words that describe it are called the *complete subject.*

> (3) Three yellow roses grew near the path.
>
> (4) A large box was delivered this morning.

- The simple subject of sentence (3) is the noun *roses.*
- The complete subject is *three yellow roses.*
- What is the simple subject of (4)? _____
- What is the complete subject of (4)? _____

Practice 2 Circle the complete subjects in these sentences. REMEMBER: The complete subject includes the *who* or *what* word (the noun or pronoun) and any words that describe it.

Example: (The typist) became a millionaire.

(1) Bette Nesmith was a good secretary. (2) However, employers constantly complained about her messy typing. (3) One day, the young office worker had an inspired idea. (4) She covered her typing errors with dots of white paint. (5) Soon other secretaries wanted to try her method. (6) Bette's kitchen became a small factory. (7) A local chemistry teacher helped her improve the formula. (8) Her son bottled the new product in the garage. (9) Quickly, orders began pouring in. (10) By 1980, six hundred people worked for the company, Liquid Paper.

Practice 3 In these sentences, the subject has been omitted. You must decide where it belongs and fill in a subject (a *who* or *what* word) that makes sense. (You may have to fill in more than one subject in a sentence.)

Example: Raced down the street.

My friend raced down the street.

1. Trained day and night for the big event.

   _____

2. Always talks about his childhood after he sees his sister.

   _____

3. Landed in the corn field.

   _____

4. After the show, applauded and screamed for fifteen minutes.

   _____

5. When the large, gray pulled up at the curb, got out.

   _____

PART B — Spotting Singular and Plural Subjects

Besides being able to spot subjects in sentences, you need to know whether a subject is singular or plural.

> (1) The man jogged around the park.

- The subject of this sentence is *the man.*
- Because *the man* is one person, the subject is *singular.*

Singular means only one of something.

> (2) The man and his friend jogged around the park.

- The subject of sentence (2) is *the man and his friend.*
- Because *the man and his friend* refers to more than one person, the subject is *plural.*

Plural means more than one of something.

Practice 1 Here is a list of possible subjects of sentences. If the subject is singular, put a check in the Singular column; if the subject is plural, put a check in the Plural column.

	Possible Subjects	Singular (one)	Plural (more than one)
Examples:	an elephant	✓	
	the computers		✓
	children		✓
1.	our cousins		
2.	a large ruby		
3.	shoulder pads		
4.	a saxophone and a trumpet		
5.	Horace		
6.	pecan pie		
7.	their trophy		
8.	his three pickup trucks		
9.	women		
10.	a rock star and her band		

Practice 2 Circle the complete subjects in these sentences. Then in the space at the right, write *S* if the subject is singular or *P* if the subject is plural.

Example: (Spike Lee) has inspired a new generation of African-American filmmakers.   S

1. Lee's first hit was *She's Gotta Have It* in 1986. _____

2. Many black moviemakers have had success since then. _____

3. These young artists write, direct, and even act in their own movies. _____

4. Often, their goal is to combine exciting entertainment with a social message. _____

5. John Singleton wrote and directed the acclaimed *Boyz N the Hood* at age twenty-three. _____

56 Unit 2 The Complete Sentence

6. *Sidewalk Stories* and *True Identity* were created by

   Charles Lane.   _____

7. Reading turned another young man into a moviemaker.   _____

8. At nineteen, Matty Rich made *Straight Out of Brooklyn*,

   after studying more than 250 film books!   _____

9. Hollywood loves Reginald and Warrington Hudlin.   _____

10. These talented brothers produced *House Party*,

    Boomerang, and *Bebe's Kids*.   _____

PART C   Spotting Prepositional Phrases

One group of words that may confuse you as you look for subjects is the prepositional phrase. A *prepositional phrase* contains a *preposition* (a word like *at, from, in,* or *of*) and its *object* (a *noun* or *pronoun*). Here are some prepositional phrases:*

Prepositional Phrase	=	Preposition	+	Object
at work		at		work
behind her		behind		her
of the students		of		the students
on the blue table		on		the blue table

The object of a preposition *cannot* be the subject of a sentence. Therefore, crossing out prepositional phrases can help you find the real subject.

> (1) On summer evenings, girls in white dresses stroll under the trees.
> (2) ~~On summer evenings~~, girls ~~in white dresses~~ stroll ~~under the trees~~.
> (3) From dawn to dusk, we hiked.
> (4) The president of the college will speak tonight.

- In sentence (1), you may have trouble spotting the subject. However, once the prepositional phrases are crossed out in (2), the subject, *girls*, is easy to see.

_____
*For more work on prepositions, see Chapter 21.

Chapter 4 Subjects and Verbs 57

- Cross out the prepositional phrases in sentence (3). What is the subject of the sentence? _____
- Cross out the prepositional phrase in sentence (4). What is the subject of the sentence? _____

Here are some common prepositions you should know:

Common Prepositions		
about	beside	off
above	between	on
across	by	over
after	during	through
against	except	to
along	for	toward
among	from	under
around	in	until
at	into	up
before	like	with
behind	of	without

Practice Cross out the prepositional phrase or phrases in each sentence. Then circle the subject of the sentence.

Example: (The boots) ~~in the window~~ are expensive.

1. ~~In the contest~~, (Wanda) won $500.
2. (News) ~~of the salary cuts~~ spread quickly.
3. ~~In five minutes~~, the (popovers) will pop.
4. (Three members) ~~of the team~~ scored more than twenty points each.
5. On ~~Sunday morning~~, at ~~414 Bret Street~~, (we) held a garage sale.
6. The box ~~of diskettes~~ was full ~~on Friday~~.
7. (Two) ~~of my uncles~~ are musicians.
8. ~~All night~~, (crates) ~~of fresh pineapples~~ were unloaded ~~on the dock~~.
9. (The tree) ~~between those houses~~ is a royal poinciana.
10. Through the woods and over the field, the (cross-country runners) raced.

11. Men and women with excellent writing skills often get good jobs.

12. ~~With your brains,~~ (you) should have no trouble passing calculus.

13. ~~In the closet by the door,~~ (Dick) keeps his baseball cap.

14. (Scientists) ~~from the United States~~ and Russia worked together on the ~~project.~~

15. ~~From one end of the block to the other,~~ (people) danced.

PART D Defining and Spotting Action Verbs

> (1) The pears _*rot*_ on the trees.
> (2) Robert _*bit*_ his customer's hand and _____ her dog on the head.

These sentences tell you what or who the subject is—*the pears* and *Robert*—but not what each subject does.

- In sentence (1), what do the pears do? Do they *grow, ripen, rot, stink,* or *glow*?

- All these *action verbs* fit into the blank space in sentence (1), but the meaning of the sentence changes depending on which action verb you use.

- In sentence (2), what actions does Robert perform? Does he *shake, ignore, kiss, pat,* or *scratch*?

- Depending on which verb you use, the meaning of the sentence changes.

- Some sentences, like sentence (2), contain two or more action verbs.

For a sentence to be complete, it must have a *verb*. An *action verb* tells what action the subject is performing.

Practice 1 Fill in each blank with an action verb.

1. Michael Jordan _____ through the air for a slam dunk.

2. An artist _____ the scene at the waterfront.

3. Anita _____ the small package in green foil.

4. When Francine _____, the waiter _____.

5. A fierce wind _____ and _____.

6. The audience _____ as the rapper _____.

7. The carpenters _____ the leftover wood before leaving the job.

8. This new kitchen gadget _____ and _____ any vegetable you can think of.

9. When the dentist _____ his drill, Earl _____.

10. David Bowie _____ and _____ across the stage.

Practice 2 Circle the action verbs in these sentences. Some sentences contain more than one action verb.

(1) Despite great handicaps, Christy Brown (wrote) two popular books about his life, *My Left Foot* and *Down All These Days*. (2) From birth, this crippled Irishman (suffered) from cerebral palsy. (3) As a child, he (spoke) mainly in grunts. (4) His young body (jerked) and (shook). (5) Only his left foot (moved) under his control. (6) Christy's family (nurtured) him, however. (7) His mother (saw) his intelligence and (tutored) him at home. (8) His twelve brothers and sisters (wheeled) him around Dublin in a homemade cart. (9) Christy Brown (created) his books, poems, and essays in an unusual way. (10) He (typed) with his left foot. (11) He also (painted) with a brush between his toes. (12) In 1990, a movie about Brown's life (inspired) millions of viewers and (won) an Academy Award.

PART E Defining and Spotting Linking Verbs

The verbs you have been examining so far show action, but a second kind of verb simply links the subject to words that describe or rename it.

> (1) Aunt Claudia sometimes seems a little strange.

- The subject in this sentence is *Aunt Claudia*, but there is no action verb.
- Instead, *seems* links the subject, *Aunt Claudia*, with the descriptive words *a little strange*.

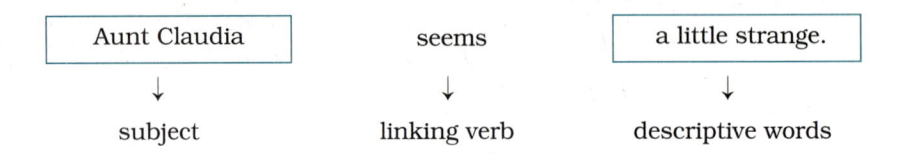

Aunt Claudia	seems	a little strange.
↓	↓	↓
subject	linking verb	descriptive words

> (2) They are reporters for the newspaper.

- The subject is *they*. The word *reporters* renames the subject.
- What verb links the subject, *they*, with the word *reporters*?

_____

For a sentence to be complete, it must contain a *verb*. A *linking verb* links the subject with words that describe or rename that subject.

The box below lists linking verbs you should know.

Common Linking Verbs

be (am, is, are, was, were)	look
act	seem
appear	smell
become	sound
feel	taste
get	

- The most common linking verbs are the forms of *to be*, but verbs of the senses, such as *feel, look,* and *smell,* also may be used as linking verbs.

Chapter 4 Subjects and Verbs 61

Practice 1 The subjects and descriptive words in these sentences are boxed. Circle the linking verbs.

1. [Jerry] (sounds) [sleepy] today.
2. [Ronda] always (was) [the best debater] on the team.
3. [His brother] often (appeared) [relaxed and happy.]
4. By evening, [Harvey] (felt) [confident] about the exam.
5. [Mr. Forbes] (became) [a long-distance runner.]

Practice 2 Circle the linking verbs in these sentences. Then underline the subject and the descriptive word or words in each sentence.

1. The sweet potato pie (tastes) delicious.
2. You often (seem) worried.
3. During the summer, she (looks) calm.
4. Under heavy snow, the new dome roof (appeared) sturdy.
5. Frankly, the jewelry robbery (was) mysterious.
6. This sunny weather (is) a pleasant surprise.
7. Raphael (is) a gifted writer.
8. Lately, I feel very competent at work.
9. Luz (became) a medical technician.
10. Yvonne (acted) surprised at her baby shower.

PART F Spotting Verbs of More Than One Word

All the verbs you have dealt with so far have been single words—*look*, *walked*, *saw*, *are*, *were*, and so on. However, many verbs consist of more than one word.

(1) Sarah is walking to work.

- The subject is *Sarah*. What is *Sarah* doing?
- Sarah is walking.

62 Unit 2 The Complete Sentence

- *Walking* is the *main verb*. *Is* is the *helping verb;* without *is, walking* is not a complete verb.

> (2) Should I have written sooner?

- The subject is *I.*
- *Should have written* is the *complete verb.*
- *Written* is the *main verb. Should* and *have* are the *helping verbs;* without *should have, written* is not a complete verb.

> (3) Do you eat fish?

- What is the subject? _____
- What is the main verb? _____
- What is the helping verb? _____

The *complete verb* in a sentence consists of all the helping verbs and the main verb.

Practice 1

The blanks following each sentence tell you how many words make up the complete verb. Fill in the blanks with the complete verb, and then circle the main verb.

Example: He has been studying for several hours. __has__ __been__ __(studying)__

1. At last, an honest person is (running) for mayor. _____

2. Do you wear false eyelashes? _____ _____

3. Joseph should have (typed) his résumé. _____ _____

4. The producers have (changed) their minds. _____ _____

5. She will be chief executive officer someday. _____ _____

Chapter 4   Subjects and Verbs   63

6. Wild geese have been nesting on the island. _____

7. Has anyone read this horoscope? _____ _____

8. With luck, he could have been a great actor. _____

9. From now on, the entire family must help with the housework.

10. You should have seen the shooting stars last night. _____

11. Rebecca does sew beautifully. _____ _____

12. I had never used a lap-top computer before yesterday.

13. The engine has run much better since the tune-up. _____

14. Before his retirement, Walter had seemed grouchy. _____

15. In May, I will have worked at Kodak for ten years. _____

Practice 2   Box the subjects, circle the main verbs, and underline any helping verbs in these sentences.

Example: Most people have wondered about the beginning of the universe.

1. Scientists have developed one theory.

2. According to this theory, the universe began with a huge explosion.

3. The explosion has been named the Big Bang.

4. First, all matter must have been packed into a tiny speck under enormous pressure.

5. Then about 15 billion years ago, that speck burst with amazing force.

6. Everything in the universe has come from the original explosion.

7. In fact, the universe still is expanding from the Big Bang.

8. All the planets and stars are moving away from each other at an even speed.

9. Will the universe expand forever?

10. Scientists may be debating that question for a long time.

Chapter Highlights

- **A sentence contains a subject and a verb, and expresses a complete thought:**

       S   V
   Jennifer bakes often.

           S   V
   The two students have tutored at the writing lab.

- **An action verb tells what the subject is doing:**

   Toni Morrison *writes* novels.

- **A linking verb links the subject with words that describe or rename it:**

   Her novels *are* bestsellers.

- **Don't mistake the object in a prepositional phrase for a subject:**

        S   PP
   The red car [in the showroom] is a Corvette.

      PP   S
   [In my dream,] *a sailor and his parrot* were singing.

Chapter Review

Circle the subjects, crossing out any confusing prepositional phrases. Then underline the complete verbs. If you have difficulty with this review, consider rereading the lesson.

Nobel Peace Prize Winners

(1) In 1895, a committee presented the first yearly Nobel Peace Prize. (2) This important prize honors one person for outstanding work toward world peace. (3) Politicians and government officials frequently have won the award for single acts of good will. (4) Several times, however, it has been given to people like Linus Pauling or Mother Teresa. (5) These champions of peace have devoted their lives to the welfare of others.

(6) Dr. Linus Pauling received two Nobel Prizes. (7) In 1954, this talented scientist was awarded the Nobel Prize in Chemistry. (8) Then in 1962, he won the Nobel Peace Prize for his opposition to nuclear weapons. (9) During World War II, Pauling and other distinguished scientists had worried about the terrible danger of atomic bombs. (10) For more than fifteen years, Pauling campaigned against the manufacture, testing, and use of nuclear weapons. (11) His message of peace was central to his life.

(12) In 1979, Mother Teresa won the Nobel Prize for her help to the homeless people of Calcutta, India. (13) Since 1948, this "Saint of the Gutters" had gone into the streets of one of the poorest neighborhoods in the world. (14) She had saved babies, hopeless mothers, and suffering people. (15) Several hundred Missionaries of Charity are following her example in countries throughout the world.

Chapter 5

Avoiding Sentence Fragments

PART A Writing Sentences with Subjects and Verbs
PART B Writing Sentences with Complete Verbs
PART C Completing the Thought

PART A   Writing Sentences with Subjects and Verbs

Which of these groups of words is a sentence? Be prepared to explain your answers.

> (1) He left at 9 a.m.
> (2) The orange cheetah.
> (3) Was swinging a gold cane.
> (4) Scratches his head.
> (5) My cousin teaches economics on Tuesdays.

- In (2), you probably wanted to know what the orange cheetah *did*. The idea is not complete because there is no *verb*.

- In (3), you probably wanted to know *who* was swinging a gold cane. The idea is not complete because there is no *subject*.

Chapter 5 Avoiding Sentence Fragments   67

- In (4), you probably wanted to know *who* scratches his head. The idea is not complete. What is missing? _____
- But in sentences (1) and (5), you knew *who did what.* These ideas are complete. Why? _____
  _____

Every *sentence* **must have both a subject and a verb, and must express a complete thought.**

A *fragment* **lacks either a subject or a complete verb—or does not express a complete thought.**

Practice   All of the following are *fragments*; they lack a subject, a verb, or both. Add a subject, a verb, or both in order to make the fragments into sentences.

Example: Was painting the dresser green.

Rewrite: *Charles was painting the dresser green.*

1. Cleared the last hurdle and raced to the finish line.

   Rewrite: _____

2. Melts easily.

   Rewrite: _____

3. The two-year-old in the red overalls.

   Rewrite: _____

4. One of the fans.

   Rewrite: _____

5. Manages a Software City store.

   Rewrite: _____

6. The tip of her nose.

   Rewrite: _____

7. A VCR with remote control.

   Rewrite: _____

8. Makes me nervous.

    Rewrite: _____

9. Closer and closer.

    Rewrite: _____

10. Were picking blackberries near the bridge.

    Rewrite: _____

11. The cost of tuition.

    Rewrite: _____

12. A person who likes to take risks.

    Rewrite: _____

PART B Writing Sentences with Complete Verbs

Do not be fooled by incomplete verbs.

> (1) She leaving for the city.
> (2) The students gone to the cafeteria for dessert.

- *Leaving* seems to be the verb in (1).
- *Gone* seems to be the verb in (2).

But . . .

- An *-ing* word like *leaving* is not by itself a verb.
- A word like *gone* is not by itself a verb.

> (1) She {is / was} leaving for the city.
> (2) The students {have / had} gone to the cafeteria for dessert.

- To be a *verb*, an *-ing word* (called a *present participle*) must be combined with some form of the verb *to be*.*

Helping Verb	Main Verb
am is are was were has been have been had been	jogging

- To be a *verb*, a word like *gone* (called a *past participle*) must be combined with some form of *to have* or *to be*.**

Helping Verb	Main Verb
am is are was were has have had has been have been had been	forgotten

Practice 1 All of the following are fragments; they have only a partial or an incomplete verb. Complete each verb in order to make these fragments into sentences.

Example: The children grown taller this year.

Rewrite: <u>The children have grown taller this year.</u>

1. Steffi Graf winning the tennis match.

    Rewrite: _____

2. My friends gone to a dude ranch.

    Rewrite: _____

---

*For a detailed explanation of present participles, see Chapter 9.
**For a detailed explanation of past participles, see Chapter 8.

3. Steve's letter published in *The Miami Herald*.

   Rewrite: _____

4. My physics professor always forgetting the assignment.

   Rewrite: _____

5. These shirts made in Korea.

   Rewrite: _____

6. For two years, Joan working as a word processor.

   Rewrite: _____

7. You ever been to San Francisco?

   Rewrite: _____

8. Yesterday, Ed's wet gloves taken from the radiator.

   Rewrite: _____

9. Ducks quacking all over the front porch.

   Rewrite: _____

10. Unemployment rising recently.

    Rewrite: _____

Practice 2 All of the following are fragments; they lack a subject, and they contain only a partial verb. Make these fragments into sentences by adding a subject and by completing the verb.

Example: Written by Ray Bradbury.

Rewrite: <u>This science fiction thriller was written by Ray Bradbury.</u>

1. Forgotten the codeword.

   Rewrite: _____

2. Now running the copy center.

   Rewrite: _____

3. Making a quilt out of scraps.

   Rewrite: _____

4. Been working at the brewery.

   Rewrite: _____

5. Talking about the good old days.

   Rewrite: _____

6. Soon taking the band on a national tour.

   Rewrite: _____

7. Driven that tractor for years.

   Rewrite: _____

8. All morning, reading on the sun porch.

   Rewrite: _____

9. Broken the computer through carelessness.

   Rewrite: _____

10. Been to Japan.

    Rewrite: _____

Practice 3 Fragments are most likely to occur in paragraphs or longer pieces of writing. Proofread the paragraph below for fragments; check for missing subjects or incomplete verbs. Circle the number of any fragments, and then write your corrections above the lines.

(1) Mozart one of the greatest musical geniuses of all time. (2) He was born Wolfgang Amadeus Mozart in Salzburg, Austria, in 1756. (3) By the age of four, he played the harpsichord like an adult. (4) At five, he already writing complex musical compositions. (5) When Mozart was just six, he and his sister performing for the kings and queens of Europe. (6) Luckily, his father recognized Mozart's genius. (7) Devoted his life to the boy's career. (8) Mozart died at age thirty-six. (9) However, he written twenty-two operas, more than forty symphonies, church music, and chamber music. (10) Today, many of these pieces still considered the finest ever composed.

PART C Completing the Thought

Can these ideas stand by themselves?

> (1) Because oranges are rich in vitamin C.
> (2) Although Sam is sleepy.

- These ideas have a subject and a verb (find them), but they cannot stand alone because you expect something else to follow.
- Because oranges are rich in vitamin C, then *what*? Should you *eat them, sell them,* or *make marmalade*?
- Although Sam is sleepy, *what will he do*? Will he *work on the computer, walk the dog,* or *go to the gym*?

> (1) Because oranges are rich in vitamin C, *I eat one every day.*
> (2) Although Sam is sleepy, *he will work late tonight.*

- These sentences are now complete.
- Words like *because* and *although* make an idea incomplete unless another idea is added to complete the thought.*

Practice 1 Make these fragments into sentences by adding some idea that completes the thought.

Example: Because I miss my family, __I am going home for the weekend.__

1. As May stepped off the elevator, _____
2. Whenever somebody whistles at me, _____
3. While Jennifer studied chemistry, _____
4. Because you believe in yourself, _____
5. Although spiders scare most people, _____
6. Until the snow stops falling, _____
7. Unless the operation is absolutely necessary, _____
8. If Ronald sings "True Colors" one more time, *I go away*

---

*For more work on this type of sentence, see Chapter 12.

Chapter 5 Avoiding Sentence Fragments   73

9. Although it is the duty of every good citizen to vote, _____
_____

10. As Maya took control of the plane, _____
_____

Can these ideas stand by themselves?

> (3) Graciela, who has a one-year-old daughter.
>
> (4) A course that I will always remember.

- In each of these examples, you expect something else to follow. Graciela, who has a one-year-old daughter, *is doing what?* Does she *attend PTA meetings, knit sweaters,* or *fly planes?*

- A course that I will always remember *is what?* The thought must be completed.

> (3) Graciela, who has a one-year-old daughter, *attends Gordon College.*
>
> (4) A course that I will always remember *is documentary filmmaking.*

- These sentences are now complete.*

Practice 2   Make these fragments into sentences by completing the thought.

Example: Kent, who is a good friend of mine, _rarely writes to me._

1. The horoscopes that appear in the daily papers _____

2. Couples who never argue _____

3. Robert, who is a superb pole vaulter, _____

4. Radio programs that explore important issues _____
_____

5. A person who has overcome great loss _____

6. Potholes, which can cause accidents, _____
_____

---

*For more work on this type of sentence, see Chapter 16, Part A.

74 Unit 2 The Complete Sentence

7. Doctors who spend a lot of time with their patients _____

_____

8. The video that we watched last night _____

9. A person who becomes upset over little things _____

_____

10. A country that I have always wanted to visit _____

Practice 3 To each fragment, add a subject, a verb, or whatever is required to complete the thought.

1. Visiting the Vietnam Memorial.

   Rewrite: _____

2. That digital clock blinking for hours.

   Rewrite: _____

3. People who never say no to their children.

   Rewrite: *should never so no to their children*

4. Wanted to become a chiropractor.

   Rewrite: _____

5. If that is the right answer.

   Rewrite: _____

6. Over the roof and into the garden.

   Rewrite: _____

7. Dave been to Costa Rica, but he back now.

   Rewrite: _____

8. Chess, which is a difficult game to play.

   Rewrite: _____

9. It's only October, but already snow falling.

   Rewrite: _____

10. Whenever Dolly starts to yodel.

    Rewrite: *I leave the room* _____

Practice 4 Proofread the paragraph for fragments. Circle the numbers of any fragments, and then write your corrections above the lines.

(1) A hurricane is a violent, whirling storm. (2) That hits land with winds up to 200 miles per hour. (3) The fierce winds swirl around an eye. (4) Which is a calm area about twenty miles across. (5) Although hurricanes eventually weaken once they pass over land. (6) They bring heavy rains and deadly tornados. (7) Huge ocean waves, called a storm surge, can increase the destruction. (8) In 1900, before the National Weather Service began tracking hurricanes and warning communities. (9) A hurricane killed 6,000 people in Galveston, Texas. (10) On August 24, 1992, Hurricane Andrew, one of the most destructive of the century, hit Miami, Florida. (11) This monster storm caused $20 billion in damage. (12) And left 160,000 people homeless.

Chapter Highlights

A sentence fragment is an error because it lacks

- **a subject:**   Was buying a gold ring. *(incorrect)*
  Diamond Jim was buying a gold ring. *(correct)*

- **a verb:**   The basketball game Friday at noon. *(incorrect)*
  The basketball game *was played* Friday at noon. *(correct)*

- **or a complete thought:**   While Teresa was swimming. *(incorrect)*
  While Teresa was swimming, she lost a contact lens. *(correct)*

  The woman who bought your car. *(incorrect)*
  The woman who bought your car is walking down the highway. *(correct)*

Chapter Review

Proofread each paragraph below for fragments. Circle the numbers of any fragments, and then correct the fragments in any way that makes sense, making them into separate ideas or adding them to other sentences. Write your corrections above the lines.

A. (1) Rap music first performed by African Americans in New York in the 1970s. (2) The roots of this popular musical style can be traced to African chanting, Jamaican reggae. (3) And the chatter of disc jockeys. (4) Because rappers do not really sing. (5) This music became known by the slang word *rap*. (6) Which means "to talk." (7) Rappers recite catchy rhymes. (8) While music with a strong beat plays in the background. (9) Today many rappers dealing with political issues, such as urban violence and poverty. (10) Successful rappers like Hammer and Queen Latifah deliver their insights to huge audiences.

B. (1) In 1986, people in the Ganges Delta of India began wearing masks to protect themselves from Bengal tigers. (2) These deadly tigers protected in the region. (3) Killing up to sixty people a year. (4) Someone noticed. (5) That the big cats attacked only from behind.

UNIT 2

Review

Proofreading and Revising

Proofread the following essay to eliminate all sentence fragments. Circle the numbers of any fragments, and then correct them in any way you choose—by connecting them to a sentence before or after, by completing any incomplete verbs, and so on. Make your corrections above the lines.

The Greatest Athlete of All

(1) James Francis Thorpe was probably the most talented American athlete of all time. (2) Born in Oklahoma in 1888. (3) The future sports great was named Bright Path by his parents, who were both half Native American. (4) Thorpe first achieved national recognition in 1911. (5) When he played halfback for the Carlisle Indian School in Pennsylvania. (6) He led his team to an upset victory against the undefeated Harvard team. (7) In the Carlisle-Army game. (8) Thorpe scored twenty-two of twenty-seven winning points. (9) Running ninety-seven yards at amazing speed for one of his touchdowns. (10) In that year, and again in 1912, he was named to the All-American football team.

(11) In track as well, 1912 was a banner year for Thorpe. (12) He won the pentathlon and decathlon in the Olympics in Sweden. (13) An incredible achievement never matched before or since. (14) In the pentathlon, Thorpe took four out of a possible five first places—in the 200-meter dash, the 1,500-meter run, the broad jump, and the discus throw. (15) He placed third in the javelin throw. (16) Although he had

79

never picked up a javelin until two months before the meet. (17) At six feet tall, weighing 180 pounds. (18) Thorpe was at the peak of his powers.

(19) Then tragedy struck. (20) In 1913, Thorpe admitted that he had earned $15 a week as a semiprofessional pitcher. (21) During the summer before his Olympic victories. (22) Thorpe had violated his amateur status. (23) The Amateur Athletic Association took away his gold medals and wiped his name from the Olympic records.

(24) Although he was down. (25) He was not out. (26) Thorpe played baseball for the New York Giants, Cincinnati Reds, and Boston Braves. (27) Between 1913 and 1919. (28) Then he began one of the longest professional football careers ever. (29) When he retired in 1934. (30) He was forty-one.

(31) Thorpe died in 1953. (32) In that same year, sportswriters from all over the country voted him the greatest American athlete. (33) Of the first half of the twentieth century. (34) Thirty years later, Thorpe's name was cleared. (35) His gold medals were returned to his family, and his Olympic victories were officially accepted again.

UNIT 3

Verbs

Chapter 6

Present Tense (Agreement)

PART A   Defining Agreement
PART B   Troublesome Verb in the Present Tense: TO BE
PART C   Troublesome Verb in the Present Tense: TO HAVE
PART D   Troublesome Verb in the Present Tense: TO DO (+ NOT)
PART E   Changing Subjects to Pronouns
PART F   Practice in Agreement
PART G   Special Problems in Agreement

PART A   Defining Agreement

A subject and a present tense verb *agree* if you use the correct form of the verb with each subject. The chart shows what form of the verb to use for each kind of pronoun subject (we discuss other kinds of subjects later).

84   Unit 3   Verbs

Verbs in the Present Tense

(example verb: to write)

Singular		Plural	
If the subject is	the verb is	If the subject is	the verb is
1st person: I	write	1st person: we	write
2nd person: you	write	2nd person: you	write
3rd person: he, she, it	writes	3rd person: they	write

Practice 1   Fill in the correct present tense form of the verb.*

1. You *ask* questions.
2. They *decide*.
3. I *travel*.
4. They *wear* glasses.
5. We *hope* so.
6. You *practice* karate.
7. I *laugh* often.
8. They *drive* slowly.
9. We *study* daily.
10. He *interests* me.

1. He _asks_ questions.
2. She _decides_.
3. He _travels_.
4. She _wears_ glasses.
5. He _hopes_ so.
6. She _practices_ karate.
7. She _laughs_ often.
8. He _drives_ slowly.
9. He _studyes_ daily.
10. It _interests_ me.

Add *-s* or *-es* to a verb in the present tense only when the subject is *third person singular (he, she, it)*.

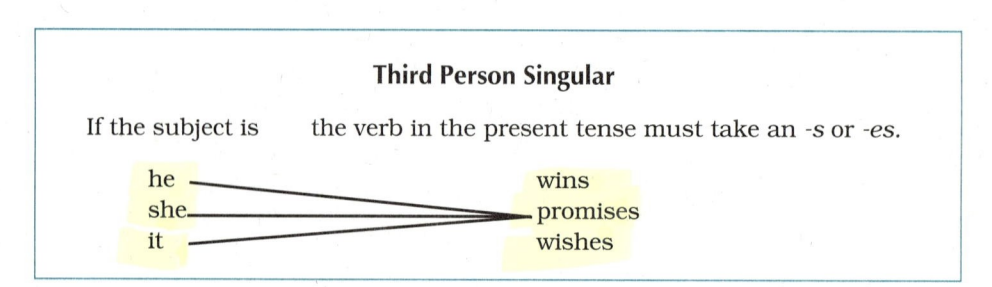

Third Person Singular

If the subject is   the verb in the present tense must take an *-s* or *-es*.

he ⟶ wins
she ⟶ promises
it ⟶ wishes

---

*If you have questions about spelling, see Chapter 30, Part G.

Chapter 6 Present Tense (Agreement) 85

Practice 2 Write the correct form of the verb in the space to the right of the pronoun subject.

Example: **to see**

I _____ see _____

they _____ see _____

she _____ sees _____

to fall

he ___ fall ___

they ___ fall ___

it ___ fall ___

to ask

I ___ ask ___

she ___ ask ___

he ___ ask ___

to go

he ___ go ___

you ___ go ___

we ___ go ___

to rest

I ___ rest ___

they ___ rest ___

she ___ rest ___

to hold

it ___ hold ___

we ___ hold ___

you ___ hold ___

to purchase

she ___ purchase ___

he ___ purchase ___

I ___ purchase ___

Practice 3 First, underline the subject or subjects in each sentence below. Then circle the correct verb form. REMEMBER: If the subject of the sentence is *he, she,* or *it* (third person singular), the verb must end in *-s* or *-es* to agree with the subject.

1. He (manage, **manages**) other people's money.
2. Pick these tomatoes first; they (seem, **seems**) ripe.
3. I always (**carry**, carries) a toothbrush.
4. He never (carry, **carries**) a toothbrush.
5. She (plan, **plans**) to buy a cattle ranch.
6. We (**hitchhike**, hitchhikes) to the beach on Saturdays.
7. He (like, **likes**) his chili hot.
8. They (love, **loves**) exercise because it (help, **helps**) them lose weight.
9. You usually (arrive, **arrives**) one minute before class.
10. Don't buy that computer; it (cost, **costs**) too much.

11. They (cross, *crosses*) Canada by train.

12. Every Christmas, we (fly, *flies*) to Santo Domingo.

13. They (*enjoy*, enjoys) dancing the Texas Two-Step.

14. He usually (ask, *asks*) excellent questions.

15. It (seem, *seems*) that more women are pumping iron these days.

16. She always (swim, *swims*) fifty laps in the morning.

17. We (*wear*, wears) contact lenses because they (*feel*, feels) more comfortable than glasses.

18. By tomorrow, he (*hope*, hopes) to complete the spreadsheet.

19. If you (*prefer*, prefers) an aisle seat, tell the travel agent.

20. She (think, *thinks*) that he (act, *acts*) young for his age.

21. Whenever she (work, *works*) the night shift, she (receive, *receives*) overtime pay.

22. After class, he (jump, *jumps*) into his car, (zoom, *zooms*) to the gym, and (work, works) out.

23. It sometimes (hurt, *hurts*) to hear the truth.

24. He (*smoke*, smokes) constantly, but I (*hate*, hates) smoking.

25. We (*like*, likes) to work outdoors: He (clip, *clips*) hedges, she (pull, *pulls*) weeds, and I (smell, *smells*) the roses.

PART B Troublesome Verb in the Present Tense: TO BE

A few present tense verbs are formed in special ways. The most common of these verbs is *to be*.

Chapter 6   Present Tense (Agreement)   87

Reference Chart: TO BE
(present tense)

Singular		Plural	
If the subject is	the verb is	If the subject is	the verb is
1st person: I	am	1st person: we	are
2nd person: you	are	2nd person: you	are
3rd person: he, she, it	is	3rd person: they	are

The chart also can be read like this:

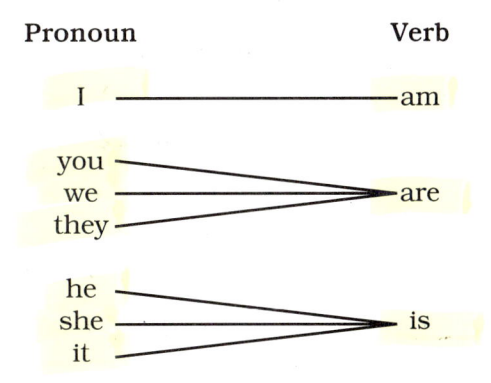

Pronoun	Verb
I	am
you, we, they	are
he, she, it	is

Practice 1   Use the charts to fill in the correct form of *to be* in each blank.

1. he __is__
2. we __are__
3. you __are__
4. I __am__
5. she __is__
6. they __are__
7. it __is__
8. he __is__

Practice 2   Use the charts to fill in the present tense form of *to be* that agrees with the subject.

1. She __is__ a member of the Olympic volleyball team.
2. We __are__ both jewelers, but he __is__ more skilled than I.
3. He __is__ usually late, but this time we __are__ not going to wait for him.

88   Unit 3   Verbs

4. We __are__ sorry about your accident; you __are__ certainly unlucky with roller skates.

5. They __are__ salmon fishermen.

6. He __is__ a musician in the firefighters' band.

7. I __am__ a weekend seamstress.

8. Because she __is__ a native of Morocco, she __is__ able to speak both Arabic and French.

9. I __am__ too nervous to sleep because we __are__ having an accounting exam tomorrow.

10. So you __are__ the one we have heard so much about!

11. We __are__ renewing our lease because you _____ a responsible landlord.

12. When you __are__ willing to do your best, they usually __are__ too.

13. It __is__ quite cool today, but she __is__ sunbathing.

14. She __is__ too quiet, and he __is__ too talkative.

15. I guess you __are__ the best public speaker here.

PART C   Troublesome Verb in the Present Tense: TO HAVE

Reference Chart: TO HAVE

(present tense)

Singular		Plural	
If the subject is	the verb is	If the subject is	the verb is
1st person: I	have	1st person: we	have
2nd person: you	have	2nd person: you	have
3rd person: he, she, it	has	3rd person: they	have

The chart also can be read like this:

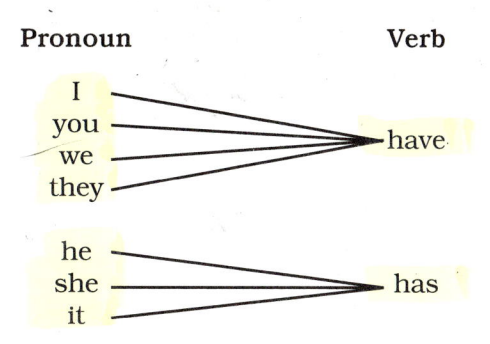

Pronoun → Verb

I, you, we, they → have

he, she, it → has

Practice 1 Fill in the correct form of *to have* in the blank to the right of the subject. Use either chart to make sure the verb agrees with the subject.

1. he _has_
2. we _have_
3. you _have_
4. I _have_
5. they _have_
6. she _has_
7. it _has_
8. we _have_

Practice 2 Fill in the present tense form of *to have* that agrees with the subject. Use the charts.

1. I _have_ a secret.
2. You _have_ a secret too.
3. We _have_ to protect our rivers, lakes, and oceans.
4. It _has_ to be spring because the cherry trees _has_ pink blossoms.
5. She _has_ a great sense of humor.
6. You _have_ a suspicious look on your face, and I _have_ to know why.
7. They _have_ doubts about the plan, but we _have_ none.
8. Soon we _have_ to switch to daylight-saving time.
9. You _have_ one ruby earring, and she _has_ the other.
10. It _has_ to be repaired, and I _have_ just the person to do it for you.

11. She _have_ the questions, and I _have_ the answers.
12. They _have_ a log cabin on Lake Superior.
13. It _have_ twelve rooms and a ping-pong table.
14. You certainly _have_ an excellent sense of direction.
15. If you _have_ $50, I _have_ an offer you can't refuse.

PART D — Troublesome Verb in the Present Tense: TO DO (+ NOT)

Reference Chart: TO DO
(present tense)

Singular		Plural	
If the subject is	the verb is	If the subject is	the verb is
1st person: I	do	1st person: we	do
2nd person: you	do	2nd person: you	do
3rd person: he, she, it	does	3rd person: they	do

The chart also can be read like this:

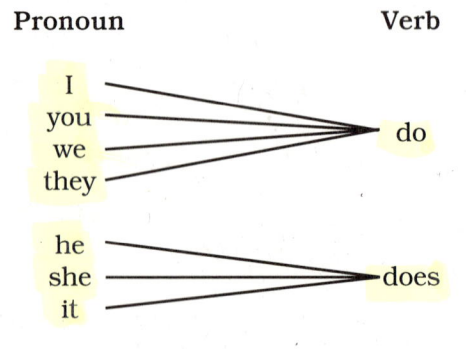

Pronoun	Verb
I, you, we, they	do
he, she, it	does

Practice 1 Fill in the correct form of *to do* in the blanks below. Use either chart to make sure the verb agrees with the subject.

1. he _have_
2. we _have_
3. you _have_
4. I _do_

5. they __are__ drive   7. we __do__ tap dance
6. she __is__ plan   8. it __has__ succeed

As you see in 5 through 8, *do* and *does* often are used as helping verbs.

Practice 2 Use the charts to fill in the correct present tense form of *to do*.

1. She always __do__ the best she can.
2. I always __do__ badly under pressure.
3. It __does__ matter if you forget to vote.
4. They __do__ recycle glass, plastic, and newspaper.
5. You __do__ what I say, or you will be sorry.
6. If you __do__ the dishes, I'll __do__ the laundry.
7. She __do__ have perfect pitch.
8. We most certainly __do__ sell muscle shirts.
9. You really __do__ irritate me.
10. He __do__ prepare income tax forms quickly.
11. He always __do__ well in history courses.
12. She __do__ drug counseling in a high school.
13. He __do__ seem sorry about forgetting your dog's birthday.
14. __do__ they dance the mambo?
15. __do__ she like being a salesperson?

To Do + Not

Once you know how to use *do* and *does*, you are ready for *don't* and *doesn't*.

do + not = don't
does + not = doesn't

Practice 1 In the Positive columns, fill in the correct form of *to do* (*do* or *does*) to agree with the pronoun. In the Negative columns, fill in the correct form of *to do* with the negative *not* (*don't* or *doesn't*).

Unit 3 Verbs

	Pronoun	Positive	Negative		Pronoun	Positive	Negative
1.	he	*does*	*do*	5.	she	*does*	*do*
2.	we	*do*	*does*	6.	they	*do*	*does*
3.	I	*do*	*does*	7.	it	*does*	*do*
4.	they	*do*	*does*	8.	you	*do*	*does*

Practice 2 Fill in either *doesn't* or *don't* in each blank.

1. If they *don't* turn down that music, I'm calling the police.
2. It just *doesn't* make sense.
3. You *don't* have to reply in writing.
4. I *don't* always lock my door at night.
5. They *doesn't* want to miss *60 Minutes*.
6. If you *don't* stop calling collect, I *don't* want to talk to you.
7. He *doesn't* want to know the whole truth.
8. They *don't* realize how lucky they are.
9. Although you *don't* like biking five miles a day to work, it *don't* do your health any harm.
10. It *doesent* fit.
11. When I *don't* try, I *don't* succeed.
12. Although he *doesent* drive fast himself, he *doesent* mind when she does.
13. I *don't* want my boss to transfer me to Toledo, but he *don't* care.
14. *don't* they have ramps for the disabled yet?
15. Even though you *don't* watch *Murphy Brown*, it *don't* mean we can't be roommates.

PART E — Changing Subjects to Pronouns

So far, you have worked on pronouns as subjects *(I, you, he, she, it, we, they)* and on how to make verbs agree with them. Often, however, the subject of a sentence is not a pronoun but a noun—like *dog, banjo, Ms. Callas, José and Robert, swimming* (as in *Swimming keeps me fit*).

To be sure that your verb agrees with your subject, *mentally* change the subject into a pronoun, and then select the correct form of the verb.

If the subject is	it can be changed to the pronoun
1. the speaker himself or herself	I
2. masculine and singular (Bill, one man)	he
3. feminine and singular (Sondra, a woman)	she
4. neither masculine nor feminine and singular (a thing or an action) (this pen, love, running)	it
5. a group that includes the speaker (I) (the family and I)	we
6. a group of persons or things not including the speaker (Jake and Wanda, several pens)	they
7. the person or persons spoken to	you

Practice 1 Change the subjects into pronouns. REMEMBER: If you add *I* to a group of people, the correct pronoun for the whole group is *we*; if you add *you* to a group, the correct pronoun for the whole group is *you*.

Possible Subject	Changed to	Pronoun
Example: Frank	=	he
1. a huge moose	=	she
2. an elevator and a staircase	=	they
3. Mr. McNut	=	he
4. my buddies and I	=	they
5. you and the other nurses	=	we
6. the silk blouse	=	it

94 Unit 3 Verbs

Possible Subject	Changed to	Pronoun
7. his daughter	=	*she*
8. their tent	=	*they*
9. deep sea fishing	=	*they*
10. a calculator and a checkbook	=	*it*

Practice 2 **Review** Change each subject into a pronoun. Then circle the present tense verb that agrees with that subject. (Use the reference chart if you need to.)

Examples: Harry = ____he____   Harry (whistle, (whistles)).

Sam and I = ____we____   Sam and I ((walk), walks).

1. Camilla = *they*   1. Camilla (own, (owns)) a horse farm.

2. Their concert = *it*   2. Their concert ((is), are) sold out.

3. Tod and you = *you*   3. Tod and you ((look), looks) alike.

4. The pilots = *they*   4. The pilots ((take), takes) a break.

5. The men and I = *it*   5. The men and I ((repair), repairs) potholes.

6. This blender = *they*   6. This blender ((grate), grates) cheese.

7. This church = *it*   7. This church ((is), are) very old.

8. Her father = *they*   8. Her father (live, (lives)) in Louisiana.

9. My winter coats = *they* 9. My winter coats (have, (has)) to be cleaned.

10. Our printer = *it*   10. Our printer (jam, (jams)) too often.

Chapter 6 Present Tense (Agreement) 95

11. My roommate = _she_

11. My roommate (disappear, (disappears)) when the dishes need washing.

12. Scuba diving = _is_

12. Scuba diving ((is,) are) her one passion.

13. The house and garden = _are_

13. The house and garden (is, (are)) well cared for.

14. This ring = _she_

14. This ring (seal, (seals)) our love.

15. Aunt Lil and I = _we_

15. Aunt Lil and I ((give,) gives) Swedish massages.

PART F   Practice in Agreement

Practice 1   **Review**   Circle the correct verb in each sentence, making sure it agrees with its subject.

The World's Richest Person

(1) The richest person in the world ((is,) are) the Sultan of Brunei.* (2) The sultan (rule, (rules)) a small, independent kingdom nestled in northern Borneo, a large island in Southeast Asia. (3) His wealth (come, comes) from huge oil and gas deposits. (4) Experts (estimate, estimates) his worth at $25 billion.

(5) The sultan's new palace (rise, rises) above the capital city like a mirage. (6) Its 1,788 rooms (cover, covers) over 300 acres. (7) The garage (hold, holds) 800 cars. (8) The gold-arched dining room (seat, seats) 4,000 people. (9) Miles of air conditioning (run, runs) through

---
*Pronounced *broon eye.*

the palace walls. (10) The sultan and his family (occupy, occupies) 700 of the rooms. (11) In the others, the government (conduct, conducts) its business. (12) Shy and withdrawn, the sultan (keep, keeps) the palace closed to all outsiders.

(13) The whole country (profit, profits) from the oil that (make, makes) the sultan so rich. (14) Citizens (earn, earns) an average of $18,000 a year, more than the average American. (15) The country (has, have) a welfare system that (pay, pays) for health, housing, and education for everyone. (16) Other government programs (supply, supplies) loans for cars and even color televisions. (17) Large shopping centers (sprawl, sprawls) everywhere. (18) The people of Brunei definitely (live, lives) in the twentieth century.

Practice 2

Review In each blank below, write the *present tense* form of one of the verbs from this list. Your sentences can be funny; just make sure that each verb agrees with each subject.

~~talk~~	punch	tickle	~~drink~~
~~kiss~~	arrive	~~sing~~	~~dance~~

(1) Many famous people _drink_ at the party. (2) Charles Barkley _kiss_ Princess Diana. (3) Madonna and I _dance_ near the punchbowl, not far from the Vice President, who _talk_ with a small poodle. (4) Several rock stars _sing_ in one corner of the room. (5) Then Sly Stallone _arrive_, and everybody goes home.

Practice 3

Review The sentences that follow have singular subjects and verbs. To gain skill in verb agreement, rewrite each sentence, changing the subject from *singular* to *plural*. Then make sure the verb agrees with the new subject. Keep all verbs in the present tense.

Chapter 6 Present Tense (Agreement) 97

Example: The train stops at Cold Spring.

Rewrite: *The trains stop at Cold Spring.*

1. The store opens at 9 a.m.

    Rewrite: *The stores opens at 9 a.m.*

2. The movie ticket costs too much.

    Rewrite: *The movie tickets costs too much*

3. The pipeline carries oil from Alaska.

    Rewrite: *The pipelines carries oil from Alaska.*

4. A white horse grazes by the fence.

    Rewrite: *A white horse grazes by fences*

5. My brother owns a variety store.

    Rewrite: *My brothers owns a variety store*

6. The family needs good health insurance.

    Rewrite: *The family needs good health insurance*

7. The beaver builds a dam.

    Rewrite: *The beavers builds a dam.*

8. The backup singer wears green contact lenses.

    Rewrite: *The backups singer wears green contact lenses.*

9. My daughter wants lace knee socks.

    Rewrite: *My daughters want lace knee socks*

10. A wave laps softly against the dock.

    Rewrite: *A waves lap softly against the dock.*

Practice 4 **Review** The sentences that follow have plural subjects and verbs. Rewrite each sentence, changing the subject from *plural* to *singular*. Then make sure the verb agrees with the new subject. Keep all verbs in the present tense.

1. My neighbors vacation in Bermuda.

    Rewrite: _____

2. The engines roar loudly.

   Rewrite: _____

3. The students invest in the stock market.

   Rewrite: _____

4. The inmates watch *America's Most Wanted*.

   Rewrite: _____

5. Overhead, seagulls ride on the wind.

   Rewrite: _____

6. Good card players know when to bluff.

   Rewrite: _____

7. The farmers plant two crops each spring.

   Rewrite: _____

8. On Saturday, the pharmacists stay late.

   Rewrite: _____

9. The welders prefer working on an assembly line.

   Rewrite: _____

10. The jewels from Bangkok are on display.

    Rewrite: _____

Practice 5

Review Rewrite this paragraph in the present tense by changing the verbs.

(1) Ralph loved to shop. (2) Night after night, he dreamed of spending a month at the West Edmonton Mall in Edmonton, Canada. (3) He needed that much time in the biggest shopping mall in the world. (4) Its 800 shops fascinated him. (5) In his dream, Ralph eyed merchandise, tried on clothing, and bargained with salespeople. (6) He dashed around the mall's 110 acres while he thought about other purchases he wanted to make. (7) When he finished shopping, he and a friend went to a different theater every night and ate in a different restaurant. (8) They did all this without ever leaving the mall. (9) Only one thing was wrong with Ralph's dream. (10) Every morning, Ralph woke up totally exhausted.

PART G   Special Problems in Agreement

So far, you have learned that if the subject of a sentence is third person singular *(he, she, it)* or a word that can be changed into *he, she,* or *it,* then the verb takes *-s* or *-es* in the present tense.

In special cases, however, you will need to know more before you can make your verb agree with your subject.

Focusing on the Subject

> (1) A box of chocolates sits on the table.

- *What* sits on the table?
- Don't be confused by the prepositional phrase before the verb—*of chocolates.*
- Just one *box* sits on the table.
- *A box* is the subject. *A box* takes the third person singular verb—*sits.*

A box (of chocolates) sits on the table.
↓ ↓
subject   verb
(singular) (singular)

> (2) The children in the park play for hours.

- *Who* play for hours?
- Don't be confused by the prepositional phrase before the verb—*in the park*.
- The *children* play for hours.
- *The children* is the subject. *The children* takes the third person plural verb—*play*.

$$\text{The children (in the park) play for hours.}$$
$$\downarrow \qquad\qquad\qquad\qquad \downarrow$$
$$\text{subject} \qquad\qquad\qquad \text{verb}$$
$$\text{(plural)} \qquad\qquad\qquad \text{(plural)}$$

> (3) The purpose of the exercises is to improve your spelling.

- *What* is to improve your spelling?
- Don't be confused by the prepositional phrase before the verb—*of the exercises*.
- The *purpose* is to improve your spelling.
- *The purpose* is the subject. *The purpose* takes the third person singular verb—*is*.

$$\text{The purpose (of the exercises) is to improve your spelling.}$$
$$\downarrow \qquad\qquad\qquad\qquad \downarrow$$
$$\text{subject} \qquad\qquad\qquad \text{verb}$$
$$\text{(singular)} \qquad\qquad\qquad \text{(singular)}$$

As you can see from these examples, sometimes what seems to be the subject is really not the subject. Prepositional phrases (groups of words beginning with *of, in, at,* and so on) *cannot* contain the subject of a sentence. One way to find the subject of a sentence that contains a prepositional phrase is to ask yourself *what makes sense as the subject.*

> My friends from the old neighborhood often { visits / visit } me.

- Which makes sense as the subject of the sentence: *my friends* or *the old neighborhood?*

> (a) My friends . . . visit me.

> (b) The old neighborhood . . . visits me.

- Obviously, sentence (a) makes sense; it clearly expresses the intention of the writer.

Practice Now try these sentences. Cross out any confusing prepositional phrases, and circle the correct verb.

1. The houses in that neighborhood (cost, *costs*) too much.
2. The traffic lights along Clark Street (*blink*, blinks) to a salsa beat.
3. The price of the repairs (seem, *seems*) high.
4. His lack of knowledge (amaze, *amazes*) me.
5. The coffee stains on his résumé (*show*, shows) his carelessness.
6. The secret of her success (*is*, are) persistence.
7. The cause of many illnesses (*is*, are) poor diet.
8. The polar bears in the zoo (*miss*, misses) the Arctic.
9. One American in ten (drink, *drinks*) too much.
10. The pizza at Rosario's (have, *has*) lots of cheese.
11. The red dress on the rack (look, *looks*) stylish.
12. The laboratories on the fifth floor (*need*, needs) cleaning.

Spotting Special Singular Subjects

Either of the students
Neither of the students
Each of the students   seems happy.
One of the students
Every one of the students

- *Either, neither, each, one,* and *every one* are the real subjects of these sentences.
- *Either, neither, each, one,* and *every one* are special singular subjects. They always take a singular verb.
- REMEMBER: The subject is never part of a prepositional phrase, so *the students* cannot be the subject.

Practice 1 Circle the correct verb.

1. One of our satellites (**is**, are) lost in space.
2. Each of my brothers (wear, **wears**) cinnamon after-shave lotion.
3. Neither of the muffins (**is**, are) made with oat bran.
4. Each of us (carry, **carries**) a snakebite kit.
5. Neither of those excuses (sound, **sounds**) believable.
6. One of the mirrors (have, **has**) a thick gold frame.
7. Either of the radios (cost, **costs**) about $30.
8. Each of the towns (celebrate, **celebrates**) its own holiday.
9. Neither of those cities (**is**, are) the capital of Brazil.
10. One of the butlers (commit, **commits**) the crime, but which one?
11. One of the desserts in front of you (do, **does**) not contain sugar.
12. Each of the taxi drivers (speed, **speeds**).

Practice 2 Write five sentences using the special singular subjects. Make sure your sentences are in the present tense.

1. _____
2. _____
3. _____
4. _____
5. _____

Using THERE to Begin a Sentence

(1) *There* is a squirrel in the yard.

(2) *There* are two squirrels in the yard.

- Although sentences sometimes begin with *there*, *there* cannot be the subject of a sentence.

Chapter 6 Present Tense (Agreement)

- Usually, the subject *follows* the verb in sentences that begin with *there.*

To find the real subject (so you will know how to make the verb agree), mentally drop the *there*, and rearrange the sentence to put the subject at the beginning.

(1) There is a squirrel in the yard.

becomes

A squirrel   *is* in the yard.
↓   ↓
subject   verb
(singular)   *(singular)*

(2) There are two squirrels in the yard.

becomes

Two squirrels   *are* in the yard.
↓   ↓
subject   verb
(plural)   *(plural)*

BE CAREFUL: Good writers avoid using *there* to begin a sentence. Whenever possible, they write more directly: *Two squirrels are in the yard.*

Practice 1   In each sentence, mentally drop the *there*, and rearrange the sentence to put the subject at the beginning. Then circle the verb that agrees with the subject of the sentence.

1. There (is, are) a day-care center on campus.

2. There (is, are) a beluga whale in the city aquarium.

3. There (is, are) two beluga whales in the city aquarium.

4. There (is, are) one good reason to quit this job—my supervisor.

5. There (is, are) six customers ahead of you.

6. There (is, are) a water fountain in the lounge.

7. There (is, are) a house and a barn in the wheat field.

8. There (is, are) only two shopping days left before my birthday.

9. There (is, are) thousands of plant species in the rain forest.

10. There (is, are) a single blue egg in the nest over the kitchen door.

Practice 2

On a separate sheet of paper, rewrite each sentence in Practice 1 so that it does not begin with *there is* or *there are*. Sentences (1) and (2) are done for you.

Examples:
1. A day-care center is on campus.
2. A beluga whale swims in the city aquarium.

Choosing the Correct Verb in Questions

(1) Where is Bob?

(2) Where are Bob and Lee?

(3) Why are they singing?

(4) Have you painted the hall yet?

- In questions, the subject usually *follows* the verb.
- In sentence (1), the subject is *Bob*. *Bob* takes the third person singular verb *is*.
- In sentence (2), the subject is *Bob and Lee*. *Bob and Lee* takes the third person plural verb *are*.
- What is the subject in sentence (3)? __*bob*__ What verb does it take? _____
- What is the subject in sentence (4)? _____ What verb does it take? _____

If you can't find the subject, mentally turn the question around:

(1) Bob is . . .

(2) Bob and Lee are . . .

Practice 1

Circle the correct verb.

1. Where (**is**, are) my bomber jacket?

2. (**Have**, Has) the waiter gone to lunch?

3. Why (is, **are**) so many children taking drugs?

4. How (do, **does**) Igor like working downtown?

5. Who (is, **are**) those people on the fire escape?

6. Which (is, **are**) your day off?

7. What (**do**, does) she think about studying dentistry?

8. What (have, **has**) that child done with his peanut butter sandwich?

9. (**Have**, Has) you considered taking a cruise to Alaska?

10. Where (**is**, are) Don's power tools?

11. (**Have**, Has) the groundhog raided the zucchini patch today?

12. Well, what (**do**, does) you know about that?

Practice 2 Write five questions of your own. Make sure that your questions are in the present tense and that the verbs agree with the subjects.

1. _____

2. _____

3. _____

4. _____

5. _____

Using WHO, WHICH, and THAT as Relative Pronouns

When you use a relative pronoun—*who, which,* or *that*—to introduce a dependent idea, make sure you choose the correct verb.*

> (1) I know a woman *who* plays expert chess.

- Sentence (1) uses the singular verb *plays* because *who* relates or refers to *a woman* (singular).

> (2) Suede coats, *which* stain easily, should not be worn in the rain.

- Sentence (2) uses the plural verb *stain* because *which* relates to the subject *suede coats* (plural).

---

*For work on relative pronouns, see Chapter 16.

106 Unit 3 Verbs

> (3) Computers *that* talk make me nervous.

- Sentence (3) uses the plural verb *talk* because *that* relates to what word? _____

Practice 1 Write the word that the *who, which,* or *that* relates or refers to in the blank at the right; then circle the correct form of the verb.

Example: I like people who (is, **are**) clever. .... *people*

1. My office has a robot that (fetch, **fetches**) the mail. .... *has*

2. Always choose lemons that (**have**, has) smooth skins. .... *that*

3. My husband, who (take, **takes**) marvelous photographs, won the Nikon Prize. .... *who*

4. He likes women who (is, **are**) very ambitious. .... *He*

5. The old house, which (sit, **sits**) on a cliff above the sea, is called Balston Heights. .... *on*

6. I like a person who (think, **thinks**) for himself or herself. .... *for*

7. People who (love, **loves**) to read usually write well. .... *who*

8. Refined foods, which (**include**, includes) white sugar and white flour, have few vitamins. .... *which*

9. The only airline that (fly, **flies**) to Charlottesville is booked solid. .... *that*

10. People who (**live**, lives) in glass houses should invest in blinds. .... *in*

11. Most students want jobs that (challenge, challenges) them.

12. Carotene, which (protect, protects) against cancer, is found in carrots and sweet potatoes.

Practice 2 Proofread the following paragraph for a variety of verb agreement errors. First underline all present tense verbs. Then correct any errors above the lines.

(1) Police detectives who works on difficult cases collect physical evidence, track down clues, and interview witnesses. (2) But how does police solve a crime when few clues exist? (3) Today, a number of police departments hires psychics to help them. (4) There is several techniques that psychics use to solve crimes. (5) One of these methods is psychometry, or sensing information from objects. (6) A psychic often gets strong impressions from jewelry or clothing belonging to the victim. (7) Nancy Czetli of Greensburg, Pennsylvania, a psychic who sometimes use this method, has worked on 200 homicide cases. (8) Many psychics also use telepathy, which is the ability to sense another person's thoughts. (9) A psychic at a crime scene pick up the thoughts of both the victim and the criminal. (10) Either of these methods allow the psychic to tell police what happened, to locate a missing person, or to provide an exact description of a murderer. (11) Nancy Czetli feels that psychic ability is more common than many people believes. (12) She calls it a survival skill that is more developed in some people than in others.

108 Unit 3 Verbs

Chapter Highlights

- A subject and a present tense verb must agree:
    The light flickers. *(singular subject, singular verb)*
    The lights flicker. *(plural subject, plural verb)*

- Only third person singular subjects *(he, she, it)* take verbs ending in *-s* or *-es*.

- Three troublesome present tense verbs are *to be*, *to have*, and *to do*.

- When a prepositional phrase comes between a subject and verb, the verb must agree with the subject.
    The *chairs* on the porch *are* painted white.

- The subjects *either, neither, each, one,* and *every one* are always singular.
    Neither of the mechanics *repairs* transmissions.

- In a sentence beginning with *there is* or *there are*, the subject follows the verb.
    There are three *oysters* on your plate.

- In questions, the subject usually follows the verb.
    Where are *Kimi and Fred?*

- Relative pronouns (*who, which,* and *that*) refer to the word with which the verb must agree.
    A *woman who* has children must manage time skillfully.

Chapter Review

Proofread this essay carefully for verb agreement. First, underline all present tense verbs. Then correct any verb agreement errors in the space above the error.

The Killer Whales of Sea World

(1) Sea World maintains large parks in San Diego, California; Aurora, Ohio; and Orlando, Florida.   (2) The show at each park star a killer whale, which is also called an orca.   (3) Audiences gasp when one of these fierce animals leaps twenty feet into the air and plant a gentle kiss on someone's cheek.   (4) At first, this amazing trick seems hard to understand.

(5) Killer whales certainly deserves their name. (6) Other whales weigh more, and killer whales rarely grow longer than thirty feet, but they is the surest killers in the sea. (7) Only the great white shark challenges them. (8) The orca lives in every ocean of the world. (9) It is a successful predator because it outsmarts and outraces all its prey. (10) It also have powerful teeth designed for tearing flesh. (11) Though it usually eats fish, a hungry killer whale think nothing of feasting on a sea lion or even an elephant seal, which weighs as much as two tons. (12) Even giant hundred-ton blue whales are known to fall prey to the powerful orca.

(13) However, killer whales are also very sociable. (14) They lives and hunts in groups, or pods, of up to twenty-five animals. (15) They enjoy close family relationships. (16) Children nurses for almost two years, and older males protect youngsters and females. (17) Like other whales, killer whales help one another when there are trouble.

(18) Animal trainers at Sea World understands that the desire for companionship in killer whales are almost as great as the need for food. (19) When regular feeding satisfies the hunting instinct, the social urge becomes very important. (20) Using food and kindness as rewards, trainers teaches killer whales to perform tricks that combine great physical skill and gentleness.

Chapter 7

Past Tense

PART A   Regular Verbs in the Past Tense
PART B   Irregular Verbs in the Past Tense
PART C   Troublesome Verb in the Past Tense: TO BE
PART D   Review

PART A   Regular Verbs in the Past Tense

Verbs in the past tense express actions that occurred in the past. The italicized words in the following sentences are verbs in the past tense.

> (1) They *noticed* a dent in the fender.
> (2) She *played* the guitar very well.
> (3) For years I *studied* yoga.

- What ending do all these verbs take? _____
- In general, then, what ending do you add to put a verb in the past tense? _____
- Verbs that add *-d* or *-ed* to form the past tense are called *regular verbs*.

Chapter 7 Past Tense 111

Practice 1 Some of the verbs in these sentences are in the present tense; others are in the past tense. Circle the verb in each sentence. Write *present* in the column at the right if the verb is in the present tense; write *past* if the verb is in the past tense.

1. James stroked his beard. _past_
2. Light travels 186,000 miles in a second. _present_
3. They play jazz on weekends. _past_
4. Magellan sailed around the world. _present_
5. These morning glories bloom at dawn. _present_
6. The lake looks calm as glass. _present_
7. All morning, Jerome studied French. _present_
8. Sheila loves Arnold Schwarzenegger films. _past_
9. Mount St. Helens erupted in 1980. _past_
10. After school, Jennifer works in the bookstore. _present_
11. That chemical plant pollutes our water. _present_
12. Ellen floated on her back. _past_
13. A committee of five selected the new auditor. _past_
14. A robin nested in the mailbox. _past_
15. He owns two exercise bikes. _present_

Practice 2 The short sentences in the left-hand column are in the present tense. In the column on the right, fill in the past tense form of each verb.*

Present Tense	Past Tense
1. They succeed.	1. They _succeed_.
2. The brakes squeak.	2. The brakes _squeak_.
3. We canoe often.	3. We _canoe_ often.
4. You shop for hours.	4. You _shop_ for hours.
5. I need a doughnut.	5. I _need_ a doughnut.

*If you have questions about spelling, see Chapter 30.

112 Unit 3 Verbs

6. He tries too hard.
7. The bees buzz loudly.
8. The shop closes at eight.
9. The pitcher hurls a curve ball.
10. A taxi roars past.
11. The soup boils over.
12. We believe you.
13. The snowplow passes.
14. She dresses very conservatively.
15. Ollie memorizes his notes.

6. He _tries_ too hard.
7. The bees _buzz_ loudly.
8. The shop _closes_ at eight.
9. The pitcher _hurls_ a curve ball.
10. A taxi _roars_ past.
11. The soup _boils_ over.
12. We _believe_ you.
13. The snowplow _passes_.
14. She _dresses_ very conservatively.
15. Ollie _memorizes_ his notes.

As you can see from this exercise, many verbs form the past tense by adding either -d or -ed.

Furthermore, in the past tense, agreement is not a problem, except for the verb *to be*. This is because verbs in the past tense have only one form, no matter what the subject is.

Practice 3   The verbs have been omitted from this paragraph. Choose verbs from the list below, and write the past tense form of each verb in the blank spaces. Do not use a verb twice.

approach	wink	shriek	stay ✓
rustle	cry ✓	leap ✓	cook ✓
move ✓	burn	chase	help
camp ✓	arrive ✓	climb ✓	laugh

(1) Last December, Tom and I _camp_ overnight in Everglades National Park. (2) We _arrive_ at sunset and _cook_ eggs and beans over a campfire. (3) Suddenly, the dry grass near us _move_, and a very large alligator _leap_. (4) We _cry_ and _climb_ into the van, where we _stay_ all night.

Practice 4

Fill in the past tense of each verb.

1. In 1923, Luis Angel Firpo __challenged__ (challenge) Jack Dempsey.

2. Firpo __wanted__ (want) to be the new heavyweight champion of the world.

3. The two boxers __battled__ (battle) in the fiercest title bout ever.

4. Excitement __filled__ (fill) the air as 85,000 fans __crowded__ (crowd) into New York City's Polo Grounds.

5. Scalpers __charged__ (charge) as much as $150 for a ticket.

6. From the opening bell, the fighters __slugged__ (slug) it out.

7. Dempsey __knocked__ (knock) Firpo down seven times and __closed__ (close) in to end the fight.

8. To everyone's surprise, Firpo __unloaded__ (unload) a powerful right-hand punch to Dempsey's jaw.

9. The champion __sailed__ (sail) through the ropes and out of the ring.

10. Only his legs __remained__ (remain) in view as they __twisted__ (twist) in the air.

11. The dazed Dempsey __staggered__ (stagger) back into the ring and barely __managed__ (manage) to finish the round.

12. Dempsey __opened__ (open) the second round by quickly flooring Firpo twice.

13. Then the champ __flattened__ (flatten) Firpo with a left to the jaw.

14. Bleeding, Firpo __tryed__ (try) hard to get up, but he __stiffened__ (stiffen) and __passed__ (pass) out.

15. The whole match __lasted__ (last) just three minutes and fifty-seven seconds.

PART B Irregular Verbs in the Past Tense

Instead of adding *-d* or *-ed*, some verbs form the past tense in other ways.

> (1) He *threw* a knuckle ball.
>
> (2) She *gave* him a dollar.
>
> (3) He *rode* from his farm into the town.

- The italicized words in these sentences are also verbs in the past tense.
- Do these verbs form the past tense by adding *-d* or *-ed*? _____
- *Threw, gave,* and *rode* are the past tense of verbs that do not add *-d* or *-ed* to form the past tense.
- Verbs that do not add *-d* or *-ed* to form the past tense are called *irregular verbs*.

A chart listing common irregular verbs follows.

Reference Chart: Irregular Verbs

Simple Form	Past	Simple Form	Past
be	was, were	forgive	forgave
become	became	freeze	froze
begin	began	get	got
blow	blew	give	gave
break	broke	go	went
bring	brought	grow	grew
build	built	have	had
buy	bought	hear	heard
catch	caught	hide	hid
choose	chose	hold	held
come	came	hurt	hurt
cut	cut	keep	kept
dive	dove (dived)	know	knew
do	did	lay	laid
draw	drew	lead	led
drink	drank	leave	left
drive	drove	let	let
eat	ate	lie	lay
fall	fell	lose	lost
feed	fed	make	made
feel	felt	mean	meant
fight	fought	meet	met
find	found	pay	paid
fly	flew	put	put
forget	forgot	quit	quit

Reference Chart: Irregular Verbs *(continued)*

Simple Form	Past	Simple Form	Past
read	read	spring	sprang
ride	rode	stand	stood
ring	rang	steal	stole
rise	rose	strike	struck
run	ran	swim	swam
say	said	take	took
see	saw	teach	taught
seek	sought	tear	tore
sell	sold	tell	told
send	sent	think	thought
set	set	throw	threw
shake	shook	understand	understood
shine	shone (shined)	wake	woke
sing	sang	wear	wore
sit	sat	win	won
sleep	slept	wind	wound
speak	spoke	write	wrote
spend	spent		

Learn the unfamiliar past tense forms by grouping together verbs that change from present tense to past tense in the same way. For example, some irregular verbs change *ow* in the present to *ew* in the past:

blow	blew
grow	grew
know	knew
throw	threw

Another group changes from *i* in the present to *a* in the past:

begin	began
drink	drank
ring	rang
sing	sang
spring	sprang
swim	swam

As you write, refer to the chart. If you are unsure of the past tense form of a verb that is not in the chart, check a dictionary. For example, if you look up the verb *go* in the dictionary, you will find an entry like this:

go \ went \ gone \ going

The first word listed is used to form the *present* tense of the verb (I *go*, he *goes*, and so on). The second word is the *past* tense (I *went*, he *went*, and so on). The third word is the *past participle (gone)*, and the last word is the *present participle (going)*.

Some dictionaries list different forms only for irregular verbs. If no past tense is listed, you know that the verb is regular and that its past tense ends in *-d* or *-ed*.

116 Unit 3 Verbs

Practice 1 Use the chart to fill in the correct form of the verb in the past tense.

1. Beryl Markham _grew_ (grow) up in Kenya, East Africa.
2. As a child, this adventurer _went_ (go) hunting with African tribesmen.
3. Once, while a lion attacked her, she _lay_ (lie) still, thus saving her own life.
4. At age seventeen, she _sought_ (seek) a license to train horses, becoming the first woman trainer in Kenya.
5. Her friend Tom Black _taught_ (teach) her how to fly a small plane, the D. H. Gipsy Moth.
6. By her late twenties, she _was_ (be) a licensed pilot.
7. As Africa's first female bush pilot, Markham regularly _flew_ (fly) across East Africa, carrying supplies, mail, and passengers.
8. In 1936, she _made_ (make) a solo flight across the Atlantic Ocean.
9. Despite poor flying conditions, fatigue, and low fuel, she _kept_ (keep) her plane in the air for more than twenty hours.
10. Markham _set_ (set) a record as the first woman to fly alone nonstop from England to Nova Scotia.
11. In 1942, she _wrote_ (write) *West with the Night*, a book about her thrilling life.
12. Reprinted in 1983, this book _became_ (become) a great success.

Practice 2 Use the chart to fill in the correct past tense form of each verb.

(1) The story of the famous Hope diamond _began_ (begin) in India in 1701. (2) Jean Baptiste Tavernier, a French jeweler and traveler, _bought_ (buy) a huge blue diamond and _brought_ (bring) it home with him. (3) The jewel _became_ (become) known as the Blue Tavernier and eventually

Chapter 7 Past Tense 117

wound (wind) up in the French royal collection. (4) During the French Revolution, someone _stole_ (steal) it. (5) Most people quickly _forgot_ (forget) about the stone. (6) However, forty years later, part of the diamond _did_ (do) show up in England. (7) H. T. Hope, a banker, _paid_ (pay) a great sum for it. (8) He _left_ (leave) it to his son, who soon _spent_ (spend) his fortune and _sold_ (sell) the diamond to the sultan of Turkey. (9) Finally, the Hope diamond _came_ (come) into the possession of Mrs. Edward B. McLean. (10) Soon after buying the jewel, she _lost_ (lose) a child in an accident, _saw_ (see) her family break up, and _went_ (go) bankrupt. (11) In the end, Mrs. McLean _took_ (take) her own life. (12) In 1958, the last private owner of the unlucky stone _sent_ (send) it to one of the Smithsonian museums in Washington, D.C., where it still can be seen.

Practice 3 Look over the list of irregular verbs on pages 114 and 115. Pick out the ten verbs that give you the most trouble, and list them here.

Simple	Past	Simple	Past
dive	dove (dived)		
shine	shone (shined)		

Now on a separate sheet of paper, write one paragraph using *all ten* verbs. Your paragraph may be humorous; just make sure your verbs are correct.

PART C — Troublesome Verb in the Past Tense: TO BE

Reference Chart: TO BE
(past tense)

	Singular		Plural
1st person:	I was	→	we were
2nd person:	you were	→	you were
3rd person:	he, she, it was	→	they were

- Note that the first and third person singular forms are the same—*was*.

Practice In each sentence, circle the correct past tense form of the verb *to be*—either *was* or *were*.

1. Our instructor (**was**, were) a pilot and skydiver.
2. You always (was, **were**) a good friend.
3. Georgia O'Keeffe (**was**, were) a great twentieth-century American painter.
4. Why (was, **were**) they wearing red ribbons?
5. Bonnie Raitt (**was**, were) a Grammy Award winner in 1990.
6. You (was, **were**) right, and I (**was**, were) wrong.
7. The president and the first lady (was, **were**) both here.
8. I (**was**, were) seven when my sister (was, **were**) born.
9. Carmen (**was**, were) a Republican, but her cousins (was, **were**) Democrats.
10. Some people say that Greg Louganis (**was**, were) the world's greatest diver.
11. The bride and groom (was, **were**) present, but where (**was**, were) the minister?
12. (Was, **Were**) you happy working in sales?

13. The weather (**was**, were) perfect for hiking.
14. Either they (was, **were**) late, or she (**was**, were) early.
15. Who (**was**, were) the woman we saw you with last night?
16. The watch and the necklace (was, **were**) her favorite possessions.
17. You (was, **were**) on my mind.
18. At this time last year, Sarni (**was**, were) in Egypt.
19. How (**was**, were) Professor Stein's lecture yesterday?
20. That man (**was**, were) selling tires when I (**was**, were) a child.

To Be + Not

Be careful of verb agreement if you use the past tense of *to be* with *not* as a contraction.

was + not = wasn't
were + not = weren't

Practice In each sentence, fill in the blank(s) with either *wasn't* or *weren't*.

1. The printer ribbons _wasn't_ on sale.
2. That papaya _wasn't_ cheap.
3. He _weren't_ happy about the opening of the nuclear power plant.
4. _Wasn't_ you here for the midterm?
5. When they finally arrived at our house, we _wasn't_ there.
6. She _wasn't_ bored, was she?
7. Dave and I _weren't_ in New Orleans at the same time.
8. This fireplace _wasn't_ built properly.
9. The last time I saw Bonnie, she and Clyde _wasn't_ speaking.
10. The parents _weren't_ willing to tolerate drug dealers near the school.
11. That _wasn't_ the point!

120 Unit 3 Verbs

12. My car keys _wasn't_ in my pocket.
13. Three of the finalists _wasn't_ at the awards ceremony.
14. It _wasn't_ the best movie I ever saw; it _wasn't_ the worst either.
15. That history quiz _wasn't_ so bad.
16. If she knew the answer, she _wasn't_ talking.
17. He and I liked each other, but we _wasn't_ able to agree about anything.
18. That remark _wasn't_ very funny.
19. If you _wasn't_ there, you can't understand what I mean.
20. Many young couples _wasn't_ able to afford homes.

PART D Review

Practice 1 **Review** Rewrite this paragraph, changing the verbs to the past tense.*

(1) Above the office where I work is a karate studio. (2) Every day as I go through my files, make out invoices, and write letters, I hear loud shrieks and crashes from the studio above me. (3) All day long, the walls tremble, the ceiling shakes, and little pieces of plaster fall like snow onto my desk. (4) Sometimes, the noise does not bother me; other times, I wear earplugs. (5) If I am in a very bad mood, I stand on my desk and pound out reggae rhythms on the ceiling with my shoe. (6) However, I do appreciate one thing. (7) The job teaches me to concentrate, no matter what.

_____
_____
_____
_____
_____

*See also Chapter 22, "Consistent Tense," for more practice.

Chapter 7 Past Tense 121

_____

_____

_____

_____

Practice 2 **Review** Read the following paragraph for meaning. Then fill in a different past tense verb in every blank.

(1) In 1861, a French naturalist _fly_ through a dense jungle of Cambodia in Southeast Asia. (2) He _dove_ to a clearing and _____ across the treetops. (3) He _____ in amazement. (4) Five enormous towers _____ above him. (5) With a pounding heart, he _____ to the most gorgeous temple imaginable. (6) He _____ 250 feet to the top of the highest tower. (7) A huge abandoned city _____ for miles all around him. (8) Carvings of gods and goddesses _____ the palaces and monuments. (9) Unlike the ruins of Greece and Rome, every stone in these buildings _____ in place. (10) Local people _____ this marvelous lost city Angkor. (11) Five hundred years before, it had been the largest city in Asia. (12) Then for unknown reasons, its entire population _____ .

Chapter Highlights

- **Regular verbs add -d or -ed in the past tense:**
    We *decided*.
    The frog *jumped*.
    He *outfoxed* the fox.

- **Irregular verbs in the past tense change in irregular ways:**
    We *took* a marketing course.
    Owen *ran* fast.
    Jan *brought* dessert.

- *To be* is the only verb that takes more than one form in the past tense:

    I was   we were
    you were   you were
    he
    she } was   they were
    it

Chapter Review

Fill in the past tense form of each verb in parentheses. Some verbs are regular; others are irregular.

Madame Curie

(1) Marie Curie _lead_ (lead) a heroic life. (2) Honored as one of the most brilliant scientists of the twentieth century, she also _triumph_ (triumph) over great hardship and loss.

(3) Born in Poland in 1867, Marie Curie _begin_ (begin) life as the daughter of a poor chemistry professor. (4) While a young woman, she _postpone_ (postpone) her own studies and _finance_ (finance) her older sister's medical education with the money she _earned_ (earn) as a governess. (5) Then Marie's turn _come_ (come). (6) She _moved_ (move) to Paris in 1891 and _become_ (become) the first woman to enroll in the Sorbonne, the greatest university in France. (7) For three years, she _study_ (study) hard and _live_ (live) in poverty. (8) Her work _pay_

Chapter 7 Past Tense 123

(pay) off. (9) The young scholar _graduate_ (graduate) first in her class with a degree in physical science. (10) One year later, she _completed_ (complete) another degree, in mathematics.

(11) The eleven years from 1895 to 1906 _be_ (be) the happiest of her life. (12) She _marry_ (marry) Pierre Curie, a well-known scientist. (13) The devoted couple _raise_ (raise) two daughters and _works_ (work) together every day on their research in radiation. (14) In 1898, Madame Curie _find_ (find) two new radioactive elements. (15) One _be_ (be) radium. (16) The other she _call_ (call) polonium, after her native land. (17) In 1903, the Curies _share_ (share) the Nobel Prize in physics. (18) When the French Legion of Honor _offer_ (offer) Pierre membership, he _refuse_ (refuse) it because his wife _be_ (be) left out.

(19) A truck _striked_ (strike) and _killed_ (kill) Pierre in 1906. (20) This bitter blow _drive_ (drive) Madame Curie further into her work. (21) She _step_ (step) into Pierre's professorship to become the first woman teacher at the Sorbonne. (22) Then in 1911, she _achieved_ (achieve) a second Nobel Prize, this one in chemistry.

(23) During World War I, the world-famous doctor _risk_ (risk) her life driving an ambulance and treating soldiers at the battlefront. (24) Later, she _establish_ (establish) research centers in Paris and Warsaw, _lecture_ (lecture) in many countries, and _continued_ (continue) her studies. (25) Madame Curie _die_ (die) in 1934 of cancer, caused by years of exposure to radioactivity.

Chapter 8

The Past Participle in Action

PART A Defining the Past Participle
PART B Past Participles of Regular Verbs
PART C Past Participles of Irregular Verbs
PART D Using the Present Perfect Tense
PART E Using the Past Perfect Tense
PART F Using the Passive Voice
PART G Using Past Participles as Adjectives

PART A Defining the Past Participle

Every verb has one form that can be combined with helping verbs like *has* and *have* to make verbs of more than one word. This form is called the *past participle*.

(1) She has solved the problem.
(2) I have solved the problem.
(3) He had solved the problem already.

Chapter 8 The Past Participle in Action 125

- Each sentence on the previous page contains a two-part verb. Circle the *first* part, or *helping verb*, in each sentence, and write each helping verb in the blanks that follow:

    (1) _____

    (2) _____

    (3) _____

- Underline the *second* part, or *main verb*, in each sentence. This word, a form of the verb *to solve*, is the same in all three. Write it here:

    _____

- *Solved* is the past participle of *to solve*.

The past participle never changes, no matter what the subject is, no matter what the helping verb is.

PART B — Past Participles of Regular Verbs

Fill in the past participle in each series below:

Present Tense	Past Tense	Helping Verb + Past Participle
(1) Beth dances.	(1) Beth danced.	(1) Beth has _danced_.
(2) They decide.	(2) They decided.	(2) They have _decided_.
(3) He jumps.	(3) He jumps.	(3) He has _jumped_.

- Are the verbs *to dance*, *to decide*, and *to jump* regular or irregular?

    _____ How do you know? _____

- What ending does each verb take in the past tense? _____

- Remember that any verb that forms its past tense by adding *-d* or *-ed* is a *regular* verb. What past participle ending does each verb take?

    _____

The past participle forms of regular verbs look exactly like the past tense forms. Both end in *-d* or *-ed*.

Practice 1 The first sentence in each of these pairs contains a one-word verb in the past tense. Fill in the past participle of the same verb in the blank in the second sentence.

Example: She designed jewelry all her life.

She has _____designed_____ jewelry all her life.

1. *Batman* earned more than any other motion picture.

   ✓ *Batman* has ___earned___ more than any other motion picture.

2. The pot of soup boiled over.

   ✓ The pot of soup has ___boiled___ over.

3. The mirror cracked.

   ✓ The mirror has ___cracked___.

4. We congratulated Jorgé.

   ✓ We have ___congratulated___ Jorgé.

5. Nelson always studied in the bathtub.

   ✓ Nelson has always ___studied___ in the bathtub.

6. Many Chinese people moved to the United States.

   ✓ Many Chinese people have ___moved___ to the United States.

7. The landlord asked for a rent increase.

   ✓ The landlord has ___for___ for a rent increase.

8. Sylvia tackled the man who took her purse.

   ✓ Sylvia has ___tackled___ the man who took her purse.

9. The satellite circled Jupiter.

   ✓ The satellite has ___circled___ Jupiter.

10. They signed petitions to save the seals.

    ✓ They have ___signed___ petitions to save the seals.

Practice 2 Write the missing two-part verb in each of the following sentences. Use the helping verb *has* or *have* and the past participle of the verb written in parentheses.

Example: __Have__ you ever __wished__ (to wish) for a new name?

1. Some of us __have wished__ (to want) new names at one time or another.
2. Many famous people __have wish__ (to fulfill) that desire.
3. Some __have wished__ (to use) only their first names.
4. Madonna Louise Ciccone __have wished__ (to drop) everything but Madonna.
5. Prince Roger Nelson __have wished__ (to remain) simply Prince.
6. Cherilyn LaPiere __have wished__ (to shorten) her name to Cher.
7. Other celebrities __have retained__ (to retain) their first names and taken new last names.
8. Raquel Tejada __have wished__ (to convert) her last name to Welch.
9. Steveland Judkinds __have__ _____ (to turn) into Stevie Wonder.
10. Still others __have wished__ (to replace) their names altogether.
11. Annie Mae Bullock __have wished__ (to rename) herself Tina Turner.
12. Jerome Silberman __have wished__ (to transform) himself into Gene Wilder.
13. For many years, Eunice Kathleen Waymoa __have wished__ (to call) herself Nina Simone.
14. Gordon Matthew Sumner __have wished__ (to change) into Sting.
15. What new name would you __have wished__ (to pick) for yourself?

PART C: Past Participles of Irregular Verbs

Present Tense	Past Tense	Helping Verb + Past Participle
(1) He sees.	(1) He saw.	(1) He has seen.
(2) I take vitamins.	(2) I took vitamins.	(2) I have taken vitamins.
(3) We sing.	(3) We sang.	(3) We have sung.

- Are the verbs *to see*, *to take*, and *to sing* regular or irregular?

  _____

- Like all irregular verbs, *to see*, *to take*, and *to sing* do not add *-d* or *-ed* to show past tense.

- Most irregular verbs in the past tense are also irregular in the past participle—like *seen*, *taken*, and *sung*.

- Remember that past participles must be used with helping verbs.*

Because irregular verbs change their spelling in irregular ways, there are no easy rules to explain these changes. Here is a list of some common irregular verbs.

Reference Chart: Irregular Verbs

Simple Form	Past	Past Participle
be	was, were	been
become	became	become
begin	began	begun
blow	blew	blown
break	broke	broken
bring	brought	brought
build	built	built
buy	bought	bought
catch	caught	caught
choose	chose	chosen
come	came	come
cut	cut	cut
dive	dove (dived)	dived
do	did	done
draw	drew	drawn
drink	drank	drunk
drive	drove	driven
eat	ate	eaten
fall	fell	fallen
feed	fed	fed

---

*For work on incomplete verbs, see Chapter 5, Part C.

Reference Chart: Irregular Verbs *(continued)*

Simple Form	Past	Past Participle
feel	felt	felt
fight	fought	fought
find	found	found
fly	flew	flown
forget	forgot	forgotten
forgive	forgave	forgiven
freeze	froze	frozen
get	got	gotten (got)
give	gave	given
go	went	gone
grow	grew	grown
have	had	had
hear	heard	heard
hide	hid	hidden
hold	held	held
hurt	hurt	hurt
keep	kept	kept
know	knew	known
lay	laid	laid
lead	led	led
leave	left	left
let	let	let
lie	lay	lain
lose	lost	lost
make	made	made
mean	meant	meant
meet	met	met
pay	paid	paid
put	put	put
quit	quit	quit
read	read	read
ride	rode	ridden
ring	rang	rung
rise	rose	risen
run	ran	run
say	said	said
see	saw	seen
seek	sought	sought
sell	sold	sold
send	sent	sent
set	set	set
shake	shook	shaken
shine	shone (shined)	shone (shined)
sing	sang	sung
sit	sat	sat
sleep	slept	slept
speak	spoke	spoken
spend	spent	spent
spring	sprang	sprung
stand	stood	stood

Reference Chart: Irregular Verbs *(continued)*

Simple Form	Past	Past Participle
steal	stole	stolen
strike	struck	struck
swim	swam	swum
take	took	taken
teach	taught	taught
tear	tore	torn
tell	told	told
think	thought	thought
throw	threw	thrown
understand	understood	understood
wake	woke (waked)	woken (waked)
wear	wore	worn
win	won	won
wind	wound	wound
write	wrote	written

You already know many of these past participle forms. One way to learn the unfamiliar ones is to group together verbs that change from the past tense to the present participle in the same way. For example, some irregular verbs change from *ow* in the present to *ew* in the past to *own* in the past participle.

blow	blew	blown
grow	grew	grown
know	knew	known
throw	threw	thrown

Another group changes from *i* in the present to *a* in the past to *u* in the past participle:

begin	began	begun
drink	drank	drunk
ring	rang	rung
sing	sang	sung
spring	sprang	sprung
swim	swam	swum

As you write, refer to the chart. If you are unsure of the past participle form of a verb that is not on the chart, check a dictionary. For example, if you look up the verb *see* in the dictionary, you will find an entry like this:

see \ saw \ seen \ seeing

The first word listed is the present tense form of the verb (*I see, she sees,* and so on). The second word listed is the past tense form (*I saw, she saw,* and so on). The third word is the past participle form (*I have seen, she has seen,* and so on), and the last word is the present participle form.

Chapter 8 The Past Participle in Action 131

Some dictionaries list different forms only for irregular verbs. If no past tense or past participle form is listed, you know that the verb is regular and that its past participle ends in -d or -ed.

Practice 1 The first sentence in each pair contains an irregular verb in the past tense. Fill in *has* or *have* plus the past participle of the same verb to complete the second sentence.

Example: I ate too much.

I __have__ __eaten__ too much.

1. The river rose over its banks.

   ✗ The river __have__ __rose__ over its banks.

2. She took a short break.

   ✗ She __have__ __took__ a short break.

3. For years, we sang in a gospel group.

   ✓ For years, we __have__ __sung__ in a gospel group.

4. Interest rates fell recently.

   ✗ Interest rates __have__ __fell__ recently.

5. Ralph gave me a red satin bowling jacket.

   ✓ Ralph __have__ __gave__ me a red satin bowling jacket.

6. They thought carefully about the problem.

   ✓ They __have__ __thought__ carefully about the problem.

7. I kept all your love letters.

   ✓ I __have__ __kept__ all your love letters.

8. The Joneses forgot to confirm the reservation.

   ✓ The Joneses __have__ __forgot__ to confirm the reservation.

9. San Diego grew quickly.

   San Diego __have__ __grown__ quickly.

10. The police knew about the drug ring for months.

    The police __have__ __know__ about the drug ring for months.

132   Unit 3   Verbs

Practice 2   Now you will be given only the first sentence with its one-word verb in the past tense. Rewrite the entire sentence, changing the verb to a two-word verb: *has* or *have* plus the past participle of the main verb.

Example: He took his credit cards with him.

He has taken his credit cards with him.

1. They brought their parrot to the party.

✓ They brought their parrot to a party

2. T. J. drove a city bus for two years.

? T. J. has drove a city bus for two years

3. She paid cash for a cellular phone.

✗ She have paid cash for a cellular phone

4. I saw a white fox near the barn.

✓ I have saw a white fox near the barn

5. A tornado tore through the shopping center.

✗ A tornado has tore through the shopping center.

6. Margo became more self-confident.

Margo have became more self-confident

7. Councilman Gomez ran a fair campaign.

✗ Councilman Gomez has ran a fair campaign.

8. The old barn stood there for years.

✓ The old barn has stood there for years

9. Spring came to New England.

✗ Spring has come to New English.

10. Our conversations were helpful.

✗ Our conversations have were helpful

Practice 3   Review   For each verb in the chart on the opposite page, fill in the present tense (third person singular form), the past tense, and the past participle. BE CAREFUL: Some of the verbs are regular, and some are irregular.

Chapter 8   The Past Participle in Action   133

Simple	Present Tense (he, she, it)	Past Tense	Past Participle
know	knows	knew	known
catch	*catchs*	*caught*	*caught*
stop			
break			
reach			
bring			
fly			
fall			
feel			
take			
go			
see			
do			
buy			
make			
answer			
hold			
say			

134 Unit 3 Verbs

Practice 4

Review Complete each sentence by filling in the helping verb *has* or *have* and the past participle of the verb in parentheses. Some verbs are regular, and some are irregular.

Examples: Millions __have__ __heard__ (hear) her sing.

She __has__ __used__ (use) words and music to make us think.

Tracy Chapman

(1) The songs of Tracy Chapman __have__ __heard__ (capture) America's ear. (2) Tracy __has__ __used__ (put) her life and experience into her music. (3) Born in Cleveland in 1964, she __have__ _____ (know) periods of poverty, but her mother always made sure that there was music in the house.

(4) Tracy __has__ __used__ (write) songs and __have__ __heard__ (play) the guitar since she was a child. (5) However, she __has__ __used__ (be) famous only since 1988, when her first album was released. (6) That album won three Grammy Awards. (7) Although Tracy's second and third albums __have__ not __heard__ (sell) as many copies, her songs __has__ __used__ (touch) many listeners and __has__ __used__ (make) them think more about social problems. (8) Critics __her__ __heard__ (describe) her music as pure, yet tough. (9) Tracy __has__ __heard__ (say) that some of her favorite singers are U2, Aretha Franklin, Al Green, Miriam Makeba, and Bob Dylan.

(10) This talented singer __have__ __heard__ (perform) in many places, from street corners to coffeehouses to the gigantic Wembley Stadium in England. (11) She usually appears on stage alone; however,

Tracy _have heard_ (sing) with such superstars as Bruce Springsteen and Sting. (12) Reviewers _has used_ (notice) Tracy's shyness. (13) Although she _have_ always _heard_ (be) forceful when singing and playing, only recently _has_ she _used_ (begin) to talk to her audiences.

Now check your work in the preceding exercises, or have it checked. Do you see any patterns in your errors? Do you tend to miss regular or irregular verbs? To help you learn, copy all four forms of each verb that you missed into the review chart below, and use it to study.

Personal Review Chart

Simple	Present Tense (he, she, it)	Past Tense	Past Participle
go	goes	went	gone

PART D — Using the Present Perfect Tense

The *present perfect tense* is composed of the present tense of *to have (has* or *have)* plus the past participle.

Present Perfect Tense	
Singular	**Plural**
I *have* spoken	we *have* spoken
you *have* spoken	you *have* spoken
he ⎫	
she ⎬ *has* spoken	they *have* spoken
it ⎭	

Let us see how this tense is used.

(1) They *sang* together last Saturday.

(2) They *have sung* together for three years now.

- In sentence (1), the past tense verb *sang* tells us that they sang together on one occasion, Saturday, but are no longer singing together. The action began and ended in the past.

- In sentence (2), the present perfect verb *have sung* tells us something entirely different: that they have sung together in the past and *are still singing together now.*

(3) Janet *sat* on the beach for three hours.

(4) Valerie *has* just *sat* on the beach for three hours.

- Which woman is probably still sunburned? _____

- In sentence (3), Janet's action began and ended at some time in the past. Perhaps it was ten years ago that she sat on the beach.

- In (4), the present perfect verb *has sat* implies that although the action occurred in the past, it *has just happened,* and Valerie had better put some lotion on her sunburn *now.*

- Notice how the word *just* emphasizes that the action occurred very recently.

Use the *present perfect tense* to show either (1) that an action began in the past and has continued until now or (2) that an action has just happened.

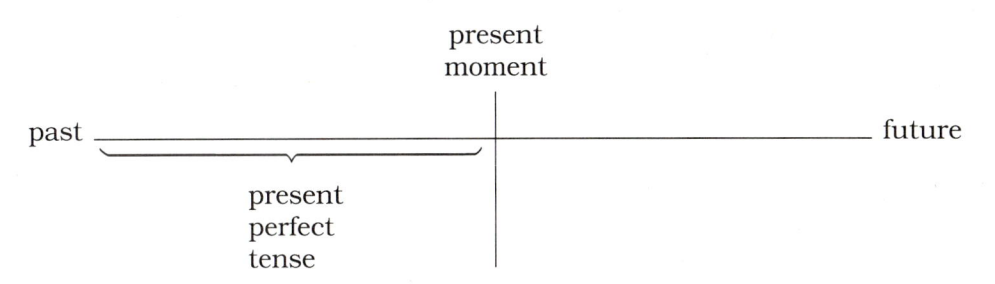

```
                              present
                              moment
past ─────────────────────────┬───────────────────── future
          ╲_____╱
              present
              perfect
              tense
```

In writing about an action that began in the past and is still continuing, you will often use time words like *for* and *since*.

> (5) We have watched the fireworks *for* three hours.
>
> (6) John has sung in the choir *since* 1980.

In writing about an action that has just happened, you will often use words like *just, recently, already,* and *yet*.

> (7) I have *just* finished the novel.
>
> (8) They have *already* gone to the party.

Practice 1

Paying close attention to meaning, circle the verb that best completes each sentence.

Examples: Ten years ago, American automobiles ((were), have been) very different from those of today.

For one year now, I (was, (have been)) a waitress.

1. She flew to Charleston and then ((drove), has driven) to the farm.
2. Nick is my next-door neighbor; he (lived, (has lived)) here for five years.
3. Yesterday, Ted ((bought), has bought) life insurance.
4. Since Tuesday, my throat (hurt, (has hurt)).
5. On May 5, 1983, he ((became), has become) an American citizen.
6. Everett loves horn-rimmed glasses; he (wore, (has worn)) them for years.

138 Unit 3 Verbs

✓ 7. I dialed his number and (got, have gotten) a busy signal.

✓ 8. Georgina works in a hospital; she (worked, has worked) there since 1979.

✗ 9. My interest in old clocks (began, has begun) four years ago.

✓ 10. Since then, I (wander, have wandered) far and wide.

Practice 2 Fill in either the *past* tense or the *present perfect* tense form of each verb in parentheses.

✓ (1) Lisa Rogers ___has worked___ (to work) as a nutritionist in the public schools since 1982. (2) That was the year her son first

✓ ___to complain___ (to complain) about the poor quality of food in the

½ school cafeteria. (3) Lisa ___apply___ (to apply) for a job as a

nutritional adviser and ___got it___ (to get) it. (4) Since then,

✗ she ___teach___ (to teach) nutrition courses for staff members.

✓ (5) Lisa's hard work ___has pay___ (to pay) off. (6) Last year, her

✓ school system ___win___ (to win) an award for its excellent

food.

PART E Using the Past Perfect Tense

The *past perfect tense* is composed of the past tense of *to have (had)* plus the past participle.

Past Perfect Tense

Singular	Plural
I *had* spoken	we *had* spoken
you *had* spoken	you *had* spoken
he ⎫	
she ⎬ *had* spoken	they *had* spoken
it ⎭	

Let us see how this tense is used.

> (1) Because Bob *had broken* his leg, he *wore* a cast for six months.

- The actions in both parts of this sentence occurred entirely in the past, but one occurred before the other.
- At some time in the past, Bob *wore* (past tense) a cast on the leg that he *had broken* (past perfect tense) at some time before that.

When you are writing in the past tense, use the past perfect tense to show that something happened at an even earlier time.

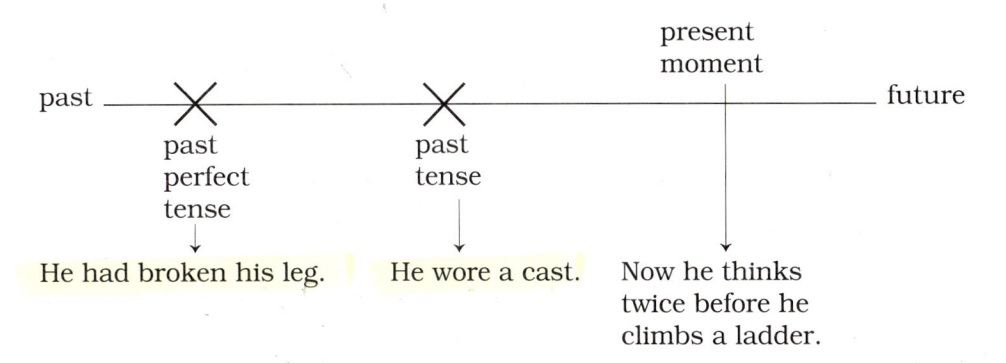

```
past ———X————————X———————|————————— future
        past           past      present
        perfect        tense     moment
        tense
        ↓              ↓         ↓
        He had broken  He wore   Now he thinks
        his leg.       a cast.   twice before he
                                 climbs a ladder.
```

As a general rule, the present perfect tense is used in relation to the present tense, and the past perfect tense is used in relation to the past tense. Read the following pairs of sentences, and note the time relation.

> (2) Sid *says* (present) he *has found* (present perfect) a good job.
>
> (3) Sid *said* (past) he *had found* (past perfect) a good job.
>
> (4) Grace *tells* (present) us she *has won* (present perfect) first prize.
>
> (5) Grace *told* (past) us she *had won* (past perfect) first prize.

Practice Choose either the present perfect or the past perfect tense of the verb in parentheses to complete each sentence. Match present perfect tense with present tense and past perfect tense with past tense.

1. The newspaper reports that the dictator _____ (to leave) the country.

2. The newspaper reported that the dictator _____ (to leave) the country.

3. I plan to buy a red convertible; I _____ (to want) a convertible for three years now.

4. Last year, I bought a red convertible; I _____ (to want) a convertible for three years before that.

5. Jerry ~~to forget~~ (to forget) to pay his electric bill; he was unable to watch the news.

6. Jerry ~~to forget~~ (to forget) to pay his electric bill; he is unable to watch the news.

7. I am worried about my cat; she ~~to drink~~ (to drink) bubble bath.

8. I was worried about my cat; she ~~to drink~~ (to drink) bubble bath.

9. Sam told us he ~~how decide~~ (to decide) to major in English literature.

10. Sam tells us he ~~to decide~~ (to decide) to major in English literature.

PART F — Using the Passive Voice

So far in this chapter, you have combined the past participle with forms of *to have*. But the past participle also can be used with forms of *to be* (*am, is, are, was, were*).

> (1) That jam was made by Aunt Clara.

- The subject of the sentence is *that jam*. The verb has two parts: the helping verb *was* and the past participle *made*.
- Note that the subject, *that jam*, does not act but is acted on by the verb. *By Aunt Clara* tells us who performed the action.

That jam *was made* by Aunt Clara.

When the subject is acted on or receives the action, it is passive, and the verb (*to be* + past participle) **is in the** *passive voice*.

Now compare the passive voice with the active voice in these pairs of sentences:

> (2) **Passive voice:** Free gifts are given by the bank.
>
> (3) **Active voice:** The bank gives free gifts.
>
> (4) **Passive voice:** We were robbed by a street gang.
>
> (5) **Active voice:** _____

Chapter 8   The Past Participle in Action   141

- In sentence (2), the subject, *free gifts*, is passive; it receives the action. In sentence (3), *the bank* is active; it performs the action.
- Note the difference between the passive verb *are given* and the active verb *gives*.
- However, the tense of both sentences is the same. The passive verb *are given* is in the present tense, and so is the active verb *gives*.
- Rewrite sentence (4) in the active voice. Be sure to keep the same verb tense in the new sentence!

Write in the passive voice only when you want to emphasize the receiver of the action rather than the doer. Usually, however, write in the active voice because sentences in the active voice are livelier and more direct.

Practice 1   Underline the verb in each sentence. In the blank at the right, write *A* if the verb is written in the active voice and *P* if the verb is in the passive voice.

Example: Benjamin Franklin <u>lived</u> a very productive life.   _A_

1. Benjamin Franklin <u>succeeded</u> in many careers.   _A_ ✓

2. Born poor, he first <u>made</u> his mark as a printer and newspaper owner.   _P_ ✗

3. Franklin <u>is remembered</u> by many people for his experiments with electricity.   _P_ ✓

4. Some of his inventions <u>are</u> still <u>used</u> today.   _A_ ✗

5. He <u>invented</u> the lightning rod and bifocals.   _A_ ✓

6. Franklin <u>is known</u> as the author of *Poor Richard's Almanac*.   _P_ ✗

7. Of course, he <u>signed</u> the Declaration of Independence.   _P_ ✗

8. He <u>served</u> as America's first postmaster general too.   _P_ ✗

9. With others, Franklin <u>started</u> the first American hospital and the first lending library.   _P_ ✗

10. The first antislavery <u>group</u> in America was also headed by Franklin.   _A_ ✗

Practice 2 In each sentence, underline both parts of the passive verb, and circle the subject. Then draw an arrow from the verb to the word or words it acts on.

Example: (I) was approached by a lost tourist.

1. The skaters were applauded vigorously by the crowd.
2. The corn is picked fresh every morning.
3. These flowered bowls were imported from Mexico.
4. Milos, my cat was ignored by the mouse.
5. Truer words were never spoken.
6. An antique train set was sold at the auction.
7. The computer was understood by only one person.
8. Customers are lured into the store by loud music and bright signs.
9. Dutch is spoken on Curaçao.
10. Our quarrel was quickly forgotten.

Practice 3 Rewrite each sentence, changing the verb into the passive voice. Make all necessary verb and subject changes. Be sure to keep each sentence in the original tense.

Example: Smith broke the world record.
The world record was broken by Smith.

1. Thick makeup hides her beauty.

   Thick makeup was h

2. Paula Abdul first sang the song.

   Paula Abdul sang the first son

3. The FDA took that drug off the market.

4. Spain gave Florida to the United States in 1819.

   Spain gave Florida .

5. My grandmother wore this wedding dress.

   This wedding dress was My grandmother,

6. Your comments encouraged me.

   Your comments help encouraged me.

7. The Navy pays for his education.

   The Navy help pays for his education.

8. Someone in this room ate my sandwich.

   In this room someone ate my sandwich.

Practice 4 Rewrite each sentence, changing the verb from the passive to the active voice. Make all necessary verb and subject changes. Be sure to keep each sentence in the original tense.

Example: The popcorn was burned by Bernie.

Bernie burned the popcorn.

1. Corn was popped by Native Americans more than five thousand years ago.

2. In fact, popcorn was made by Native American women in many different ways.

3. Popcorn necklaces were bought by Columbus in the West Indies.

4. Bags of popcorn were brought to the first Thanksgiving by the Wampanoag natives.

5. In 1907, the first electric corn popper was manufactured by an American company.

144   Unit 3   Verbs

6. By 1947, the snack was sold in movie houses all over the country.

_____

7. Sure-fire popcorn was developed by Orville Redenbacher in the 1950s.

_____

8. Now over one billion dollars' worth of popcorn is munched by Americans each year.

_____

_____

PART G   Using Past Participles as Adjectives

Sometimes the past participle is not a verb at all, but an *adjective*, a word that describes a noun or pronoun.*

> (1) Jay is *married*.
> (2) The *broken* window looks terrible.
> (3) Two *tired* students slept in the hall.

- In sentence (1), *married* is the past participle of the verb *to marry*, but here it is not a verb. Instead, it describes the subject, *Jay*.
- *Is* links the subject, *Jay*, with the descriptive word, *married*.
- In sentence (2), *broken* is the past participle form of *to break*, but it is used as an adjective to describe the noun *window*.
- In sentence (3), what past participle is an adjective? _____
- Which word does it describe? _____

Past participles like *married*, *broken*, and *tired* are often used as adjectives.
Some form of the verb *to be* usually links descriptive past participles with the subjects they describe, but here are a few other common linking verbs that you learned in Chapter 4, Part E.

_____
*For more work on adjectives, see Chapter 20.

Chapter 8   The Past Participle in Action   145

```
           Subject        Linking Verb       Past Participle
                          (simple form)      (used as adjective)

                              act
                              appear
                              become
            They    →         feel          →    surprised.
                              get
                              look
                              seem
                              sound
```

Practice 1   Underline the linking verb in each sentence. Then circle the descriptive past participle or participles that complete the sentence.

Examples: The window was (polish, (polished)).

Harry seems very (worry, (worried)) these days.

1. This product is (guarantee, guaranteed) not to explode.
2. Nellie seems (qualify, qualified) for the job.
3. My employer appears (prejudice, prejudiced).
4. After we read the chapter, we were still (confuse, confused).
5. The science laboratory is (air-condition, air-conditioned).
6. David feels (trap, trapped) in a low-paying job.
7. Did you know that one out of two American couples gets (divorce, divorced)?
8. We were (thrill, thrilled) to see Niagara Falls.
9. During the holidays, Paul feels (depress, depressed).
10. She is (interest, interested) in women's history.
11. You look so (dignify, dignified) in that tuxedo.
12. The garnet ring she wore was (borrow, borrowed).
13. I can't help you; my hands are (tie, tied).

14. Are the potatoes (fry, fried), (bake, baked), or (boil, boiled)?

15. After the trip, we felt, (rest, rested), (pamper, pampered), and (relax, relaxed).

Practice 2 Below is a list of verbs. Use the past participles of the verbs as adjectives, to describe each noun in the exercise. Then use your adjective-noun combination in a sentence. Use a different past participle for each noun.

bore	freeze	park	train
delight	hide	pollute	wear
dry	lose	tire	worry
embarrass	mask	toast	wrinkle

Example: the _____dried_____ fruit

We served the dried fruit for dessert.

1. a(n) _____ bandit

2. a(n) _____ sheet

3. the _____ river

4. a(n) _____ man

5. the _____ emeralds

6. these _____ muffins

7. that _____ bear

8. a(n) _____ nurse

9. several _____ cars

_____

10. a(n) _____ woman

_____

Practice 3 Proofread the following ad copy for past participle errors. First, underline all the past participles. Then make any corrections above the line.

(1) We are pleased to bring you the new Neurotic, the car of the 1990s. (2) The Neurotic is make in America. (3) It comes fully equip with a fuel-injected engine, balanced suspension, and a five-speed transmission. (4) It is designed for your every comfort. (5) Contoured bucket seats and tint glass are featured. (6) Each Neurotic is tested on the roughest roads and in the worst weather conditions. (7) Guarantee for two years, the Neurotic was named "Car of the Year" by *Road and Trail* magazine. (8) Test-drive the new Neurotic at your local car dealer.

Practice 4 Combine each pair of short sentences. First, find and underline the past participle. Then rewrite the two short sentences as one smooth sentence, using the past participle as an adjective.

Example: The book is lost. It is worth $1,000.
The lost book is worth $1,000.

1. The car was rented. Desi drove it into a fence.

_____

2. This rug has been dry-cleaned. It looks new.

_____

3. Your wallet was stolen. It is at the police station.

_____

4. The envelope was sealed. Harriet opened it.

_____

5. The player was injured. The coach took him out of the game.

 _____

6. Your report is typed. It looks very neat.

 _____

7. This bowl is broken. Can you fix it?

 _____

8. The weather forecast was revised. It calls for sunshine.

 _____

9. These gold chains are overpriced. Do not buy them.

 _____

10. The box was locked. Divers brought it to the surface.

 _____

Practice 5   The sentences in the left column are in the present tense; those in the right column are in the past tense. If the sentence is shown in the present tense on the left, write the sentence in the past tense on the right, and vice versa. REMEMBER: Only the *linking verb*, never the past participle, changes to show tense.

	Present Tense	**Past Tense**
Examples:	Smoking is forbidden.	Smoking was forbidden.
	Lunches are served.	Lunches were served.
	1. Your piano is tuned.	1. _____
	2. _____	2. The store looked closed.
	3. _____	3. My feelings were hurt.
	4. The seats are filled.	4. _____
	5. She is relaxed.	5. _____
	6. _____	6. You seemed qualified for the job.

7. He is supposed to meet us.* 7. _____

8. She is used to city life.* 8. _____

9. _____ 9. It was written in longhand.

10. You are expected to win. 10. _____

Chapter Highlights

- **Past participles of regular verbs add *-d* or *-ed*, just like their past tense forms:**

Present	Past	Past Participle
decide	decided	decided
jump	jumped	jumped

- **Past participles of irregular verbs change in irregular ways:**

Present	Past	Past Participle
bring	brought	brought
see	saw	seen
take	took	taken

- **Past participles can combine with *to have*:**

    He *has edited* many articles for us. *(present perfect tense)*
    He *had edited* many articles for us. *(past perfect tense)*

- **Past participles can combine with *to be*:**

    The report *was edited* by Mary. *(passive voice)*

- **Past participles can be used as adjectives:**

    The *edited* report arrived today. *(adjective)*

*For more work on *supposed* and *used*, see Chapter 31, "Look-alikes/Sound-alikes."

Chapter Review

Proofread the following essay for past participle errors. Then correct each error above the line.

Three Ways to Save the Elephants

(1) The ivory tusks of elephants have always brought high prices. (2) Poachers are lured by the chance to make a quick dollar. (3) These illegal hunters have recently took the lives of so many African elephants that soon all of them may die out. (4) Seventy percent of the elephant population of Kenya has been kill in the past ten years. (5) Concerned people have thought of three ways to save the elephants of Kenya.

(6) One way is to catch poachers in the act. (7) Game wardens, who are now given automatic weapons, are telled to shoot poachers on sight. (8) This method has gotten results. (9) Within a few months, the number of elephant deaths dropped greatly. (10) However, critics have claim that this method cannot solve the problem. (11) After all, poachers are poor people who have no other way to earn a living.

(12) Alarmed by the danger to elephants, the United States and Western Europe have join together to stop the sale of ivory. (13) They have argued that ivory is no longer use. (14) Plastic has replaced ivory for billiard balls and piano keys. (15) Some countries have refuse to support the ban; they argue that their elephants are protect.

(16) Richard Leakey, a well-knowed Kenyan, has proposed a third way to save the elephants. (17) Nearly 700,000 visitors a year have make tourism Kenya's largest industry. (18) Most tourists come to see the elephants. (19) Leakey wants to use the money these visitors spend to help both the elephants and the people of Kenya. (20) Meanwhile, too many elephants are still being shooted.

Chapter 9

Progressive Tenses (TO BE + -ING Verb Form)

PART A   Defining and Writing the Present Progressive Tense
PART B   Defining and Writing the Past Progressive Tense
PART C   Using the Progressive Tenses
PART D   Avoiding Incomplete Progressives

PART A   Defining and Writing the Present Progressive Tense

Verbs in the *present progressive tense* have two parts: the present tense form of *to be (am, is, are)* plus the *-ing* (or present participle) of the main verb.

Unit 3 Verbs

Present Progressive Tense

(example verb: to play)

Singular	Plural
I am playing	we are playing
you are playing	you are playing
he } is playing	they are playing
she	
it	

Compare the present tense with the present progressive tense below.

(1) Larry works at the bookstore.
(2) Larry is working at the bookstore.

- Sentence (1) is in the present tense. Which word tells you this?

    works

- Sentence (2) is also in the present tense. Which word tells you this?

    working

- Note that the main verb in sentence (2), *working*, has no tense. Only the helping verb *is* shows tense.

Practice 1

Change each one-word present tense verb in the left-hand column to a two-part present progressive verb in the right-hand column. Do this by filling in the missing helping verb (*am, is,* or *are*).

Present Tense   **Present Progressive Tense**

Examples: I fly.   I __am__ flying.

He wears my sweater.   He __is__ wearing my sweater.

1. Elsa and I set goals together.   1. Elsa and I __are__ setting goals together.

2. You write rapidly.   2. You __are__ writing rapidly.

3. He plans the wedding.   3. He __is__ planning the wedding.

4. Our work begins to pay off.   4. Our work __is__ beginning to pay off.

Chapter 9   Progressive Tenses (TO BE + -ING Verb Form)   153

5. We pose for the photographer.
6. Maryann smiles.
7. Sal does his Elvis impression.
8. I speak Portuguese to Manuel.
9. Frank gets lazy.
10. You probably wonder why.

5. We _are_ posing for the photographer.
6. Maryann _is_ smiling.
7. Sal _is_ doing his Elvis impression.
8. I _am_ speaking Portuguese to Manuel.
9. Frank _is_ getting lazy.
10. You _are_ probably wondering why.

REMEMBER: Every verb in the present progressive tense must have two parts: a helping verb (*am*, *is*, or *are*) and a main verb ending in *-ing*. The helping verb must agree with the subject.

Practice 2   Below are sentences in the regular present tense. Rewrite each one in the present progressive tense by changing the verb to *am, is,* or *are* + the *-ing* form of the main verb.

Example: We play cards.

We are playing cards.

1. The telephone rings.

   The telephone is rings.

2. Dexter wrestles with his math homework.

   Dexter wrestlesing with his math homework.

3. James and Judy work in the emergency room.

   James and Judy are in the emergency room.

4. I keep a journal of thoughts and observations.

   I am keeping a journal of thoughts and observations.

5. We build a house.

   We are building a house.

PART B — Defining and Writing the Past Progressive Tense

Verbs in the *past progressive tense* have two parts: the past tense form of *to be* (*was* or *were*) plus the *-ing* form of the main verb.

Past Progressive Tense
(example verb: to play)

Singular	Plural
I was playing	we were playing
you were playing	you were playing
he }	
she } was playing	they were playing
it }	

Compare the past tense with the past progressive tense below.

---

(1) Larry worked at the bookstore.

(2) Larry was working at the bookstore.

- Sentence (1) is in the past tense. Which word tells you this?

  _____

- Sentence (2) is also in the past tense. Which word tells you this?

  _____

- Notice that the main verb in sentence (2), *working*, has no tense. Only the helping verb *was* shows tense.

Practice 1 Change each one-word past tense verb in the left-hand column to a two-part past progressive verb in the right-hand column. Do this by filling in the missing helping verb (*was* or *were*).

	Past Tense	Past Progressive Tense
Examples:	I flew.	I __was__ flying.
	He wore my sweater.	He __was__ wearing my sweater.

Chapter 9   Progressive Tenses (TO BE + -ING Verb Form)   155

	Past Tense	Past Progressive Tense
1.	Elsa and I set goals together.	Elsa and I *was* setting goals together.
2.	You wrote rapidly.	You *was* writing rapidly.
3.	He planned the wedding.	He *were* planning the wedding.
4.	Our work began to pay off.	Our work *was* beginning to pay off.
5.	We posed for the photographer.	We *were* posing for the photographer.
6.	Maryann smiled.	Maryann *was* smiling.
7.	Sal did his Elvis impression.	Sal *was* doing his Elvis impression.
8.	I spoke Portuguese to Manuel.	I *was* speaking Portuguese to Manuel.
9.	Frank got lazy.	Frank *was* getting lazy.
10.	You probably wondered why.	You *were* probably wondering why.

Practice 2   Below are sentences in the past tense. Rewrite each sentence in the past progressive tense by changing the verb to *was* or *were* + the *-ing* form of the main verb.

Example: You cooked dinner.

You were cooking dinner.

1. The two linebackers growled at each other.

   The two linebackers were growled at each other.

2. Leroy examined his bank receipt.

   Leroy examined his banking receipt

3. We watched the news.

   We were watcheding the news

4. Marsha decided on a career.

   Marsha were decided on a career.

5. He acted like a patient, not a doctor!

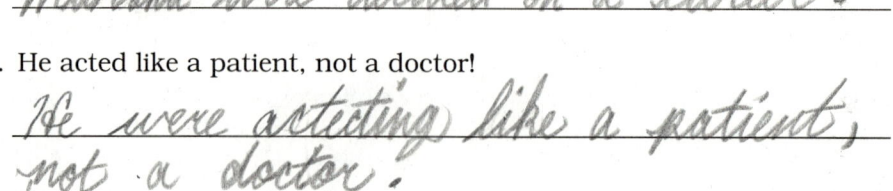

   He were actecting like a patient, not a doctor.

PART C — Using the Progressive Tenses

As you read these sentences, do you hear the differences in meaning?

> (1) Lenore *plays* the piano.
>
> (2) Al *is playing* the piano.

- Which person is definitely at the keyboard right now?

- If you said Al, you are right. He is *now in the process of playing* the piano. Lenore, on the other hand, *does* play the piano; she may also paint, write novels, and play center field, but we do not know from the sentence what she *is doing right now*.

- The present progressive verb *is playing* tells us that the action is *in progress*.

Here is another use of the present progressive tense:

> (3) Tony *is coming* here later.

- The present progressive verb *is coming* shows *future* time: Tony is going to come here.

> (4) Linda *washed* her hair last night.
>
> (5) Linda *was washing* her hair when we arrived for the party.

- In sentence (4), *washed* implies a completed action.

- The past progressive verb in sentence (5) has a special meaning: that Linda was *in the process* of washing her hair when something else happened (we arrived).

- To say, "Linda *washed* her hair *when* we arrived for the party" means that first we arrived, and then Linda started washing her hair.

Writers in English use the progressive tenses *much less often* than the present tense and past tense. Use the progressive tense only when you want to emphasize that something is or was in the process of happening.

Use the *present progressive tense (am, is, are + -ing)* to show that an action is in progress now or that it is going to happen in the future.

Use the *past progressive tense (was, were + -ing)* to show that an action was in progress at a certain time in the past.

Practice Read each sentence carefully. Then circle the verb or verbs that best express the meaning of the sentence.

Example: Right now, we (write, **are writing**) letters.

1. Last week, we (**saw**, were seeing) a fantastic play, *The Skin of Our Teeth*.
2. Donald (**loves**, is loving) to solve problems.
3. Where is Nell? She (drives, **is driving**) to Omaha.
4. Most mornings we (**get**, are getting) up at 7 a.m.
5. Believe it or not, Leroy (does, **is doing**) the laundry right now.
6. My dog Gourmand (**eats**, is eating) anything at all.
7. At this very moment, Gourmand (eats, **is eating**) the sports page.
8. Max (fried, **was frying**) onions when the smoke alarm (**went**, was going) off.
9. Please don't bother me now; I (study, **am studying**).
10. Newton (sat, **was sitting**) under a tree when he (**discovered**, was discovering) gravity.
11. When she lived in Nevada, she often (**drove**, was driving) through the desert.
12. The *Andrea Doria*, a huge pleasure ship, (**sank**, was sinking) on July 25, 1956.
13. Right now, she (takes, **is taking**) a nap.

158 Unit 3 Verbs

14. Through a scheduling error, runner Eddie Hart (**missed**, was missing) his race at the 1972 Olympics.

15. The last time I (**saw**, was seeing) Sandy, he (headed, **was heading**) toward the Lone Star Café.

PART D — Avoiding Incomplete Progressives

Now that you can write both present and past progressive verbs, here is a mistake you should not make:

> We having fun. *(incomplete)*

- Can you see what is missing?
- All by itself, the *-ing* form *having* is not a verb. It has to have a helping verb.
- Because the helping verb is missing, *we having fun* has no time. It could mean *we are having fun* or *we were having fun*.
- *We having fun* is not a sentence. It is a fragment of a sentence.*

Practice

Each group of words below is incomplete. Put an *X* over the exact spot where a word is missing. Then in the Present Progressive column, write the word that would complete the sentence in the *present progressive tense*. In the Past Progressive column, write the word that would complete the sentence in the *past progressive tense*.

	Present Progressive	Past Progressive
Example: He X having fun.	**is** (He is having fun.)	**was** (He was having fun.)
1. Mario balancing his checkbook.	X	X
2. Fran and I watching the sunrise.	X	X
3. You taking a computer course.	X	X
4. A big log floating down the river.	X	X

---

*For more on this type of fragment, see Chapter 5, Part B.

5. Those women always playing poker. _____ ✗
6. The tulips blooming. ✗ _____
7. I trying to give up caffeine. _____ ✗
8. Fights about money getting me down. _____ ✗
9. Jean and Marie opening a café. ✗ _____
10. Thick fog blanketing the city. _____ ✗
11. He fixing up old cars. ✗ _____
12. That child reading already. _____ ✗
13. Your ice cream melting. ✗ _____
14. Her skills improving. ✗ _____
15. They discussing the terms of the new contract. ✗ _____

Chapter Highlights

- The progressive tenses combine *to be* with the *-ing* verb form.
    present progressive tense: I *am reading*. He *is reading*.
    past progressive tense: I *was reading*. He *was reading*.

- The *-ing* verb form must have a helping verb to be complete:
    She playing the tuba. *(incorrect)*
    She *is playing* the tuba. *(correct)*

- The present progressive tense shows that an action is in progress now:
    Aunt Belle *is waxing* her car.

- The present progressive tense can also show that an action will take place in the future:
    Later today, Aunt Belle *is driving* us to the movies.

- The past progressive tense shows that an action was in progress at a certain time in the past:
    Aunt Belle *was waxing* her van when she heard thunder.

Chapter Review

Proofread this paragraph for incomplete progressive verbs. Then write any missing verbs above the lines.

(1) To save lives, many car manufacturers installing "passive restraint" devices that work without any action by the passenger. (2) Automatic seat belts, for example, move into place as the car door closing. (3) Already these new belts saving lives because they take choice away from the passenger. (4) When automobile passengers are given a choice, only about 20 percent fasten their seatbelts. (5) Air bags, another passive restraint, being used more and more. (6) The purpose of air bags protecting front-seat occupants from hitting the dashboard, windshield, or steering column during a crash. (7) If air bags functioning properly, they pop out of the steering column or dashboard and inflate fast, like giant balloons. (8) Because air bags are relatively expensive to install, some car makers putting only one air bag on the driver's side, and only in their higher-priced models. (9) But many consumers saying that they would pay a little more for increased safety. (10) It won't be long before most car manufacturers providing "dual" airbags—for driver and passenger—just as they now provide seatbelts.

Chapter 10

Fixed-Form Helping Verbs and Verb Problems

PART A   Defining and Spotting the Fixed-Form Helping Verbs
PART B   Using the Fixed-Form Helping Verbs
PART C   Using CAN and COULD
PART D   Using WILL and WOULD
PART E   Writing Infinitives
PART F   Revising Double Negatives

PART A   Defining and Spotting the Fixed-Form Helping Verbs

You already know the common—and changeable—helping verbs: *to have, to do,* and *to be.* Here are some helping verbs that do not change:

161

Unit 3 Verbs

> **Fixed-Form Helping Verbs**
>
> | can ✓ | could ✓ |
> |---|---|
> | will ✓ | would ✓ |
> | may ✓ | might ✓ |
> | shall | should ✓ |
> | must | |

The fixed-form helping verbs do not change, no matter what the subject is. They always keep the same form.

Practice Fill in each blank with a fixed-form helping verb.

1. You __can__ do it!
2. This __might__ be the coldest day of the year.
3. I __will__ buy the tickets while you park the car.
4. Rico __may__ win a basketball scholarship.
5. In South America, the elephant beetle __could__ grow to twelve inches long.
6. If the committee __would__ meet today, we __should__ have a new budget on time.
7. This computer __must__ last another few years.
8. Violent films __could__ frighten young children.
9. You __should__ have no difficulty finding a sales position.
10. Your friend __might__ attend Ohio University.

PART B Using the Fixed-Form Helping Verbs

> (1) Al will stay with us this summer.
>
> (2) Susan can shoot a rifle well.

- *Will* is the fixed-form helping verb in sentence (1). What main verb does it help? __stay__

- *Can* is the fixed-form helping verb in sentence (2). What main verb does it help? _shoot_

- Notice that *stay* and *shoot* are the simple forms of the verbs. They do not show tense by themselves.

When a verb has two parts—a fixed-form helping verb and a main verb—the main verb keeps its simple form.

Practice In the left column, each sentence contains a verb made up of some form of *to have* (the changeable helping verb) and a past participle (the main verb).

Each sentence in the right column contains a fixed-form helping verb and a blank. Write the form of the main verb from the left column that correctly completes each sentence.

Have +
Past Participle

Fixed-Form Helping Verb +
Simple Form

Examples: I have talked to him.

I may ___talk___ to him.

She has taken so long.

She will ___take___ so long.

1. Irma has written a song.
2. We have begun.
3. Joy has arrived.
4. He has slept all day.
5. I have gone there.
6. We have seen an eclipse.
7. It has drizzled.
8. Fred has fastened his seat belt.
9. Has he studied?
10. Della has been promoted.

1. Irma must ___written___ a song.
2. We can ___begun___.
3. Joy will ___arrived___.
4. He could ___slept___ all day.
5. I will ___gone___ there.
6. We might ___seen___ an eclipse.
7. It may ___drizzled___.
8. Fred could ___fastened___ his seat belt.
9. Should he ___studied___?
10. Della might ___been___ promoted.

PART C — Using CAN and COULD

> (1) He said that I *can* use any tools in his garage.
>
> (2) He said that I *could* use any tools in his garage.

- What is the tense of sentence (1)? __can__
- What is the tense of sentence (2)? __could__
- What is the helping verb in (1)? __He__
- What is the helping verb in (2)? __He__
- As you can see, *could* may be used as the past tense of *can*.

> **Present tense:** Today, I *can* touch my toes.
>
> **Past tense:** Yesterday, I *could* touch my toes.

Can means *am/is/are able*. It may be used to show present tense.

Could means *was/were able* when it is used to show the past tense of *can*.

> (3) If I went on a diet, I *could* touch my toes.
>
> (4) Rod wishes he *could* touch his toes.

- In sentence (3), the speaker *could* touch his toes *if* . . . Touching his toes is a possibility, not a certainty.
- In sentence (4), Rod *wishes* he *could* touch his toes, but probably he cannot. Touching his toes is a wish, not a certainty.

Could also means *might be able,* a possibility or a wish.

Practice 1

Fill in the present tense helper *can* or the past tense *could*, whichever is needed. To determine whether the sentence is present or past, look at the other verbs in the sentence, or look for words like *now* and *yesterday*.

1. When I am rested, I __could__ study for hours.
2. When I was rested, I __could__ study for hours.
3. Renard claims that he __can__ fly a plane.
4. Renard claimed that he __can__ fly a plane.

Chapter 10 Fixed-Form Helping Verbs and Verb Problems 165

5. A year ago, Zora __could__ jog for only five minutes at a time.
6. Now Zora __can__ jog for nearly an hour at a time.
7. If you're so smart, how come you __can__ never find your own socks?
8. If you were so smart, how come you __can__ never find your own socks?
9. When the air was clear, you __can__ see the next town.
10. When the air is clear, you __can__ see the next town.

Practice 2   Circle either *can* or *could*.

1. Sue thinks that she ((can), could) carry a tune.
2. Yesterday, we (can, (could)) not go to the town meeting.
3. I wish I ((can), could) play with the Lakers.
4. You should meet Tony: he ((can), could) lift a two-hundred-pound weight.
5. Nobody I know ((can), could) change a flat tire.
6. Until the party, everyone thought that Harry (can, (could)) cook.
7. She ((can), could) ice skate better now than she (can, could) last year.
8. On the night that Smithers disappeared, the butler ((can), could) not be found.
9. When my brother was younger, he ((can), could) name every car on the road.
10. I hope that the snow leopards ((can), could) survive in captivity.

Practice 3   Now write two sentences using *can* to show present tense and two sentences using *could* to show past tense.

1. _I can play football ov_
2. _Not to many can play football._
3. _A year a go I could not wor_
4. _A year go I could play basket_

PART D Using WILL and WOULD

> (1) You know you *will* do well in that class.
>
> (2) You knew you *would* do well in that class.

- Sentence (1) says that *you know* now (present tense) that you *will* do well in the future. *Will* points to the future from the present.

- Sentence (2) says that *you knew* then (past tense) that you *would* do well after that. *Would* points to the future from the past.

Would **may be used as the past tense of** *will*, **just as** *could* **may be used as the past tense of** *can*.

> (3) *If* you studied, you *would* pass physics.
>
> (4) Juanita *wishes* she *would* get an A in French.

- In sentence (3), the speaker *would* pass physics *if* . . . Passing physics is a possibility, not a certainty.

- In sentence (4), Juanita *wishes* she *could* get an A, but this is a wish, not a certainty.

Would **can also express a possibility or a wish.**

Practice 1
Fill in the present tense *will* or the past tense *would*.

1. The weather forecaster predicts that it __will__ snow Friday.
2. The weather forecaster predicted that it __will__ snow Friday.
3. John said that he __would__ move to Florida.
4. John says that he __would__ move to Florida.
5. Roberta thinks that she __will__ receive financial aid.
6. Roberta thought that she __will__ receive financial aid.
7. I __would__ marry you if you propose to me.
8. Unless you stop adding salt, no one __would__ want to eat that chili.

Chapter 10 Fixed-Form Helping Verbs and Verb Problems 167

9. Hugo thinks that he ___will___ be a millionaire someday.

10. Because she hated blind dates, she said she ___would___ never go on another one.

Practice 2 Circle either *will* or *would*.

1. You (**will**, would) find the right major once you start taking courses.
2. When the house is painted, you (will, **would**) see how lovely the old place looks.
3. Yolanda wishes that her neighbor (will, **would**) call her for a date.
4. The instructor assumed that everyone (**will**, would) improve.
5. They insisted that they (**will**, would) pick up the check.
6. The whole town assumed that they (will, **would**) live happily ever after.
7. When you get off the bus, you (will, **would**) see a diner.
8. If I had a million dollars, I (will, **would**) buy a big house on the ocean.
9. Your dinner (**will**, would) be ready in fifteen minutes.
10. Because we hated waiting in long lines, we decided that we (**will**, would) shop somewhere else.

PART E   Writing Infinitives

Every verb can be written as an *infinitive*. An infinitive has two parts: *to* + the simple form of the verb—*to kiss, to gaze, to sing, to wonder, to help.* Never add endings to the infinitive form of a verb: no *-ed*, no *-s*, no *-ing*.

(1) Roberta has *to finish* dental school this summer.

(2) Neither dictionary seems *to contain* the words I need.

- In sentences (1) and (2), the infinitives are *to finish* and *to contain*.
- *To* is followed by the simple form of the verb: *finish, contain*.

Don't confuse an infinitive with the preposition *to* followed by a noun or a pronoun.

> (3) Robert spoke *to Sam*.
>
> (4) I gave the award *to her*.

- In sentences (3) and (4), the preposition *to* is followed by the noun *Sam* and the pronoun *her*.
- *To Sam* and *to her* are prepositional phrases, not infinitives.*

Practice 1

Find the infinitives in the following sentences, and write them in the blanks at the right.

Infinitive

Example: Many people don't realize how hard it is to write a funny essay. — *to write*

1. Our guests started to leave at midnight. — *to leave*
2. Barbara has decided to become a landscape gardener. — *to become*
3. Hal has to get a B on his final exam, or he will not pass the course. — *to get*
4. It is hard to think with that radio blaring. — *to think*
5. The man wanted to buy a silver watch to give to his son. — *to buy*

Practice 2

Write an infinitive in each blank in the following sentences. Use any verb that makes sense. Remember that the infinitive is made up of *to* plus the simple form of the verb.

1. They began _to eat_ in the cafeteria.
2. My three-year-old niece loves _it_.
3. Few people know how _to_ well.
4. Would it be possible for me _to_ now?

---

*For more work on prepositions, see Chapter 4, Part C, and Chapter 21.

Chapter 10   Fixed-Form Helping Verbs and Verb Problems   169

5. No one wants ____?____ the haunted house.
6. Try not __do__ that hornets' nest.
7. I enjoy people who like __to play__.
8. He hopes __to find__ a nurse.
9. They wanted __me__ a better relationship.
10. We have __to finish__ by four o'clock.
11. As a child, I wasn't allowed __playing__ alone.
12. Fiona refused __play__ with me.
13. __Ready__ or not __my__: This is the question.
14. Len learned how __write__ yesterday.
15. It will be hard ____?____ the bank, but you can do it.

Practice 3   The verbs below are listed in the present, past, past participle, or -ing form. Put each one in the infinitive form. Then create a sentence using the infinitive.

	Word	Infinitive	Sentence
Example:	helping	to help	I want to help you.
1.	shouting	to shouting	stop shouting
2.	drove	to drove	I the drove the c
3.	wiggles		
4.	heard		
5.	tried		
6.	found		
7.	leading		
8.	rumble		
9.	decided		
10.	discovers		

PART F Revising Double Negatives

The most common *negatives* are *no, none, not, nowhere, no one, nobody, never,* and *nothing.*

The negative *not* is often joined to a verb to form a contraction: *can't, didn't, don't, hasn't, haven't,* and *won't,* for example.

However, a few negatives are difficult to spot. Read these sentences:

(1) There are hardly any beans left.

(2) By noon, we could scarcely see the mountains on the horizon.

- The negatives in these sentences are *hardly* and *scarcely.*
- They are negatives because they imply that there are *almost no* beans left and that we *almost couldn't* see the mountains.

Use only one negative in each idea. The double negative is an error you should avoid.

(1) **Double negative:** I *can't* eat *nothing.*

- There are two negatives in this sentence—*can't* and *nothing*—instead of one.
- Double negatives cancel each other out.

To revise a double negative, simply drop one of the negatives.

(2) **Revised:** I *can't* eat anything.

(3) **Revised:** I can eat *nothing.*

- In sentence (2), the negative *nothing* is changed to the positive *anything.*
- In sentence (3), the negative *can't* is changed to the positive *can.*

When you revise double negatives that include the words *hardly* and *scarcely,* keep those words and change the other negatives to positives.

(4) **Double negative:** They *couldn't hardly* finish their papers on time.

- The two negatives are *couldn't* and *hardly.*

Chapter 10   Fixed-Form Helping Verbs and Verb Problems   171

> (5) **Revised:** They could hardly finish their papers on time.

- Change *couldn't* to *could*.

Practice   Revise the double negatives in the following sentences.

Example: I don't have no more homework to do.

Revised: I don't have any more homework to do.

1. I can't hardly wait for Christmas vacation.
   Revised: *I can't wait for Christmas hardly*

2. Ms. Chandro hasn't never been to Los Angeles before.
   Revised: _____

3. Sonia was so tired, she couldn't do nothing.
   Revised: *She couldn't do nothing, Sonia was so tired.*

4. Nat won't talk to nobody until his lawyer arrives.
   Revised: *Until his lawyer arrives. nat won't to nobody.*

5. Yesterday's newspaper didn't contain no ads for color television sets.
   Revised: _____

6. I don't have no credit cards with me.
   Revised: _____

7. If Harold were smart, he wouldn't answer no one in that tone of voice.
   Revised: *He wouldn't answer no one in that tone of voice*

8. Kylie claimed that she hadn't never been to a rodeo before.
   Revised: *She hadn't never been to a rodeo before Kylie claimed that.*

9. Some days, I can't seem to do nothing right.

   Revised: *I can't seem to do nothing right some days.*

10. Umberto searched, but he couldn't find his gold bow tie nowhere.

    Revised: *but he couldn't find his gold bow tie nowhere Umberto searched.*

Chapter Highlights

- **Fixed-form verbs do not change, no matter what the subject is:**

  I *can*.

  He *can*.

  They *can*.

- **The main verb after a fixed-form helping verb keeps the simple form:**

  I will *sleep*.

  She might *sleep*.

  Sally should *sleep*.

- **An infinitive has two parts, *to* + the simple form of a verb:**

  to dance

  to exclaim

  to read

- **Do not write double negatives:**

  I didn't order no soup. *(incorrect)*

  I didn't order any soup. *(correct)*

  They couldn't hardly see. *(incorrect)*

  They could hardly see. *(correct)*

Chapter Review

Proofread the following essay for errors in fixed-form verbs, infinitives, and double negatives. Cross out each incorrect word, and correct the error above the line.

The Great Houdini

(1) Harry Houdini began to study magic as a child. (2) He became very famous as an escape artist. (3) He could free himself from ropes, chains, and locked containers. (4) Nobody couldn't keep Harry where he

didn't want to be. (5) He could get out of any jail. (6) Once, the head of Scotland Yard handcuffed Houdini's arms around a thick post and then locked him in a prison cell. (7) Houdini managed free himself immediately. (8) Another time, some of the best locksmiths in Europe attempted to trick him with a foolproof lock. (9) Houdini was able open it in seconds. (10) In one of the master's favorite stunts, the police will first put him in a straitjacket and bind him with ropes and chains; then they would hang him by his feet. (11) Even in that position, Houdini can wiggle free.

(12) Houdini continued to amazing people with his incredible feats. (13) He once jumped in midair from one airplane to another while handcuffed. (14) He leaped from a bridge into San Francisco Bay with his hands tied behind his back and a seventy-five-pound ball and chain tied to his feet. (15) People expected to found him dead, but he survived the ordeal. (16) In the most daring feat of all, he asked to be sealed in a coffin and lowered into a swimming pool. (17) He stayed locked up underwater for ninety minutes and then emerged in perfect health. (18) No doubt, Houdini's fame would last. (19) Probably, we won't never see another escape artist as daring as he.

UNIT 3

Writing Assignments

Writing Assignment 1: *Describe a lively scene.* To practice using verbs in the present tense, go where the action is—to a sports event, a busy store, a public park, even woods or a field. Observe carefully as you take notes and freewrite. Capture specific sounds, sights, colors, actions, and smells. Then write a description of what takes place, using lively verbs. Underline all your verbs. Make sure that they are in the present tense and agree with their subjects.

Writing Assignment 2: *Retell an early experience.* Choose an incident from your childhood or adolescence that deeply affected you—for instance, an experience that determined your career choice (or lack of choice). First, using past tense verbs, tell exactly what happened. Then discuss the meaning of this experience for you. Let the reader know precisely why it was so important. You may want to let a classmate read your paper and offer suggestions before you write your final draft. Check all verb endings.

Writing Assignment 3: *Tell a family story.* Many of us heard family stories as we were growing up—how our grandmother escaped from Poland, how Uncle Chester took his sister for a joyride in the Ford when he was six. Assume that you have been asked to write such a story for a scrapbook that will be given to your grandmother on her eightieth birthday. Choose a story that reveals something important about a member of your family. Jot or freewrite the story in interesting detail. Then rewrite carefully. Be sure that all your verbs are correct.

Writing Assignment 4: *Capture a few exciting moments.* Read paragraphs A and B in the Unit 3 Review. Both use lively verbs to describe just a few moments of intense action. Both use the present tense as if the exciting events were happening now. Choose a few intense moments from your life—an accident, a scene in a hospital room, an athletic contest—and write about them. Decide whether using the present or past tense works best. Use varied, interesting verbs; make sure they are correct.

Writing Assignment 5: *Write to Abby.* Think of a problem with love, marriage, parents, or school that might prompt you or someone you know to write to "Dear Abby." Then as if you are the person with the problem, write a letter. In your first sentence, state the problem clearly. Then explain it. Remember, you are confused and don't know what to do. You want to give Abby enough information so that she can answer you wisely. Proofread your letter carefully. Don't let grammatical errors or incorrect verbs stand between you and happiness!

UNIT 3

Review

Transforming

A. Rewrite this paragraph, changing every *I* to *she*, every *me* to *her*, and so forth. Keep all verbs in the present tense. Be sure all verbs agree with the new subjects, and make any other necessary changes.

(1) The race is about to begin. (2) My heart pounds as I peel off my sweatpants and jacket and drop them on the grass. (3) I step onto the new, all-weather track and enter my assigned lane. (4) Next I check my track shoes for loose laces. (5) By now, the athletes around me are stretching backwards, forwards, and sideways. (6) I extend one leg, then the other, and bend low, giving my hamstrings a final stretch. (7) Although I never come eye to eye with my opponents, I feel their readiness as they exhale loudly. (8) Their energy charges the air like electricity. (9) I plant my feet in the blocks. (10) Off to one side, a coach starts to speak. (11) My mind is flashing. (12) How will my opponents kick off? (13) How will they start? (14) The seconds swell, thick and dreamlike. (15) The gun sounds.

SHEILA GRANT, STUDENT

B. Rewrite this paragraph, changing the verbs from present tense to past tense.

(1) It is the morning of April 18, 1906. (2) Alfred Hunt sleeps peacefully in the Palace Hotel in San Francisco. (3) At 5:12 a.m., a violent jolt suddenly shakes his room and sends him rolling from bed. (4) The shaking lasts for forty-five seconds. (5) During the calm of the

next ten seconds, Hunt staggers to the window. (6) Another tremor rocks the city for twenty-five more seconds. (7) Hunt watches in terror. (8) The whole city looks like breaking waves. (9) Buildings reel and tumble to the ground. (10) Then fires break out and start to spread. (11) Hunt quickly dresses, throws open his door, and runs downstairs into the street. (12) Crowds of rushing people block his path. (13) Some people carry screaming children while others struggle under loads of furniture and other valuable objects. (14) It takes Hunt four hours to push through the four blocks from his hotel to the safety of the Oakland ferry. (15) Later, he will learn that the great San Francisco earthquake has destroyed 520 city blocks and has killed more than seven hundred people.

Proofreading The following essay contains a number of past tense errors and past participle errors. First, proofread for verb errors, underlining all incorrect verbs. Then correct any errors above the lines.

They Made Computer History

(1) Charles Babbage is sometimes called the grandfather of the computer, and Ada Lovelace is knowed as the first computer programmer. (2) Ada met Charles in June 1833. (3) She was only eighteen; he were over forty. (4) Together, they make computer history.

(5) Ada Lovelace was the only legal child of Lord Byron, the great English poet. (6) However, she never knew her father. (7) He had separated from her mother thirty-six days after her birth and then had leaved England forever. (8) Ada's mother raise her with a strong hand, but she encouraged her daughter's natural talent for mathematics. (9) Ada was taught at home. (10) She also wrote to famous mathematicians and scientists, among them Charles Babbage.

(11) By the time he met Ada Lovelace, Babbage had already design a machine that could perform any mathematical operation. (12) He called it the analytical engine. (13) The British government had promise him money to build it. (14) Ada give him both money and support. (15) She also created the system of punch cards for feeding information into the machine. (16) Some people said that she want to use the machine to win at the horse races. (17) However, the analytical engine was never build. (18) No one at that time could make the necessary parts.

(19) The analytical engine was almost forgotten until 1937 when Howard H. Aiken discovered Babbage's plans. (20) Aiken use them to help design the first modern computer. (21) In the 1980s, ADA become the name of a programming language.

UNIT 4

Joining Ideas Together

Chapter 11

Coordination

As a writer, you will sometimes want to join short, choppy sentences to form longer sentences. One way to join two ideas is to use a comma and a *coodinating conjunction*.

> (1) This car has many special features, and it costs less than $9,000.
>
> (2) The television picture is blurred, but we will watch the football game anyway.
>
> (3) She wants to practice her Italian, so she is going to Italy.

- Can you break sentence (1) into two complete and independent ideas or thoughts? What are they? Underline the subject and verb in each.
- Can you do the same with sentences (2) and (3)? Underline the subjects and verbs.
- In each sentence, circle the word that joins the two parts of the sentence together. What punctuation mark comes before that word?
- *And*, *but*, and *so* are called *coordinating conjunctions* because they coordinate, or join together, ideas. Other coordinating conjunctions are *for*, *nor*, *or*, and *yet*.

182 Unit 4 *Joining Ideas Together*

To join two complete and independent ideas, use a coordinating conjunction preceded by a comma.

Now let's see just how coordinating conjunctions connect ideas:

Coordinating Conjunctions

and	means	in addition
but, yet	mean	in contrast
for	means	because
nor	means	not either
or	means	either, a choice
so	means	as a result

BE CAREFUL: *Then, also,* and *plus* are not coordinating conjunctions. By themselves, they cannot join two ideas.

Incorrect: He studied, then he went to work.

Correct: He studied, and then he went to work.

Practice 1

Read these sentences for meaning. Then punctuate them correctly, and fill in the coordinating conjunction that best expresses the relationship between the two complete thoughts. REMEMBER: Do you want to *add, contrast, give a reason, show a result,* or *indicate a choice?* Some sentences may take more than one conjunction. Punctuate correctly!

1. I bought a CD player _but_ I never use it.

2. My daughter wants to skate like Kristi Yamaguchi _so_ she practices at the rink every day.

3. She will go to Sacramento City College, _or_ she will attend the University of California at Davis.

4. The stock market crashed in 1929 _and so_ the Great Depression began soon after.

5. Ruth loves flowers, _so_ let's give her these violets.

6. On her vacation, Julie will snorkel in Hawaii, _and_ she will backpack in Colorado.

7. My washing machine just broke down _and_ the guarantee expired yesterday.

8. Dr. Donovan teaches fiction and drama classes _and_ both are excellent.

9. The temperature may fall to zero, _so_ you had better wear your long underwear.

10. I love the paintings of Matisse, _for_ he uses such brilliant colors.

11. In 1912, the *Titanic* was hailed as the world's safest liner, _so_ it sank after hitting an iceberg on April 12.

12. The Hansons have a snowblower, _so_ they never have to shovel snow.

13. Darryl uses a lap-top computer, _for_ he has to work while traveling.

14. We looked everywhere for him; he was not at home _nor_ was he at work.

15. Paul's wife works the day shift, _and_ he works the night shift, _so_ they rarely see each other.

Practice 2 Every one of these thoughts is complete by itself, but you can join them together to make more interesting sentences. Combine pairs of these thoughts, using _and, but, for, nor, or, so,_ or _yet_, and write six new sentences on the lines below. Punctuate correctly.

    teeth fascinate Jack

    live models danced in the store window

    in the 1840s, American women began to fight for the right to vote

    I will write my essay at home tonight

    the ancient Chinese valued peaches

    a curious crowd gathered on the sidewalk

    they are the best pool players on the block

    he has decided to become a dentist

    I will write it tomorrow in the computer lab

    they did not win that right until 1920

    they can't beat my cousin from Cleveland

    they believed that eating peaches made a person immortal

1. _____

    _____

2. _____

    _____

3. _____

4. _____

5. _____

6. _____

Practice 3 Finish these sentences by adding a second complete idea after the coordinating conjunction.

1. America is a rich country, but *America is so rich*

2. Please help me carry these packages, or _____

3. Yuri has lived in the U.S. for ten years, so _____

4. Len has been married three times, and _____

5. These are my favorite sneakers, for *I like to wear them*

6. He loves to tell people what to do, so _____

7. She carries her math book everywhere, yet _____

8. This curry had better be hot, or _____

Chapter 11   Coordination   185

9. I like owning a car, for _____

_____

10. I like owning a car, but _____

_____

Practice 4   Write seven sentences of your own using each of the coordinating conjunctions—*and, but, for, nor, or, so,* and *yet*—to join two independent ideas. Punctuate correctly.

1. _____

_____

2. _____

_____

3. _____

_____

4. _____

_____

5. _____

_____

6. _____

_____

7. _____

_____

Chapter Highlights

- A comma and a coordinating conjunction join two independent ideas:

    The fans booed, *but* the umpire paid no attention.

    Independent idea { , and / , but / , for / , nor / , or / , so / , yet } independent idea.

- Note: *Then, also,* and *plus* are not coordinating conjunctions.

Chapter Review

Read this paragraph of short, choppy sentences. Then rewrite it, using different coordinating conjunctions to combine some pairs of sentences. Keep some short sentences for variety. Copy your revised paragraph on a fresh sheet of paper. Punctuate with care.

(1) Victory was sweet for Wilma Rudolph. (2) She won three gold medals at the 1960 Olympic games. (3) Rudolph finished first in the 100-meter and 200-meter dashes. (4) She ran the anchor leg for the 400-meter relay team. (5) Everyone praised and admired the powerful runner. (6) She had not always been athletic. (7) When she was born, Rudolph weighed less than five pounds. (8) She was very weak. (9) This great runner also had a paralyzed leg. (10) She developed grace, power, and speed through hard work. (11) To train herself, Rudolph ran track. (12) She exercised every day. (13) Her routine helped her gain strength. (14) It was her determination that made her a champion. (15) Wilma Rudolph made Olympic history. (16) She proved that continuing dedication can lead to extraordinary achievements.

Chapter 12

Subordination

PART A Defining and Using Subordinating Conjunctions
PART B Punctuating Subordinating Conjunctions

PART A Defining and Using Subordinating Conjunctions

Another way to join ideas together is with a *subordinating conjunction*. Read this paragraph:

> A great disaster happened in 1857. The S.S. *Central America* sank. This steamship was carrying six hundred wealthy passengers from California to New York. Many of them had recently struck gold. Battered by a storm, the ship began to flood. Many people on board bailed water. Others prayed and quieted the children. Thirty hours passed. A rescue boat arrived. Almost two hundred people were saved. The rest died. Later, many banks failed. Three tons of gold had gone down with the ship.

This could have been a good paragraph, but notice how dull the writing is because the sentences are short and choppy.

188 Unit 4 Joining Ideas Together

Here is the same paragraph rewritten to make it more interesting:

> A great disaster happened in 1857 *when* the S.S. *Central America* sank. This steamship was carrying six hundred wealthy passengers from California to New York. Many of them had recently struck gold. Battered by a storm, the ship began to flood. Many people on board bailed water *while* others prayed and quieted the children. *After* thirty hours passed, a rescue boat arrived. Almost two hundred people were saved *although* the rest died. Later, many banks failed *because* three tons of gold had gone down with the ship.

Notice that the paragraph now reads more smoothly and is more interesting because the following words were used to join some of the choppy sentences: *when, while, after, although,* and *because.*

When, while, after, although, and *because* are part of a large group of words called *subordinating conjunctions.* As you can see from the paragraph, these conjunctions join ideas.

BE CAREFUL: Once you add a subordinating conjunction to an idea, that idea can no longer stand alone as a complete and independent sentence. It has become a subordinate or dependent idea; it must rely on another independent idea to complete its meaning.*

> (1) Because he is tired, *he won't go out*
>
> (2) As I left the room, *some one come in the room*
>
> (3) If you know Spanish, *You help my with my spanish work*

- Note that each of these ideas is dependent and must be followed by something else—a complete and independent thought.

- Sentence (1), for example, could be completed like this: Because he is tired, *he won't go out.*

- Add an independent idea to complete each dependent idea on the lines above.

On the next page is a partial list of subordinating conjunctions.

---

*For more work on sentence fragments of this type, see Chapter 5, Part C.

Common Subordinating Conjunctions		
after	even though	when
although	if	whenever
as	since	where
as if	so that	whereas
as though	though	wherever
because	unless	whether
before	until	while

Practice 1 Read these sentences for meaning. Then fill in the subordinating conjunction that best expresses the relationship between the two ideas.

✓ 1. The Berlin Wall was torn down __because__ it was a symbol of oppression.

✓ 2. __after__ Harold turned forty, he started lifting weights each day.

✗ 3. Please light the candles __since__ I pour the wine.

✓ 4. __when__ Billy the Kid burst into the room, everyone dove for cover.

✓ 5. I have to get the boiler fixed __so that__ we can get some heat in this house.

✓ 6. __since__ you revise your papers carefully, you get an excellent grade.

✓ 7. __if__ I had the money, I would open a summer camp for city kids.

✗ 8. __since__ Veronica pulled away, a blue cloud of exhaust rose from the car.

✗ 9. My mother refuses to use a sewing machine __unless__ hand stitching is difficult.

✓ 10. Apples had been America's favorite fruit __until__ citrus fruit became popular in the twentieth century.

✗ 11. __since__ the guests were dancing downstairs, a thief was helping himself to the valuables.

✓ 12. __since__ subway fares are going up tomorrow, I will buy extra tokens tonight.

✓ 13. They are good friends __although__ they fight constantly.

Unit 4   Joining Ideas Together

14. She entered the room ___when___ she were Cleopatra on her barge.

15. ___Although___ my dog Fang is usually friendly, he growls and drools ___until___ he sees you.

Practice 2   Now that you understand how subordinating conjunctions join thoughts together, try these sentences. Here you have to supply one idea. Make sure that the ideas you add have subjects and verbs.

1. The cafeteria food improved when ___The food change and it service.___

2. Because Mark and Joel both love basketball, ___They play basketball all night___

3. If ___They stop send me magizes___, I'll cancel my subscription.

4. When ___it herad for her to sty___, Harriet laughed.

5. The history class cheered after ___The History class win the History contests.___

6. Whenever Ken looks in the mirror, ___He is alway sing___

7. I was washing stacks of dirty dishes while ___My cusin the football game on TV.___

8. Although he is usually very shy, ___He likes to be a fenny person.___

9. Before ___it can be a easy mistake___, you had better get all the facts.

10. After ___I work out with weight___, I always feel wonderful.

PART B Punctuating Subordinating Conjunctions

As you may have noticed in the preceding exercises, some sentences with subordinating conjunctions use a comma while others do not. Here is how it's done.

> (1) Because it rained very hard, we had to leave early.
>
> (2) We had to leave early because it rained very hard.

- Sentence (1) has a comma because the dependent idea comes before the independent idea.

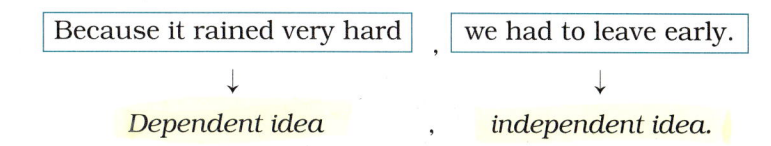

Because it rained very hard	,	we had to leave early.
↓		↓
Dependent idea	,	*independent idea.*

- Sentence (2) has no comma because the dependent idea follows the independent idea.

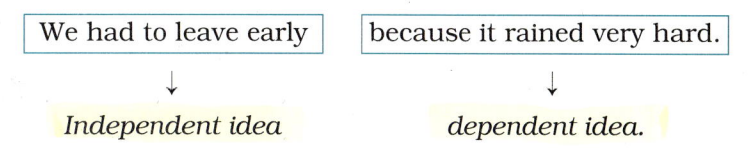

We had to leave early	because it rained very hard.
↓	↓
Independent idea	*dependent idea.*

Use a comma after a dependent idea; do not use a comma before a dependent idea.

Practice 1

If a sentence is punctuated correctly, write *C* in the blank. If not, punctuate it correctly by adding a comma.

1. Whenever Americans get hungry, they want to eat quickly. _____

2. When McDonald's opened in 1954, it started a trend that has continued. _____

3. Whether you are talking about hamburgers or pizza, fast food is big business—more than $60 billion a year. _____ *C*

4. While Americans spend $15 billion on pizza each year, they spend another $7 billion on fast-food chicken. _C_

5. About eight million bagels are sold each day although only one out of four Americans has ever eaten one. _C_

6. Fast-food profits have recently dropped because Americans can eat faster at home. _C_

7. Whereas only 25 percent of Americans had microwave ovens ten years ago, now more than 75 percent own them. _____

8. When you buy frozen hamburgers, you can pop them into the microwave and sit down to eat in three minutes. _____

9. You will spend much more time if you have to travel to a restaurant. _C_

10. Because they want to meet the microwave challenge, fast-food chains are trying to produce food even faster. _____

11. In some restaurants, waiters take orders while you wait in line. _C_

12. In other restaurants, computers are available so that you can order without talking. _C_

13. In some others, as you walk through the door, you may see robots making French fries. _____

14. Unless we reverse the trend, Americans will continue to eat more and more quickly. _____

15. Perhaps the trend won't end until we eat only nutrition pills. _C_

Chapter 12 Subordination 193

Practice 2 Combine each pair of sentences below by using a subordinating conjunction. Write each combination two ways: once with the subordinating conjunction at the beginning of the sentence and once with the conjunction in the middle of the sentence. Punctuate correctly.

Example: We sat on the porch.
The sun went down.

Until the sun went down, we sat on the porch.

We sat on the porch until the sun went down.

1. We will not sign the lease
   We study the fine print.

   We are not sign the lease
   We are study the fine print.

2. Fred arrived.
   The meeting started.

   Fred plane arrived late
   The meeting started late

3. Rico is a good typist.
   He cannot take dictation.

   Rico is a verry good typist
   He always cannot take dictation.

4. Tourism is booming.
   Linda has enrolled in the new travel and tourism curriculum.

   That year tourism is booming
   That Linda has in the new travel and tourism curriclum

194 Unit 4 Joining Ideas Together

5. The scientist was falling asleep.
   She solved the problem.

   The scientist was always fall a

6. Books of poetry do not sell well.
   Very few poetry books are published.

   Meny of books of poetry do not sell well. Very few poetry books are not published.

7. Our boss stormed out of the office.
   We laughed nervously.

   O.

8. Sir Walter Scott wrote a novel about an unlucky opal.
   Opals quickly went out of fashion.

9. Phil has good ideas.
   He has trouble expressing them.

10. She is bothered by her son's drinking.
    She attends Al-Anon.

Chapter 12 Subordination 195

Practice 3 Now try writing sentences of your own. Fill in the blanks, being careful to punctuate correctly. Do not use a comma when the independent idea precedes the dependent idea.

1. _I like to which move_ because _It ejoyng to which_.

2. Although _my mine was laze_.

3. Since _I start lift weight. My body feel good_.

4. _____ whenever _____.

5. Unless _you study you can pass_.

Chapter Highlights

- **A subordinating conjunction joins a dependent idea and an independent idea:**

    When I registered, all the math courses were closed.

    All the math courses were closed *when* I registered.

- **Use a comma after a dependent idea.**

    { After / Because / Before / If / Since / Unless / When / While } *dependent idea, independent idea.*

- **Do not use a comma before a dependent idea.**

    Independent idea { after / because / before / if / since / unless / when / while } *dependent idea.*

Chapter Review

Read this paragraph of short, choppy sentences. Then rewrite it on the lines below, using different subordinating conjunctions to combine pairs of sentences. Keep some short sentences for variety. Punctuate with care.

(1) An Wang was both a great inventor and a brilliant businessman. (2) The founder of Wang Laboratories was born in China in 1920. (3) He earned a doctorate in physics from Harvard University. (4) He was twenty-eight years old. (5) China was torn by civil war. (6) He stayed in the United States. (7) Wang had only $600 in 1951. (8) He began Wang Laboratories. (9) This company produced his revolutionary word-processing system. (10) Wang is best known for this accomplishment. (11) He also invented a magnetic-core memory for computers and a fast desktop calculator. (12) By 1983, sales of these inventions had made him one of the five richest Americans. (13) Wang believed in giving, not just taking. (14) He donated much of his wealth to education and to people in need. (15) An Wang was elected to the National Inventors Hall of Fame. (16) He was also one of twelve naturalized Americans to receive the President's Medal of Liberty.

Chapter 13

Avoiding Run-ons and Comma Splices

Now that you have had practice joining ideas together, here are two errors to watch out for: the *run-on* and the *comma splice*.

> **Run-on:** Herb talks too much nobody seems to mind.

- There are two complete ideas here: *Herb talks too much* and *nobody seems to mind*.
- A run-on incorrectly runs together two complete ideas without using a conjunction or punctuation.

> **Comma splice:** Herb talks too much, nobody seems to mind.

- A comma splice incorrectly joins two complete ideas with a comma but no conjunction.

Here are three ways to correct a run-on and a comma splice.

1. Write two separate sentences, making sure that each is complete.

> Herb talks too much. Nobody seems to mind.

2. Use a comma and a coordinating conjunction *(and, but, for, nor, or, so, yet).**

> Herb talks too much, *but* nobody seems to mind.

3. Use a subordinating conjunction (for example, *although, because, if, since,* or *when).***

> *Although* Herb talks too much, nobody seems to mind.

Practice 1 Many of these sentences contain run-ons or comma splices. If a sentence is correct, write *C* in the right-hand column. If it contains a run-on or a comma splice, write either *RO* or *CS.* Then correct the error in any way you wish. Use each method at least once.

Example: Many celebrities have admitted their addictions public awareness of addiction has increased. — Because many addictions,   RO

1. Many famous people today have struggled with alcoholism or drug abuse, *but* some have overcome these problems.   C RO

2. Often politicians, athletes, and actors hide their addiction and their recovery, they do not want to risk ruining their careers.   C

3. They also feel that going public might interfere with the success of their treatment.   C

4. Other celebrities choose to go public in their battles with alcohol or drugs.   C

---
*For more work on coordinating conjunctions, see Chapter 11.
**For more work on subordinating conjunctions, see Chapter 12.

5. They feel that their struggles may help others, they want to act as positive role models.

6. One such person is Betty Ford, a former First Lady, she is one of the best-known women in America.

7. In 1978, Ford's whole family confronted her about her addiction with their love and support, she became sober at age sixty.

8. Her recovery was successful. Ford agreed to help several friends create a treatment center.

9. The Betty Ford Center opened in 1982 in Rancho Mirage, California.

10. At the Betty Ford Center, alcoholics and addicts receive counseling and support for their new way of life, thousands have been treated there.

11. Another celebrity who once denied his alcohol abuse is Chris Mullin, this NBA star now believes education is the best way to fight addiction.

12. Mullin did not think he was an alcoholic. he drank only beer.

13. His coach, Don Nelson, demanded that Mullin take care of his drinking problem, Mullin attended a thirty-day drug treatment program in 1988.

14. Mullin continues to be sober, for he takes his recovery very seriously.

15. He is now a superstar for the Golden State Warriors, in 1992, he played on the U.S. Olympic Basketball "Dream Team."

200 Unit 4 *Joining Ideas Together*

16. Today younger and younger people are becoming addicted the talented actress Drew Barrymore is just one example.   _C_

17. At six years old, Barrymore acted in *E.T.: The Extra-Terrestrial* by age nine she was addicted to drugs and alcohol.   _RO_

18. Her mother forced her into treatment when she was thirteen, the two tried to keep her problems a secret.   _CS_

19. When a gossip magazine ran a story about her drug treatment, Barrymore decided to speak for herself.   _C_

20. She wrote a book called *Little Girl Lost*, she appeared on television talk shows and gave interviews.   _RO_

21. Barrymore believes that addiction is nothing to be embarrassed about, she wants to speak out.   _CS_

22. Alcohol and drugs harm millions of Americans, when someone truly recovers, his or her triumph can give others the courage to seek help.   _CS_

Practice 2 Correct each run-on or comma splice in two ways. Be sure to punctuate correctly.

Example: Two cars raced down the street no one paid any attention to them.

  a. Two cars raced down the street. No one paid any attention to them.

  b. Two cars raced down the street, but no one paid any attention to them.

1. They took classes in marketing, they started a soft drink business.

  a. *They took classes in marketing.*
  b. *They started up a soft drink business.*

2. She sat in the dentist's waiting room, she studied the tank of tropical fish.

   a. *She sat in the dentist's waiting room, she studied the tank tropical fi[sh]*

   b. *She sat in the dentist's waiting roo[m] So she she studied the tank of tropical fish.*

3. My dad has few material possessions he is happy.

   a. *My dad has few material possession h[e]*

   b. *My has a lot of material possession h[e] is happy.*

4. They were uninvited guests, they had to settle for leftovers.

   a. *They were uninvited guests, they had to sett[le] for leftovers.*

   b. *They were uninvited guests, they had to settle for leftovers food from the party.*

5. Eric was swimming in the water hole Amy hid his clothes.

   a. *Eric was swimming in the water hol[e] amy h[id] his clothes.* (come back)

   b. _____

6. We followed the signs we still got lost.

   a. _____

   b. _____

7. Employment agencies sometimes help you find a job, their fees can be quite high.

   a. _____
   _____

   b. _____
   _____

8. I like the film course we are studying the work of Kurosawa.

   a. _____

   b. _____

9. It thunders loudly, I get nervous.

   a. _____

   b. _____

10. The concert had been well planned everything went smoothly.

    a. _____

    b. _____

    _____

Chapter Highlights

Avoid run-ons and comma splices:

> Her house faces the ocean the view is breathtaking. *(run-on)*
>
> Her house faces the ocean, the view is breathtaking. *(comma splice)*

Use these techniques to avoid run-ons and comma splices.

- **Write two complete sentences:**

    Her house faces the ocean. The view is breathtaking.

- **Use a coordinating conjunction:**

    Her house faces the ocean, *so* the view is breathtaking.

- **Use a subordinating conjunction:**

    Because her house faces the ocean, the view is breathtaking.

Chapter Review

Run-ons and comma splices are most likely to occur in paragraphs or longer pieces of writing. Proofread each paragraph for run-ons and comma splices. Correct the run-ons and the comma splices in any way that makes sense: Make two separate sentences, add a coordinating conjunction, or add a subordinating conjunction. Then write a revised version of the paragraph on a separate sheet of paper. Punctuate with care.

A. (1) The U.S. government first investigated unidentified flying objects, or UFOs, during the 1940s. (2) In 1947, President Truman formed a secret panel of scientists and military officers to research

UFOs, that same year, one of the most bizarre cases occurred. (3) Between June 27 and July 2, more than a dozen witnesses in western states saw bright, disk-shaped objects in the sky. (4) On July 2, a sheep rancher named William Brazel heard a huge explosion the next day he found the wreckage of a crash. (5) He notified local Air Force officials, who issued a press release about the discovery of an alien spaceship both national and international newspapers carried the story. (6) Near Roswell, New Mexico, unusual tinfoil-like metal and the bodies of space aliens were supposedly found, almost immediately, the Air Force changed its story and denied its own report. (7) Officials said a weather balloon had crashed, top-secret documents finally released in 1987 say that a weird spacecraft and its crew were in fact found. (8) The government no longer officially investigates UFOs, many think such investigations are taking place in secret.

B. (1) José Clemente Orozco was a brilliant twentieth-century Mexican painter. (2) He became interested in art when he was seven years old, on his way to school, Orozco watched printmaker Jose Guadalupe Posada. (3) He begged his mother to let him take art classes. (4) Orozco became the youngest student to study drawing at the Academia de San Carlos, he was soon able to draw better than the older students. (5) At seventeen, Orozco lost his left hand in an accident the young artist continued to take classes. (6) In his late thirties, he began to paint large, colorful murals on building walls, these murals made him famous. (7) Although Orozco was driven out of Mexico several times for publicly criticizing the government, he won praise and awards, his work helped draw international attention to Mexican art.

C. (1) The Leaning Tower of Pisa is one of the most unusual buildings in the world, it was begun in 1174. (2) When the builders reached the third of its eight stories, the marble bell tower started to tilt toward the south attempts to correct the slant only made it lean more. (3) Many ideas to keep the tower from toppling have been suggested over the centuries. (4) One was to build a huge statue to prop it up, another was to freeze the marshy ground on which the structure rests. (5) One inventor thought of installing a large wind machine to keep the building from falling. (6) During the 1930s, the Italian government pumped in concrete to strengthen the foundations. (7) However, the tilt of the 179-foot tower keeps increasing today the Leaning Tower is 16.5 feet off center and still standing.

D. (1) What do you do every night before you go to sleep and every morning when you wake up? (2) You probably brush your teeth, most people in the United States did not start brushing their teeth until after the 1850s. (3) People living in the nineteenth century did not have toothpaste, Dr. Washington Wentworth Sheffield developed a toothcleaning substance, which soon became widely available. (4) With the help of his son, this Connecticut dentist changed our daily habits by making the first toothpaste it was called Dr. Sheffield's Creme Dentifrice. (5) The product was not marketed cleverly enough, the idea of using toothpaste caught on slowly. (6) Then toothpaste was put into tin tubes everyone wanted to try this new product. (7) Think of life without tubes of mint-flavored toothpaste then thank Dr. Sheffield for his idea.

E. (1) The first semester of college is difficult for many students they must take on many new responsibilities. (2) For instance, they must create their own schedules. (3) New students get to select their courses in addition, they have to decide when they will take them. (4) Students also must purchase their own textbooks, colleges do not distribute textbooks each term as high schools do. (5) No bells ring to announce when classes begin and end students are supposed to arrive on time. (6) Furthermore, many professors do not call the roll they expect students to attend classes regularly and know the assignments. (7) Above all, new students must be self-disciplined. (8) No one stands over them telling them to do their homework or to visit the writing lab for extra help, they must balance the temptation to have fun and the desire to build a successful future.

Chapter 14

Semicolons

So far you have learned to join ideas together in two ways.

Coordinating conjunctions *(and, but, for, nor, or, so, yet)* can join ideas:

> (1) This is the worst food we have ever tasted, *so* we will never eat in this restaurant again.

Subordinating conjunctions (for example, *although, as, because, if,* and *when)* can join ideas:

> (2) *Because* this is the worst food we have ever tasted, we will never eat in this restaurant again.

Chapter 14 Semicolons 207

comeback

Another way to join ideas is with a semicolon:

> (3) This is the worst food we have ever tasted; we will never eat in this restaurant again.

A *semicolon* **joins two related independent ideas without a conjunction; do not capitalize the first word after a semicolon.**

Use the semicolon for variety. In general, use no more than one or two semicolons in a paragraph.

Practice 1 Each independent idea below is the first half of a sentence. Add a semicolon and a second complete idea, one that can stand alone.

Example: Ken was a cashier at Food City ; now he manages the store.

1. My cat spotted a mouse *He startcae to the mouses*

2. The garage was filled with new tires *He use them for my car*

3. Beatrice has an unlisted phone number *Because Beatrice has an unlisted phone number* [come back]

4. The man wore a tattered coat *c6*

5. I felt sure someone was in the room *When I left out*

6. P.J. is majoring in philosophy *Because he want to a docther*

7. Roslyn's first car had a stick shift *?*

8. The batter takes a hard swing at the ball _____

_____

9. Be careful repairing the roof _____

_____

10. The windows of the house were dark _____

_____

BE CAREFUL: Do not use a semicolon between a dependent idea and an independent idea.

> Although he is never at home, he is not difficult to reach at the office.

- You cannot use a semicolon in this sentence because the first idea (*although he is never at home*) cannot stand alone.
- The word *although* requires that another idea be added in order to make a complete sentence.

Practice 2

Which of these ideas can be followed by a semicolon and an independent thought? Check them (✓).

1. The sun seemed to pop up from the horizon ✓
2. The library has installed new computers ✓
3. After he finishes cleaning the fish _____
4. When I left, she was laughing ✓
5. My answer is simple ✓
6. Because I could not find my car keys _____
7. The contact lens cracked ✓
8. When the health fair is over _____
9. Unless you arrive early _____
10. The town of Montclair recycles its newspapers and glass ✓

Now copy the sentences you have checked, add a semicolon, and complete each sentence with a second independent idea. You should have checked sentences 1, 2, 4, 5, 7, and 10.

1. *The sun seemed to pop up from the horizon In morning sun seemed to pop up from*
2. *The library has installed new computers all the library has installed new compute*
4. *When I left, she was laughing When I in the room, she was seal laug*
5. *My answer is simple. The answer from the test is simp*
7. *The contact lens cracked. Both of my contact lens cracked*
10. *The town of Montclair recycles its newspapers and glass Many small town recycles its newspa and glass.*

Chapter Highlights

- **A semicolon joins two independent ideas:**
    I like hiking; she prefers fishing.

- **Do not capitalize the first word after a semicolon.**

    | Independent idea | ; | independent idea. |

Chapter 14 Semicolons 209

Chapter Review

Proofread for incorrect semicolons or capital letters. Make any corrections above the lines.

(1) The Swiss Army knife is carried in the pockets and purses of millions of travelers, campers, and just plain folks. (2) Numerous useful gadgets are folded into its famous red handle; These include knife blades, tweezers, scissors, toothpick, screwdriver, bottle opener, fish scaler, and magnifying glass. (3) The handy Swiss Army knife was created for Swiss soldiers in 1891; and soon became popular all over the world. (4) Now it comes in many models and colors; although many people prefer the classic original. (5) The Swiss Army knife has earned a reputation for beautiful design and usefulness; a red one is on permanent display in New York's famous Museum of Modern Art.

Chapter 15

Conjunctive Adverbs

PART A Defining and Using Conjunctive Adverbs
PART B Punctuating Conjunctive Adverbs

PART A Defining and Using Conjunctive Adverbs

Another excellent method of joining ideas is to use a semicolon and a special kind of adverb. This special adverb is call a *conjunctive adverb* because it is part *conjunction* and part *adverb*.

> (1) (a) He received an A on his term paper; *furthermore,*
>
>   (b) the instructor exempted him from the final.

- *Furthermore* adds idea (b) to idea (a).
- The sentence might have been written, "He received an A on his term paper, *and* the instructor exempted him from the final."
- But *furthermore* is stronger, more emphatic.
- Note the punctuation.

> (2) (a) Jane has never studied finance; *however*,
>
> (b) she plays the stock market like a pro.

- *However* contrasts ideas (a) and (b).
- The sentence might have been written, "Jane has never studied finance, *but* she plays the stock market like a pro."
- But *however* is stronger, more emphatic.
- Note the punctuation.

> (3) (a) The complete dictionary weighs thirty pounds; *therefore*,
>
> (b) I bring my pocket edition to school.

- *Therefore* shows that idea (a) is the cause of idea (b).
- The sentence might have been written, "*Because* the complete dictionary weighs thirty pounds, I bring my pocket edition to school."
- But *therefore* is stronger, more emphatic.
- Note the punctuation.

A *conjunctive adverb* joins ideas in an *emphatic* way. It may be used with a semicolon only when both ideas are independent and can stand alone.

Here are some common conjunctive adverbs and their meanings:

Common Conjunctive Adverbs

consequently	means	as a result
furthermore	means	in addition
however	means	in contrast
instead	means	in place of
meanwhile	means	at the same time
nevertheless	means	in contrast
otherwise	means	as an alternative
therefore	means	for that reason

Conjunctive adverbs are also called *transitional expressions*. They help the reader see the transitions, or changes, in meaning from one idea to the next.

Practice Add an idea after each conjunctive adverb. The idea you add must make sense in terms of the entire sentence, so keep in mind the meaning of each conjunctive adverb. If necessary, refer to the chart.

Example: I hate eating pretzels when I have a sore throat; however, <u>I love ice cream any time at all.</u>

1. Anthony ran to get help; meanwhile, <u>meanwhile he give aid to that person.</u>

2. Anna says whatever is on her mind; consequently, _____

3. I refuse to wear those red cowboy boots again; furthermore, <u>I hate wearing those red cowboy boots</u>

4. Travis is having trouble with calculus; otherwise, <u>I to see a tutor for help.</u>

5. Her birthday is the day before Christmas; nevertheless, <u>She her birthday on Christmas.</u>

6. Kim wanted to volunteer at the hospital; however, <u>She to work long hours at work.</u>

7. My mother carried two huge pieces of luggage off the plane; furthermore, _____

8. Jason hoped to graduate in June 1990; instead, _____

9. My parents rarely read; however, _____

10. The gas gauge on my car does not work properly; therefore, _____

PART B Punctuating Conjunctive Adverbs

Notice the punctuation pattern:

> Complete idea; conjunctive adverb, complete idea.

- The conjunctive adverb is preceded by a semicolon.
- It is followed by a comma.

Practice 1 Punctuate these sentences correctly.

1. In the 1990s, the fastest-growing occupations will require much training; therefore, a college degree will be important.
2. Many jobs needing little education will be in less demand; consequently, high school dropouts will find fewer positions.
3. Service jobs will increase at a greater rate than jobs that produce goods; furthermore, growth will be faster in some services than in others.
4. There will be many openings for jobs in retail and wholesale; however, there will be fewer openings in government and communications.
5. Transportation and public utilities will also expand slowly; meanwhile, job growth in legal services will be rapid.
6. Business services will also grow; furthermore, this growth will be greatest in such areas as word processing and computer support.
7. Employment in health services will increase; however, the increase will not occur in hospitals, but in outpatient clinics and doctors' offices.
8. The manufacturing, mining, and agricultural industries will not expand much; nevertheless, the number of construction jobs will rise.

Chapter 15 Conjunctive Adverbs 215

9. For more information about the future job market, go to your college library; otherwise, you can go to your town library.

10. Studying the *Occupational Outlook Handbook* will give you valuable career information; furthermore, it may help you find a rewarding job.

Practice 2 Combine each set of sentences into one, using a conjunctive adverb. Choose a conjunctive adverb that expresses the relationship between the two ideas. Punctuate with care.

1. (a) Marilyn fell asleep on the train.

    (b) She missed her stop.

    Combination: *She missed her stop when fell asleep on the train.*

2. (a) Last night, Channel 20 televised a special about gorillas.

    (b) I did not get home in time to see it.

    Combination: *I did not get home in time to see it last night, on channel 20 televised a special about gorillas.*

3. (a) Roberta wrote her nephew every month.

    (b) She received answers infrequently.

    Combination: *Roberta wrote her nephew every mo— she received answers infrequently.*

4. (a) The pay at Ace Shoe isn't high.

    (b) The employers make working there a pleasure.

    Combination: *The employers make working there a pleasure. The pay at ace shoe isn't high.*

5. (a) Luke missed work on Monday.

    (b) He did not proofread the quarterly report.

    Combination: *Luke missed work on Monday He did not proofread the quarterly report.*

BE CAREFUL: Never use a semicolon when a conjunctive adverb does not join together two independent ideas.

> (1) *However*, I don't like him.
>
> (2) I don't, *however*, like him.
>
> (3) I don't like him, *however*.

- Why aren't semicolons used in sentences (1), (2), and (3)?
- These sentences contain only one independent idea; therefore, a semicolon cannot be used.

Never use a semicolon to join two ideas if one of the ideas is subordinate to the other.

> (4) If I were you, *however*, I would never talk to him again.

- Are the two ideas in sentence (4) independent?
- *If I were you* cannot stand alone as an independent idea; therefore, a semicolon cannot be used.

Practice 3

Write four sentences, using a different conjunctive adverb in each one. Make sure both ideas in each sentence are independent.

1. _____

2. _____

3. _____

4. _____

Chapter Highlights

- **A semicolon and a conjunctive adverb join two independent ideas:**
  We can't go rowing now; *however*, we can go on Sunday.
  Lou earned an 83 on the exam; *therefore*, he passed physics.

  Independent idea {; consequently, ; furthermore, ; however, ; instead, ; meanwhile, ; nevertheless, ; therefore,} independent idea.

- **Use a semicolon *only* when the conjunctive adverb joins two independent ideas:**
  I wasn't sorry; however, I apologized. *(two independent ideas)*
  I apologized, however. *(one independent idea)*
  If you wanted to go, however, you should have said so.
  (one dependent idea + one independent idea)

Chapter Review

Proofread the following paragraph for conjunctive adverb errors and punctuation errors. Then correct each error above the line.

(1) You might not know that the largest museum of Native American culture in the world is in New York City however, it is.   (2) The National Museum of the American Indian owns more than one million objects furthermore, it contains more than seventy-five thousand photographs and forty thousand books.   (3) The first floor has exhibits about such tribes as the Navajo, Algonquin, Hopi, Creek, Cherokee, and Seminole. (4) The Iroquois show, the largest anywhere, features fascinating masks of imaginary forest creatures, as well as a fine collection of wampum belts.   (5) The second floor contains displays about other North American tribes meanwhile: South American culture is represented in rich detail on the third floor.   (6) This remarkable collection has grown so large that the New York museum can no longer hold it.   (7) It has been moved; therefore, to larger quarters downtown, and a second museum will be created in Washington, D.C.

Chapter 16

Relative Pronouns

PART A Defining and Using Relative Pronouns
PART B Punctuating Ideas Introduced by WHO, WHICH, or THAT

PART A Defining and Using Relative Pronouns

To add variety to your writing, you sometimes may wish to use *relative pronouns* to combine two sentences.

> (1) My father is eighty years old.
> (2) He collects stamps.

- Sentences (1) and (2) are grammatically correct.
- They are so short, however, that you may wish to combine them.

> (3) My father, who is eighty years old, collects stamps.

- Sentence (3) is a combination of (1) and (2).

- *Who* has replaced *he*, the subject of sentence (2). *Who* introduces the rest of the idea, *is eighty years old.*
- *Who* is called a *relative pronoun* because it *relates* "is eighty years old" to "my father."*

BE CAREFUL: An idea introduced by a relative pronoun cannot stand alone as a complete and independent sentence. It is dependent; it needs an independent idea (like "My father collects stamps") to complete its meaning.

Here are some more combinations:

(4) He gives great singing lessons

(5) All his pupils love them.

(6) He gives great singing lessons, *which* all his pupils love.

(7) I have a large living room.

(8) It can hold two grand pianos.

(9) I have a large living room *that* can hold two grand pianos.

- As you can see, *which* and *that* also can be used as relative pronouns.
- In sentence (6), what does *which* relate or refer to?

  _____

- In sentence (9), what does *that* relate or refer to?

  _____

When *who, which,* and *that* are used as relative pronouns, they usually come directly after the words they relate to.

My father, who . . .

. . . singing lessons, which . . .

. . . living room that . . .

BE CAREFUL: *Who, which,* and *that* cannot be used interchangeably.

Who refers to people.

Which refers to things.

That refers to people or things.

---

*For work on subject-verb agreement with relative pronouns, see Chapter 6, Part G.

Practice Combine each set of sentences into one sentence. Make sure to use *who*, *which*, and *that* correctly.

Example: a. The garden is beginning to sprout.
b. I planted it last week.

Combination: The garden that I planted last week is beginning to sprout.

1. a. My uncle is giving me diving lessons.
   b. He was a state champion.

   Combination: _____

2. a. Laser printers are fast and silent.
   b. They are also very expensive.

   Combination: _____

3. a. The manatee is a sea mammal.
   b. It lives along the Florida coast.

   Combination: _____

4. a. Donna's house has a terrace.
   b. The terrace overlooks the bay.

   Combination: _____

5. a. This shopping mall has two hundred stores.
   b. It is the largest one in the state.

   Combination: _____

6. a. Hockey is a fast-moving game.
   b. It often becomes violent.

   Combination: _____

7. a. Andrew Jackson was the seventh American president.
   b. He was born in South Carolina.

   Combination: _____

   _____

8. a. Dancing is my favorite pastime.
   b. It relaxes me after a long day of studying.

   Combination: _____

   _____

9. a. Henry caught a trout.
   b. It was the largest fish ever recorded in Idaho.

   Combination: _____

   _____

10. a. We climbed into the antique car.
    b. It had a crank starter with a rumble seat.

    Combination: _____

    _____

PART B — Punctuating Ideas Introduced by WHO, WHICH, or THAT

Ideas introduced by relative pronouns can be one of two types, either *restrictive* or *nonrestrictive*. Punctuating them must be done carefully.

Restrictive

> Never eat peaches *that are green.*

- What is the relative clause in this sentence? _____
- Can you leave out *that are green* and still keep the basic meaning of the sentence?
- *No!* You are not saying *don't eat peaches,* but don't eat *certain kinds* of peaches—*green* ones.

- Therefore, *that are green* is *restrictive*; it restricts the meaning of the sentence.

A *restrictive clause* **is not set off by commas; it is necessary to the meaning of the sentence.**

Nonrestrictive

> My guitar, *which is a Martin,* was given to me as a gift.

- In this sentence, the relative clause is _____.
- Can you leave out *which is a Martin* and still keep the basic meaning of the sentence?
- *Yes! Which is a Martin* merely adds a fact. It does not change the basic idea of the sentence, that *my guitar was given to me as a gift.*
- Therefore, *which is a Martin* is called *nonrestrictive* because it does not restrict or change the meaning of the sentence.

A *nonrestrictive clause* **is set off by commas; it is not necessary to the meaning of the sentence.**

Note: *Which* **is often used as a nonrestrictive relative pronoun.**

Practice 1

Punctuate correctly. Write a *C* next to each correct sentence.

1. The herb that Ruth planted last month smells wonderful. _____
2. People who need people are the luckiest people in the world. _____
3. This scarlet leaf which has three points fell from a sugar maple tree. _____
4. Ovens that clean themselves are the best kind. _____
5. Paint that contains lead can be dangerous to children. _____
6. This silver coin which is a rare one comes from Korea. _____
7. Edward's watch which tells the time and the date was a gift from his wife. _____
8. Carol who is a flight attendant has just left for Pakistan. _____

9. Joel Upton who is a dean of students usually sings in the yearly talent show. _____

10. Exercise that causes severe exhaustion is dangerous. _____

Practice 2 Complete each sentence by completing the relative clause.

Example: Boxing is a sport that _____*frightens me*_____.

1. My aunt, who _____, rescued a cat last week.

2. People who _____ usually succeed.

3. They seldom buy videos that _____.

4. This T-shirt, which _____, was a gift from my husband.

5. Chicago, which _____, is fun to visit.

6. James, who _____, just enlisted in the Air Force.

7. I cannot resist stores that _____.

8. You, who _____, have ruined our plans!

9. I like friends who _____.

10. The fireworks, which _____, began at nine o'clock.

Practice 3 Write four sentences using restrictive relative clauses and four using nonrestrictive relative clauses. Punctuate with care.

Restrictive

1. _____
2. _____
3. _____
4. _____

Nonrestrictive

1. _____
2. _____
3. _____
4. _____

Chapter Highlights

- **Relative pronouns** *(who, which,* and *that)* **can join two independent ideas:**
    We met Krizia Stone, *who* runs an advertising agency.
    Last night, I had a hamburger *that* was too rare.
    My favorite radio station, *which* is WQDF, plays mostly jazz.

- **Restrictive relative clauses change the meaning of the sentence. They are not set off by commas:**
    The uncle *who is helping me through college* lives in Texas.
    The car *that we saw Ned driving* was not his.

- **Nonrestrictive relative clauses do not change the meaning of the sentence. They are set off by commas:**
    My uncle, *who lives in Texas,* owns a supermarket.
    Ned's car, *which is a 1985 Mazda,* was at the repair shop.

Chapter Review

Proofread the following paragraph for relative pronoun errors and punctuation errors. Then correct each error above the line.

(1) Frida Kahlo (1907–1954) was a Mexican artist and the wife of Diego Rivera who was the most famous Mexican artist of his time. (2) Kahlo's brightly colored paintings explored her Mexican identity and her physical suffering. (3) At the age of eighteen, she was in a terrible bus accident which, left her physically disabled. (4) She began painting in bed after the accident and sent her work to the man, who soon would become her husband. (5) Rivera and Kahlo shared a stormy marriage.

(6) Both had many lovers, but they always came back to each other. (7) Many famous politicians and artists were their friends. (8) The French artist Magritte, which admired Kahlo's work described her painting as "a ribbon around a bomb." (9) In the 1980s, several of Kahlo's shows, which thousands of people attended increased her popularity. (10) Today the work of this controversial painter has admirers all over the world.

Chapter 17

-ING Modifiers

PART A   Using -ING Modifiers
PART B   Avoiding Confusing Modifiers

PART A   Using -ING Modifiers

Another way to join ideas together is with an *-ing* modifier, or present participle.

> (1) Beth was learning to ski. She broke her ankle.
>
> (2) Learning to ski, Beth broke her ankle.

- It seems that *while* Beth was learning to ski, she had an accident. Sentence (2) emphasizes this time relationship and also joins two short sentences in one longer one.

- Remember that in sentence (2), *learning*, without its helping verb *was*, is no longer a verb. Instead, *learning to ski* refers to or modifies *Beth*, the subject of the new sentence.

Chapter 17 -ING Modifiers 227

> Learning to ski, Beth broke her ankle.

- Note that a comma follows the introductory *-ing* modifier, setting it off from the independent idea.

Practice Combine the two sentences in each pair, using the *-ing* modifier to connect them. Drop unnecessary words. Draw an arrow from the *-ing* word to the word or words it refers to.

Example: Tom was drinking champagne. He stood on the deck.

Drinking champagne, Tom stood on the deck.

1. Kyla was going through the old chest. She found her grandmother's love letters.

   Kyla was going through the old chest, Kyla found her grandmother's love letters.

2. Herb was singing in the shower. He woke the neighbors.

   Herb singing in the shower, Herb woke the neighbors.

3. They were traveling in the Orient. They made many new friends.

   Traveling the Orient, They made new friends.

4. I was studying Greek. I had to learn a new alphabet.

   I studying Greek, I had to learn new alphabet.

5. She was visiting Santa Fe. She decided to move there.

   She was visiting Santa Fe, She decided to move.

6. You are loading your camera. You spot a grease mark on the lens.

   You are loading your camera, You sopt a greaseing mark on the lens.

7. Seth was mumbling to himself. He memorized Emily Dickinson's poem.

   Seth mumbling to himself, Seth memorized Emily Dickinson's poems.

8. Scientists are tagging sea birds. They hope to study flock movements.

   Tagging sea birds, Scientists hope to study flocking movements.

9. Judge Smithers was pounding his gavel. He called a recess.

   Judge Smithers pounding his gavel, Judge Smithers called a recess.

10. The students enjoyed the evening together. They were listening to classical guitar and eating grapes.

    Students enjoyed the evening together, students were listening to classical guitar and eating grapes.

PART B — Avoiding Confusing Modifiers

Be sure that your *-ing* modifiers say what you mean!

> (1) Hanging by the toe from the dresser drawer, Joe found his sock.

- Probably the writer did not mean that Joe spent time hanging by his toe. What, then, was hanging by the toe from the dresser drawer?
- *Hanging* refers to the *sock*, of course, but the order of the sentence does not show this. We can clear up the confusion by turning the ideas around.

> Joe found his sock hanging by the toe from the dresser drawer.

Read your sentences in the previous exercise to make sure the order of the ideas is clear, not confusing.

> (2) Visiting my cousin, our house was robbed.

- Does the writer mean that *our house* was visiting my cousin? Who or what, then, does *visiting my cousin* refer to?
- *Visiting* seems to refer to *I*, but there is no *I* in the sentence. To clear up the confusion, we would have to add or change words.

> Visiting my cousin, I learned that our house was robbed.

Chapter 17 -ING Modifiers 229

Practice 1   Rewrite the following sentences to clarify any confusing -ing modifiers.

1. Huffing and puffing, Jack's last race was finished.

   come ✓ Rewrite: _Huffing and puffing, Jack's last racing was finished._

   ✗ 2. Leaping from tree to tree, Professor Thomas spotted a monkey.

   Rewrite: _Professor Thomas leaping from tree to tree spotted a monkey._

3. Drinking from the mud hole, the safari group watched the elephants.

   Rewrite: _The safari group watched the elephants Drinking from the mud hole._

4. My son spotted our dog playing baseball in the schoolyard.

   Rewrite: _Playing baseball in the schoolyard, My son spotted our dog._

5. Lying in the driveway, Teresa discovered her lost glove.

   Rewrite: _Teresa discovered her lost glove lying in the driveway._

Practice 2   Write three sentences of your own, using -ing modifiers to join ideas.

1. _Playing football is a lot of fun_
2. _Sometimes I might go to bating_
3. active your _Passing driving test is importan_

Chapter Highlights

- **An *-ing* modifier can join two ideas:**
    (1) Sol was cooking dinner.
    (2) He started a small fire.
    (1) + (2) *Cooking* dinner, Sol started a small fire.

- **Avoid confusing modifiers:**
    I finally found my cat riding my motorcycle. *(incorrect)*
    Riding my motorcycle, I finally found my cat. *(correct)*

Chapter Review

Proofread the following paragraph for comma errors and confusing modifiers. Then correct each error above the line.

(1) What happened in the shed behind Patrick O'Leary's house to start the Great Chicago Fire of 1871? (2) No one knows for sure. (3) Smoking in the shed, some people say the fire was started by careless boys. (4) In another story, poker-playing youngsters accidentally kicked over an oil lamp. (5) However, the blame usually is placed on Mrs. O'Leary's cow. (6) At 8:45 p.m., swinging a lantern at her side Mrs. O'Leary went out to milk the unruly cow. (7) The cow tipped the lantern wagging its tail. (8) Recalling the incident Mrs. Nellie Hayes branded the cow theory "nonsense." (9) In fact, she said that the O'Leary's neighbors were having a party on the hot night of October 7. (10) Looking for some fresh milk a thirsty guest walked into the shed and dropped a lit candle along the way. (11) Whatever happened, the fire

was the greatest calamity of nineteenth-century America.　(12) Killing three hundred people and destroying more than three square miles of buildings it left ninety thousand people homeless.

UNIT 4

Writing Assignments

Writing Assignment 1: *Be a witness.* You have just witnessed a fender bender involving a car and an ice cream truck. No one was badly hurt, but the police have asked you to write a brief eyewitness report explaining what you saw. First, close your eyes and "see" the accident occurring, noticing as many details as possible. Freely jot these down. Then using conjunctions that indicate time—*when, as, while, after, before,* and so on—write a clear description of what you saw so that someone who was not there would be able to understand exactly what happened. Proofread your work for run-ons and comma splices.

Writing Assignment 2: *Explain an accomplishment.* Have you ever accomplished something that you thought you could not do—like passing a difficult course, becoming proficient at a musical instrument, or learning to drive? Explain why you felt you could not accomplish this goal, what you did to accomplish it, and how you felt afterward. Did your success have an effect on the way you see yourself? Use as many of the techniques for joining ideas as you can. Proofread for run-ons and comma splices.

Writing Assignment 3: *Discuss an important lesson.* Remember a day when you learned something about yourself, about someone else, or about life in general. Preferably, discuss a lesson that you learned outside of school. Freewrite or cluster for at least ten minutes. In your first sentence, tell what lesson you learned. Then explain the lesson in detail, describing who was involved, what happened, and so on. Use as many of the techniques for joining ideas as you can. Proofread for run-ons and comma splices.

Writing Assignment 4: *Describe your favorite age.* What has been your favorite age so far? Eight, when you lived on a ranch with your grandfather? Fifteen, when your social life began to flower? Thirty-one, when you changed careers? In your first sentence, use this form: "My favorite age so far has been _____." Then explain the statement in detail. Did something change? Was the change outer (you inherited $10,000), inner (you overcame your shyness), or both? You may wish to show your first draft to a classmate; ask for an honest response and specific suggestions. Rewrite, and then proofread for run-ons and comma splices.

Writing Assignment 5: *Discuss a person you admire.* Choose a celebrity or an acquaintance whose achievements, values, or personal qualities you admire. Freewrite or brainstorm to focus your ideas. In your first sentence, say why you admire the person. Then with examples and details, explain exactly what makes this person special. Exchange papers with a classmate, and give each other feedback, saying which parts you especially like and which could be improved with more explanation or details. Join ideas in a variety of ways. Check for run-ons and comma splices.

UNIT 4

Review

Five Useful Ways to Join Ideas

In this unit, you have combined simple sentences by means of a **coordinating conjunction**, a **subordinating conjunction**, a **semicolon**, and a **semicolon** and **conjunctive adverb**. Here is a review chart of the sentence patterns discussed in this unit.

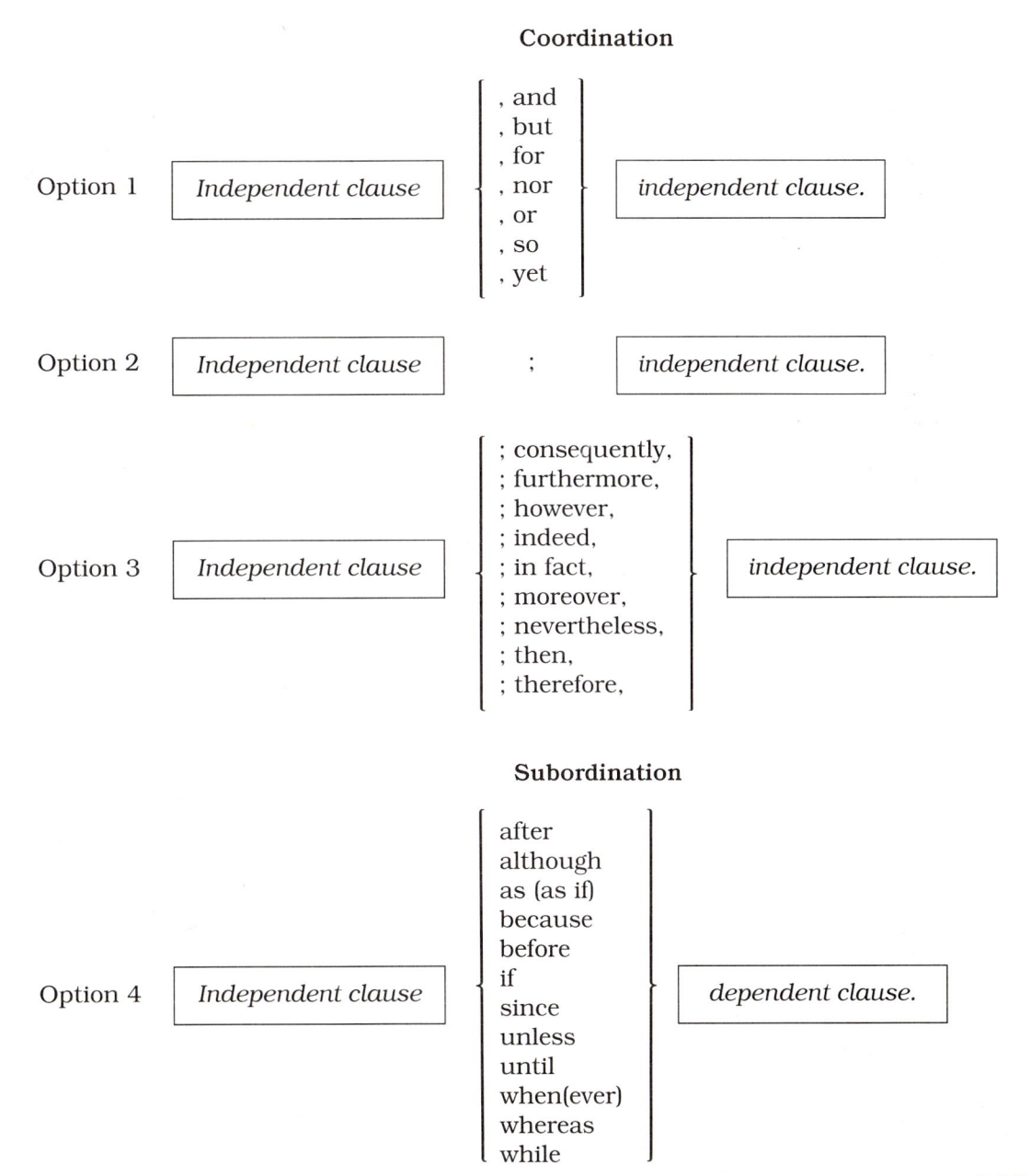

Coordination

Option 1 Independent clause { , and / , but / , for / , nor / , or / , so / , yet } independent clause.

Option 2 Independent clause ; independent clause.

Option 3 Independent clause { ; consequently, / ; furthermore, / ; however, / ; indeed, / ; in fact, / ; moreover, / ; nevertheless, / ; then, / ; therefore, } independent clause.

Subordination

Option 4 Independent clause { after / although / as (as if) / because / before / if / since / unless / until / when(ever) / whereas / while } dependent clause.

233

Option 5 { After / Although / As (as if) / Because / Before / If / Since / Unless / Until / When(ever) / Whereas / While } *dependent clause, independent clause.*

Proofreading We have changed the composition below so that it contains run-ons, comma splices, and misused semicolons. Proofread for these errors. Then correct them above the lines in any way you choose.

Managing Time in College

(1) When I started college, time was a problem. (2) I was always desperately reading an assignment just before class or racing to get to work on time. (3) The stress became too much. (4) It took a while now I know how to manage my time. (5) The secret of my success is flexible planning.

(6) At the beginning of each semester, I mark a calendar with all the due dates for the term these include deadlines for assignments, papers, and tests. (7) I also write in social events and obligations, therefore; I know at a glance when I need extra time during the next few months.

(8) Next I make out a model weekly study schedule. (9) First, I block in the hours when I have to sleep, eat, work, go to class, and tend to my family then I decide what time I will devote to study and relaxation. (10) Finally, I fill in the times I will study each subject, making sure I plan at least one hour of study time for each hour of class time. (11) Generally, I plan some time just before or after a class that way I can prepare for a class or review my notes right after a lecture.

(12) In reality, I don't follow this schedule rigidly, I vary it according to the demands of the week and day. (13) In addition, I spend more time on my harder subjects and less time on the easy ones. (14) I also try to study my harder subjects in the morning, when I am most awake.

(15) I find that by setting up a model schedule but keeping it flexible, I can accomplish all I have to do with little worry. (16) This system may not help everyone, it has certainly worked for me.

JESSE ROSE, STUDENT

Combining

Read each pair of sentences below to determine the relationship between them. Then join each pair in *two* different ways, using the conjunctions shown. Punctuate correctly.

1. No lifeguard was on duty.
   We went swimming.

   (although) _____

   _____

   (but) _____

   _____

2. Fans love watching Michael Jordan play.
   He seems to fly.

   (for) _____

   _____

   (because) _____

   _____

3. Alexis plays the trumpet very well.
   She hopes to have her own band someday.

   (and) _____

   _____

   (furthermore) _____

   _____

4. The lecture starts in five minutes.
   We had better get to our seats.

   (because) _____

   _____

   (so) _____

   _____

5. He knows how to make money. He doesn't know how to save it.

   (although) _____

   _____

   (however) _____

   _____

Revising Read through this paragraph of short, choppy sentences. Then revise it, combining some sentences. Use one coordinating conjunction, one subordinating conjunction, and any other ways you have learned to join ideas together. Keep some short sentences for variety. Make corrections above the lines, and punctuate with care.

(1) Nature lovers should watch out for a common danger, poison ivy. (2) Poison ivy looks harmless. (3) Its leaves, stems, and roots contain an allergy-producing oil. (4) This oil is very potent. (5) One drop can affect more than five hundred people. (6) Most people develop skin reactions from the oil. (7) It is best to avoid any contact with poison ivy. (8) The potency of poison ivy oil lasts a long time. (9) In fact, scientists once found a jar. (10) The jar had been buried for ten centuries. (11) Handling this artifact. (12) They developed skin rashes.

(13) Then they realized the jar had been coated with poison ivy sap one thousand years earlier! (14) Outdoor enthusiasts should learn to recognize poison ivy and avoid it.

UNIT 5

Nouns, Pronouns, Adjectives, Adverbs, and Prepositions

Chapter 18

Nouns

PART A Defining Singular and Plural
PART B Signal Words: Singular and Plural
PART C Signal Words with OF

PART A Defining Singular and Plural

A *noun* names a person, a place, a thing, or an idea. Nouns may be singular or plural.

Singular **means one.** *Plural* **means more than one.**

Singular	Plural
a reporter	the reporters
a pear	pears
the boss	the bosses

- Nouns usually add *-s* or *-es* to form the plural.

Practice 1

Make these nouns plural.*

	Singular	Plural		Singular	Plural
1.	necktie	neckties	6.	watch	watches
2.	purse	purses	7.	friend	friends
3.	radiator	radiators	8.	pot	pots
4.	tax	taxes	9.	secretary	secretaries
5.	birdcage	birdcages	10.	headache	headaches

Some nouns form their plurals in other ways. Below is a partial list:

Singular	Plural
child	children
foot	feet
goose	geese
man	men
mouse	mice
tooth	teeth
woman	women

- Many nouns ending in *-f* or *-fe* change their endings to *-ves* in the plural:

Singular	Plural
half	halves
knife	knives
leaf	leaves
life	lives
scarf	scarves
shelf	shelves
wife	wives
wolf	wolves

---

* For help with spelling, see Chapter 30, Part G.

Other nouns do not change at all to form the plural. Below is a partial list:

Singular	Plural
deer	deer
fish	fish
moose	moose
sheep	sheep

Hyphenated nouns usually form plurals by adding -s or -es to the first word:

Singular	Plural
brother-in-law	brothers-in-law
maid-of-honor	maids-of-honor
mother-in-law	mothers-in-law
runner-up	runners-up

If you are ever unsure about the plural of a noun, check a dictionary. For example, if you look up the noun *woman* in the dictionary, you will find an entry like this:

woman \ women

The first word listed, *woman*, is the singular form of the noun; the second word, *women*, is the plural.

Some dictionaries list the plural form of a noun only if the plural is unusual. If no plural is listed, the noun probably adds -s or -es.

Practice 2
Make these nouns plural.

Singular	Plural	Singular	Plural
1. man	*men*	6. knife	*knives*
2. child	*children*	7. father-in-law	*son-in-law*
3. deer	*deer*	8. woman	*women*
4. shelf	*shelves*	9. half	*half*
5. mouse	*mice*	10. foot	*feet*

Singular	Plural	Singular	Plural
11. skyscraper	*skyscraper*	16. leaf	*leaves*
12. planet	*planets*	17. fish	*fish*
13. boy	*boys*	18. moose	*moose*
14. mother-to-be	*mother-to-be*	19. wife	*wives*
15. sheep	*sheeps*	20. mayor-elect	*mayors-elect*

REMEMBER: Do not add an -s to words that form plurals by changing an internal letter or letters. For example, the plural of *man* is *men*, not *mens*; the plural of *woman* is *women*, not *womens*; the plural of *foot* is *feet*, not *feets*.

PART B — Signal Words: Singular and Plural

A *signal word* tells you whether a singular or a plural noun usually follows.

These signal words tell you that a *singular noun* usually follows:

Signal Words

a(n)
another
a single
each
every
one
} motorboat

These signal words tell you that a *plural noun* usually follows:

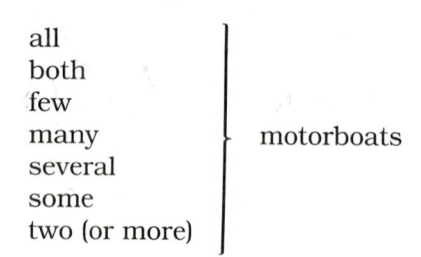

Signal Words

all
both
few
many
several
some
two (or more)
} motorboats

Chapter 18   Nouns   245

Practice 1   In the blank following each signal word, write either a singular or a plural noun. Use as many different nouns as you can think of.

Examples: a single ____stamp____

most ____fabrics____

1. a(n) _____
2. some _bathroom_
3. few _men_
4. nine _dog_
5. some _tables_
6. one _mouse_
7. several _moose_
8. each _light_
9. four _girls_
10. another _time_
11. a single _women_
12. few _tree_
13. every _left_
14. both _men_
15. another _time_
16. most _day_
17. every _moose_
18. few _people_
19. all _doors_
20. many _books_

Practice 2   Write three sentences using signal words that show singular nouns.

1. _All the boys play basketball._
2. _Several people lost their money._
3. _Some but not all play football._

Write three sentences using signal words that show plural nouns.

1. _Both toys are the same._
2. _I no a few people in army._
3. _In each room was fill with boxs._

PART C — Signal Words with OF

Many signal words are followed by *of . . .* or *of the . . .* Usually, these signal words are followed by a *plural* noun (or a collective noun) because you are really talking about one or more from a larger group.*

many of the
a few of the } houses are . . .
lots of the

one of the
each of the } houses is . . .

BE CAREFUL: The signal words *one of the* and *each of the* are followed by a *plural* noun, but the verb is *singular* because only the signal word *(one, each)* is the real subject.**

(1) *One* of the apples *is* spoiled.

(2) *Each* of the trees *grows* quickly.

- In sentence (1), *one* is the subject, not *apples*.
- In sentence (2), *each* is the subject, not *trees*.

Practice 1

Fill in your own nouns in the following sentences. Use a different noun in each sentence.

1. Many of the _students_ found the take-home final easy.
2. Larry lost one of his _shoes_ at the beach.
3. Mr. Thompson bought a few of the _items_ on sale last week.
4. This is one of the _things_ that surprised everyone.
5. Each of the _person_ carried a sign.
6. You are one of the few _people_ who can do somersaults.

---

*For more work on collective nouns, see Chapter 19, Part D.
**For more work on this type of construction, see Chapter 6, Part G.

Chapter 18 Nouns **247**

7. Each of the _agents_ has found a good home.
8. Lots of the _papers_ gave long, dull speeches.
9. Many of the _clock's_ don't work properly.
10. I found a few of my old _tapes_.

Practice 2 Use a different noun in each sentence. Write five sentences using signal words with *of*.

Example: (many of those . . .)   I planted many of those flowers myself.

1. (one of my . . .) _I fown one of my shoe in the box_
2. (many of the . . .) _For many of the buildings in the city has a parking lots._
3. (lots of the . . .) _Yesterday I bort lots of the wood for the fire places._
4. (each of these . . .) _For each of these house has a pool in the back._
5. (a few of your . . .) _Can my brother brow a few of your books._

248   Unit 5   *Nouns, Pronouns, Adjectives, Adverbs, and Prepositions*

Chapter Highlights

- Most plural nouns are formed by adding *-s* or *-es* to the singular noun:
    egg/eggs, watch/watches

- Some plurals are formed in other ways:
    child/children, woman/women, wolf/wolves

- Some nouns have identical singular and plural forms:
    fish/fish, deer/deer

- Hyphenated nouns usually add *-s* or *-es* to the first word:
    sister-in-law/sisters-in-law

- Signal words indicate whether a singular or a plural noun usually follows:
    another musician, many of the musicians

Chapter Review

Proofread the following essay for incorrect singular and plural nouns. Cross out any errors, and correct them above the lines.

The Effects of Alcohol on Pregnancy

(1) All mother-to-bes who drink alcohol run the risk of harming an innocent children. (2) When a pregnant women takes a drink, the alcohol goes straight from her bloodstream into the bloodstream of her child. (3) When she has several drink, the blood-alcohol level of her child rises as high as her own.

(4) Newborns can be harmed by alcohol in many way. (5) Some infant are born addicted to alcohol and will become alcoholics as adults. (6) Other children are born mentally retarded. (7) In fact, most doctor believe that exposure to alcohol before birth is one of the major cause of mental retardation. (8) In the worst cases, babies are born with a disease called fetal alcohol syndrome. (9) These unfortunate children are not only mentally retarded but can also have many physical deformity as well. (10) In milder cases, the children's problems don't

show up until they go to school.   (11) For instance, they may have poor memories and short attention spans.   (12) Later, they may have trouble holding a jobs.

(13) Too many young life have been ruined before birth because of alcohol consumption.   (14) All unborn child need and deserve a chance to have a healthy, normal futures.   (15) If you are a women who is expecting a baby, stop drinking alcohol now!

Chapter 19

Pronouns

PART A   Defining Pronouns and Antecedents
PART B   Referring to Indefinite Pronouns
PART C   Referring to Collective Nouns
PART D   Referring to Special Singular Constructions
PART E   Avoiding Vague and Repetitious Pronouns
PART F   Using Pronouns as Subjects, Objects, and Possessives
PART G   Choosing the Correct Case after AND or OR
PART H   Choosing the Correct Case in Comparisons
PART I   Using Pronouns with -SELF and -SELVES

PART A   Defining Pronouns and Antecedents

Pronouns take the place of or refer to nouns or other pronouns. The word or words that a pronoun refers to are called the *antecedent* of the pronoun.

(1) *Bob* said that *he* was tired.

- *He* refers to *Bob*.
- *Bob* is the antecedent of *he*.

> (2) *Sonia* left early, but I did not see *her* until later.

- *Her* refers to *Sonia*.
- *Sonia* is the antecedent of *her*.

> (3) *Robert and Tyrone* have been good friends ever since *their* college days.

- *Their* refers to *Robert and Tyrone*.
- *Robert and Tyrone* is the antecedent of *their*.

A pronoun must agree with its antecedent. In sentence (1), the antecedent *Bob* requires the singular, masculine pronoun *he*. In sentence (2), the antecedent *Sonia* requires the singular, feminine pronoun *her*. In sentence (3), the antecedent *Robert and Tyrone* requires the plural pronoun *their*.

Practice 1 In each of these sentences, a pronoun is circled. In the columns on the right, write the pronoun and its antecedent as shown in the example.

	Pronoun	Antecedent
Example: Susan B. Anthony promoted women's rights before (they) were popular.	they	rights
1. Susan B. Anthony deserves praise for (her) accomplishments.	her	Susan B. Anthony
2. Anthony became involved in the antislavery movement because of (her) principles.	her	Anthony
3. She helped President Lincoln develop (his) plans to free the slaves during the Civil War.	his	plans

Unit 5 Nouns, Pronouns, Adjectives, Adverbs, and Prepositions

	Pronoun	Antecedent
4. Eventually, Anthony realized that women wouldn't be fully protected by the law until (they) could vote.	they	women
5. When Anthony voted in the presidential election of 1872, (she) was arrested.	she	was
6. She was found guilty and given a $100 fine, but she refused to pay (it).	it	she
7. The judge did not sentence Anthony to jail because a sentence would have given (her) grounds for an appeal.	her	grounds
8. If the Supreme Court had heard her appeal, (it) might have ruled that women had the right to vote.	it	might
9. Audiences in England and Germany showed (their) appreciation of Anthony's work with standing ovations.	their	
10. Unfortunately, women in the United States had to wait until 1920 before (they) could legally vote.	They	

Practice 2   Read this paragraph for meaning, and then write the antecedent of each boxed pronoun above it.

(1) In 1935, a Hungarian journalist got tired of the ink blotches $\boxed{\text{his}}$ fountain pen made. (2) So László Biro and $\boxed{\text{his}}$ brother developed a pen with a rolling ball at the point. (3) $\boxed{\text{It}}$ wrote without making blotches. (4) $\boxed{\text{Their}}$ pen wasn't the first ballpoint, but it was the first one that worked well. (5) The new pens got a big boost during World War II. (6) Pilots needed a pen $\boxed{\text{they}}$ could use at high altitudes. (7) Only ballpoints did the job. (8) In 1945, a department store in New York City introduced these pens to $\boxed{\text{its}}$ shoppers. (9) The store sold ten thousand ballpoints the first day. (10) $\boxed{\text{They}}$ cost $12.50 each! (11) Today, people buy almost two *billion* ballpoints a year, for as little as ten cents apiece.

PART B   Referring to Indefinite Pronouns

Indefinite pronouns do not point to a specific person.

anybody anyone each everybody everyone no one nobody somebody someone	Indefinite pronouns are usually *singular*. A pronoun that refers to an indefinite pronoun should also be singular.

(1) *Everyone* should do what *he* or *she* can to help.

- *Everyone* is a singular antecedent and must be used with the singular pronoun *he* or *she*.

(2) *Each* wanted to read *his* or *her* composition aloud.

- *Each* is a singular antecedent and must be used with the singular pronoun *his* or *her*.

> (3) If *someone* smiles at you, give *him* or *her* a smile in return.

- *Someone* is a singular antecedent and must be used with the singular pronoun *him* or *her*.

In the past, writers used *he, his,* or *him* to refer to both men and women. Now, however, many writers use *he or she, his or her,* or *him or her*. Of course, if *everyone* is a woman, use *she* or *her*; if *everyone* is a man, use *he, his,* or *him*.*

Someone left *her* purse in the classroom.

Someone left *his* necktie on the bus.

Someone left *his or her* glasses on the back seat.

It is often best to avoid the repetition of *his or her* and *he or she* by changing the indefinite pronoun to a plural.

> (4) *Everyone* in the club agreed to pay *his or her* dues on time.
>
> or
>
> (5) The club *members* agreed to pay *their* dues on time.

Practice 1

Fill in the blanks with the correct pronouns. Then write the antecedent of each pronoun in the column on the right.

Antecedent

Example: Everyone should do his ___his or her___ best.   ___everyone___

1. The average citizen does not take ___his___ right to vote seriously enough.   _____

2. If a person chooses to take a science course, ___he___ must complete the lab assignments.   _____

3. Each player gave ___his___ best in the women's basketball finals.   ___everyone___

4. Juan lettered some of the signs with ___his___ left hand.   _____

---
*For more work on pronoun reference, see Chapter 23, "Consistent Person."

5. Anyone can learn to drive if __she__ has a patient instructor.

6. My friends always leave __his__ keys under the mat.

7. An individual should always be given a chance to develop __his__ potential.

8. Someone left __his__ fingerprints on the windshield.

9. The sales managers asked me to attend __his__ meeting tomorrow.

10. Everyone should see __her__ dentist at least once a year.

11. Randolph always makes sure that __her__ ties match __his__ socks.

12. You should renew __her__ membership before the end of the month.

13. Each witness gave __his__ account of the accident.

14. No one wanted to devote __his__ time to the neighborhood safety patrol.

15. Everybody is welcome to try __her__ luck in the lottery.

Practice 2

Some of the following sentences contain errors in pronoun reference. Revise the incorrect sentences. Place a *C* in the blank next to each correct sentence.

Example: Everyone must provide ~~their~~ lunch.   *his or her*   __his__

1. Somebody put ~~their~~ wet umbrella on the table.   __her__

2. A person should not try to impose ~~their~~ ideas on others.   __his__

3. Many people are returning to school in order to further ~~their~~ careers. *her*

4. Someone dropped ~~their~~ wallet on the library steps. *her*

5. Everybody can take ~~their~~ choice of two dishes from column A and one from column B. *his*

6. No one works harder at ~~their~~ paramedic job than my brother-in-law. *her*

7. Everyone should memorize ~~their~~ social security number. *his*

8. Each state has ~~their~~ own flag. *his*

9. Anyone can conquer his or her fear of speaking in public. *his*

10. Does anybody want ~~their~~ picture taken? *her*

Practice 3 Write three sentences using indefinite pronouns as antecedents.

1. _____

_____

2. _____

_____

3. _____

_____

PART C — Referring to Collective Nouns

Collective nouns imply more than one person but are generally considered *singular*. Here is a partial list:

Common Collective Nouns

board	family	panel
class	flock	school
college	government	society
committee	group	team
company	jury	tribe

Chapter 19 Pronouns 257

> (1) The *jury* meets early today because *it* must decide on a verdict.

- *Jury* is a singular antecedent and is used with the singular pronoun *it*.

> (2) *Society* must protect *its* members from violence.

- *Society* is a singular antecedent and is always used with the singular pronoun *it*.
- Use *it* or *its* when referring to collective nouns.
- Use *they* or *their* only when referring to collective nouns in the plural (*schools*, *companies*, and so forth).

Practice 1 Write the correct pronoun in the blank. Then write the antecedent of the pronoun in the column on the right.

Antecedent

Example: The committee sent __its__ report to the president of the college.   committee

1. Wanda's company will have __its__ annual picnic next week.   _____

2. The two teams picked up __their__ gloves and bats and walked off the field.   _____

3. My high school class will soon have __its__ tenth reunion.   _____

4. The city is doing __its__ best to build new low-cost housing.   _____

5. Many soap operas count on __their__ viewers' loving to cry.   _____

6. Each group has __its__ insiders and outsiders.   _____

7. The panel made __its__ financial recommendations to the president.   _____

8. This college needs to increase __its__ course offerings in African studies.   _____

9. The men's soccer team played ~~its~~ most
ferocious game yesterday.

10. The housing committee must reach ~~its~~
decision before Monday.

Practice 2 Some of the following sentences contain errors in pronoun reference. Cross out the incorrect pronoun, and write the correct pronoun above the line. Place a *C* in the blank next to each correct sentence.

Examples: The committee will present ~~their~~ report today. [its]

The jury has reached its verdict. ___C___

1. The computer company retrains ~~their~~ employees for new jobs. [its]

2. Central Technical College wants to double ~~their~~ enrollment by 1996. [its]

3. That rock group has changed ~~their~~ name again. [its]

4. The plumbing crew did its best to finish by 4 a.m. ___C___

5. The telephone company plans to raise ~~their~~ rates again. [its]

6. A jury must be very careful in ~~their~~ deliberations. [its]

7. The Robinson family moved into its new apartment last week. ___C___

8. The class decided to give ~~their~~ teacher a surprise birthday party. [its]

Practice 3 Write three sentences using collective nouns as antecedents.

1. _____

_____

2. _____

_____

3. _____

_____

PART D — Referring to Special Singular Constructions

> each of . . .
> either of . . .
> every one of . . .
> neither of . . .
> one of . . .

Each of these constructions is *singular*. Pronouns that refer to them must also be singular.

> (1) *Each* of the women did *her* work.

- *Each* is a singular antecedent and is used with the singular pronoun *her*.
- Do not be confused by the prepositional phrase *of the women*.

> (2) *Neither* of the men finished *his* meal.

- *Neither* is a singular antecedent and is used with the singular pronoun *his*.
- Do not be confused by the prepositional phrase *of the men*.

> (3) *One* of the bottles is missing from *its* place.

- *One* is a singular antecedent and is used with the singular pronoun *its*.
- Do not be confused by the prepositional phrase *of the bottles*.*

Practice 1 Fill in the blanks with the correct pronouns. Then write the antecedent of each pronoun in the column on the right.

Antecedent

Example: Each of my nephews did ___his___ homework.   ___each___

1. One of the hikers filled ___his___ canteen.   ___One___
2. The hikers filled ___their___ canteens.   ___hikers___

---

*For more work on these special constructions, see Chapter 6, Part G.

260 Unit 5 Nouns, Pronouns, Adjectives, Adverbs, and Prepositions

Antecedent

3. Every one of the women scored high on ___his___ entrance examination.

4. Each of the puzzles has ___his___ own solution.

5. Either of them should be able to learn ___his___ lines before opening night.

6. Neither of the dental technicians has had ___his___ lunch yet.

7. Each of the contestants knew that ___his___ had won a year's supply of Tacky Taco Chips.

8. Both divers bring ___his___ scuba gear when they visit the Gulf Coast.

9. Each of the administrative assistants takes pride in ___his___ work.

10. Lin Li and her mother opened ___their___ boutique in 1993.

11. Each musician kept time by tapping ___her___ foot.

12. One of the ambulances has a dent in ___its___ hood.

Practice 2 Some of the following sentences contain errors in pronoun reference. Cross out the incorrect pronoun, and write the correct pronoun above it. Place a *C* in the blanks next to the correct sentences.

Example: One of the uncles made ~~their~~ *his* opinion known.

1. One of the women at the hardware counter hasn't made ~~their~~ *his* purchase yet.

2. Each of the birds has ~~their~~ *his* distinctive mating ritual.

3. Many Asian cooks use cilantro in ~~their~~ *his* dishes.

4. I hope that neither of the senators will change ~~their~~ *his* vote.

5. Both supermarkets now carry Superfizz Carrot Juice for

   ~~their~~ *his* health-conscious customers. _____

6. Neither of the men found ~~their~~ *his* job challenging. _____

7. One of the ski sweaters was still in its box. __C__

8. Each of the children has ~~their~~ *his* own bedroom. _____

Practice 3 Write three sentences that use the special singular constructions as antecedents.

1. *Each of his books are old looking*
2. *The cards in his book bag are*
3. *The new his open to day.*

PART E — Avoiding Vague and Repetitious Pronouns

Vague Pronouns

Be sure that all pronouns *clearly* refer to their antecedents. Be especially careful of the pronouns *they* and *it*. If *they* or *it* does not refer to a *specific* antecedent, change *they* or *it* to the exact word you have in mind.

> (1) **Vague pronoun:** At registration, they said I should take Math 101.
>
> (2) **Revised:** At registration, an adviser said I should take Math 101.

- In sentence (1), who is *they*? The pronoun *they* does not clearly refer to an antecedent.
- In sentence (2), the vague *they* has been replaced by *an adviser*.

> (3) **Vague pronoun:** On the beach, it says that no swimming is allowed.
>
> (4) **Revised:** On the beach, a sign says that no swimming is allowed.

- In sentence (3), what is *it*? The pronoun *it* does not clearly refer to an antecedent.
- In sentence (4), the vague *it* has been replaced by *a sign*.

Repetitious Pronouns

Don't repeat a pronoun directly after its antecedent. Use *either* the pronoun *or* the antecedent—not both.

> (1) **Repetitious pronoun:** The doctor, he said that my daughter is in perfect health.

- The pronoun *he* unnecessarily repeats the antecedent *doctor*, which is right before it.

> (2) **Revised:** *The doctor* said that my daughter is in perfect health.
>
> or
>
> *He* said that my daughter is in perfect health.

- Use either *the doctor* or *he*, not both.

Practice Revise the following sentences by removing vague or repetitious pronouns.

Examples: They get lots of snow in Vermont.

Revised: Vermont gets lots of snow.

My friend Charlie, he loves to play bridge.

Revised: My friend Charlie loves to play bridge.

1. In the article, it says that Americans didn't start paying income tax until 1913.

    Revised: *It says in the article, that Americans didn't start paying income tax until 1913.*

2. At the stadium box office, they said that the wrestling matches had been canceled.

    Revised: *They said the stadium box office, that the wrestling matches had been canceled.*

3. It says in the cookbook that tortillas can be made with either cornmeal or wheat flour.

    Revised: *In the cookbook it says that tortillas can be made with either cornmeal or wheat flour.*

4. My brother and I, we grew up on a farm.

    Revised: *He and my brother grew up on a farm.*

5. It reported on the six o'clock news that snow is expected.

    Revised: *The six o'clock news reported that snow is expected.*

6. At the bank, they get many compliments about the friendly service.

    Revised: *They get many compliments about the friendly service at the bank.*

7. Maria, she is studying to become a laboratory technician.

    Revised: *Maria is studying to become a laboratory technician.*

8. In Denver, they have three museums that display old locomotives, trolleys, and fire engines.

    Revised: *They have three museums that display old locomotives, trolleys and fire engines in Denver.*

PART F — Using Pronouns as Subjects, Objects, and Possessives

Pronouns have different forms depending on how they are used in a sentence. Pronouns can be *subjects* or *objects* or *possessives*. They can be in the *subjective case*, *objective case*, or *possessive case*.

Pronouns as Subjects

A pronoun can be the *subject* of a sentence:

> (1) *He* loves the summer months.
>
> (2) By noon, *they* reached the top of the hill.

- In sentences (1) and (2), the pronouns *he* and *they* are subjects.

Pronouns as Objects

A pronoun can be the *object* of a verb:

> (1) Gertrude kissed *him*.
>
> (2) Sheila moved *it* to the corner.

- In sentence (1), the pronoun *him* tells whom Gertrude kissed.
- In sentence (2), the pronoun *it* tells what Sheila moved.
- These objects answer the questions *kissed whom?* or *moved what?*

A pronoun can also be the *object* of a preposition, a word like *to*, *for*, or *at*.*

> (3) The umpire stood between *us*.
>
> (4) Near *them*, the children played.

- In sentences (3) and (4), the pronouns *us* and *them* are the objects of the prepositions *between* and *near*.

Sometimes the prepositions *to* and *for* are understood, usually after words like *give*, *send*, *tell*, and *bring*.

> (5) I gave *her* the latest sports magazine.
>
> (6) Carver bought *him* a cowboy hat.

- In sentence (5), the preposition *to* is understood before the pronoun *her*: I gave *to* her . . .
- In sentence (6), the preposition *for* is understood before the pronoun *him*: Carver bought *for* him . . .

---

*See the list of prepositions on page 290.

Pronouns That Show Possession

A pronoun can show *possession* or ownership.

> (1) Bill took *his* report and left.
>
> (2) The climbers spotted *their* gear on the slope.

- In sentences (1) and (2), the pronouns *his* and *their* show that Bill owns *his* report and that the climbers own *their* gear.

The chart below can help you review all the pronouns discussed in this part.

Pronoun Case Chart

	Singular Pronouns			Plural Pronouns	
Subjective	Objective	Possessive	Subjective	Objective	Possessive
1st person: I	me	my (mine)	we	us	our (ours)
2nd person: you	you	your (yours)	you	you	your (yours)
3rd person: he	him	his	they	them	their (theirs)
she	her	her (hers)			
it	it	its			

Practice In the sentences below, underline the pronouns. Then over each pronoun, write an *S* if the pronoun is in the subjective case, an *O* if it is in the objective case, and a *P* if it is in the possessive case.

Example: I sent them my résumé.
          S   O   P

1. My best friend and I had our first job interviews the same day.
     P   S   P

2. To prepare, we had attended a job interviewing workshop.
                     S

3. Until then, I hadn't realized the importance of a first impression.

4. Our workshop leader explained that we had to make a good first
    P

   impression or we wouldn't get a chance to make a second.

5. A few days before my interview, I had my hair cut.
                          P   S

6. Tom helped me decide what to wear, and I helped him.
              O   S   O

7. We looked very professional when we headed for the Astra
    S

   Insurance Company.

8. I chew gum occasionally, and Tom smokes, but we left our gum and cigarettes at home.

9. Tom was offered a job in customer service because he was polite and professional.

10. He asked thoughtful questions about the responsibilities of the job before he accepted it.

11. I was offered a trainee position in the accounting department.

12. To celebrate, we took our families out to dinner.

PART G Choosing the Correct Case after AND or OR

When nouns or pronouns are joined by *and* or *or*, be careful to use the correct pronoun case after the *and* or the *or*.

> (1) **Incorrect:** *Bob* and *me* have to leave soon.

- In sentence (1), the pronoun *me* should be in the *subjective case* because it is part of the subject of the sentence.

> (2) **Revised:** *Bob* and *I* have to leave soon.

- Change *me* to *I*.

> (3) **Incorrect:** The dean congratulated *Charles* and *she*.

- In sentence (3), the pronoun *she* should be in the *objective case* because it is the object of the verb *congratulated*.
- The dean congratulated *whom*? The dean congratulated *her*.

> (4) **Revised:** The dean congratulated *Charles* and *her*.

- Change *she* to *her*.

> (5) **Incorrect:** Is that letter for *me* or *he*?

- In sentence (5), both objects of the preposition *for* must be in the *objective case.* What should *he* be changed to? _____

One simple way to make sure that you have the right pronoun case is to leave out the *and* or the *or*, and the word before it. You probably would not write these sentences:

> (6) **Incorrect:** *Me* have to leave soon.
>
> (7) **Incorrect:** The dean congratulated *she*.
>
> (8) **Incorrect:** Is that letter for *he*?

The sentences above look and sound strange, and you would know that they have to be corrected.

Practice 1 Circle the correct pronoun in the parentheses. If the pronoun is a *subject*, use the *subjective case*. If it is the *object* of a verb or a preposition, use the *objective case*.

1. Frieda and (**I**, me) were born in Bogotá, Colombia. ✓
2. Will Dominic or (**he**, him) bring the keys to the shop? ✓
3. My brother gave Kylee and (I, **me**) a ride to the subway. ✓
4. Why don't you give (we, **us**) short people a chance to play basketball? ✓
5. For (we, **us**), there is nothing like lemonade on a hot day. ✓
6. If it were up to Angelo and (she, **her**), they would spend all their time searching for out-of-print l.p.'s. ✓
7. My supervisor took Pete and (I, **me**) out to lunch. ✓
8. (**We**, Us) women deserve equal pay for equal work. ✓
9. Isaac and (he, **him**) play in a jazz band. ✗
10. I'm going to the movies tonight with Yolanda and (she, **her**). ✓
11. The foreman chose Ellen and (he, **him**). ✓

Unit 5 Nouns, Pronouns, Adjectives, Adverbs, and Prepositions

12. We took Nicole and (he, **him**) to see the Navajo sand paintings. ✓
13. Between you and (I, **me**), I don't like spinach.
14. Robert and (he, **him**) have decided to go to Rocky Mountain National Park with James and (I, me).
15. Either (he, **him**) or (she, **her**) must work overtime.

Practice 2 Revise those sentences in which the pronoun is in the wrong case. Write a *C* in the blanks next to the correct sentences.

1. Between you and I, I have a crush on my karate instructor. _____
2. Him and me think that the National League will win. _C_
3. That knapsack must belong either to me or to him. _C_
4. Bonnie and me love listening to Johnny Cash records. _C_
5. Joseph and her will be named this year's winners. _C_
6. Those crickets kept Lena and me up all night. _____
7. The construction job will go to us or to they. _C_
8. In May, Bill and him drove to Lynchburg, Virginia. _C_

PART H — Choosing the Correct Case in Comparisons

Pronouns in comparisons usually follow *than* or *as*.

> (1) Ferdinand is taller *than* I.
> (2) These guidelines help you as much *as* me.

- In sentence (1), the comparison is completed with a pronoun in the subjective case, *I*.
- In sentence (2), the comparison is completed with a pronoun in the objective case, *me*.

(1) Ferdinand is taller than I . . . (am tall).

(2) These guidelines help you as much as . . . (they help) . . . me.

- A comparison is really a kind of shorthand that omits repetitious words.

By completing the comparison mentally, you can choose the correct case for the pronoun.

BE CAREFUL: The case of the pronoun you place after *than* or *as* can change the meaning of the sentence.

(3) Diana likes Tom more than *I* . . . (more than *I* like him).

or

(4) Diana likes Tom more than *me* . . . (more than she likes *me*).

- Sentence (3) says that Diana likes Tom more than I like Tom.
- Sentence (4) says that Diana likes Tom more than she likes me.*

Practice 1 Circle the correct pronoun in these comparisons.

1. Rena exercises more often than (I, *me*).
2. Anthony received more on-the-job training than (we, *us*).
3. The verdict surprised you more than it did (he, *him*).
4. Barbara looks as old as (I, *me*).
5. She ran a better campaign for the local school board than (he, *him*).
6. Stan cannot type faster than (he, *him*).
7. The ringing of a telephone disturbs her more than it disturbs (they, *them*).
8. They may think they are sharper than (she, *her*), but wait until they tangle with her and find out the truth.

---

*For more work on comparisons, see Chapter 20, Part C.

9. I hate doing laundry more than (they, (them)). ✗
10. Sometimes our children are more mature than (we, (us)). ✗
11. Learning English often seems easier for me than for (he, (him)). ✓
12. Usually Ronald is more careful than (I, (me)). ✓

Practice 2 Revise only those sentences in which the pronoun after the comparison is in the wrong case. Write a *C* in the blanks next to the correct sentences.

1. Raoul moved to San Diego six months earlier than them. _C_
2. Jean can sing Haitian folk songs better than me. _C_
3. Nobody, but nobody, can whistle louder than she. _C_
4. Sarah was glad that Joyce arrived later than her. _____
5. In a crowd, you would notice her faster than you would him. _C_
6. Before switching jobs, I wanted to know if Rose would be as good a boss as him. _C_
7. The night shift suits her better than I. _____
8. Antoinette is six feet tall; no one on the loading dock is taller than her. _C_

Practice 3 Write three sentences using comparisons that are completed with pronouns. Choose case carefully.

1. _____
2. _____
3. _____

PART I — Using Pronouns with -SELF and -SELVES

Pronouns with -*self* and -*selves* are used in two ways.

> (1) José admired *himself* in the mirror.

- In sentence (1), José did something to *himself*; he admired *himself*. In this sentence, *himself* is called a *reflexive* pronoun.

> (2) The teacher *herself* thought the test was too difficult.

- In sentence (2), *herself* emphasizes the fact that the teacher—much to her surprise—found the test too hard. In this sentence, *herself* is called an *intensive* pronoun.

This chart will help you choose the right reflexive or intensive pronoun.

	Antecedent	Reflexive or Intensive Pronoun
Singular	I	myself
	you	yourself
	he	himself
	she	herself
	it	itself
Plural	we	ourselves
	you	yourselves
	they	themselves

Note that in the plural -*self* is changed to -*selves*.

Practice 1 Write the correct reflexive or intensive pronoun in each sentence. Be careful to match the pronoun with the antecedent.

Examples: I could have kicked ____myself____.

Roberta ____herself____ made this bracelet.

1. Dimitri cooked the black beans ____himself____.
2. She ____myself____ was surprised to discover that she had a green thumb.

3. We gave _ourselves_ a party after we graduated.
4. Rick, look at _himself_ in the mirror!
5. I think of _myself_ as a very practical person.
6. Don't bother; Don and André will hang the pictures _themselves_.
7. The guide _himself_ was amazed at the length of the Appalachian Trail.
8. Sonia found _themselves_ in a difficult situation.
9. He wanted the tickets for _himself_.
10. These new lamps turn _themselves_ on and off.
11. The oven cleans _herself_.
12. We _myself_ decided to rearrange the furniture.

Practice 2 Write three sentences using either a reflexive or an intensive pronoun in each.

1. _Sometimes I treat myself to nights then_
2. _The car that have cut itself off._
3. _Mike himself drew that picture of Michael Jorhon._

Chapter Highlights

- **A pronoun takes the place of or refers to a noun or another pronoun.**

    Louise said *she* would leave work early.

- **The word that a pronoun refers to is its antecedent:**

    I have chosen *my* seat for the concert.
    (*I* is the antecedent of *my*.)

- **A pronoun that refers to an indefinite pronoun or a collective noun should be singular:**

    Everyone had cleared the papers off *his* or *her* desk.

    The *committee* will give *its* report Friday.

- **A pronoun after *and* or *or* is usually in the subjective or objective case.**

    Dr. Smythe and *she* always work as a team. *(subjective)*

    The bus driver wouldn't give the map to Ms. Tallon or *me*. *(objective)*

- **Pronouns in comparisons usually follow *than* or *as*.**

    Frank likes Sally more than *I*.
    (*subjective:* . . . more than I like Sally)

    Frank likes Sally more than *me*.
    (*objective:* . . . more than he likes me)

- **A pronoun ending in *-self* (singular) or *-selves* (plural) may be used as a reflexive or an intensive pronoun. A reflexive pronoun shows that someone did something to himself or to herself; an intensive pronoun shows surprise:**

    On his trip, Martin bought nothing for *himself*.

    The musicians *themselves* were almost late for the street fair.

Chapter Review

Proofread the following essay for pronoun errors. Cross out any incorrect, vague, or repetitious pronouns, and make corrections above the lines. Use nouns to replace vague pronouns.

A New Beginning

(1) Martha Andrews, she was a good student in high school. (2) After graduation, she found a job as a bank teller in order to save money for college. (3) She liked her job because she knew her regular customers and enjoyed handling his or her business. (4) When she was nineteen, Patrick Kelvin, another teller, and her fell in love and married. (5) By

the time she was twenty-two, she had become the mother of three children.   (6) Martha's plans for college faded.

(7) As her fortieth birthday approached, Martha began thinking about going to college in order to study accounting; however, she had many fears.   (8) Would she remember how to study after so many years?   (9) Would the younger students be smarter than her?   (10) Would she feel out of place with them?   (11) Worst of all, her husband, he worried that Martha would neglect him.   (12) He thought that everyone who goes to college forgets their family.   (13) He also feared that Martha would be more successful than him.

(14) One of Martha's children, who attended college hisself, encouraged her.   (15) With his help, Martha got the courage to visit Middleton College.   (16) In the admissions office, they told her that older students were valued at Middleton.   (17) Older students often enriched classes because he or she brought a wealth of life experiences with them.   (18) Martha also learned that the college had a special program to help their older students adjust to school.

(19) Martha enrolled in college the next fall.   (20) To their credit, her and her husband soon realized that they had made the right decision.

Chapter 20

Adjectives and Adverbs

PART A Defining and Writing Adjectives and Adverbs
PART B A Troublesome Pair: GOOD/WELL
PART C Writing Comparatives
PART D Writing Superlatives
PART E Troublesome Comparatives and Superlatives
PART F Demonstrative Adjectives: THIS/THAT and THESE/THOSE

PART A Defining and Writing Adjectives and Adverbs

Adjectives and adverbs are two kinds of descriptive words. An *adjective* describes a noun or a pronoun. It tells *which one*, *what kind*, or *how many*.

(1) The *red* coat belongs to me

(2) He looks *healthy*.

- In sentence (1), the adjective *red* describes the noun *coat*.
- In sentence (2), the adjective *healthy* describes the pronoun *he*.

276 Unit 5 Nouns, Pronouns, Adjectives, Adverbs, and Prepositions

An *adverb* describes a verb, an adjective, or another adverb. Adverbs often end in *-ly*. They tell *how, to what extent, why, when,* or *where*.

> (3) Laura sings *loudly*.
> (4) My biology instructor is *extremely* short.
> (5) Lift this box *very* carefully.

- In sentence (3), *loudly* describes the verb *sings*. How does she sing? She sings *loudly*.
- In sentence (4), *extremely* describes the adjective *short*. How short is he? *Extremely* short.
- In sentence (5), *very* describes the adverb *carefully*. How carefully should you lift the box? *Very* carefully.

Practice 1

Complete each sentence with an appropriate adjective from the list below.

funny ✓   yellow   sarcastic ✓   attractive ✓
old ✓   tired   bitter   little ✓

1. Janet is _little_.
2. She always carries a(n) _yellow_ duffel bag.
3. _Sarcastic_ remarks will be his downfall.
4. My daughter loves _old_ houses.
5. This coffee tastes _funny_.

Practice 2

Complete each sentence with an appropriate adverb from the list below.

quietly   loudly   wildly   convincingly
sadly   quickly   constantly   happily

1. We danced _wildly_.
2. Mr. Huff smokes _constantly_.
3. The lawyer spoke _convincingly_.
4. He gazed _quietly_ at his empty wallet.
5. _Quickly_, he entered the rear door of the church.

Chapter 20 Adjectives and Adverbs 277

Many adjectives can be changed into adverbs by adding an *-ly* ending. For example, *glad* becomes *gladly*, *thoughtful* becomes *thoughtfully*, and *wise* becomes *wisely*.

Be especially careful of the adjectives and adverbs in this list; they are easily confused.

Adjective	Adverb	Adjective	Adverb
awful	awfully	quiet	quietly
bad	badly	real	really
poor	poorly	sure	surely
quick	quickly		

(6) This chair is a *real* antique.

(7) She has a *really* bad sprain.

- In sentence (6), *real* is an adjective describing the noun *antique*.
- In sentence (7), *really* is an adverb describing the adjective *bad*. How bad is the sprain? The sprain is *really* bad.

✓ **Practice 3** Change each adjective in the left-hand column into its adverb form.*

Adjective	Adverb
Example: You are smart.	You dress ___smartly___.
1. She is honest.	1. She speaks ___honestly___.
2. They are quiet.	2. They play ___quietly___.
3. It is easy.	3. It turns ___easy___.
4. We are careful.	4. We decide ___carefully___.
5. You are attractive.	5. You dress ___attractively___.
6. He is creative.	6. He thinks ___creatively___.
7. She was quick.	7. She acted ___quickly___.
8. It is perfect.	8. It fits ___perfectly___.
9. She was eager.	9. She spoke ___eagerly___.
10. It is real.	10. It is ___really___ hot.
11. He is poor.	11. He plays ___poorly___.

*If you have questions about spelling, see Chapter 30, Part E.

Adjective	Adverb
12. You are cheerful.	12. You laugh _cheerfully_.
13. We are joyful.	13. We watch _joyfully_.
14. We are angry.	14. We shout _angryly_.
15. You seemed confident.	15. You waved _confidently_.

Practice 4 Circle the adjective or adverb form of the word in parentheses.

Example: The office is ((quiet), quietly) on a snowy Sunday afternoon.

1. On the couch, a young man snores ((noisy), noisily).
2. A ((tired), tiredly) young woman slumps in a chair.
3. ((Sudden), Suddenly), the telephone rings.
4. Grunting ((sleepy), sleepily), the man rolls over.
5. By the time he answers the phone, he is (full, (fully)) awake.
6. He takes notes ((hasty), hastily) and nods to his partner.
7. She puts on her (official, (officially)) jacket and grabs her bag of tools.
8. This is another ((typical), typically) call for two (high, (highly)) skilled technicians.
9. The man rereads his notes aloud while the panel truck moves (quick, (quickly)) through the streets.
10. In a ((calm), calmly) voice, the man describes the problem to his partner.
11. Sam and Terri Phillips have been (anxious, (anxiously)) awaiting their arrival.
12. They point (sad, (sadly)) to the blank TV screen and say, "The game starts in exactly one hour."
13. The technicians examine the set (careful, (carefully)); the problem is not a ((serious), seriously) one.

14. In fifty-five minutes, the screen is (**bright**, brightly) lit, and the game is about to begin.

15. "Another job well done," they (happy, **happily**) whisper to each other as they leave.

Practice 5 Use each adjective and adverb in a sentence of your own.

Example: (sweet) He is a sweet child.

(sweetly) He sings sweetly.

1. (quick) *He is a quick learner*
   (quickly) *He became house hold name in the*
2. (bad) *He a bad boy in class.*
   (badly) *He can be a badly person.*
3. (happy) *He all ways happy a people.*
   (happily) *Say happily whisper to each other.*
4. (real) *The jewelry I buy is real 14ct go*
   (really) *My leg was really hurting.*
5. (easy) *I easy finish the long race.*
   (easily) *I easy pass the final test*

PART B — A Troublesome Pair: GOOD/WELL

Unlike most adjectives, *good* does not add *-ly* to become an adverb; it changes to *well*.

> (1) **Adjective:** Peter is a *good* student.
> (2) **Adverb:** He writes *well*.

- In sentence (1), the adjective *good* describes or modifies *student*.
- In sentence (2), the adverb *well* describes or modifies *writes*.

Note, however, that *well* can be used as an adjective to mean *in good health*—for example, *He felt well after his long vacation.*

Practice Write either *good* or *well* in each sentence.

Example: Charles plays ball very ___well___.

1. Lucille is a ___good___ pilot.
2. She handles a plane ___well___.
3. How ___well___ do you understand computers?
4. Pam knows my bad habits very ___well___.
5. It is a ___good___ thing we ran into each other.
6. He works ___well___ with all kinds of people.
7. How ___good___ or how badly did you do at the tryouts?
8. Were the cherry tarts ___good___ or tasteless?
9. Aretha Franklin is a ___good___ blues singer.
10. Those lamps do not light the room very ___well___.
11. Carole doesn't look as though she takes ___good___ care of herself.
12. He asked ___good___ questions at the meeting, and she answered them ___well___.

PART C Writing Comparatives

(1) John is *tall*.

(2) John is *taller* than Mike.

- Sentence (1) describes John with the adjective *tall*, but sentence (2) *compares* John and Mike in terms of how tall they are: John is the *taller* of the two.

Taller is called the *comparative* of *tall*.

Chapter 20 Adjectives and Adverbs

Use the comparative when you want to compare two people or things.

To Form Comparatives

Add *-er* to adjectives and adverbs that have *one syllable:**

short	shorter
fast	faster
thin	thinner

Place the word *more* before adjectives and adverbs that have *two or more syllables:*

foolish	more foolish
rotten	more rotten
happily	more happily

✓ Practice 1

Write the comparative form of each word. Either add *-er* to the word or write *more* before it. Never add both *-er* and *more!*

Examples: _____ dumb _er_

more willing _____

1. _____ fast _er_
2. _more_ interesting _____
3. _more_ hopeful _____
4. _____ quick _er_
5. _____ poor _er_
6. _____ fat _er_
7. _more_ foolish _____
8. _more_ valuable _____
9. _____ cold _er_
10. _____ clean _er_

Here is one important exception to the rule that two-syllable words use *more* to form the comparative:

To show the comparative of two-syllable adjectives ending in *-y,* change the *y* to *i* and add *-er.***

cloudy	cloudier
sunny	sunnier

---

*If you have questions about spelling, see Chapter 30, Part C.
**For more work on spelling, see Chapter 30, Part F.

Practice 2
Write the comparative form of each adjective.

Example: happy _____happier_____

1. shiny _shinier_
2. friendly _friendlier_
3. lazy _lazier_
4. easy _easier_
5. heavy _heavier_
6. curly _curlier_
7. lucky _luckier_
8. skinny _skinnier_
9. drowsy _drowsier_
10. crazy _crazier_

Practice 3
The following sentences use both *more* and *-er* incorrectly. Decide which one is correct, and write your revised sentences on the lines provided.
REMEMBER: Write comparatives with either *more* or *-er*—not both!

Examples: Jan is more younger than her brother.

Jan is younger than her brother.

She is more attractiver with glasses than without.

She is more attractive with glasses than without.   _comeback study_

1. No one can run the hundred-yard-dash more faster than she.

   No run the hundred-yard-dash more faster than she.

2. The trail was more rockier than we expected.

   The trail more rockier than we expected

3. The people in my new neighborhood are more friendlier than those in my old one.

   The people in my new neighborhood are friendlier than those in my old one

4. Sonia has a more cheerfuler personality than her sister.

   Sonia has more cheerful personality than her sister.

Chapter 20 Adjectives and Adverbs 283

5. When the children are in bed and the house is more quieter, I can study. *When, then children are in bed the hous is more quieter, I can study.*

6. The audience at this theater is more noisier than usual. *The audience at this theater is noisier than usual.*

7. His down jacket is more newer than Rudy's. *He down jacket is newer than Rudy's.*

8. If today is more warmer than yesterday, we'll picnic on the lawn. *If today is warmer than yesterday, we'll picnic on the lawn.*

Practice 4 Write a sentence of your own using the *comparative* form of the adjective or adverb given.

Example: (funny) This play is funnier than the one we saw last week.

1. (dark) *This tunnal is dark to out of.*
2. (noisy) *The class today is noisy.*
3. (handsome) *The girl I saw last week is handsom.*
4. (slowly) *The tiptic is realy more slowly.*
5. (wet) *My boot got realy wet.*

PART D Writing Superlatives

(1) Tim is the *tallest* player on the team.
(2) Juan was voted the *most useful* player.

- In sentence (1), Tim is not just *tall* or *taller than* someone else; he is the *tallest* of all the players on the team.
- In sentence (2), Juan was voted the *most useful* of all the players.

Tallest **and** *most useful* **are called** *superlatives*.

Use the superlative when you wish to compare more than two people or things.

> **To Form Superlatives**
>
> Add *-est* to adjectives and adverbs of *one syllable*:
>
> short   shortest
>
> Place the word *most* before adjectives and adverbs that have *two or more syllables*:
>
> foolish   most foolish
>
> *Exception:* With two-syllable adjectives ending in *-y*, change the *y* to *i* and add *-est.**
>
> happy   happiest

Practice 1

Write the superlative form of each word. Either add *-est* to the word or write *most* before it, not both.

Examples: _____ tall *est*

most ridiculous _____

1. _____ loud *est*
2. *most* colorful _____
3. _____ brave *est*
4. _____ thick *est*
5. *more* brilliant _____
6. _____ wild *est*
7. *most* intelligent _____
8. *most* frightening _____
9. _____ green *est*
10. _____ hazy *est*

Practice 2

The following sentences use both *most* and *-est* incorrectly. Decide which one is correct, and write your revised sentences on the lines provided. REMEMBER: Write superlatives with either *most* or *-est*—not both!

Examples: Jane is the most youngest of my three children.

Jane is the youngest of my three children.   *comeback*

He is the most skillfulest guitarist in the band.

He is the most skillful guitarist in the band.

---

*For more work on spelling, see Chapter 30, Part F.

1. This mattress feels like the most comfortablest one in the store.

   This mattress feels the most comfortablest one in the store.

2. The World Trade Center towers are the most tall buildings in New York City.

   The World Trade Center are the most tallst buildings in New York City.

3. He asks the most oddest questions I have ever heard.

   He asks the most odd questions I have ever heard.

4. Jackie always makes us laugh, but she is most funniest when she hasn't had enough sleep.

   Jackie always makes us laugh, she is most funniest when she hasn't had enough sleep.

5. When I finally started college, I was the most eagerest student on campus.

   When I finally started college, I was the most eager student on campus.

6. Professor Deitz gives the most boringest lectures at the college.

   Professor Deitz gives the most born lectures at the college

7. My daughter is the most thoughtfulest teenager I know.

   My daughter is the most thoughtful teenager I know.

8. He thinks that the most successfulest people are just lucky.

   He thinks that the most successful people are just lucky.

PART E — Troublesome Comparatives and Superlatives

These comparatives and superlatives are some of the trickiest you will learn:

	Comparative	Superlative
Adjective: good	better	best
Adverb: well	better	best
Adjective: bad	worse	worst
Adverb: badly	worse	worst

Practice Fill in the correct comparative or superlative form of the word in parentheses. REMEMBER: *Better* and *worse* compare *two* persons or things. *Best* and *worst* compare three or more persons or things.

Examples: Is this theme ____better____ (good) than my last one?
(Here two themes are compared.)

It was the ____worst____ (bad) movie I have ever seen.
(Of *all* movies, it was the *most* awful.)

1. He likes driving __better__ (well) than walking.
2. I like country and western music __best__ (well) of all.
3. My uncle's arthritis is __worst__ (bad) than it was last month.
4. That is the __worse__ (bad) joke I have ever heard!
5. The volleyball team played __worst__ (badly) than it did last year.
6. He plays the piano __better__ (well) than he plays the guitar.
7. The traffic is even __worst__ (bad) on Fridays than on Mondays.
8. Static electricity is __worst__ (bad) in winter than in summer.
9. That was the __worst__ (bad) storm Kansas has had in years.
10. Sales are __better__ (good) this year than last.
11. Of the two, Dawn is the __better__ (good) keyboarder.
12. Of all of us, Dawn is the __better__ (good) keyboarder.
13. He is the __better__ (good) mechanic in the shop.
14. He is also the __worst__ (bad) slob.
15. Do you take this person for __better__ (good) or for __worst__ (bad)?

PART F — Demonstrative Adjectives: THIS/THAT and THESE/THOSE

This, that, these, and *those* are called *demonstrative adjectives* because they point out, or demonstrate, which noun is meant.

> (1) I don't trust *that* wobbly front wheel.
>
> (2) *Those* toys are not as safe as their makers claim.

- In sentence (1), *that* points to a particular wheel, the wobbly front one.
- In sentence (2), *those* points to a particular group of toys.

Demonstrative adjectives are the only adjectives that change to show singular and plural:

Singular	Plural
this book	these books
that book	those books

This and *that* are used before singular nouns; *these* and *those* are used before plural nouns.

Practice

In each sentence, circle the correct form of the demonstrative adjective in parentheses.

1. **(This**, These) chairs belong in the hallway. ✓
2. Mr. Lathorpe is sure **(this**, these) address is correct. ✓
3. You can find (that, **those)** maps in the reference room. ✓
4. Can you catch **(that**, those) waiter's eye? ✓
5. Let's order what (that, **those)** people are eating. ✓
6. I like (this, **these)** leather gloves best of all. ✗
7. The learning center is in **(that**, those) gray building. ✓
8. (These, **This)** biography tells the story of Charles Curtis, the first ✓ Native American elected to the Senate.
9. (That, **Those)** gyms remain open until midnight. ✓
10. Does **(this**, these) sweatshirt come in pink? ✓

288 Unit 5 *Nouns, Pronouns, Adjectives, Adverbs, and Prepositions*

Chapter Highlights

- Most adverbs are formed by adding *-ly* to an adjective:
  quick/quickly, bright/brightly, *but* good/well

- Comparative adjectives and adverbs compare two persons or things:
  I think Bill Cosby is *funnier* than Eddie Murphy.
  Laura can balance a checkbook *more quickly* than I can.

- Superlative adjectives and adverbs compare more than two persons or things:
  Last winter, Ingrid had the *worst* cold of her life.
  That was the *most carefully* prepared speech I have ever heard.

- The adjectives *good* and *bad* and the adverbs *well* and *badly* require special care in the comparative and the superlative:
  good/better/best
  bad/worse/worst
  well/better/best
  badly/worse/worst

- Demonstrative adjectives can be singular or plural:
  this/that (chair)
  these/those (chairs)

Chapter Review

Proofread these paragraphs for adjective and adverb errors. Cross out any errors, and then correct them above the lines.

A. (1) The most famousest comet, Halley's comet, appears regular every seventy-six years. (2) This mass of gas and dust has caused panic and fear because its appearance has often coincided with the baddest events in history. (3) During the Middle Ages, people believed that Halley's comet was a surely omen of destruction. (4) The most silly notions about Halley's comet came about during its 1910 appearance when people bought pills and bottled oxygen to protect themselves. (5) Although that sounds real foolish, they believed that poisonous gas was contained in the comet's brilliantly tail. (6) Despite the most wildest superstitions, Halley's comet has given us more better information about comets and our solar system.

B. (1) It is awful easy to forget that artificial satellites have been circling the Earth for only thirty or so years. (2) The first and probably bestest known artificial satellite was *Sputnik I*, launched by the former Soviet Union in 1957. (3) The next year, the United States sent a satellite to gather real important information about radiation around the equator. (4) Now more than five thousand artificial satellites orbit the Earth. (5) As they move quiet across the night sky, we take them for granted.

(6) We also take for granted the ways in which many of this satellites make our lives more easier. (7) Because of communications satellites, for example, a caller in the United States can get through quick to someone in Brazil—or even Senegal! (8) Weather satellites help weather stations receive more earlier warnings about hurricanes. (9) Navigation satellites guide ships when visibility is poor. (10) Other satellites design more accurater maps of the Earth to help find scarce minerals. (11) Soon satellites may enable scientists to forecast earthquakes. (12) These forecasts will help authorities prepare for the baddest effects of the quakes. (13) Within thirty years, this list of practical uses will probably grow much more longer.

Chapter 21

Prepositions

PART A   Defining Prepositions
PART B   Troublesome Prepositions
PART C   Words Requiring Certain Prepositions

PART A   Defining Prepositions

A preposition is a word like *at, from, in,* or *of.* Below is a partial list of common prepositions:*

Common Prepositions		
about	beside	off
above	between	on
across	by	over
after	during	through
against	except	to
along	for	toward
among	from	under
around	in	until
at	into	up
before	like	with
behind	of	without

---
*For more work on prepositions, see Chapter 4, Part C.

Chapter 21 Prepositions

A preposition is usually followed by a noun or pronoun. The noun or pronoun is called the *object* of the preposition. Together, the preposition and its object are called a *prepositional phrase.* Here are some prepositional phrases:

Prepositional Phrase	=	Preposition	+	Object
after the movie		after		the movie
at Kean College		at		Kean College
beside them		beside		them
between you and me		between		you and me

Below are some sentences with prepositional phrases:

(1) Ms. Kringell arrived *at noon.*

(2) A man *in a gray suit* bought three lottery tickets.

(3) The huge moving van sped through the tunnel.

- In sentence (1), the prepositional phrase *at noon* tells when Ms. Kringell arrived. It describes *arrived.*

- In sentence (2), the prepositional phrase *in a gray suit* describes how the man was dressed. It describes *man.*

- What is the prepositional phrase in sentence (3)? _____

    Which word does it describe? _____

Practice

Underline the prepositional phrases in the following sentences.

1. Bill collected some interesting facts about human biology.

2. Human eyesight is sharpest at midday.

3. In extreme cold, shivering produces heat, which can save lives.

4. A pound of body weight equals 3,500 calories.

5. Each of us has a distinguishing odor.

6. Fingernails grow fastest in summer.

7. One of every ten people is left-handed.

8. The human body contains approximately ten pints of blood.

Unit 5 Nouns, Pronouns, Adjectives, Adverbs, and Prepositions

9. Beards grow more rapidly than any other hair <u>on the human body</u>.

10. Most people <u>with an extra rib</u> are men.

PART B Troublesome Prepositions ✓

IN/ON for Time

Use *in* before seasons of the year, before months not followed by specific dates, and before years that do not include specific dates.

> (1) *In the summer*, most of us like to laze around in the sun.
>
> (2) No classes will meet *in January*.
>
> (3) Rona was a student at Centerville Business School *in 1988*.

Use *on* before days of the week, before holidays, and before months if a date follows.

> (4) *On Thursday*, the gym was closed for renovations.
>
> (5) The city looked deserted *on Christmas Eve*.
>
> (6) We hope to arrive in Burlington *on October 3*.

Practice Write either *in* or *on* in the following sentences.

Example: Professor Bradshaw will talk about the War between the States __on__ Monday.

1. South Carolina seceded from the United States __in__ December 1860.

2. President Lincoln sat in the White House __on__ Christmas Eve wondering what would happen next.

3. __In__ the winter of 1861, other southern states from Virginia to Texas joined South Carolina to form the Confederate States of America.

4. The war actually began __on__ April 12, 1861, when the Confederates fired on Fort Sumter, South Carolina.

5. After four years of fierce fighting, the war finally ended __in__ 1865.

IN/ON for Place

In means *inside of*.

> (1) Raoul slept *in the spare bedroom.*
>
> (2) The exchange student spent the summer *in Sweden.*

On means *on top of* or *at a particular place*.

> (3) The spinach pie *on the table* is for tonight's book discussion group.
>
> (4) Dr. Helfman lives *on Marblehead Road.*

Practice Write either *in* or *on* in the following sentences.

Example: Here's how you can make raspberry sherbet right __in__ your own kitchen.

1. Lay out all the ingredients you need __on__ a counter top: 3/4 cup of sugar, 1 cup warm water, 1/2 cup light corn syrup, 1/4 cup lemon juice, 1 container of strained raspberries, and 2 egg whites.

2. Dissolve the sugar __in__ the warm water; then add the corn syrup, lemon juice, and raspberries, and freeze the mixture until the edges are hard.

3. __In__ a separate container, beat the egg whites until they are stiff.

4. Whip the partly frozen mixture __in__ a chilled bowl so that it is smooth but not melted.

5. After folding in the egg whites quickly, place the mixture __on__ a shelf __in__ your refrigerator freezer until the sherbet is firm.

LIKE

Like is a preposition that means *similar to*. Therefore, it is followed by an object (usually a noun or a pronoun).

> (1) *Like you,* I prefer watching films on a VCR rather than going to a crowded movie theater.

Do not confuse *like* with *as* or *as if*. *As* and *as if* are subordinating conjunctions.* They are followed by a subject and a verb.

> (2) *As the instructions explain,* insert flap B into slit B before folding the bottom in half.
>
> (3) Robert sometimes acts *as if he has never made a mistake.*

Practice Write *like, as,* or *as if* in the following sentences.

Example: George grinned ___as___ he approached the door.

1. ___like___ his friends, Kirk plays basketball at least once a week.
2. Joyce came home ___as___ I was leaving, but she persuaded me to stay a bit longer.
3. Mr. Porter acts ___as if___ he is in charge.
4. Penny's voice sounds ___like___ her mother's.
5. ___As___ the weather forecaster predicted, six inches of snow fell overnight.

PART C — Words Requiring Certain Prepositions

Prepositions often are combined with other words to form fixed phrases or expressions. These combinations can sometimes be confusing. Below is a list of some troublesome combinations. If you are in doubt about others, consult a dictionary.

---

*For more work on subordinating conjunctions, see Chapter 12.

Expressions with Prepositions

Expression	Example
acquainted with	He became *acquainted with* his duties.
addicted to	I am *addicted to* chocolate.
agree on (a plan)	They finally *agreed on* a sales strategy.
agree to (another's proposal)	Did she *agree to* their demands?
angry about or at (a thing)	The subway riders are *angry about* (or *at*) the delays.
angry with (a person)	The manager seems *angry with* Jake.
apply for (a position)	You should *apply for* this job.
approve of	Does he *approve of* the proposed budget?
consist of	The plot *consisted of* both murder and intrigue.
contrast with	The red lettering *contrasts* nicely *with* the gray stationery.
convenient for	Is Friday *convenient for* you?
correspond with (write)	My daughter *corresponds with* a pen pal in India.
deal with	How do you *deal with* friends who always want to borrow your notes?
depend on	He *depends on* your advice.
differ from (something)	A diesel engine *differs from* a gasoline engine.
differ with (a person)	On that point, I *differ with* the medical technician.
displeased with	She is *displeased with* all the publicity.
fond of	We are all *fond of* Sam's grandmother.
grateful for (something)	Jim was *grateful for* the two test review sessions.
grateful to (someone)	We are *grateful to* the plumber for repairing the leak on Sunday.

Expressions with Prepositions

Expression	Example
identical with	This watch is *identical with* hers.
interested in	George is *interested in* modern art.
interfere with	Does the party *interfere with* your study plans?
object to	She *objects to* the increase in the state sales tax.
protect against	This vaccine *protects* people *against* the flu.
reason with	Don't *reason with* a hungry pit bull.
reply to	Did the newspaper editor *reply to* your letter?
responsible for	Omar is *responsible for* marketing.
shocked at	We were *shocked at* the damage to the buildings.
similar to	That popular song is *similar to* another one I know.
specialize in	The shop *specializes in* clothing for large men.
succeed in	Gandhi *succeeded in* freeing India from British rule.
take advantage of	Let's *take advantage of* that two-for-one paperback book sale.
worry about	I no longer *worry about* my manager's moods.

Practice Circle the correct expressions in these sentences.

1. The amazing career of Albert Goodwill Spalding (consisted of, consisted in) baseball and business success.

2. At first, his mother did not (approve in, approve of) his playing professional ball.

3. Spalding obeyed his mother and (**applied for**, applied to) a "regular" job.

4. Eventually (**displeased with**, displeased at) the work he found, Spalding signed up with the Boston Red Stockings in 1871.

5. Over the next five years, the Boston team came to (**depend on**, depend with) his unusual underhand pitching style.

6. In fact, he was the first pitcher ever to (**succeed in**, succeed on) winning two hundred games.

7. Spalding soon became more (**interested in**, interested with) designing baseballs than in playing.

8. Pitchers were (grateful for, **grateful to**) him for marketing the ball he had designed for his own pitching use; it became the official ball of the National League.

9. Spalding became (fond for, **fond of**) designing other kinds of balls; for example, he designed the first basketball.

10. He also (dealt on, **dealt with**) the problem of what to use as goals in this new ball game.

11. He (**took advantage of**, took advantage for) peach baskets, and the new game was called "basketball."

12. By the 1890s, Spalding had been (**responsible for**, responsible to) developing one of the world's largest sporting goods companies.

298 Unit 5 Nouns, Pronouns, Adjectives, Adverbs, and Prepositions

Chapter Highlights

- **Prepositions are words like *at, from, in,* and *of*. A prepositional phrase contains a preposition and its object:**

    The tree *beneath my window* has lost its leaves.

- **Be careful of prepositions like *in, on,* and *like*:**

    I expect to graduate *in* June.
    I expect to graduate *on* June 10.

    The Packards live *in* Tacoma.
    The Packards live *on* Farnsworth Avenue.

    Like my father, I am a Cleveland Indians fan.

- **Prepositions are often combined with other words to form fixed phrases:**

    convenient *for,* different *from,* reason *with*

Chapter Review

Proofread this essay for preposition errors. Cross out the errors, and correct them above the lines.

Taking a Stand

(1) Important events often begin with a person who decides to take a stand. (2) At Thursday, December 1, 1955, Rosa Parks helped inspire the civil rights movement simply by sitting down.

(3) On 1955, city buses in Montgomery, Alabama, were segregated. (4) African-American riders had to sit in the back of the bus. (5) The African-American community and its leaders were angry with segregation. (6) They also knew that the city depended at its African-American riders for income. (7) They were waiting to take advantage about the right occasion to organize a bus boycott. (8) Rosa Parks gave them that occasion.

(9) Rosa Parks was a forty-three-year-old tailor's assistant. (10) At that December afternoon, she was tired after a hard day's work. (11) When she was told to give her seat to a white man, she objected from moving. (12) She was arrested.

(13) African-American community leaders organized a boycott, and the buses stayed empty for more than a year. (14) To deal about the lack of transportation, African Americans organized a system of car pools or just walked. (15) At last, in December 20, 1956, an order from the United States Supreme Court made Montgomery's bus laws unconstitutional. (16) The next day, Rosa Parks was photographed inside one of the first integrated buses on the city. (17) Her simple act of courage helped change the course of American history.

UNIT 5

Writing Assignments

Writing Assignment 1: *Explain your job.* Explain your job to someone who knows nothing about your kind of work. In your first sentence, tell what you do: "I run a computer for an insurance company." Then describe exactly what you do, what equipment you use, and generally how you spend your day. Proofread for correct singular and plural nouns.

Writing Assignment 2: *Look at a favorite room.* Choose your favorite room in your house or apartment. Begin by jotting down details about this room—its size, color, furnishings, and so on. Then in your first sentence, describe the mood of the room or how it makes you feel when you enter it: "My study is the most relaxing room in the apartment." Describe the room in exact detail. Proofread for correct adjectives and adverbs.

Writing Assignment 3: *Observe someone.* Pick someone to observe, preferably someone who does not know you are watching—perhaps a student in the cafeteria or library, or a child at play. As you observe, jot details. Then form an overall impression of this person and what he or she is doing. In your first sentence, state this overall impression: "This student browses a lot but never opens a book to read." Describe this person's actions for five or six minutes, noting as much detail as you can about exactly what he or she does, how he or she does it, and what instruments or equipment he or she uses. Proofread for correct adjectives and adverbs.

Writing Assignment 4: *Explore a special talent.* Most people have a special talent, something they do extremely well. In your first sentence, state your special talent. You might say, "My family often comments on how well I can relieve a tense situation." Then provide one or two instances of your talent: a case in which you were able to bring friends who had been feuding back together again, for example. Proofread for correct prepositions.

Writing Assignment 5: *Answer a personal ad.* The following personal advertisement appeared in a local newspaper: "35-year-old medical technician would like to meet someone for serious relationship and marriage. Likes cats and the outdoors, especially hiking. Not much on sports. Favorite music: rock and jazz. Loves movies, except the really violent ones; prefers spy thrillers and adventure, like Indiana Jones and James Bond. Wants large family. Goes to church on occasion."

In groups of two or three students, plan and write an answer to this ad. First, decide whether you are writing to a man or a woman. Then, working together, choose three or four points that you want to cover in your response: hobbies, pet peeves, things you like to do, and family, for example. Show why you feel that you might be an ideal match for this person, but also discuss areas of conflict in which you two would have to work out some differences. Proofread for correct nouns and pronouns.

UNIT 5

Review

Proofreading Proofread the following paragraph for incorrect use of nouns, pronouns, adjectives, adverbs, and prepositions. Cross out any errors, and then correct them above the lines.

The Last Frontier

(1) When the government of Brazil opened the Amazon rain forest for settlement on the 1970s, they created the last frontier on earth. (2) Many concerned man and woman everywhere now fear that the move has been a disasters for the land and for the people.

(3) The most large rain forest in the world, the Amazon rain forest has been hit real hard. (4) The government built highways to make it more easy for poor people to get to the land, but the roads also made investors interested to the forest. (5) Lumber companies chopped down millions of tree. (6) Ranchers and the settlers theirselves burned the forest to make room for cattle and crops. (7) All this activities have taken their toll; in some areas, one-fifth of the rain forest has already been destroyed. (8) Many kinds of plants and animals have been lost forever.

(9) The Indians of the rain forest, they are also threatened by this wholesale destruction. (10) Ranchers, miners, lumbermen, and settlers have moved onto Indian lands. (11) Contact with the outside world has changed the Indians' traditional way of life. (12) A few Indian tribe

301

have made economic and political gains; however, many tribes have totally disappeared.

(13) Many of the settler are not doing very good either. (14) People have poured into the region too rapid, and the government is unable to provide the needed services. (15) Small villages have become crowded cities, diseases (especially malaria) have spread, and lawlessness is common. (16) Worse of all, the soil beneath the rain forest is not fertile. (17) After a few years, the settlers' land, it is worthless. (18) As the settlers go into debt, businesses take advantage for the situation by buying land quick and exploiting it bad.

(19) Will the government be able to use the rain forest to improve the quality of Brazilian life? (20) Will it be able to preserve those forest—and the plant, animal, and human life it supports? (21) The world watches nervous. (22) The future of the Amazon rain forest is still uncertain.

Transforming Change the subject of this paragraph from singular to plural, changing every *the dog* to *dogs*, every *it* to *they*, and so forth. Make all necessary verb and other changes. Make your revisions above the lines.

(1) The Saint Bernard is a legendary dog famous for its many acts of bravery. (2) Bred in the wild mountains of Switzerland, it can find paths in the worst snowstorms, smell human beings buried in snow, and detect avalanches before they occur. (3) This powerful yet sensitive creature works in rescue patrols. (4) When a Saint Bernard finds a hurt traveler, it lies down next to the sufferer to keep him or her warm and licks the person's face to restore consciousness. (5) Another dog goes back to headquarters to sound the alarm and guide a rescue party to the scene. (6) In all, the Saint Bernard has saved more than two thousand

lives. (7) Oddly enough, though this dog has been known for about three hundred years, the Saint Bernard did not get its name until about a hundred years ago. (8) The Saint Bernard was named for a shelter in the Swiss Alps. (9) Monks of the shelter of Saint Bernard used this dog in rescue patrols.

UNIT 6

Consistency and Parallelism

Chapter 22

Consistent Tense

Consistent tense means using the same verb tense whenever possible within a sentence or a paragraph. As you write, avoid shifting from one tense to another—for example, from present to past—without a good reason for doing so.

(1)	**Inconsistent tense:**	We *were* seven miles from shore. Suddenly, the sky *turns* dark.
(2)	**Consistent tense:**	We *were* seven miles from shore. Suddenly, the sky *turned* dark.
(3)	**Consistent tense:**	We *are* seven miles from shore. Suddenly, the sky *turns* dark.

- Sentence (1) begins in the past tense with the verb *were* but then shifts into the present tense with the verb *turns*. The tenses are inconsistent because both actions are happening at the same time.
- Sentence (2) is consistent. Both verbs, *were* and *turned*, are in the past tense.
- Sentence (3) is also consistent. Both verbs, *are* and *turns*, are in the present tense.

Unit 6 Consistency and Parallelism

Of course, you should use different verb tenses in a sentence or paragraph if they convey the meaning you want to convey.

> (4) Two years ago, I *wanted* to be a chef, but now I *am studying* forestry.

- The verbs in sentence (4) accurately show the time relationship: In the past, I *wanted* to be a chef, but now I *am studying* forestry.

As you proofread your papers for tense consistency, ask yourself: Have I needlessly shifted from one tense to another?

Practice Underline the verbs in these sentences. Then correct any inconsistencies above the line.

Example: As soon as I get out of bed, I did fifty pushups. *Come back*
  (got)

or

As soon as I get out of bed, I did fifty pushups.
  (do)

1. We were walking near the lake when a large moose appears just ahead.

2. When we ask the time, the cab driver told us it was after six.
   (Do)

3. The man behind me was slurping soda and crunching candy. I am getting angrier by the minute.
   (got)

4. Dr. Choi smiled and welcomes the next patient.

5. This sweatshirt says "Go to Health" across the front. I wanted to buy it for my son.

6. The Oklahoma prairie stretches for miles, flat and rusty red. Here and there, an oil rig broke the monotony.

7. Whenever Fred practices the trombone, we covered our ears.

8. Linda walked in without a word and flops down in front of the TV.

9. They were walking down Main Street when the lights go out.

10. My cousins questioned me for hours about my trip. I describe the flight, my impressions of Paris, and every meal I ate.

11. We started cheering as he approaches the finish line.

12. Cynthia collapses into laughter and made us all giggle.

13. If Terry takes short naps during the day, she didn't feel tired in the evening.

14. Last year, Harold worked full time, take two courses at night, and played soccer on the weekends.

15. Yesterday, we march in the New Year's Day parade. Colorful floats accompany us. At the end of the route, Grinley's Department Store served hot chocolate to all the marchers.

Chapter Highlights

- **In general, use the same verb tense within a sentence or a paragraph:**

    She *sings* beautifully, and the audience *listens* intently.

    or

    She *sang* beautifully, and the audience *listened* intently.

- **However, at times different verb tenses are required because of meaning:**

    He *is* not working now, but he spent *sixty* hours behind the counter last week.

Chapter Review

Read each of these paragraphs for consistent tense. Correct any inconsistencies by changing the tense of the verbs. Write your corrections above the lines.

A. (1) When C. Latham Sholes read about a machine for printing letters in 1867, he decided to build a writing machine himself. (2) His first machine printed only the letter *W*, but in 1868, Sholes and two other men patent a machine that has eleven keys. (3) It typed only capitals, and the typist needs to lift the carriage to see what he or she types. (4) Over the next five years, Sholes built dozens of typewriters. (5) Each is better than the one before it. (6) When he finally produced a practical model, a manufacturer buys the patent rights to it. (7) Sholes even invents an arrangement that keeps the keys from banging into one another. (8) He also put frequently used letters within easy reach. (9) Once the typewriter catches on, it changed the business world forever.

B. (1) Yesterday, we sailed out of Provincetown Harbor aboard the *Dolphin IV* and headed north toward Stellwagon Bank, a favorite feeding ground of whales. (2) The thirty passengers are whale watchers who hope to glimpse the largest living mammals in their natural surroundings. (3) After an hour, the first cry came: "Sighting off the starboard bow!" (4) As the engines were cut, we rush to the right side of the boat. (5) Twenty yards out, two whales surface, blow their silver spouts, and sink out of sight. (6) The guide said that they looked like humpback whales, an endangered species.

(7) For long seconds, we held our breath, scanning the calm sea. (8) Suddenly, a whale rolls out of the water right beside the boat; it was sixty feet long, graceful as a dancer. (9) We gasp with delight and a little fear as it lifts its huge tail out of the water and disappears under the boat. (10) "Bravo!" shouted one of the passengers, and we break into loud applause.

C. (1) Almost every major city in the world has a subway system. (2) Underground trains speed through complex networks of tunnels and carried millions of passengers every day.

(3) Subway systems sometimes differ because of their locations. (4) In Mexico City, for example, subway cars traveled through suspended tunnels capable of absorbing earthquake shocks. (5) Residents of

Haifa, Israel, use an unusually short, straight subway that ran up and down inside a mountain. (6) The train brought people from Haifa's lower port city up a thousand feet to its upper residential city. (7) In Hong Kong, the world's first completely air-conditioned subway system offered relief from extremely hot and humid outdoor temperatures. (8) Cities like San Francisco, of course, expand the definition of subway to cover underwater as well as underground transportation. (9) The San Francisco Bay Area Rapid Transit system (BART) included several miles of track under San Francisco Bay.

(10) Some subway systems are famous for their artwork. (11) With paintings and walls of precious marble, many Moscow subway stations looked like museums. (12) Several stations in Stockholm, Sweden, seemed like elegant caverns because of granite carvings and rock in its natural state. (13) With colorful designs and all kinds of special effects, subway stations from Montreal to Tokyo resembled modern art galleries.

(14) Subways, therefore, not only provided an efficient means of public transportation. (15) They are also creative solutions to special problems as well as expressions of art and culture.

Chapter 23

Consistent Person

Consistent person means using the same person or personal pronoun throughout a sentence or a paragraph. Avoid confusing shifts from one person to another. For example, don't shift from *first person (I, we)* or *third person (he, she, it, they)* to *second person (you).**

(1)	**Inconsistent person:**	College *students* soon see that *you* are on *your* own.
(2)	**Consistent person:**	College *students* soon see that *they* are on *their* own.
(3)	**Consistent person:**	In college, *you* soon see that *you* are on *your* own.

- Sentence (1) shifts from the third person plural *students* to the second person *you* and *your*.

- Sentence (2) uses the third person plural consistently. *They* and *their* now clearly refer to *students*.

---
*For more work on pronouns, see Chapter 19.

Chapter 23   Consistent Person   313

- Sentence (3) is also consistent, using the second person *you* and *your* throughout.

Practice   Correct any inconsistencies of person in these sentences. If necessary, change the verbs to make them agree with any new subjects. Make your corrections above the lines.

Example: Each hiker should bring ~~your~~ *his or her* own lunch.

1. Jane treats me like ~~family~~ *her* when I visit her. She always makes ~~you~~ *me* feel at home.

2. A student has to show ~~their~~ *his* identification card in order to borrow books from the library.

3. The first person at the counter gets ~~their~~ *his* order filled quickly.

4. I love to go dancing. You can exercise, work off tensions, and have fun, all at the same time.

5. If a person has lived in a city, you may find the country too quiet.

6. The cast members have discovered that you have to work together to prepare for a performance.

7. A person with high blood pressure should watch ~~their~~ *her* diet.

8. When Lee and I ride our bikes to work at 6 a.m., you can see the city waking up.

9. Every mechanic should make sure they have a ~~good~~ *his* set of tools.

10. I gave birth to my daughter when I was only seventeen. In many ways, you are still a child yourself.

11. People who want to buy cars today are often stopped by high prices. You don't know which way to turn.

12. A working mother must schedule ~~your~~ *her* time carefully.

13. Many people think that ~~your~~ *his* votes don't really count.

14. Although I enjoy a day at the beach, you have to be careful about too much sun.

15. A teacher's attitude affects the performance of their students.

Chapter Highlights

- Use the same personal pronoun throughout a sentence or a paragraph:

    When *you* apply for a driver's license, *you* may have to take a written test and a driving test.

    When a *person* applies for a driver's license, *he or she* may have to take a written test and a driving test.

Chapter Review

Correct the inconsistencies of person in these paragraphs. Then make any other necessary changes. Write your corrections above the lines.

A. (1) When exam time comes, do you become anxious because you aren't sure how to study for tests? (2) They may have done all the work for their courses, but you still don't feel prepared. (3) Fortunately, he can do some things to make taking tests easier. (4) They can look through the textbook and review the material one has underlined. (5) You might read the notes you have taken in class and highlight or underline main points. (6) A person can think about some questions the professor may ask and then try writing answers. (7) Sometimes, they can find other people from your class and form a study group to compare class notes. (8) The night before a test, they shouldn't drink too much coffee. (9) They should get a good night's sleep so that your mind will be as sharp for the exam as your pencil.

B. (1) Skateboarding was an American fad of the 1960s. (2) At first, skateboarders were called sidewalk surfers because you were usually

West Coast surfers who couldn't find any good waves. (3) Soon, however, skateboarders could be found all across the country. (4) They entered national contests in which he or she performed fancy tricks. (5) Unfortunately, many skateboarders were injured or injured others. (6) By the late 1960s, we were declared public menaces in many cities. (7) This fad seemed dead. (8) However, it revived in the 1970s, as fads often do, when wheels made of polyurethane gave skateboarders more control over his boards. (9) Skateboarders were ready to make a comeback. (10) Today's skateboarders are male and female, young and old. (11) Some of you practice just to keep in shape. (12) Others enter contests, and he and she perform tricks undreamed of in the sixties, such as the one-and-a-half turn in midair. (13) Who knows? (14) Someday, skateboarders may compete for gold medals as you perform in the Olympics.

Chapter 24

Parallelism

PART A Defining and Writing Parallels
PART B Using Parallelism for Special Writing Effects

PART A Defining and Writing Parallels

Which sentence in each pair sounds better to you?

> (1) Jean is an artist, spends time at athletics, and flies planes.
>
> (2) Jean is *an artist, an athlete,* and *a pilot.*
>
> (3) He slowed down and came sliding. The winning run was scored.
>
> (4) He *slowed* down, *slid,* and *scored* the winning run.

- Do sentences (2) and (4) sound smoother and clearer than sentences (1) and (3)?
- Sentences (2) and (4) balance similar words or phrases to show similar ideas.

This technique is called *parallelism* or *parallel structure.* The italicized parts of (2) and (4) are *parallel.* When you use parallelism, you repeat similar grammatical structures in order to express similar ideas.

Chapter 24   Parallelism   317

- In sentence (2), can you see how *an artist, an athlete,* and *a pilot* are parallel? All three words in the series are singular nouns.

- In sentence (4), can you see how *slowed, slid,* and *scored* are parallel? All three words in the series are verbs in the past tense.

Now let's look at two more pairs of sentences. Note which sentence in each pair contains parallelism.

(5) The car was big, had beauty, and it cost a lot.

(6) The car was *big, beautiful,* and *expensive.*

(7) They raced across the roof, and the fire escape is where they came down.

(8) They raced *across the roof* and *down the fire escape.*

- In sentence (6), how are *big, beautiful,* and *expensive* parallel words?

  _____

- In sentence (8), how are *across the roof* and *down the fire escape* parallel phrases? _____

Certain special constructions require parallel structure:

(9) The room is *both* light *and* cheery.

(10) You *either* love geometry *or* hate it.

(11) Sonia *not only* plays the guitar *but also* sings.

(12) Richard would *rather* fight *than* quit.

Each of these constructions has two parts:

both . . . and   not only . . . but also
(n)either . . . (nor)   rather . . . than . . .

The words, phrases, or clauses following each part must be parallel:

light . . . cheery   plays . . . sings
love . . . hate   fight . . . quit

Parallelism is an excellent way to add smoothness and power to your writing. Use it in pairs or series of ideas, balancing a noun with a noun, an *-ing* verb with an *-ing* verb, a prepositional phrase with a prepositional phrase.

Practice 1 Circle the element that is *not* parallel in each list.

Example: blue

red

(colored like rust)

purple

1. broiling

    frying

    baker

    cooking

2. under the porch

    in the attic

    the basement stairs

    behind the back door

3. painting the kitchen

    cans of paint

    several brushes

    one roller

4. goodness

    strength

    love

    wise

5. standing on tiptoes

    toward the audience

    smiling with anticipation

    leaning against the table

6. sits

    watched

    listened

    thought

7. record shops

    clothing stores

    buying a birthday present

    boutiques

8. funny

    intelligent

    popularity

    cheerful

9. topped with whipped cream

    bananas and ice cream

    sprinkled with pecans

    covered with chocolate sauce

10. We shop for fruits at the market.

    We buy enough to last all week.

    We are baking a cake tonight.

    We cook special meals often.

Practice 2   Rewrite each sentence, using parallelism to accent the parallel ideas.

Example: We would break some windows and hopped a few trains. We had a few fights.

Rewrite: *We broke a few windows, hopped a few trains, and had a few fights.*

1. Tillie chose reading, drawing, and to swim as her favorite ways to relax.

    Rewrite: _____

    _____

2. The work was difficult, and there was danger in it.

    Rewrite: _____

3. Lula is a secretary, a student, and has a child too.

    Rewrite: _____

4. He wore a tweed overcoat, and his shirt was bright red. He was wearing white tennis shoes, large.

    Rewrite: _____

    _____

5. Leonardo da Vinci was an engineer. He painted pictures, and he would invent things also.

    Rewrite: _____

6. The subway rumbled, did squeal, shook, and was speeding through the tunnel.

    Rewrite: _____

    _____

7. My son wants to be either a bookkeeper or work as a disc jockey.

    Rewrite: _____

8. Julian would rather do vacuuming than polish the furniture.

    Rewrite: _____

9. From the window, he could see the barn and the bean field. The distant mountains were visible also.

   Rewrite: _____

   _____

10. Always wise and thoughtfully, my mother reminded me that I was once sixteen too.

    Rewrite: _____

    _____

11. In summer, the city air is hot and full of stickiness.

    Rewrite: _____

12. To get to grandmother's house, go over the river and through the woods is where you go next.

    Rewrite: _____

    _____

Practice 3 Fill in the blanks in each sentence with parallel words or phrases of your own. Be creative. Take care that your sentences make sense and that your parallels are truly parallel.

Example: I feel ____rested____ and ____happy____.

1. Ethan's favorite colors are _____ and _____.

2. The day of the storm, we _____, and they _____.

3. You look very _____ and _____ today.

4. In high school, _____, but in college, _____.

5. Her attitude was strange. She acted as if _____ and as if _____.

6. When you have _____ or have _____, finding a good job can be difficult.

7. It is much easier to _____ than to _____.

8. I like people who _____ and who _____.

9. Some married couples _____, while others _____.

10. Harold _____, but I just _____.

11. To reach the lake, walk _____ and _____.

12. _____ and _____ relax me.

13. We found _____, _____, and _____ on the beach.

14. He would like to _____ or to _____.

15. During the intermission, people _____ and _____.

PART B Using Parallelism for Special Writing Effects

By rearranging the order of a parallel series, you can sometimes add a little drama or humor to your sentences. Which of these two sentences is more dramatic?

(1) Jamie is a wife, a mother, and a black belt in karate.

(2) Jamie is a wife, a black belt in karate, and a mother.

- If you chose sentence (1), you are right. Sentence (1) saves the most surprising item—*a black belt in karate*—for last.

- Sentence (2), on the other hand, does not build suspense but gives away the surprise in the middle.

You can also use parallelism to set up your readers' expectations and then surprise them with humor.

> (3) The handsome cowboy saddled up, leaped on his horse, and slid off.

Practice Write five sentences of your own using parallel structure. In one or two of your sentences, arrange the parallel elements to build toward a dramatic or humorous conclusion. For ideas, look at Practice 3 in Part A, but create your own sentences.

1. _____

2. _____

3. _____

4. _____

5. _____

Chapter Highlights

- **Parallelism balances similar words or phrases to express similar ideas:**

    He left the gym *tired, sweaty,* and *satisfied.*

    Tami not only *finished the exam in record time* but also *answered the question for extra credit.*

    To celebrate his birthday, Roger *went to a dance, took in a show,* and *ate a late dinner.*

Chapter Review

This essay contains both correct and faulty parallel structures. Revise any faulty parallelism. Write your corrections above the lines.

The Flea Market

(1) Our local flea market is always lively and one has fun there. (2) Every Sunday, sellers, buyers, and just plain lookers get together in the parking lot of the Starlite Drive-In. (3) Everything imaginable is for sale—from fine jewelry to worthless junk. (4) I can find old clothes, plastic dishes, pistols that are antique, and fake-fur seat covers for my car. (5) The sellers call me over, are offering me a treasure, and will promise me a special price. (6) Eagerly or cautious, I look over the merchandise. (7) Sometimes I bargain, and sometimes I buy. (8) The food is terrific, whether it's homemade bean pies, eating chili dogs, or lemonade. (9) No matter what, there is always a lot of talking, laughing, and people socialize.

(10) Some sellers remember what I like and are saving special objects until I come by. (11) Last week, for example, Eddie Burrows was selling beautiful jewelry, and it was old. (12) He had kept aside a jade necklace with a garnet pendant and there was also a carved clasp. (13) When I held the necklace up to the sun, the light made the garnet glow and the clasp to shine. (14) Some other people came to look at the necklace. (15) Eddie was glad to see his stall attracting so many people and to hold their attention. (16) I decided to surprise my girlfriend, so I bought the necklace for her before she was coming to find me.

UNIT 6

Writing Assignments

Writing Assignment 1: *Discuss a public figure.* Choose a public person whom you admire—a civic leader or an athlete, for example. In your first sentence, focus on just one of this person's admirable qualities. Use this form: "I admire _____ because _____ possesses the courage to speak out," for example. Then explain your statement in detail, discussing two or three things the person has said or done that clearly show this quality. Proofread for consistent tense and person.

Writing Assignment 2: *Tell how you have changed.* Are you the same person you were ten years ago, or have you changed? If you are much the same, explain the ways in which you have not changed. If you are different, explain the most important changes. Brainstorm, freewrite, or cluster to get started. Then select specific examples and details so the reader can really understand your transformation. You may want to use parallelism to highlight your comparison: "In 1984, I was _____, but now I am _____." Proofread your work for consistent tense and person.

Writing Assignment 3: *Write to the mayor.* Write a letter of complaint to the mayor of your town about a local problem. In your first sentence, state the problem—a broken traffic light or infrequent garbage pickup, for example. Then explain why the issue is important to you and what action you feel the mayor should take. Before you write, decide on the best way to persuade the mayor to take action. That is, what approach is most likely to convince him or her? Use parallelism to give smoothness to your writing.

Writing Assignment 4: *Describe a person of faith.* Does religion or faith play an important part in the life of someone you know? In other words, do you know someone who not only goes to a place of worship but really seems to live by spiritual principles? Begin this way: "_____ is a truly religious person." Then describe this person, giving specific instances from his or her life that show religion (or faith) at work. Use parallelism to give smoothness to your writing.

Writing Assignment 5: *Praise a neighbor.* An old saying claims that "good fences make good neighbors." That is, neighbors should avoid becoming too friendly. Yet most of us are grateful for good neighbors. Pick a neighbor you are especially fond of because of his or her consideration, helpfulness, or concern. Begin by jotting down as many details as you can about this neighbor. These details will give you an idea about the main reason you are grateful for this person. Then in your first sentence, state your neighbor's name and why you singled him or her out: "My favorite neighbor is _____ because _____." Proofread for consistent tense and person.

UNIT 6

Review

Proofreading A. We have changed this student's composition so that it contains inconsistent tense and faulty parallelism. Proofread for these errors, and correct them above the lines.

Inspiration

(1) When I was a freshman in high school, I have a serious problem with English. (2) All day long, my head was filled with ideas for compositions, but when I arrived in English class, my mind goes blank. (3) I feared that my teacher thinks I was just another lazy student. (4) In fact, I almost gave up; thank goodness, I didn't!

(5) Then by the strangest twist of fate, I find out why my mind goes blank and why my themes were never finished. (6) One day, the English class moved from the basement to the third floor of the building. (7) The moment I stepped into the new room and the window was seen, I know what had bothered me all semester—no light, no fresh air, and the fact that there wasn't a sense of space. (8) I select a seat near the window and looked over my shoulder at the tall oak tree that stretched past the third-floor window. (9) When I pick up my pen, the writing began to flow. (10) If I ran out of things to say, I just glance over my shoulder at the tree and at the sky—and I would be inspired to continue my essay.

CHRISTOPHER MOORE, STUDENT

B. Proofread the essay below for inconsistent person and faulty parallelism. Correct the errors above the lines.

Touring Boston

(1) Boston offers visitors a rich variety of places to see and things to be doing. (2) For instance, the Freedom Trail takes visitors through the downtown area. (3) There you can find the sites of important historic events, like the Old North Church. (4) The church has copies of the lanterns that were used during the Revolutionary War to signal that British troops were coming. (5) If the guard in the steeple signaled once, the British were coming by land. (6) If he signaled twice, they were coming on their way by sea. (7) Paul Revere waited nearby in his home. (8) He watched for the signal and was carrying the news to the patriots in Lexington.

(9) In addition, the Black Heritage Trail takes visitors to sites important to the development of Boston's black community. (10) He or she can stop at the African Meeting House, the oldest black church in New England. (11) At the meeting house, William Lloyd Garrison founded the New England Anti-Slavery Society in 1832. (12) On Boston Common, you can see the Boston Massacre monument. (13) Black citizens of Boston erected this monument. (14) It commemorates the death of Crispus Attucks, a former slave and he was also the first casualty of the Boston Massacre. (15) Boston is clearly a city filled with history.

UNIT 7

Mechanics

Chapter 25

Beginning and Ending Sentences

Every sentence begins with a *capital letter*.

A sentence can end with a *period*, a *question mark*, or an *exclamation point*.

Period .

- Use a *period* at the end of a sentence that makes a statement.

> I went to the movies three times this week.

Question Mark ?

- Use a *question mark* at the end of a sentence that asks a question.

> Where are you going?

Exclamation Point !

- Use an *exclamation point* at the end of a sentence that gives a command or expresses a strong emotion.

> Get out!
> Wow!

Use the exclamation point sparingly.

Practice 1 Begin and end these sentences properly. Write your corrections above the lines.

1. where is my toothbrush ?
2. **W** watch your language !
3. **S** she borrowed an atlas from the library .
4. **D** did she borrow an atlas from the library ?
5. **T** this novel is about whaling !
6. **T** take your hands off that bike !
7. **H** he questioned his final grade .
8. **W** what is this knob for ?
9. **H** he loves to ride horses .
10. **T** this practice was easy .

Practice 2 Write two sentences ending with a period, two ending with a question mark, and two ending with an exclamation point. Make sure that you begin the sentences correctly.

1. _I study all night._
2. _My mother call me last night._
3. _he win the game light night?_
4. _In 1992 he win the NBA title?_

5. _What a game!_
6. _Say out!_

Chapter Highlights

- **A sentence begins with a capital letter:**
  The music grew louder and louder.

- **A period ends a sentence that makes a statement:**
  We borrowed a chair from your office.

- **A question mark ends a sentence that asks a question:**
  Are you going to the grocery store?

- **An exclamation point ends a sentence that commands or expresses strong emotion:**
  Put that down!
  Hooray!

Chapter Review

Begin and end these sentences correctly.

(1) are you old enough to remember drive-in movies   (2) what an invention   (3) a man named Richard M. Hollingshead started this American tradition when he set up a projector on his car roof and placed a screen a few feet away   (4) after some experimentation, he opened the world's first drive-in movie theater in New Jersey in 1933   (5) it was larger than a football field, held four hundred cars, and had an entrance fee of just one dollar   (6) viewers saw *Wife Beware* on opening night   (7) this new entertainment was informal, convenient, and cheap   (8) moreover, it appealed to people who liked their privacy   (9) whatever happened to the drive-in   (10) with the popularity of television and the VCR, it has become practically a thing of the past

Chapter 26

Capitalization

Here are the basic rules of capitalization:

1. nationality, race, language, religion → *Capitalize* → American, African American, French, English, Protestant, Jewish, Catholic, and so forth

This group is *always capitalized*.

2. names of persons, countries, states, cities, places, streets, bodies of water, and so forth → *Capitalize* → Bill Morse, New Zealand, California, Denver, Central Park, Jones Street, Pacific Ocean, and so forth

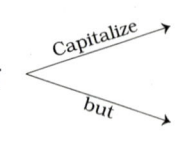

   but → a large state, a town, the lake, and so forth

If you name a specific person, state, city, street, or body of water, *capitalize*; if you don't, use small letters.

3. buildings, organizations, institutions — *Capitalize* → World Trade Center, Paradise Theater, National Organization for Women, Johnson City Library, Smithson University, and so forth

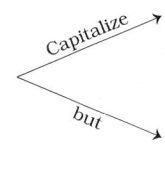

but → a tall building, an expensive theater, a feminist group, an old school, and so forth

If you name a specific building, group, or institution, *capitalize;* if you don't, use small letters.

4. historical events, periods, documents — *Capitalize* → the Spanish-American War, the Renaissance, the Constitution, and so forth

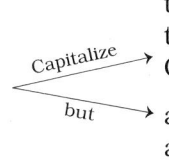

but → a terrible war, a new charter, and so forth

If you name a specific historical event, period, or document, *capitalize;* if you don't, use small letters.

5. months, days, holidays — *Capitalize* → June, Monday, the Fourth of July, and so forth

but → summer, fall, winter, spring

Always capitalize months, days, and holidays; use small letters for the seasons.

6. professional and civil titles — *Capitalize* → Dr. Smith, Professor Greenstein, Judge Alvarez, and so forth

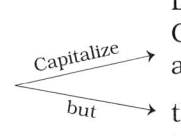

but → the doctor, the professor, the judge, and so forth

If you name the doctor, judge, and so forth, *capitalize;* if you don't, use small letters.

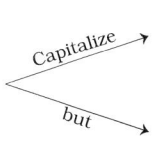

7. family names — *Capitalize* → Uncle Joe, Grandmother Stein, Cousin Beverly, Mother, Grandfather, and so forth

but → an uncle, the aunt, our cousin, my mother, her grandfather, and so forth

If you name a relative or use *Mother, Father, Grandmother,* or *Grandfather* as a name, *capitalize;* however, if these words are preceded by the word *a, an,* or *the,* a possessive pronoun, or an adjective, use small letters.

8. brand names — Capitalize → Greaso hair oil, Quick drafting ink, and so forth

Capitalize the brand name but not the type of product.

9. geographic location — Capitalize → the East, the Northwest, the South, and so forth
— but → east on the boulevard

If you mean a geographic location, *capitalize*; if you mean a direction, use small letters.

10. academic subjects — Capitalize → Mathematics 51, Sociology 11, English Literature 210, and so forth
— but → a tough mathematics course, an A in sociology, a course in English literature, and so forth

If you use the course number, *capitalize*; if you don't, use small letters. However, always capitalize languages and countries.

11. titles of books, poems, plays, films — Capitalize → *A Farewell to Arms*, "Ode to a Bat," *Major Barbara*, *Jurassic Park*, and so forth

Capitalize titles except for short words or prepositions; however, always capitalize the *first* and *last* words of the title.

Practice

Capitalize where necessary.

Example: The smithsonian consists of thirteen museums and the national zoo.

1. Judy and I took the children and aunt mae to washington last summer during the week of independence day.

2. We spent one full day visiting the museums.

3. Carl and Luke liked the national air and space museum best.

4. They thought that the tiny craft flown by orville and wilbur wright at kitty hawk, north carolina, in 1903, looked like a model plane.

5. We all marveled that charles lindbergh would dare to fly a plane as small as the *spirit of saint louis* across the atlantic ocean.

6. There was a great difference between those early planes and the model of the *Voyager* spacecraft; this modern spacecraft was designed to explore Jupiter, Saturn, and Uranus.

7. Next we walked along Constitution Avenue to the National Museum of American History.

8. There I saw my favorite car, The 1903 Winton that made the first trip across the United States.

9. We also saw the flag that inspired Francis Scott Key to write "The Star Spangled Banner."

10. This was the same flag that Mrs. Pickersgill sewed to fly over Fort McHenry in Chesapeake Bay during 1812.

11. Some of the other treasures we viewed there were President Washington's wooden false teeth, a pair of ruby slippers from the film *The Wizard of Oz*, and a copy of Thomas Paine's book *Common Sense*.

12. Finally, my family and I went to the National Museum of Natural History to stare at the African bull elephant and Bengal tiger on display.

13. Exhausted, we returned to the Ramada Inn, flopped into bed, and watched a rerun of *Star Trek*.

14. The next day, Thursday, we visited the White House and the Library of Congress.

15. We never saw any of the art museums that are also part of the Smithsonian, but we will be back soon.

Chapter Highlights

- **Capitalize nationalities, languages, races, and religions:**
  Asian, French, Caucasian, Baptist

- **Capitalize specific countries, states, cities, organizations, and buildings:**
  Belgium, Utah, Akron, United Nations, the White House

- **Capitalize months, days, and holidays, but not seasons:**
  November, Friday, Labor Day, summer

- **Capitalize professional titles only when a person is named:**
  Mayor Alexander, the mayor, Superintendent Alicia Morgan

- **Capitalize brand names, but not the type of product:**
  Dawn dishwashing detergent

- **Capitalize geographic locations, but not directions:**
  the West, west of the city

- **Capitalize academic subjects only when they are followed by a course number:**
  History 583, psychology

- **Capitalize titles of books, poems, plays, and films:**
  Lord of the Flies, "The Raven," *Hamlet, Do the Right Thing*

Chapter Review

Proofread the following paragraph for errors in capitalization; correct the errors above the lines.

The Strange Career of Deborah Sampson

(1) Few Soldiers have had a stranger army career than Deborah Sampson. (2) Sampson disguised herself as a man so that she could fight in the revolutionary war. (3) Born on december 17, 1760, she spent her early years in a Town near plymouth, massachusetts. (4) Her Father left his large family, however, and went to sea when Sampson was seven years old. (5) After living with a Cousin and then with the widow of a Minister, sampson became a servant in a wealthy family.

(6) Household tasks and hard outdoor work built up her physical strength. (7) She was taller than the average Man and more muscular than the average Woman. (8) Therefore, she was able to disguise herself successfully. (9) Sampson enlisted in the continental army on may 20, 1782, under the name of robert shurtleff.

(10) Sampson fought in several Battles and was wounded at least twice. (11) One story says that she took a bullet out of her own leg with a penknife to avoid seeing a Doctor. (12) However, after the surrender of the british, Sampson's regiment was sent to philadelphia, where she was hospitalized with a high fever and lost consciousness. (13) At the Hospital, dr. Barnabas Binney made the discovery that ended Sampson's army life. (14) She was honorably discharged by general henry knox at west point on october 28, 1783.

(15) Female again, Sampson returned to Massachusetts and eventually married a Farmer named benjamin gannett. (16) The story of Sampson's adventures spread; in 1797, a book titled *the female review* was published about her. (17) When Sampson decided to earn money by telling her own story, she became the first american woman to be paid as a Public Speaker. (18) She gave her first talk at the federal street theatre in boston in march, 1802, and toured until september. (19) Her health was poor, however, and she could not continue her appearances.

(20) In 1804, paul revere, who was a neighbor of the gannetts, wrote to a member of the united states congress. (21) He asked for a pension for this Soldier who had never been paid and was still suffering from her war wounds. (22) Congress granted deborah sampson gannett a pension of four dollars a month.

(23) Deborah Sampson died in sharon, Massachusetts, in april 1827. (24) Her story inspired the People of her own time and continues to inspire People today. (25) Two plays have been written about her: *she was there* and *portrait of deborah*. (26) On veterans day in 1989, a life-size bronze statue was dedicated in front of the sharon public library to honor her.

Chapter 27

Commas

PART A   Commas after Items in a Series
PART B   Commas after Introductory Phrases
PART C   Commas for Direct Address
PART D   Commas to Set Off Appositives
PART E   Commas for Parenthetical Expressions
PART F   Commas for Dates
PART G   Commas for Addresses
PART H   Commas for Coordination and Subordination

The comma is a pause. It gives your reader a chance to stop for a moment to think about where your sentence has been and where it is going, and to prepare to read on.

Although this chapter will cover some basic uses of the comma, always keep this generalization in mind: If there is no reason for a comma, leave it out!

PART A Commas after Items in a Series

> (1) I like apples, oranges, and pears.

- What three things do I like? _apples_, _oranges_, and _pears_

Use commas to separate three or more items in a series.

> (2) We will walk through the park, take in a film, and visit a friend.

- What three things will we do? _walk through the park_, _take in a film_, and _visit a friend_

> (3) She loves to explore new cultures sample different foods and learn foreign languages.

- In sentence (3), what are the items in the series?
  explore new cultures, _different foods_, and _learn foreign languages._

- Punctuate sentence (3).

However, if you want to join three or more items with *and* or *or* between the items, do not use commas.

> (4) She plays tennis *and* golf *and* softball.

- Note that commas are not used in sentence (4).

Practice 1 Punctuate these sentences correctly.

1. I can't find my shoes, my socks, or my hat!

2. Sylvia, Eddie, and James, have just completed a course in welding.

3. Over lunch, they discussed new accounts, marketing, strategy, and motherhood.

4. In June, July, and August, the city feels deserted.
5. Francine went to the wrestling match Harry visited the antique automobile show and Isaac caught a cold.
6. On Sunday, we repaired the porch cleaned the basement and shingled the roof.
7. The exhibit will include photographs, diaries, and love letters.
8. Body building, tennis, and roller blading have become very popular in the past ten years.
9. You will find tapes videos, and compact discs, on the third floor.
10. Paula hung her coat on the hook, Henry, draped his jacket over her coat, and Susie threw her scarf on top of the pile.

Practice 2 Write three sentences, each containing three or more items in a series. Punctuate correctly.

1. _____
   _____
2. _____
   _____
3. _____
   _____

PART B Commas after Introductory Phrases

(1) By the end of the season, our local basketball team will have won thirty games straight.

- *By the end of the season* introduces the sentence.

An introductory phrase is usually followed by a comma.

> (2) On Thursday we left for Hawaii.

However, a very short introductory phrase, like the one in sentence (2), need not be followed by a comma.

Practice 1 Punctuate these sentences correctly. One sentence is already punctuated correctly.

1. By the end of January, I'll be in Atlanta.
2. During the rainstorm, we huddled in a doorway.
3. Every Saturday, at 9 p.m. she carries her telescope to the roof.
4. After their last trip, Fred, and Nita, decided on separate vacations.
5. This wall must be completely plastered by Friday.
6. By the light of the moon, we could make out a dim figure.
7. During the coffee break, George reviewed his psychology, homework.
8. At the height of the season Joanne hurt her shoulder, and could not pitch any longer.
9. In the deep end of the pool, he found three, silver dollars.
10. In almost no time they had changed, the tire.

Practice 2 Write three sentences using introductory phrases. Punctuate correctly.

1. _The place I would like to visit is, Hawaii_
2. _____
3. _____

PART C Commas for Direct Address

> (1) Bob, you must leave now.
>
> (2) You must, Bob, leave now.
>
> (3) You must leave now, Bob.
>
> (4) Don't be surprised, old buddy, if I pay you a visit very soon.

- In sentences (1), (2), and (3), Bob is the person spoken to; he is being *addressed directly*.
- In sentence (4), *old buddy* is being *addressed directly*.

The person addressed directly is set off by commas wherever the direct address appears in the sentence.

Practice 1

Circle the person or persons directly addressed, and punctuate the sentences correctly.

1. I am happy to inform you, Mr. Forbes, that you are the father of twins.

2. We will meet in an hour, Florence.

3. It appears, my friend, that you have won two tickets to the opera.

4. Get out of my roast, you mangy old dog.

5. Tom, it's probably best that you sell the heap at a loss.

6. Have you ever ridden an elephant, Harold?

7. If I were you, Hilda, I would start my own business.

8. My child, there is no Santa Claus.

9. Bruce, it's time you learned to operate the lawn mower!

10. I am pleased to announce, ladies and gentlemen, that the Mambo Kings band will entertain you tonight.

344   Unit 7   Mechanics

Practice 2   Write three sentences using direct address. Punctuate correctly.

1. _____

2. _____

3. _____

PART D   Commas to Set Off Appositives

> (1) The Rialto, a new theater, is on Tenth Street.

- A *new theater* describes *the Rialto*.

> (2) An elderly man, my grandfather walks a mile every day.

- What group of words describes *my grandfather*? *An elderly man*

> (3) They bought a new painting, a rather beautiful landscape.

- What group of words describes *a new painting*?
  landscape

- *A new theater, an elderly man,* and *a rather beautiful landscape* are called *appositives*.

An *appositive* is usually a group of words that describes a noun or pronoun. It can occur at the beginning, middle, or end of a sentence.

An appositive is usually set off by commas.

Practice 1   Circle the appositive, and punctuate correctly.

1. That door, the one with the X on it, leads backstage.

2. A short man, he decided not to pick a fight with the basketball player.

3. Rudolph Pinderkist, a noted expert on penguins, will lecture tonight.

4. Hassim, my friend from Morocco, will be staying with me this week.

5. She expects to go to Midvale Technical College, a fine institution.

6. We borrowed Joe's truck, a lumbering monster, to move my furniture.

7. Pickles, my favorite food, make my mouth pucker.

8. George Eliot, a nineteenth-century novelist, was a woman.

9. A very close race, the election for mayor wasn't decided until 2 a.m.

10. Dr. Simpson, a specialist in ethnic music, always travels with a tape recorder.

Practice 2 Write three sentences using appositives. Punctuate correctly.

1. _____

2. _____

3. _____

PART E — Commas for Parenthetical Expressions

(1) By the way, I think that you're beautiful.
(2) I think, by the way, that you're beautiful.
(3) I think that you're beautiful, by the way.

- *By the way* modifies or qualifies the entire sentence or idea.
- It is called a *parenthetical expression* because it is a side remark, something that could be placed in parentheses: *(By the way) I think that you're beautiful.*

Set off a parenthetical expression with commas.

Below is a partial list of parenthetical expressions:

as a matter of fact	in fact
believe me	it seems to me
I am sure	it would seem
I assure you	to tell the truth

346 Unit 7 Mechanics

Practice 1 Circle the parenthetical expressions in the sentences below, and then punctuate correctly.

1. Believe me Sonia has studied hard for her driver's test.
2. She possesses it would seem an uncanny gift for gab.
3. He is in fact a black belt.
4. This computer I am sure will have enough memory for you.
5. It was I assure you an accident.
6. To tell the truth I am not pleased with my sandwich.
7. His supervisor by the way will never admit when he is wrong.
8. A well-prepared résumé as a matter of fact can help you get a job.
9. To begin with I want to see the manager.
10. Some plants surprisingly enough need almost no sunlight.

Practice 2 Write three sentences using parenthetical expressions. Punctuate them correctly.

1. _____
2. _____
3. _____

PART F   Commas for Dates

> (1) I arrived on Tuesday, March 20, 1993, and found that I was in the wrong city.

- Note that commas separate the different parts of the date.
- Note that a comma follows the last item in the date.

> (2) She saw him on Wednesday and spoke with him.

However, a one-word date *(Wednesday* **or** *1990)* **preceded by a preposition (***in, on, near,* **or** *from,* **for example) is not followed by a comma unless there is some other reason for it.**

Practice 1   Punctuate these sentences correctly. Not every sentence requires additional punctuation.

1. By Tuesday, October 6, he had outlined the whole history text.
2. Thursday, May 8, is Hereford's birthday.
3. He left Cairo on Monday, and arrived in Hartford, on Tuesday.
4. She was born on January 9, 1945, in a small, New England town.
5. He was born on July 4, 1976, the two-hundredth anniversary of the Declaration of Independence.
6. On March 18, 1987, he won the state lottery.
7. Do you think we will have finished the yearbook by, May?
8. On January 24, 1848, James Wilson Marshall found gold in California.
9. I was a full-time student between September, and June.
10. This book was due back in the library more than a year ago—on March 13, 1992.

Practice 2   Write three sentences using dates. Punctuate correctly.

1. _My cousins birthday is on Sept 5, 1969_
2. _My sisters birthday is on June 27, 1969_
3. _My birthday is on Sept 3, 1971._

PART G   Commas for Addresses

> (1) We just moved from 11 Landow Street, Wilton, Connecticut, to 73 James Street, Charleston, West Virginia.

- Commas separate different parts of an address.

- A comma generally follows the last item in an address, usually a state *(Connecticut)*.

> (2) Julio Smith *from* Queens was made district sales manager.

However, a one-word address preceded by a preposition (*in, on, at, near,* or *from,* for example) is not followed by a comma unless there is another reason for it.

> (3) Julio Smith, Queens, was made district sales manager.

Commas are required to set off a one-word address if the preposition before the address is omitted.

Practice 1

Punctuate these sentences correctly. Not every sentence requires additional punctuation.

1. Their address is 6 Great Ormond Street, London, England.
2. My cousin from Korea is having a special party for us at his house on Ventnor Street.
3. Seattle, Washington, faces the Cascade Mountains.
4. That package must be sent to 30 West Overland Street, Phoenix Arizona.
5. She lives near Valentine Avenue, around the corner from the park.
6. His father now lives in Waco, Texas, but his sister has never left Vermont.
7. How far is Kansas City, Kansas, from Independence, Missouri?
8. My old apartment at 98 Underhill Avenue, Fargo, North Dakota, was much larger than the one I have now.
9. Foster's Stationery, 483 Heebers Street Plainview, sells special calligraphy pens.
10. Both Rome, New York, and Rome, Georgia, are named after Rome, Italy.

Practice 2 Write three sentences using addresses. Punctuate correctly.

1. *My old work address or 20158 Vermont, ave*
2. *She lives near Valentine Avenue,*
3. *My cousin on 29 Ormond St,*

PART H — Commas for Coordination and Subordination

Chapters 11 and 12 covered the use of commas with coordinating and subordinating conjunctions. Below is a brief review.

> (1) Enzio enjoys most kinds of music, but heavy metal gives him a headache.
>
> (2) Although the weather bureau had predicted rain, the day turned out bright and sunny.
>
> (3) The day turned out bright and sunny although the weather bureau had predicted rain.

- In sentence (1), a comma precedes the coordinating conjunction *but*, which joins together two independent ideas.
- In sentence (2), a comma follows the dependent idea because it precedes the independent idea.
- Sentence (3) does not require a comma because the independent idea precedes the subordinate one.

Use a comma before coordinating conjunctions—*and, but, for, nor, or, so,* or *yet*—that join two independent ideas.

Use a comma after a dependent idea only when the dependent idea precedes the independent one; do not use a comma if the dependent idea follows the independent one.

Practice 1 Punctuate correctly. Not every sentence requires additional punctuation.

Example: Because scrapped cars create millions of tons of waste, recycling auto parts has become an important issue.

1. Today new cars are made from many old parts, and manufacturers are trying to increase the use of recycled, materials from old cars.

2. Scrapped cars can be easily recycled, because they mostly consist of metals.

3. After these cars are crushed, magnets draw the metals out of them.

4. However, the big problem in recycling cars is the plastic they contain.

5. Although plastic can also be recycled, the average car contains about twenty different kinds of plastic.

6. Separating the different types of plastic takes much time, but companies are developing ways to speed up the process.

7. Still, new cars need to be made differently before recycling can truly succeed.

8. Their parts should detach easily, and they should be made of plastics and metals that can be separated from each other.

9. As we develop more markets for the recycled auto parts, new cars may soon be 90 percent recycled and recyclable.

10. Our environment will benefit, and brand-new cars will really be more than fifty years old!

Practice 2 Write three sentences, one with a coordinating conjunction, one beginning with a subordinating conjunction, and one with the subordinating conjunction in the middle.

1. _____

2. _____

3. _____

Chapter Highlights

- **Commas separate three or more items in a series:**
  He bought a ball, a bat, and a fielder's glove.

- **Unless it is very short, an introductory phrase is followed by a comma:**
  By the end of January, I'll be in Australia.

- **Commas set off the name of a person directly addressed:**
  I think, Aunt Betty, that your hat is a winner.

- **Commas set off appositives:**
  My boss, the last person in line in the cafeteria, often forgets to eat lunch.

- **Commas set off parenthetical expressions:**
  My wife, by the way, went to school with your sister.

- **Commas separate the parts of a date or an address, except for a one-word date or address preceded by a preposition:**
  On January 4, 1973, I was in a terrible blizzard.
  I live at 48 Trent Street, Randolph, Michigan.
  She works in Tucson as a plumber.

- **A comma precedes a coordinating conjunction that joins two independent ideas:**
  We had planned to see a movie together, but we couldn't agree on one.

- **If a dependent idea precedes the independent idea, it is followed by a comma; if the independent idea comes first, it is not followed by a comma:**
  Although I still have work to do, my project will be ready on time.
  My project will be ready on time although I still have work to do.

Chapter Review

Proofread the following essay for comma errors—either missing commas or commas used incorrectly. Correct any errors right on the page.

Sitting Bull

(1) Sitting Bull the great Sioux chief was born about 1830. (2) From the stories of the tribal elders he learned that a Sioux must be brave strong generous and wise. (3) He also learned that a Sioux had, to earn his adult name.

(4) When he was fourteen he earned the name Sitting Bull. (5) Armed with only a coup stick, a long wooden pole, he rode into battle against the Crow tribes. (6) He was the first Sioux to touch a Crow with his coup stick. (7) This act was considered as brave as killing an enemy. (8) After that battle, his father gave him his adult name a bow arrows a spear and other weapons.

(9) When he was thirty-five years old Sitting Bull became the chief of the Hunkpapa Sioux. (10) He led, his people, across the Great Plains. (11) He saw greedy men taking away native lands ruining native holy places and destroying the buffalo.

(12) The destruction of the buffalo was disastrous for the Sioux. (13) The Sioux used every part of the buffalo the "giver of life." (14) They made leather clothes from the hide they ate the meat and they used the tendons for bow strings. (15) In fact they even used buffalo droppings for fuel. (16) Without the buffalo the Sioux could barely survive. (17) They had to fight to protect their land and their "giver of life."

(18) On June 25 1876 the Sioux fought their famous battle against General George Custer and his army. (19) In less than half an hour Custer and all his men had been killed. (20) This battle became known as "Custer's Last Stand." (21) It also was the Sioux tribes' last stand against the United States cavalry. (22) Despite their great victory most of the Sioux were forced to settle on reservations. (23) Even Sitting Bull, lived on Standing Rock Reservation.

(24) Sitting Bull was killed on December 15 1890 and buried in Fort Yates North Dakota. (25) More than sixty years later, his remains were reburied in Mobridge South Dakota. (26) Sitting Bull is remembered still for his leadership for his courage and for his wisdom.

Chapter 28

Apostrophes

PART A Using the Apostrophe for Contractions
PART B Defining the Possessive
PART C Using the Apostrophe to Show Possession (in Words That Do Not Already End in -*S*)
PART D Using the Apostrophe to Show Possession (in Words That Already End in -*S*)

PART A Using the Apostrophe for Contractions

A *contraction* is a way of combining two words and making one word out of them.

do + not = don't

- Note that the *o* of *not* is omitted in the contraction. An apostrophe (') replaces the omitted letter *o*.

should + not = shouldn't (*o* omitted)

I + have = I've (*ha* omitted)

BE CAREFUL: *Won't* is an odd contraction because it cannot be broken into parts in the same way the previous contractions can.

will + not = won't

Practice 1 Write these words as contractions.

1. you + are = *you're*
2. who + is = *who's*
3. he + is = *he's*
4. are + not = *aren't*
5. they + are = *they're*
6. can + not = *can't*
7. should + not = *shouldn't*
8. it + is = *it's*
9. I + am = *I'm*
10. will + not = *won't*

Practice 2 Insert the missing apostrophes in these contractions.

1. She'll arrive by helicopter.
2. Won't you go with us?
3. They're in the backyard.
4. What's in the locked box?
5. We'll finish by noon.
6. I don't know the answer.
7. You're gorgeous.
8. Who's playing at the Blue Bongo?
9. She's working out at the gym.
10. Aren't we early?
11. Now we're in trouble.
12. They just can't agree.
13. He'll play the trombone.
14. It's too early to leave.
15. Shouldn't we eat soon?
16. I'm nervous.
17. He's never nervous.
18. Didn't he mention his name?
19. She doesn't like blues; they don't like classical.
20. Who's sorry now?

Practice 3 Write five sentences, each using an apostrophe in a contraction.

1. _____
2. _____

Chapter 28 Apostrophes 355

3. _____

4. _____

5. _____

PART B — Defining the Possessive

A *possessive* is a way of showing that someone or something owns someone or something else.

Practice — In the following phrases, who owns what?

Example: "The hat of the man" means ___the man owns the hat___.

1. "The camera of Judson" means ___Judson owns the camera___

2. "The hopes of the people" means _____.

3. "The earring of the woman" means ___The woman owns the earring___

4. "The trophies of the home team" means ___The home team owns the trophies___

5. "The reputation of that man" means ___That man owns the reputation___

PART C — Using the Apostrophe to Show Possession (in Words That Do Not Already End in -S)

| (1) the hands of my father | becomes | (2) my father's hands |

- In phrase (1), who owns what? ___hands___

- In phrase (1), what is the *owner word*? _____

- How does the owner word show possession in phrase (2)?
  _____

- Note that what is owned, *hands*, follows the owner word.

If the *owner word* (possessive) does not end in *-s*, add an apostrophe and an *-s* to show possession.

Practice 1 Change these phrases into possessives with an apostrophe and an *-s*. (Note that the owner words do not end in *-s*.)

Example: the friend of my cousin = _____my cousin's friend_____

1. the eyes of Rona = *Rona's eyes*
2. the voice of the coach = *The coach's voice*
3. the ark of Noah = *Noah's ark*
4. the prices of today = *Today's prices*
5. the jacket of someone = *Someone's jacket*

Practice 2 Add an apostrophe and an *-s* to show possession in these phrases.

1. Judy's briefcase
2. the company's new president
3. the diver's tanks
4. Edison's invention
5. Bill's decision
6. the salesman's charm
7. the carpenter's tools
8. that man's cigars
9. the speaker's message
10. the winner's ribbon
11. somebody's umbrella
12. the parrot's vocabulary
13. everyone's dreams
14. your daughter's sandwich
15. yesterday's fashion
16. the woman's eyes
17. the horse's white mane
18. Marcia's groceries
19. anyone's guess
20. the artist's brushes

Practice 3 Write five sentences. In each, use an apostrophe and an *-s* to show ownership. Use owner words that do not already end in *-s*.

1. *Judy's briefcase was lost in airport.*
2. *Edison's invention the light bud.*
3. *Bill's decision to wash the car was his.*

Chapter 28 Apostrophes 357

4. *Yesterday the fashion show was held*
5. *Somebody lost their umbrella last night at the party.*

PART D — Using the Apostrophe to Show Possession (in Words That Already End in -*s*)

| (1) the uniforms of the pilots | becomes | (2) the pilots' uniforms |

- In phrase (1), who owns what? *pilots*
- In phrase (1), what is the owner word? *uniforms*
- How does the owner word show possession in phrase (2)? _____
- Note that what is owned, *uniforms*, follows the owner word.

If the owner word (possessive) ends in -*s*, add an apostrophe after the -*s* to show possession.*

Practice 1

Change these phrases into possessives with an apostrophe. (Note that the owner words already end in -*s*.)

Example: the helmets of the players = __the players' helmets__

1. the farm of my grandparents = *My grandparents farm*
2. the kindness of my neighbors = *My kindness neighbors*
3. the dunk shots of the basketball players = *The basketball players dunk shots*
4. the music of the Pointer Sisters = *The Pointer Sisters music*
5. the trainer of the horses = *The trainer horse*

---
*Some writers add an '*s* to one-syllable proper names that end in -*s*: *James's* book.

Practice 2 Add either 's or ' to show possession in these phrases. BE CAREFUL: Some of the owner words end in -s and some do not.

1. the models faces
2. the model face
3. that writer ideas
4. the children room
5. the singer voice
6. the runner time
7. James radio
8. the thief scheme
9. somebody watch
10. my family history
11. your parents garden
12. the men locker room
13. nobody fault
14. the students exams
15. Dana suitcases
16. the bankers plan
17. several contestants answers
18. Mr. Jones band saw
19. my brother computer
20. the women movement

Practice 3 Rewrite each of the following pairs of short sentences as *one* sentence by using a possessive.

Example: Joan has a friend. The friend comes from Chile.

Joan's friend comes from Chile.

1. Rusty has a motorcycle. The motorcycle needs new brakes.
2. Nurse Johnson had evidence. The evidence proved that the doctor was not careless.
3. Tom has a salary. The salary barely keeps him in peanut butter.
4. Lee has a job. His job in the Complaint Department keeps him busy.
5. José has a bad cold. It makes it hard for him to sleep.

6. Ms. Rose has a class. Her class will meet in the language lab.

   Ms. Rosa has a class will meet in the Language lab.

7. Lucy had a day off. The day off gave her a chance to weed the garden.

   Lucy's had a day off gave her a chance to weed the garden.

8. My sisters have a day-care center. The day-care center is open seven days a week.

   My sisters have a day care center is open seven days a week.

9. The twins have a goal. Their goal is to study flamenco dancing in Spain.

   The twins have a goal to study flamenco dancing in Spain.

10. Robert has a thank-you note. The thank-you note says it all.

    Robert has a thank-you note say it all.

Practice 4 Write six sentences that use an apostrophe to show ownership—three using owner words that do not end in -s and three using owner words that do end in -s.

1. _____
2. _____
3. _____ *Comeback*
4. _____
5. _____
6. _____

BE CAREFUL: The apostrophe is used to show possession by nouns. As the chart on the next page shows, no apostrophe is used with possessive pronouns.

> **Possessive Pronouns**
>
> | Singular | Plural |
> |---|---|
> | <u>my</u> book, <u>mine</u> | <u>our</u> book, <u>ours</u> |
> | <u>your</u> book, <u>yours</u> | <u>your</u> book, <u>yours</u> |
> | <u>his</u> book, <u>his</u> | <u>their</u> book, <u>theirs</u> |
> | <u>her</u> book, <u>hers</u> | |
> | <u>its</u> book, <u>its</u> | |
>
> Do not confuse *its* (possessive pronoun) with *it's* (contraction for *it is* or *it has*) or *your* (possessive pronoun) with *you're* (contraction for *you are*).*

REMEMBER: Use apostrophes for contractions and possessive nouns only. Do not use apostrophes for plural nouns, verbs, or possessive pronouns.

Chapter Highlights

- **An apostrophe can indicate a contraction:**
    We're glad you could come.
    They *won't* be back until tomorrow.

- **A word that does not end in -s takes an 's to show possession:**
    Is that *Barbara's* coat on the sofa?
    I like *Clint Eastwood's* movies.

- **A word that ends in -s takes just an ' to show possession:**
    That store sells *ladies'* hats with feathers.
    I depend on my *friends'* advice.

---

*See Chapter 31 for work on words that look and sound alike.

Chapter Review

Proofread this essay for apostrophe errors—missing apostrophes or apostrophes used incorrectly. Correct the errors above the lines.

The Magic Fastener

(1) Its hard to remember the world without Velcro. (2) Shoelaces had to be tied; jackets' had to be zipped and did'nt make so much noise when they were loosened. (3) We have a Swiss engineers' curiosity to thank for todays changes.

(4) On a hunting trip in 1948, Georges de Mestral became intrigued by the seedpods that clung to his clothing. (5) He knew that they we're hitching rides to new territory by fastening onto him, but he could'nt tell how they were doing it. (6) He examined the seedpods to find that their tiny hooks were catching onto the threads of his jacket.

(7) The idea of Velcro was born, but the actual product wasnt developed overnight. (8) It took eight more years' before Georges de Mestrals invention was ready for the market. (9) Today, Velcro is used on clothing, on space suits, and even in artificial hearts. (10) Velcro can not only help keep a skier warm, but it can also save a persons' life.

Chapter 29

Direct and Indirect Quotations

PART A Defining Direct and Indirect Quotations
PART B Punctuating Simple Direct Quotations
PART C Punctuating Split Quotations
PART D Ending Direct Quotations

PART A Defining Direct and Indirect Quotations

(1) John said that he was going.
(2) John said, "I am going."

- Which sentence gives the *exact words* of the speaker, John?

    John said, "I am going"

- Why is sentence (2) called a *direct quotation*?

- Why is sentence (1) called an *indirect quotation*?

Chapter 29   Direct and Indirect Quotations   363

- Note that the word *that* introduces the *indirect quotation*.

Practice   Write *D* in the blank at the right if the sentence uses a *direct quotation*. Write *I* in the blank at the right if the sentence uses an *indirect quotation*.

1. I insisted that I was first.   _D_ ✓
2. Rita asked, "Which is my chair?"   _I_ ✓
3. Ruth said that one turkey would feed the whole family.   _D_ ✗
4. The students shouted, "Get out of the building! It's on fire!"   _D_ ✓
5. "This is silly," she said, sighing.   _I_ ✓
6. I suggested that Bill continue practicing.   _D_ ✗
7. "Don't leave yet," they begged.   _I_ ✓
8. "How about a film tonight?" he asked.   _D_ ✓

PART B — Punctuating Simple Direct Quotations

Note the punctuation:

(1) Rafael whispered, "I'll always love you."

- Put a comma before the direct quotation.
- Put quotation marks around the speaker's exact words.
- Capitalize the first word of the direct quotation.
- Put the period *inside* the quotation marks.

Of course the direct quotation may come first in the sentence:

(2) "I'll always love you," Rafael whispered.

- List the rules for a direct quotation written like the sentence above:

_____

_____

_____

364 Unit 7 Mechanics

Practice Rewrite these simple direct quotations, punctuating them correctly.

1. He yelled answer the phone!
   Rewrite: *"Answer the phone!" he yelled.*

2. The usher called, "no" more seats in front.
   Rewrite: *"No more seats in front," the usher called.*

3. It's raining we mumbled angrily.
   Rewrite: *He mumbled angrily, "It's raining."*

4. Looking at the flowers, Bob said, I've never seen a lavender rose before.
   Rewrite: *Bob said, "I've never seen a lavender rose before," looking at the flowers.*

5. Something is doing the backstroke in my soup the man said.
   Rewrite: *The man said, "Something is doing the backstroke in my soup."*

6. Your jacket was already torn insisted the dry cleaner.
   Rewrite: *The dry cleaner, "your jacket was already torn," insisted.*

7. The introduction states, this book is intended for those with no background in mathematics.
   Rewrite: *"This book is intended for those with no background in mathematics," the introduction states.*

PART C — Punctuating Split Quotations

Sometimes one sentence of direct quotation is split into two parts:

(1) "Because it is 2 a.m.," he said, "you had better go."

- *He said* is set off by commas.
- The second part of the quotation—*you had better go*—begins with a small letter because it is part of one directly quoted sentence.

Chapter 29 Direct and Indirect Quotations   365

> (2) "Because it is 2 a.m. . . . you had better go."

A direct quotation can also be broken into separate sentences:

> (3) "It is a long ride to San Francisco," he said. "We should leave early."

- Because the second part of the quotation is a separate sentence, it begins with a capital letter.
- Note the period after *said*.

BE CAREFUL: If you break a direct quotation into separate sentences, be sure that both parts of the quotation are complete sentences.

Practice 1

Rewrite these split direct quotations, punctuating them correctly.

1. Before the guests arrive she said let's relax.
   Rewrite: *She said let's relax before the guests arrive.*

2. Don't drive so fast he begged I get nervous.
   Rewrite: *He begged I get nervous don't drive so fast.*

3. Whenever John sees her Sarah said he is reminded of Whitney Houston.
   Rewrite: *Whenever John; see her Sarah said he is reminded of Whitney Houston.*

4. I want to go to Hong Kong he told me I have relatives there.
   Rewrite: *I want to Hong Kong; told me I relatives there*

5. Although my new phone looks terrific he said it has a funny ring.
   Rewrite: *Although my new phone looks terrific he said it; has a funny ring*

6. Being the youngest in the family she said has its advantages.
   Rewrite: *Being the youngest in the family she said, has its; advantages*

366 Unit 7 Mechanics

7. This catalog is fantastic, the clerk said and you can have it for free.

   Rewrite: *This catalog is fantastic, the clerk said, and you can have it for free*

8. I have to read this novel by Tuesday, he moaned but I don't think I will make it.

   Rewrite: *I have to read this novel by Tuesday, he moaned but I don't think*

Practice 2 Write three sentences using split quotations.

1. _____
2. _____
3. _____

PART D — Ending Direct Quotations

A sentence can end in any of three ways:

- with a period (.)
- with a question mark (?)
- with an exclamation point (!)

The period is *always* placed inside the quotation marks:

> (1) He said, "My car cost five thousand dollars."

The question mark and the exclamation point go before or after the quotation marks—depending on the sense of the sentence.

> (2) He asked, "Where are you?"
> (3) Did he say, "I am thirty-two years old"?
> (4) She yelled, "Help!"

- The question mark in sentence (2) is placed before the end quotation marks because the direct quotation is a question.
- The question mark in sentence (3) is placed after the end quotation marks because the direct quotation itself *is not a question*.

Note that sentence (2) can be reversed:

(5) "Where are you?" he asked.

- Can you list the rules for the exclamation point used in sentence (4)?

  _____

  _____

- Note that sentence (4) can be reversed:

(6) "Help!" she yelled.

Practice Rewrite these direct quotations, punctuating them correctly.

1. Barbara asked is that your station wagon.

   Rewrite: _Barbara_ _____

2. He screamed I hate spicy foods.

   Rewrite: _____

3. Did Frank make the team he inquired.

   Rewrite: _Did Frank, make "the team he inquir_____

4. Be careful with that mirror she begged the movers.

   Rewrite: _____

5. The truck driver shouted give me a break.

   Rewrite: _____

6. Now you've done it the woman mumbled.

   Rewrite: _____

7. The man thought "how can I leave without being seen?"

   Rewrite: _____

8. The students chanted we want more English courses.

   Rewrite: _____

Chapter Highlights

- **A direct quotation requires quotation marks:**
  Benjamin Franklin said, "There never was a good war or a bad peace."

- **Both parts of a split quotation require quotation marks:**
  "It isn't fair," she argued, "for us to lose the money for the after-school programs."

- **When a direct quotation is split into separate sentences, begin the second sentence with a capital letter:**
  "It's late," he said. "Let's leave in the morning."

- **Always place the period inside the quotation marks:**
  He said, "Sometimes I talk too much."

- **A question mark or exclamation point can be placed before or after the quotation marks, depending on the meaning of the sentence:**
  She asked, "Where were you when we needed you?"
  Did she say, "Joe looks younger without his beard"?

Chapter Review

Proofread this essay for direct and indirect quotations. Punctuate the quotations correctly, and make any other necessary changes above the lines.

Satchel Paige

(1) Some people say that the great pitcher Leroy Paige was called Satchel because of his big feet. (2) Paige himself said I got the nickname as a boy in Mobile before my feet grew. (3) He earned money by carrying bags, called satchels, at the railroad station. (4) I figured out a way to

make more money by carrying several bags at a time on a pole he said. (5) Other boys began shouting at him that he looked like a satchel tree. (6) The name stuck.

(7) Unfortunately, for most of Paige's long pitching career, major league baseball excluded African-American players. (8) However, Satchel Paige pitched impressively in the black leagues and in tours against white teams. (9) In 1934, he won a thirteen-inning, one-to-nothing pitching duel against the white pitcher Dizzy Dean and a team of major league all-stars. (10) My fast ball admitted Dean looks like a change of pace alongside of that little bullet old Satchel shoots up to the plate!

(11) After Jackie Robinson broke the major league color barrier in 1948, Satchel Paige took his windmill windup to the Cleveland Indians. (12) He became the oldest rookie in major league history. (13) Some people said that he was too old, but his record proved them wrong. (14) His plaque in the Baseball Hall of Fame reads he helped pitch the Cleveland Indians to the 1948 pennant.

(15) Satchel Paige pitched off and on until he was sixty years old. (16) When people asked how he stayed young, he gave them his famous rules. (17) Everyone remembers the last one. (18) Don't look back he said. (19) Something might be gaining on you.

UNIT 7

Writing Assignments

Writing Assignment 1: *Write a letter to compliment or to complain.* Write a letter to a manufacturer, a store manager, or a dean praising an especially good product, polite salesperson, or a particularly helpful teacher. Or write a letter complaining about how poorly a product was made, how rudely a salesperson acted, or how unhelpful a teacher was. In your first sentence, state your compliment or complaint. Then describe in detail what happened. Remember, how well your letter is written will contribute to the impression you make; proofread carefully for the correct use of capitals, commas, and apostrophes.

Writing Assignment 2: *Describe a personal discovery.* Have you ever discovered that you are kinder, smarter, or more popular than you thought? Describe one such experience, explaining how and where you found out. Has this new knowledge about yourself changed the way you act toward others or toward yourself? Explain. As you proofread your work, pay special attention to the correct use of capitals, commas, and apostrophes.

Writing Assignment 3: *Explore an anxiety.* Many people find that certain situations make them nervous—for example, giving a speech or organizing a party. In your first sentence, state what upsets you. You might begin, "Whenever I have to _____, I become extremely nervous." Explain why you react this way and how you cope with your nervousness. What advice would you give to others who have similar fears? Proofread carefully for the correct use of capitals, commas, and apostrophes.

Writing Assignment 4: *Apply for a job.* You need to write a letter of application for a job—*not* a résumé. In your first sentence, name the position you are applying for and the company. Then discuss any talents or experience that make you suited for this job. Be specific. Relate your past job experience to this new position. If you have never worked before, discuss any abilities that would apply. Don't brag, but put your best foot forward. Don't hurt your chances by sending a letter with errors. Proofread for the correct use of capitals, commas, and apostrophes.

Writing Assignment 5: *Write a "hello" or "goodbye" letter.* You want to meet someone in your class but feel too shy to speak. So you decide to write a letter to say hello. Or, alas, you must write to someone to end a relationship. Begin by jotting down your feelings. From these jottings, choose the main reasons for wanting to say hello or goodbye. You should refer to specifics—for example, "I like the way you argued with the teacher last week and won!" State your feelings clearly; make the best case you can. Proofread carefully for the correct use of capitals, commas, and apostrophes.

UNIT 7

Review

Proofreading   A. Proofread the following business letter for incorrect or missing capitals, commas, apostrophes, and quotation marks. Correct all errors above the lines. BE CAREFUL: There are errors lurking everywhere.

                                                                          99 somers street

                                                                          Northfield, ohio 44056

                                                                          february 28, 1991

weird walts Discount Store

Main office

akron, Ohio 44313

Dear sir or Madam:

    On february 20 1991 I ordered a Zenith nineteen-inch color television with remote control from your store at 1101, Lakeland avenue medina ohio. The model number is 19K44P. When the delivery man brought the set to my home yesterday, he seemed impatient. He urged me to sign before I had a chance to open the box unpack it or examine the equipment. In fact, he said, "Listen, mister Im leaving now whether you open this box or not. To my dismay I later discovered that the handheld remote control was missing.

    As soon as possible please send me this remote control. I want to use my new zenith properly. For years now I have been a loyal customer of Weird walt's and would appreciate your prompt attention in this matter. thank You.

                                                                            Sincerely your's,

                                                                             Milton rainford

B. Proofread the following essay for incorrect or missing capitals, commas, apostrophes, and quotation marks. Correct the errors above the lines.

The Liberator of South America

(1) One day in 1805 Simón Bolívar made a vow. (2) He vowed that he wouldnt rest until South America was free from spanish oppression. (3) This promise changed his life and Latin American history (4) Bolívar surprisingly enough spent the first twenty-two years of his life as a rich aristocrat. (5) When he died at fifty-seven he was known as the george Washington of south america.

(6) Bolívar was born in caracas, Venezuela on July 24 1783. (7) after he became an orphan at the age of nine his uncle provided him with a tutor Simón Rodriguez (8) A fierce patriot Rodriguez wanted South American's to rule themselves. (9) However young Simón Bolívar was'nt very interested in his tutors ideas about independence. (10) Bolívars uncle sent Simón to europe to help further the young mans education. (11) during his travels in Spain, Bolívar realized that Latin America was destined to be independent of Spain.

(12) Bolívar returned to Venezuela and joined those fighting Spain. (13) His troops were defeated but Bolívar would not admit to failure. (14) In a famous letter that he wrote in 1814, he declared, "the bonds that unite us to Spain have been cut". (15) Finally, the tide turned against Spain. (16) The spaniards were driven out of Colombia Venezuela Ecuador Peru, and Bolivia (17) Bolívar, leader of much of South America wanted to unite the people under one government. (18) His idea may have been a good one yet each area preferred to become a separate nation. (19) Although his plan for a united country failed Bolívar is still remembered as South Americas greatest hero.

UNIT 8

Improving Spelling

Chapter 30

Spelling

PART A   Suggestions for Improving Your Spelling
PART B   Spotting Vowels and Consonants
PART C   Doubling the Final Consonant (in Words of One Syllable)
PART D   Doubling the Final Consonant (in Words of More Than One Syllable)
PART E   Dropping or Keeping the Final *E*
PART F   Changing or Keeping the Final *Y*
PART G   Adding *-S* or *-ES*
PART H   Choosing *IE* or *EI*
PART I   Review
Personal Spelling Lists

PART A   Suggestions for Improving Your Spelling

One important ingredient of good writing is accurate spelling. No matter how interesting your ideas are, your writing will not be effective if your spelling is sloppy.

Tips for Improving Your Spelling

1. Look closely at the words on the page.

2. Use any tricks you can to remember the right spelling: for example, "the *a*'s in *separate* are separated by an *r*," or "*dessert* has two *s*'s because you want two *desserts*."

3. Use a dictionary. Even professional writers frequently check spelling in a dictionary. As you write, underline the words you are not sure of, and look them up when you write your final draft. If locating words in the dictionary is a real problem for you, consider a "poor speller's dictionary." Ask your professor to recommend one.

4. Keep a list of the words you misspell. Look over your list whenever you can, and keep it handy as you write.

5. Look over corrected papers for misspelled words (often marked *sp*). Add these words to your list.

6. Test yourself. Use flash cards or have a friend dictate words from your list or from this chapter.

7. Read through Chapter 31, "Look-alikes/Sound-alikes," for commonly confused words (*their, there,* and *they're,* for instance). The practices in that chapter will help you eliminate some common spelling errors from your writing.

8. Review the basic spelling rules explained in this chapter. Take time to learn the material; don't rush through the entire chapter all at once.

PART B Spotting Vowels and Consonants

To learn some basic spelling rules, you must know the difference between vowels and consonants.

The vowels are *a, e, i, o,* and *u*.

The consonants are *b, c, d, f, g, h, j, k, l, m, n, p, q, r, s, t, v, w, x,* and *z*.

The letter *y* can be either a vowel or a consonant, depending on its sound.

> happy, shy

- In each of these words, *y* is a vowel because it has a vowel sound: an *ee* sound in *happy* and an *i* sound in *shy*.

> young, yawn

- In each of these words, *y* is a consonant because it has the consonant sound of *y*.

Practice Write *V* for vowel or *C* for consonant in the space over each letter. Be careful of the *y*.

Examples:

$\overset{C}{h}\overset{V}{o}\overset{C}{p}\overset{V}{e}\overset{C}{d}$

$\overset{C}{s}\overset{C}{t}\overset{V}{a}\overset{C}{r}$

1. t h e r e
2. r e l y
3. p e r h a p s
4. y a m s

5. i n s t e a d
6. j u m p
7. q u a l i f y
8. h i d d e n

PART C — Doubling the Final Consonant (in Words of One Syllable)

When you add a suffix or ending that begins with a vowel (like *-ed, -ing, -er, -est*) to a word of one syllable, double the final consonant *if* the last three letters of the word are *consonant-vowel-consonant*, or *cvc*.

> mop + ed = mopped
> swim + ing = swimming
> thin + est = thinnest
> burn + er = burner

- *Mop, swim,* and *thin* all end in *cvc*; therefore, the final consonants are doubled.
- *Burn* does not end in *cvc*; therefore, the final consonant is not doubled.

Practice 1   Which of the following words double the final consonant? Check to see whether the word ends in *cvc*. Double the final consonant if necessary, and then add the suffixes *-ed* and *-ing*.

	Word	Last Three Letters	-ed	-ing
Examples:	drop	cvc	dropped	dropping
	boil	vvc	boiled	boiling
1.	plan			
2.	brag			
3.	rip			
4.	sail			
5.	stop			
6.	peel			
7.	fish			
8.	tap			
9.	shift			
10.	skip			
11.	wrap			
12.	bat			
13.	ask			
14.	plug			
15.	can			

Practice 2   Which of the following words double the final consonant? Check for *cvc*. Then add the suffixes *-er* or *-est*.

	Word	Last Three Letters	-er	-est
Examples:	wet	cvc	wetter	wettest
	cool	vvc	cooler	coolest
1.	tall			

2. short _____ _____ _____

3. fat _____ _____ _____

4. slim _____ _____ _____

5. red _____ _____ _____

6. green _____ _____ _____

7. moist _____ _____ _____

8. clean _____ _____ _____

9. dim _____ _____ _____

10. bright _____ _____ _____

PART D — Doubling the Final Consonant (in Words of More Than One Syllable)

When you add a suffix that begins with a vowel to a word of more than one syllable, double the final consonant *if*

(1) the last three letters of the word are *cvc*, and

(2) the accent or stress is on the *last* syllable.

> begin + ing = beginning
>
> patrol + ed = patrolled

- *Begin* and *patrol* both end in *cvc*.
- In both words, the stress is on the last syllable: *be-gin'*, *pa-trol'*. (Pronounce the words aloud, and listen for the correct stress.)
- Therefore, *beginning* and *patrolled* double the final consonant.

> gossip + ing = gossiping
>
> visit + ed = visited

- *Gossip* and *visit* both end in *cvc*.
- However, the stress is *not* on the last syllable: *gos'-sip, vis'-it*.
- Therefore, *gossiping* and *visited* do not double the final consonant.

Practice

Which of the following words double the final consonant? First, check for *cvc*. Then check for the final stress, and add the suffixes *-ed* and *-ing*.

	Word	Last Three Letters	-ed	-ing
Examples:	repel	cvc	repelled	repelling
	enlist	vcc	enlisted	enlisting
1.	occur			
2.	happen			
3.	polish			
4.	admit			
5.	offer			
6.	prefer			
7.	enter			
8.	defend			
9.	travel			
10.	wonder			
11.	respond			
12.	omit			
13.	listen			
14.	commit			
15.	evict			
16.	repeat			
17.	hammer			
18.	pardon			
19.	expel			
20.	answer			

PART E Dropping or Keeping the Final *E*

When you add a suffix that begins with a vowel (like *-able, -ence,* or *-ing*), drop the final *e*.

When you add a suffix that begins with a consonant (like *-less, -ment,* or *-ly*), keep the final *e*.

> write + ing = writing
>
> pure + ity = purity

- *Writing* and *purity* both drop the final *e* because the suffixes *-ing* and *-ity* begin with vowels.

> hope + less = hopeless
>
> advertise + ment = advertisement

- *Hopeless* and *advertisement* keep the final *e* because the suffixes *-less* and *-ment* begin with consonants.

Here are some exceptions to memorize:

argument   manageable
awful   noticeable
courageous   truly
judgment

Practice 1
Add the suffix to each word.

Examples: hope + ing = __hoping__

hope + ful = __hopeful__

1. love + able = _____
2. love + ly = _____
3. time + er = _____
4. time + less = _____
5. pure + ly = _____
6. pure + er = _____
7. complete + ing = _____
8. complete + ness = _____
9. move + ment = _____
10. move + ed = _____
11. arrange + ing = _____
12. arrange + ment = _____

Practice 2   Add the suffix shown to each word.

Examples: come + ing = *coming*

rude + ness = *rudeness*

1. pleasure + able = _____
2. guide + ance = _____
3. manage + ment = _____
4. dense + ity = _____
5. complete + ly = _____
6. shine + ing = _____
7. hate + ful = _____
8. motive + ation = _____
9. relate + ing = _____
10. sincere + ly = _____
11. desire + able = _____
12. argue + ment = _____
13. home + less = _____
14. response + ible = _____
15. divide + ing = _____
16. awe + ful = _____
17. manage + er = _____
18. judge + ment = _____
19. fame + ous = _____
20. grieve + ance = _____

PART F — Changing or Keeping the Final Y

When you add a suffix to a word that ends in -*y*, change the *y* to *i* if the letter before the *y* is a consonant.

Keep the final *y* if the letter before the *y* is a vowel.

> happy + ness = happiness
>
> delay + ed = delayed

- The *y* in *happiness* is changed to *i* because the letter before the *y* is a consonant, *p*.
- However, the *y* in *delayed* is not changed to *i* because the letter before it is a vowel, *a*.

When you add -*ing* to words ending in *y*, always keep the *y*.

> copy + ing = copying
>
> delay + ing = delaying

Here are some exceptions to memorize:

day + ly = daily   pay + ed = paid
lay + ed = laid   say + ed = said

Practice 1 Add the suffix shown to each of the following words.

Examples: marry + ed = __married__

buy + er = __buyer__

1. cry + ed = _____
2. vary + able = _____
3. mercy + ful = _____
4. worry + ing = _____
5. say + ed = _____
6. juicy + er = _____
7. relay + s = _____
8. enjoy + able = _____
9. clumsy + ness = _____
10. wealthy + est = _____
11. day + ly = _____
12. duty + ful = _____
13. stay + ed = _____
14. buy + ing = _____
15. occupy + ed = _____

Practice 2 Add the suffixes in parentheses to each word.

1. pity (ful) _____
   (ed) _____
   (ing) _____
2. beauty (fy) _____
   (ful) _____
   (es) _____
3. lonely (er) _____
   (est) _____
   (ness) _____
4. deny (al) _____
   (ed) _____
   (ing) _____

5. portray (ed) _____   8. study (es) _____

(ing) _____   (ous) _____

(al) _____   (ing) _____

6. fry (ing) _____   9. busy (ness) _____

(er) _____   (er) _____

(ed) _____   (est) _____

7. angry (er) _____   10. try (es) _____

(est) _____   (ed) _____

(ly) _____   (al) _____

PART G — Adding -S or -ES

Nouns usually take an -s or an -es ending to form the plural. Verbs take an -s or -es in the third person singular (*he, she,* or *it*).

Add -es instead of -s if a word ends in *ch, sh, ss, x,* **or** *z* **(the -es adds an extra syllable to the word).**

> clutch + *es* = clutches
>
> miss + *es* = misses
>
> fox + *es* = foxes

Add -es instead of -s for most words that end in *o.*

> do + *es* = does   go + *es* = goes
> echo + *es* = echoes   potato + *es* = potatoes
> hero + *es* = heroes   veto + *es* = vetoes

Here are some exceptions to memorize:

pianos   solos
radios   sopranos

When you change the final *y* **to** *i* **in a word, add -es instead of -s:***

---

*See Part F of this chapter for more on changing or keeping the final *y*.

> fly + *es* = flies
>
> marry + *es* = marries
>
> candy + *es* = candies

Practice Add *-s* or *-es* to the following nouns and verbs.

Examples: sketch _____ sketches _____

echo _____ echoes _____

1. match _____
2. brush _____
3. baby _____
4. tomato _____
5. reply _____
6. dictionary _____
7. automobile _____
8. radio _____
9. stress _____
10. monkey _____
11. company _____
12. carry _____
13. watch _____
14. cemetery _____
15. boss _____
16. tax _____
17. necessity _____
18. buzz _____
19. do _____
20. study _____

PART H   Choosing *IE* or *EI*

Write *i* before *e*, except after *c*, or in any *ay* sound like *neighbor*:

> niece, believe
>
> conceive
>
> weigh

- *Niece* and *believe* are spelled *ie*.
- *Conceive* is spelled *ei* because of the preceding *c*.

- *Weigh* is spelled *ei* because of its *ay* sound.

However, words with a *shen* sound are spelled with an *ie* after the *c*: ancient, conscience, efficient, sufficient.

Here are some exceptions to memorize:

either	seize
foreign	society
height	their
neither	weird

Practice 1 Pronounce each word out loud. Then fill in the blanks with either *ie* or *ei*.

1. f _ _ ld
2. v _ _ n
3. effic _ _ nt
4. w _ _ ght
5. f _ _ rce
6. n _ _ ther
7. rel _ _ ve
8. th _ _ r
9. ch _ _ f
10. soc _ _ ty
11. rec _ _ ve
12. br _ _ f
13. consc _ _ nce
14. gr _ _ f
15. h _ _ ght
16. ach _ _ ve
17. anc _ _ nt
18. _ _ ght
19. for _ _ gn
20. perc _ _ ve

Practice 2 In the following sentences, write either *ie* or *ei* in the blanks.

(1) The story is anc _ _ nt history, but I can't bel _ _ ve how easy it is for parents to rel _ _ ve a child's gr _ _ f. (2) My n _ _ ce Paula was staying with me while her mother and father took a br _ _ f vacation. (3) She was _ _ ght years old and a bundle of energy. (4) All day Saturday, we played baseball in a n _ _ ghbor's f _ _ ld, so we were tired at the end of the afternoon—at least I was! (5) That night there was a f _ _ rce storm. (6) My ch _ _ f fear was that the lights would go out because I knew that Paula was afraid of the dark.

(7) At the h _ _ ght of the storm, I effic _ _ ntly got out a flashlight and candles. (8) That's all Paula needed to see! (9) She immediately burst into worr _ _ d tears. (10) I tr _ _ d to calm her; I cut us each a p _ _ ce of p _ _ . (11) However, n _ _ ther I nor my dog, who climbed into her lap, could console her. (12) Suddenly the phone rang; Paula ran to it and picked up the rec _ _ ver. (13) Her parents were calling, and just hearing th _ _ r voices made her feel much better. (14) Within seconds, she was her cheery, fr _ _ ndly self again. (15) I just stared in amazement.

PART I Review

Practice 1 Test your knowledge of the spelling rules in this chapter by adding suffixes to these words. If you have trouble, reread the part shown in parentheses.

1. fame + ous _____ (Part E)
2. feel + ing _____ (Part C)
3. beach + s/es _____ (Part G)
4. hop + ed _____ (Part C)
5. hope + ing _____ (Part E)
6. study + s/es _____ (Part G)
7. busy + ness _____ (Part F)
8. manage + ment _____ (Part E)
9. radio + s/es _____ (Part G)
10. occur + ed _____ (Part D)
11. carry+ing _____ (Part F)
12. hero + s/es _____ (Part G)
13. admit + ing _____ (Part D)

14. test + er _____ (Part C)

15. tasty + est _____ (Part F)

16. bat + ing _____ (Part C)

17. believe + able _____ (Part E)

18. commit + ment _____ (Part D)

19. deny + al _____ (Part F)

20. day + ly _____ (Part F)

Practice 2 Circle the correctly spelled word in each pair.

1. achievement, acheivement
2. writting, writing
3. begining, beginning
4. breif, brief
5. zeroes, zeros
6. niether, neither
7. resourceful, resourcful
8. admiration, admireation
9. carries, carrys
10. thier, their

Practice 3 Write the correctly spelled word in each blank.

As the two _____ _____ into the church,
      (family + s/es)   (file + ed)

the bride _____ _____ to herself. She wore the
        (hum + ed)   (happy + ly)

_____, _____ gown _____. On
(white + est)   (lacy + est)   (imagine + able)

her feet were blue _____ shoes, for she valued comfort. In
                   (jog + ing)

the next room, the _____ groom _____ his foot
                   (nerve + ous)   (tap + ed)

and _____ gum. He _____ he would feel
    (pop + ed)   (bel _ _ ved)

_____ as soon as the _____ march sounded.
(rel _ _ f)   (wed + ing)

Chapter Highlights

- **Double the final consonant in one-syllable words that end in *cvc*:**
  hop/hopped, swim/swimming

- **Double the final consonant in words of more than one syllable if they end in *cvc* and if the stress is on the last syllable:**
  begin/beginning, prefer/preferred

- **Keep the final *e* when adding a suffix that begins with a consonant:**
  hope/hopeful, time/timely

- **Drop the final *e* when adding a suffix that begins with a vowel:**
  hope/hoping, time/timer

- **Keep the final *y* when adding a suffix if the letter before the *y* is a vowel:**
  buy/buying, delay/delayed

- **Change the *y* to *i* when adding a suffix if the letter before the *y* is a consonant:**
  happy/happiest, pity/pitiful

- **Add *-es* to words that end in *ch*, *sh*, *ss*, *x*, *z*, and to most words that end in *o*. Add *-es* when you change a final *y* to *i*:**
  bench/benches, box/boxes, hero/heroes, carry/carries

- **Write *i* before *e*, except after *c*, or in any *ay* sound like *neighbor*:**
  believe, niece, *but* receive, weigh

- **Remember that there are exceptions to all of these rules. Check a dictionary whenever you are uncertain.**

Chapter Review

Proofread this essay for spelling errors. Correct the errors above the lines.

The Discovery of Penicillin

(1) Penicillin was discovered almost by accident. (2) During World War I, Alexander Fleming, a Scottish scientist, was working without succes on the problem of infected wounds. (3) The antiseptics used then to cleanse wounds probaly did more harm than good. (4) They killed germs

but ocassionally harmed the pateint. (5) Despite his hard work, Fleming made little progress.

(6) In 1928, however, his luck changed. (7) He returned to his laboratory after a vacation. (8) At first he was disapointed to find that some of his bacteria samples were spoiled. (9) One of the spoiled cultures had a noticable mold on it. (10) To his supprise, the mold had killed all the bacteria! (11) He named the bacteria-killing mold penicillin.

(12) This might have truely been the begining of the age of miracle drugs if Fleming had not stoped his research. (13) Fortunatly, Howard Florey and Ernst Chaim siezed the opportunity to perfect the drug. (14) For thier discoverys, Fleming, Florey, and Chaim were awarded the Nobel Prize for medicine in 1945. (15) Penicillin saved many lives in World War II and has gone on saveing them ever since.

Personal Spelling Lists

Commonly Misspelled Words

For your convenience as you write, there is a list of often-misspelled words on the last page of this book opposite the back cover. Please turn to that list now, noting that the *trouble spot*, the part of each word that is usually spelled incorrectly, has been italicized.

To help learn these words, you might copy each one twice, making sure to underline the trouble spot, or copy the words on flash cards and have someone test you.

Personal Spelling List

Keep a list of words that *you* misspell. Add words to your list from corrected papers and from the exercises in this chapter. First, copy each word as you misspelled it, underlining the trouble spot; then write the word correctly. Use the following form. Study your list often.

As I Wrote It **Correct Spelling**

1. _____ _____
2. _____ _____
3. _____ _____
4. _____ _____
5. _____ _____
6. _____ _____
7. _____ _____
8. _____ _____
9. _____ _____
10. _____ _____
11. _____ _____
12. _____ _____
13. _____ _____
14. _____ _____
15. _____ _____
16. _____ _____
17. _____ _____
18. _____ _____
19. _____ _____
20. _____ _____
21. _____ _____
22. _____ _____
23. _____ _____
24. _____ _____
25. _____ _____

Chapter 31

Look-alikes/Sound-alikes

A/An/And

A is used before a word beginning with a consonant or a consonant sound.

> (1) *a* man
>
> (2) *a* house
>
> (3) *a* union (the *u* in *union* is pronounced like the consonant *y*)

An is used before a word beginning with a vowel (*a, e, i, o, u*) or a silent *h*.

> (4) *an* igloo
>
> (5) *an* apple
>
> (6) *an* hour (the *h* in *hour* is silent)

And joins words or ideas together.

> (7) Edward *and* Ralph are taking the same biology class.
>
> (8) He is very honest, *and* most people respect him.

Practice 1 Fill in *a*, *an*, or *and*.

Example: Choosing __a__ career is __an__ important step for __a__ college student.

1. Don Miller has used each summer vacation to try out __a__ different career choice.

2. Last summer, he worked in __a__ law office.

3. He filled in for __an__ administrative assistant on leave.

4. He found the work __an__ the atmosphere very stimulating.

5. In fact, he had never liked __a__ job so much.

6. Because Don was eager to learn, __a__ young lawyer let him proofread some important documents.

7. The lawyer was impressed by how carefully Don worked __an__ suggested that Don consider __a__ law career.

8. Don returned to school in the fall __an__ spent time researching his new career.

9. He talked to his adviser about becoming _____ paralegal.

10. _____ paralegal investigates the facts of cases, prepares documents, _____ does other background work for lawyers.

11. His adviser could see that Don had both _____ interest in law _____ the ability to succeed.

12. With his adviser's help, Don found _____ course of study to prepare for his career.

13. Next summer, he hopes to work for _____ public interest law firm _____ to learn about environmental law.

14. He is happy to have found _____ worthwhile career _____ looks forward to the future.

394 Unit 8 Improving Spelling

Practice 2 Write two sentences using *a*, two using *an*, and two using *and*.

1. _____
2. _____
3. _____
4. _____
5. _____
6. _____

Accept/Except

Accept means "to receive."

> (1) Please *accept* my apologies.
>
> (2) I *accepted* his offer of help.

Except means "other than" or "excluding."

> (3) Everyone *except* Ron thinks it's a good idea.

Practice 1 Fill in *accept* or *except*.

1. Did Steve *accept* the collect call from his brother?
2. Every road *except* that one leads to Milwaukee.
3. Mr. Francis will *accept* the package in the mailroom.
4. Did Meg *accept* Ron's explanation?
5. Helping customers find the right tie makes me feel useful, *except* when they don't like anything in the store.
6. *Accept* for Cynthia, the whole family is vacationing in North Carolina.
7. The athlete proudly _____ his award.

8. The tornado left every building standing, _____ for the barn.

9. _____ for Jean, we all had tickets for the movie.

10. My science professor agreed to _____ my late lab report.

Practice 2 Write two sentences using *accept* and two using *except*.

1. _____
2. _____
3. _____
4. _____

Been/Being

Been is the past participle form of *to be*. *Been* is usually used after the helping verb *have*, *has*, or *had*.

(1) I *have been* to that restaurant before.

(2) She *has been* in Akron for ten years.

- *Being* is the *-ing* form of *to be*. *Being* is usually used after the helping verbs *is*, *are*, *am*, *was*, and *were*.

(3) They *are being* helped by the salesperson.

(4) Rhonda *is being* courageous and independent.

Practice 1 Fill in *been* or *being*.

1. Shirley has *been* very quiet all evening.
2. We have *been* to Mexico three times.
3. What good films are *being* shown on television tonight?
4. This building is *being* turned into a homeless shelter.
5. I haven't *been* in such a good mood for a week.

6. A sea monster has _____ spotted in Scotland.

7. Manuel thinks he is _____ funny when he dances with the dog.

8. Is the battery _____ changed right now?

9. Has Roberta _____ asleep on the sofa all night?

10. His last offer has _____ on my mind all day.

11. Which elevator is _____ inspected now?

12. Because you are _____ honest with me, I admit that I have _____ seeing someone else.

Practice 2 Write two sentences using *been* and two using *being*.

1. _____

2. _____

3. _____

4. _____

Buy/By

Buy means "to purchase."

> (1) She *buys* new furniture every five years.

By means "near," "before," or "by means of."

> (2) He walked right *by* and didn't say hello.
>
> (3) *By* sunset, we had finished the harvest.
>
> (4) We prefer traveling *by* bus.

Practice 1 Fill in *buy* or *by*.

1. Where did you *buy* that CD?

2. Pat trudged through the storm to *buy* a Sunday paper.

3. These quilted potholders were made _____ hand.

4. He stood _____ the cash register and waited his turn to _____ a cheeseburger.

5. _____ next month, you should have finished all the chemistry experiments in the book.

6. Sean hopes to finish painting the studio _____ Friday.

7. We don't need to _____ any more Christmas decorations.

8. The red convertible _____ the corner is mine.

9. She finds it hard to walk _____ a bookstore without going in to browse.

10. It's expensive to _____ imported cheeses.

11. I need a two-week vacation _____ the ocean.

12. Please answer this letter _____ October 10.

Practice 2   Write two sentences using *buy* and two using *by*.

1. _____

2. _____

3. _____

4. _____

Fine/Find

Fine means "good" or "well." It can also mean "a penalty."

(1) He wrote a *fine* analysis of the short story.

(2) She paid a $10 *fine*.

Find means "to locate."

(3) I can't *find* my red suspenders.

Practice 1 Fill in *fine* or *find*.

1. You will have to pay a ___fine___ if you drive without a seat belt.

2. As soon as we _____ your lost suitcase, we'll send it to you.

3. How did you manage to _____ strawberries in December?

4. Can you _____ time to help post these notices?

5. Harold made a _____ impression on the assistant buyer.

6. If you lost the key, you will have to _____ it, or else we will have to climb in through the window.

7. Bears eat honey whenever they can ___find___ it.

8. It's _____ weather for handball.

9. When Maria _____ a new job, she will resign from her old one.

10. Although she can _____ the flaws in other people's characters, she has trouble spotting flaws in her own.

Practice 2 Write two sentences using *fine* and two using *find*.

1. _____
2. _____
3. _____
4. _____

It's/Its

It's is a contraction of *it is* or *it has*. If you cannot substitute *it is* or *it has* in the sentence, you cannot use *it's*.

> (1) *It's* a ten-minute walk to my house.
> (2) *It's* been a nice party.

Its is a possessive and shows ownership.

> (3) The bear cub rolled playfully on *its* side.
>
> (4) Industry must do *its* share to curb inflation.

Practice 1   Fill in *it's* or *its*.

1. If _____ sunny, we'll rent a rowboat.

2. The government is doing _____ best to mail tax refunds early.

3. _____ been hard for him to accept the fact that he can no longer play ball.

4. _____ been years since Evelyn used a manual typewriter.

5. I can't open this window because _____ been nailed shut.

6. "Everything in _____ place" was my grandmother's motto.

7. If _____ a good idea, I'm all for it.

8. The kitten used _____ paws to pull the ball from under the stove.

9. _____ a boy!

10. _____ a chocolate cake with your social security number in pink frosting.

11. The sales force thinks _____ been a successful first year.

12. The *Daily News* reporter was lucky because the jury reached _____ verdict just before her deadline.

13. _____ a sure thing! Gladys Robertson will win the election.

14. _____ amazing how devious Ray is.

15. My family is at _____ best when there is work to be done.

Practice 2 Write three sentences using *it's* and three using *its*.

1. _____
2. _____
3. _____
4. _____
5. _____
6. _____

Know/Knew/No/New

Know means "to have knowledge or understanding." *Knew* is the past tense of the verb *to know*.

> (1) Carl *knows* he has to finish by 6 p.m.
>
> (2) The police officer *knew* the quickest route to the pier.

No is a negative.

> (3) He is *no* longer dean of academic affairs.

New means "fresh" or "recent."

> (4) I like your *new* belt.

Practice 1 Fill in *know, knew, no,* or *new*.

1. We need a _____ slogan to keep people involved.

2. I wish I _____ where he found that _____ waterproof briefcase.

3. Tim has _____ time to repair the garage door.

4. She didn't _____ the lid was loose.

5. I _____ I need to find _____ jokes because no one laughs when I tell my old ones.

6. Because she _____ the answer, she won a pool table and two hundred dish towels.

7. Sorry, there is _____ room in the auditorium for latecomers.

8. Have you seen the _____ automated teller machines?

9. Because you really _____ the _____ material, why don't you take the final early?

10. Charlene thinks there's _____ way we can do it, but I _____ we'll be speaking Italian by June.

11. He didn't _____ whether they went to San Francisco or San Diego.

12. Rosalyn _____ that she would win the fifty-yard freestyle.

13. We have _____ way of knowing how well you scored on the civil service examination.

14. Do you _____ how many people are in the waiting room?

15. I wish I _____ then what I _____ now.

Practice 2 Write two sentences using *know*, two using *knew*, two using *no*, and two using *new*.

1. _____
2. _____
3. _____
4. _____
5. _____
6. _____
7. _____
8. _____

Lose/Loose

Lose means "to misplace" or "not to win."

> (1) Be careful not to *lose* your way on those back roads.
>
> (2) George hates to *lose* at cards.

Loose means "ill fitting" or "too large."

> (3) That's not my size; it's *loose* on me.

Practice 1 Fill in *lose* or *loose*.

1. Those shoes were so _Loose_ that he walked right out of them.

2. When the children _Lose_ a volleyball game, they become extremely irritable.

3. Because the plug is _____ in the socket, the television keeps blinking on and off.

4. If Irene doesn't tighten that _____ hubcap, she will _____ it.

5. Emily had nothing to _____, so she called the manager and asked for an interview.

6. We may _____ the battle, but we'll win the war.

7. I like wearing _____ clothing in the summer.

8. Before finals, I always _____ my appetite.

9. This belt is too _____.

10. I'm surprised you didn't _____ those _____ quarters.

Practice 2 Write two sentences using *lose* and two using *loose*.

1. _____

2. _____

3. _____

4. _____

Mine/Mind

Mine is a possessive and shows ownership.

> (1) This is your umbrella, but where is *mine*?

Mind means "intelligence." It can also be a verb meaning "to object" or "to pay attention to."

> (2) What's on your *mind*?
>
> (3) I don't *mind* if you come late.

Practice 1 Fill in *mine* or *mind*.

1. _____ is the one with the polka dots.

2. Will Doris _____ if Roger joins us?

3. Sherlock put his _____ to work and solved the mystery.

4. Her road test is tomorrow; _____ was yesterday.

5. I really _____ when you crack your knuckles in church.

6. As I read that novel, my _____ was filled with images of ancient Greece.

7. My _____ is made up! I'm going to ask for a raise.

8. Don't interrupt him; he really _____ when someone breaks his train of thought.

9. Don't _____ him; he always snores in public.

10. Camping out in the woods wasn't his idea; it was _____.

Practice 2 Write two sentences using *mine* and two using *mind*.

1. _____

2. _____

3. _____

4. _____

Past/Passed

Past is that which has already occurred; it is over with.

> (1) His *past* work has been satisfactory.
>
> (2) Never let the *past* interfere with your hopes for the future.

Passed is the past tense of the verb *to pass*.

> (3) She *passed* by and nodded hello.
>
> (4) The wild geese *passed* overhead.

Practice 1 Fill in *past* or *passed*.

1. He asked for the butter, but I absentmindedly _____ him the mayonnaise.

2. Forget about failures in the _____, and look forward to success in the future.

3. Yesterday Ruth _____ the West Virginia bar exam.

4. I have _____ this same corner every Saturday morning for a year.

5. I am sure we _____ through this town an hour ago.

6. In the _____, Frieda and Rose used to talk on the phone once a week.

7. Is your _____ catching up with you?

8. We couldn't resist a glance as we _____ the bakery.

9. In the _____, people were friendlier than they are now.

10. The gray limo _____ us doing eighty.

Practice 2 Write two sentences using *past* and two using *passed*.

1. _____
2. _____
3. _____
4. _____

Quiet/Quit/Quite

Quiet means "silent, still."

> (1) The woods are *quiet* tonight.

Quit means "to give up" or "to stop doing something."

> (2) Last year, I *quit* smoking.

Quite means "very" or "exactly."

> (3) He was *quite* tired after playing handball for two hours.
>
> (4) That's not *quite* right.

Practice 1 Fill in *quiet*, *quit*, or *quite*.

1. I love a _____ evening at home.
2. She is _____ a good dentist.
3. I can't concentrate when my apartment is too _____.
4. They _____ their jobs when they didn't get raises.
5. Minding children can be _____ tiring.
6. Please be _____; I'm trying to listen to the news.
7. Don't _____ now; you're almost finished!
8. If she _____ now, she will jeopardize her vacation pay.
9. Dwight asked the crew to be absolutely _____ while the magicians performed.

10. City people are surprised by the _____ nights in the country.

11. That is not _____ what I meant.

12. She _____ pushing when people in the line began to stare at her.

Practice 2 Write two sentences using *quiet*, two using *quit*, and two using *quite*.

1. _____

2. _____

3. _____

4. _____

5. _____

6. _____

Rise/Raise

Rise means "to get up by one's own power." The past tense of *rise* is *rose*. The past participle of *rise* is *risen*.

> (1) The sun *rises* at 6 a.m.
>
> (2) Daniel *rose* early yesterday.
>
> (3) He *has risen* from the table.

Raise means "to lift an object" or "to grow or increase." The past tense of *raise* is *raised*. The past participle of *raise* is *raised*.

> (4) *Raise* your right hand.
>
> (5) She *raised* the banner over her head.
>
> (6) We have *raised* $1,000.

Practice 1 Fill in *rise* or *raise*.

1. When the moon _____, we'll be able to see the path better.
2. Farmers in Vermont don't _____ as many dairy cows as they once did.
3. During the meeting, she _____ the possibility of a strike.
4. She _____ at 6 a.m. to begin her daily three-mile jog.
5. The jet _____ off the runway and roared into the clouds.
6. At noon yesterday, Fred _____ the flag.
7. The butcher _____ his prices again.
8. Don't _____ your voice.
9. He couldn't _____ from his chair because of the chewing gum stuck to his pants.
10. She _____ an eyebrow to signal that she would continue bidding for the antique vase.
11. He _____ to his feet and shuffled out the door.
12. The loaves of homemade bread have _____.
13. A flock of birds _____ out of the salt marsh.
14. Can you _____ that picture an inch or two?
15. To do this dance step, _____ your left foot and hop on your right.

Practice 2 Write two sentences using some form of *rise* and two using some form of *raise*.

1. _____
2. _____
3. _____
4. _____

Sit/Set

Sit means "to seat oneself." The past tense of *sit* is *sat*. The past participle of *sit* is *sat*.

> (1) *Sit* up straight!
>
> (2) He *sat* down on the porch and fell asleep.
>
> (3) She has *sat* reading that book all day.

Set means "to place" or "to put something down." The past tense of *set* is *set*. The past participle of *set* is *set*.

> (4) Don't *set* your books on the dining room table.
>
> (5) She *set* the package down and walked off without it.
>
> (6) He had *set* the pot on the stove.

Practice 1   Fill in *sit* or *set*.

1. Marcy _____ her glasses on the seat next to her.

2. Antique stores do not allow browsers to _____ on the expensive furniture.

3. Tyrone likes to _____ in a recliner.

4. _____ the cans of paint in the corner.

5. I would have _____ in the front row, but the sign said "Reserved."

6. Please _____ that box of clothes by the door.

7. Walk across the stage, and _____ the vase on the table.

8. We usually _____ in the bleachers.

9. I would have _____ your bracelet on the counter, but I was afraid someone might walk off with it.

10. _____ down, and let me _____ this Hawaiian feast before you!

Practice 2 Write two sentences using some form of *sit* and two using *set*.

1. _____

2. _____

3. _____

4. _____

Suppose/Supposed

Suppose means "to assume" or "to guess." The past tense of *suppose* is *supposed*. The past participle of *suppose* is *supposed*.

> (1) Brad *supposes* that the teacher will give him an A.
>
> (2) We all *supposed* she would win first prize.
>
> (3) I had *supposed* Dan would win.

- *Supposed* means "ought" or "should"; it is followed by *to*.

> (4) He is *supposed to* meet us after class.
>
> (5) You were *supposed to* wash and wax the car.

REMEMBER: When you mean *ought* or *should*, always use the *-ed* ending—*supposed*.

Practice 1 Fill in *suppose* or *supposed*.

1. How do you _____ he will get himself out of this mess?

2. You were _____ to buy your ticket at the box office.

3. My father-in-law was _____ to arrive last night.

4. I _____ I'll find my car keys in my other pants.

5. Everett is _____ to meet her after work.

6. Why do you _____ that cereal is so expensive?

7. You are not _____ to open presents until Christmas.

8. Diane was _____ to check the bus schedule.

9. What do you _____ we saw on Buford Road?

10. What are we _____ to do with these 3-by-5-inch cards?

11. I _____ I could help you move your television set.

12. Mindy _____ that the factory would reopen in the fall.

Practice 2 Write two sentences using *suppose* and two using *supposed to*.

1. _____

2. _____

3. _____

4. _____

Their/There/They're

Their is a possessive pronoun and shows ownership.

---

(1) They couldn't find *their* wigs.

(2) *Their* children are charming.

There indicates a direction.

---

(3) I wouldn't go *there* again.

(4) Put the lumber down *there*.

There is also a way of introducing a thought.

---

(5) *There* is a fly in my soup.

(6) *There* are two ways to approach this problem.

They're is a contraction: *they* + *are* = *they're*. If you cannot substitute *they are* in the sentence, you cannot use *they're*.

---

(7) *They're* the best poems I have read in a long time.

(8) If *they're* coming, count me in.

Practice 1 Fill in *their*, *there*, or *they're*.

1. If you move over _____, I can get everyone into the picture.
2. _____ are three suspicious people selling gold watches on the corner.
3. If _____ here, we can set out the food.
4. Please hang your coats over _____.
5. My uncle and aunt always helped _____ children with _____ homework.
6. _____ apartment faces a courtyard.
7. _____ preparing for a hot, sticky summer.
8. Is _____ a faster route to Topeka?
9. _____ never on time when it comes to paying _____ phone bills.
10. _____ products contain no sugar and no preservatives.
11. _____ here to discuss raises and health insurance.
12. Is _____ a wrench in the toolbox?
13. _____ sorry now that they didn't take _____ exams on time.
14. _____ bananas, I guess, but why are they purple?
15. Is _____ a good reason for Mr. Spence's strange behavior?

Practice 2 Write two sentences using *their*, two using *there*, and two using *they're*.

1. _____
2. _____
3. _____
4. _____
5. _____
6. _____

Then/Than

Then means "next" or "at that time."

> (1) First, we went to the theater, and *then* we went for pizza.
>
> (2) I was a heavyweight boxer *then*.

Than is used in a comparison.

> (3) She is a better student *than* I.

Practice 1 Fill in *then* or *than*.

1. Carlos is older ~~than~~ Maria, but he isn't as mature.
2. San Francisco has colder winters ~~than~~ San Diego.
3. She seems easier to talk to ~~then~~ her brother.
4. First, separate the eggs, _____ mix the batter, and finally, grease the pan.
5. Thinking you are better _____ everyone else can get you into trouble.
6. Get your first paycheck, and _____ think about moving into your own apartment.
7. If you receive straight A's this semester, will you _____ apply for a scholarship?
8. If I'm taller _____ Roslyn and Roslyn is taller _____ Herb, then I must be taller _____ Herb.
9. You asked me a question and _____ interrupted me before I could answer.
10. It appears, _____, that we will have to hire three new computer programmers.
11. It's harder to rollerblade _____ to swim.
12. Now I'm ready for marriage; _____ I was confused.
13. This automobile uses less gas _____ any other V-6 on the road.

14. She plans to join the army and _____ learn electronics.

15. Bill was more pessimistic _____ _____ he is now.

Practice 2 Write two sentences using *then* and two using *than*.

1. _____

2. _____

3. _____

4. _____

Thought/Taught

Thought is the past tense of the verb *to think*. It can also mean "an idea."

(1) She *thought* it was an interesting idea.

(2) Now that's a strange *thought!*

Taught is the past tense of the verb *to teach*.

(3) Last summer, Ned *taught* his daughters how to swim.

(4) She once *taught* mathematics at Stanford Community College.

Practice 1 Fill in *thought* or *taught*.

1. Nora _____ me to play the guitar.

2. I _____ about the company's offer but decided to refuse it and wait for a better one.

3. Perry _____ that he could make extra money driving a cab.

4. The judge _____ that she would be reelected.

5. Francine _____ learning-disabled children to read.

6. Charlie _____ he could always borrow anything he needed.

7. What a fascinating _____!

8. Who _____ you how to balance your checkbook?

9. When she _____ about next summer, Louisa promised herself that she would learn to relax.

10. Mr. Gold _____ carpentry for three years before he opened his own shop.

Practice 2 Write three sentences using *thought* and three using *taught*.

1. _____
2. _____
3. _____
4. _____
5. _____
6. _____

Threw/Through

Threw is the past tense of the verb *to throw*.

> (1) Charleen *threw* the ball into the bleachers.

Through means "in one side and out the other" or "finished."

> (2) He burst *through* the front door laughing.
>
> (3) If you are *through* eating, we can leave.

Practice 1 Fill in *threw* or *through*.

1. Whenever Conrad was happy, he _____ his hat in the air.

2. I went _____ my notes, but I couldn't find any reference to Guatemala.

3. He _____ the pillow on the floor and plopped down in front of the TV.

4. Gail _____ her raincoat over her head and ran out into the storm.

5. We finally got _____ the crowd and found our seats.

6. He _____ the broken toy into the trash can.

7. You go _____ that door to get to the editor's office.

8. Are you _____ talking to those detectives?

9. I am not sure why he _____ the towel over the mirror.

10. I can see _____ the window although it's frosted.

11. Even when Andrea _____ the Frisbee right to me, I couldn't catch it.

12. It took Beverly over an hour to go _____ airport security.

Practice 2 Write two sentences using *threw* and two using *through*.

1. _____
2. _____
3. _____
4. _____

To/Too/Two

To means "toward."

> (1) We are going *to* the stadium.

To can also be combined with a verb to form an infinitive.

> (2) Where do you want *to go* for lunch?

Too means "also" or "very."

> (3) Roberto is going to the theater *too*.
> (4) They were *too* bored to stay awake.

Two is the number 2.

> (5) Ms. Palmer will teach *two* new accounting courses this term.

Practice 1 Fill in *to*, *too*, or *two*.

1. If you want _____ enroll in college this fall, you will need _____ letters of recommendation.

2. This humid weather is _____ much for my French poodle.

3. It will be _____ awkward _____ leave the dinner before dessert is served.

4. They selected _____ volumes on ecology.

5. Algebra may be _____ advanced for me this semester.

6. She _____ has a birthday in June.

7. By mistake, I bought _____ left-handed gloves.

8. It's _____ early _____ leave for the football game.

9. No one is _____ old to learn.

10. They went _____ see Judge Granger about a marriage license.

11. The _____ students worked all night preparing for the debate.

12. On the express bus, there were _____ many people in the front and _____ few in the back.

13. Are they filing for a tax refund _____?

14. After _____ weeks in space, the astronauts were homesick.

15. Albert wants _____ become a nurse.

16. Even the students admitted that the test was _____ easy.

17. Jimmy and I have _____ build the drawers by Friday if we want _____ stain the chest on Monday.

18. _____ whom did you give my credit card?

19. The salesperson took out a thick catalog _____ show me.

20. If there were _____ more people with us, we could move _____ a larger table.

21. She plans _____ trade in her motorcycle.

22. It's _____ much trouble to make my own salad dressing.

23. She _____ likes _____ watch professional wrestling.

24. There are only _____ weeks left until we leave for vacation.

25. We saw _____ undercover agents talking quietly _____ the bartender.

Practice 2 Write three sentences using *to*, three using *too*, and three using *two*.

1. _____
2. _____
3. _____
4. _____
5. _____
6. _____
7. _____
8. _____
9. _____

Use/Used

Use means "to make use of." The past tense of *use* is *used*. The past participle of *use* is *used*.

> (1) Why do you *use* green ink?
> (2) He *used* the wrong paint in the bathroom.
> (3) I have *used* that brand of toothpaste myself.

Used means "in the habit of" or "accustomed"; it is followed by *to*.

> (4) I am not *used to* getting up at 4 a.m.
>
> (5) They got *used to* the good life.

REMEMBER: When you mean *in the habit of* or *accustomed*, always use the *-ed* ending—*used*.

Practice 1 Fill in *use* or *used*.

1. Terry is _____ to long bus rides.
2. It may take a few days to get _____ to this high altitude.
3. May I _____ your portable television tonight?
4. Don't _____ aspirin for allergies.
5. He _____ the wrong key and damaged the lock.
6. Vera hopes to get _____ to her grumpy father-in-law.
7. Please _____ the main entrance on Globe Avenue.
8. Carlotta and Roland still _____ the laundromat on the corner.
9. We _____ the self-service pump; it was cheaper.
10. Marguerite _____ my telephone every time she visits.
11. _____ your head!
12. He _____ a dictaphone because he cannot take shorthand.
13. Never _____ big words to try to impress people.
14. If we _____ any more water before it rains, the well may run dry.
15. Some people find it hard to get _____ to success.

Practice 2 Write two sentences using *use* and two using *used to*.

1. _____
2. _____

3. _____

4. _____

Weather/Whether

Weather refers to atmospheric conditions.

> (1) In June, the *weather* in Spain is lovely.

Whether implies a question.

> (2) *Whether* or not you pass is up to you.

Practice 1 Fill in *weather* or *whether*.

1. Rainy *weather* makes me lazy.

2. Be sure to tell the employment agency *whether* or not you plan to take the job.

3. This March _____ is so unpredictable!

4. You never know _____ Celia will be happy or sad.

5. I don't know _____ to go to the bank or to Ruby's house first.

6. Norman wasn't sure _____ or not his boss would let him use the copier after 5 p.m.

7. Good _____ always brings joggers to the park.

8. The real estate agent must know by 10 a.m. _____ or not you intend to rent the house.

9. I wonder _____ we have time to go shopping before the stores close.

10. We're going to the beach _____ or not the _____ cooperates.

Practice 2   Write two sentences using *weather* and two using *whether*.

1. _____

2. _____

3. _____

4. _____

Where/Were/We're

Where implies place or location.

> (1) *Where* have you been all day?
>
> (2) Home is *where* you hang your hat.

Were is the past tense of *are*.

> (3) We *were* on our way when the hurricane hit.

We're is a contraction: *we* + *are* = *we're*. If you cannot substitute *we are* in the sentence, you cannot use *we're*.

> (4) *We're* going to leave now.
>
> (5) Because *we're* in the city, let's go to the zoo.

Practice 1   Fill in *where*, *were*, or *we're*.

1. The desk was scratched, but _____ not sure who did it.

2. _____ did you put the tape measure?

3. Ted and Gloria _____ childhood sweethearts.

4. If _____ such a good team, why do we always lose?

5. When you _____ at your aunt's house, _____ did your cat stay?

6. My convertible is not _____ I left it.

7. The librarians _____ very helpful in showing us

   _____ things _____.

8. Alaska and Hawaii _____ granted statehood in 1959.

9. Let's go to New Orleans, _____ we can sample some Cajun cooking.

10. When _____ the storm windows installed?

11. The clouds _____ blocking the sun in exactly the spot

    _____ we _____ sitting.

12. Our children want a story every night, but sometimes _____ too tired to read them one.

13. Where _____ your sisters born?

14. Everyone needs a little hideaway, a place _____ he or she can be absolutely alone.

15. _____ not sure _____ the motel is.

Practice 2 Write three sentences using *where*, three using *were*, and three using *we're*.

1. _____
2. _____
3. _____
4. _____
5. _____
6. _____
7. _____
8. _____
9. _____

Whose/Who's

Whose implies ownership and possession.

> (1) *Whose* term paper is that?

Who's is a contraction of *who is* or *who has*. If you cannot substitute *who is* or *who has*, you cannot use *who's*.

> (2) *Who's* knocking at the window?
>
> (3) *Who's* seen my new felt hat with the green bows?

Practice 1   Fill in *whose* or *who's*.

1. _____ going to see the play tonight?

2. Terry is someone _____ instincts I trust.

3. _____ tapping on the window?

4. We found a puppy in the vacant lot, but we don't know _____ it is.

5. _____ been eating my porridge?

6. _____ car is double-parked by the barbershop?

7. He's a physician _____ diagnosis can be trusted.

8. Grace admires the late Marian Anderson, _____ singing always moved her.

9. I'm not sure _____ coming and _____ not.

10. _____ going to try the mambo with me?

Practice 2 Write two sentences using *whose* and two using *who's*.

1. _____
2. _____
3. _____
4. _____

Your/You're

Your is a possessive and shows ownership.

> (1) *Your* knowledge is astonishing!

You're is a contraction: *you* + *are* = *you're*. If you cannot substitute *you are* in the sentence, you cannot use *you're*.

> (2) *You're* the nicest person I know.

Practice 1 Fill in *your* or *you're*.

1. Where is _____ bottle opener?
2. If _____ pregnant, don't smoke!
3. Does _____ daughter like her new school?
4. I hope _____ children haven't forgotten Father's Day.
5. Since _____ driving north, would you drop me at the mall?
6. If _____ in a rush, we can mail _____ scarves to you.
7. _____ foreman was just transferred.

8. Please keep _____ Saint Bernard out of my rose garden.

9. Is that _____ rain hat or Shelley's?

10. When _____ optimistic about life, everything seems to go right.

11. I see _____ point.

12. The supervisor thinks that _____ due for a promotion and a big raise.

13. The audience enjoyed _____ rendition of "St. Louis Blues."

14. Although _____ not sure about all the rules of grammar, _____ paper shows that you have a flair for writing.

15. Please send me _____ résumé today.

Practice 2 Write three sentences using *your* and three using *you're*.

1. _____

2. _____

3. _____

4. _____

5. _____

6. _____

Chapter Highlights

Some words look and sound alike. Below are a few of them:

- **it's/its**

    It's the neatest room I ever saw.
    Everything is in *its* place.

- **their/they're/there**

    They found *their* work easy.
    They're the best actors I have ever seen.
    Put the lumber down *there*.

- **then/than**

    I was a heavyweight boxer *then*.
    He is a better cook *than* I.

- **to/too/two**

    We are going *to* the stadium.
    No one is *too* old to learn.
    I bought *two* hats yesterday.

- **whose/who's**

    Whose Italian dictionary is this?
    I'm not sure *who's* leaving early.

- **your/you're**

    Is *your* aunt the famous mystery writer?
    You're due for a promotion and a big raise.

Chapter Review

Proofread this essay for look-alike/sound-alike errors. Make your corrections above the lines.

The Olympic Games

(1) Although the Olympic games are almost three thousand years old, scholars now of an athlete who was and Olympic champion in 776 B.C.

(2) Coroebus was his name. (3) He won the two-hundred-yard footrace,

the only event in the Olympics at that time.   (4) Buy the fourteenth Olympic games, in 720 B.C., knew events, including boxing and discus throwing, had been added.   (5) At these early games, women weren't allowed to set in the stadium as spectators.   (6) A woman who broke this law could loose her life.   (7) Eventually, women were excepted as spectators and even as participants.   (8) After the decline of ancient Greece, the games were abolished.   (9) Although the last games were held in the fourth century A.D., the idea of the Olympic games was not dead.

(10) In 1896, the first modern Olympic games where held in Athens, Greece.   (11) Of all the events, the marathon attracted the most attention. (12) The marathon was suppose to represent the ancient games. (13) Actually, it commemorates a real event.   (14) In 490 B.C., the Greeks defeated the Persians at the Battle of Marathon.   (15) Legend says that Pheidippides, a professional runner, ran to Athens, told of the victory, an fell to the ground dead.   (16) Weather or not the legend is true, the marathon has being the major attraction of the modern Olympic games.

(17) At the first modern games, the Greek spectators were unhappy. (18) By the last day of the games, none of there athletes had won an event.   (19) Their were twenty-five runners in the final event, the marathon.   (20) One of the runners was an Greek shepherd who's name was Spiridon Louis.   (21) He was use to running great distances, and he taught about winning the marathon and bringing glory to Greece. (22) For the first part of the race, a Frenchman led.   (23) Than runners began dropping out from exhaustion, and Louis past many of them.

(24) About seven kilometers from the Olympic stadium, Louis took the lead. (25) When word reached the stadium, the Greek crowd went wild. (26) Louis entered the stadium to they're cheers. (27) The second- and third-place winners were Greeks to. (28) Spiridon Louis excepted his honors quitely and modestly. (29) He returned to his life as a shepherd, but he left his mark on the Greek language. (30) The expression *egine Louis,* which means "became Louis," also means "ran quickly."

UNIT 8

Writing Assignments

Writing Assignment 1: *Define being a success.* Everybody wants to be a success, but success means different things to different people. For you, does success mean earning a lot of money, raising a happy family, finishing school, or something else? In your first sentence, define what success means to you: "Success means _____." Then explain how you plan to achieve this success. Do your plans include a special person, further education, or even a particular attitude toward life? Proofread for spelling.

Writing Assignment 2: *Discuss giving and getting advice.* We all give advice to and get advice from others. Sometimes that advice can have a great impact. Have you received advice that changed your life? Were you advised to return to school, marry, or change careers? Did you give advice to others that changed their lives? Begin by jotting or freewriting as many details as you can remember. In your first sentence, explain who advised whom to do what. What happened? What were the consequences of the advice? End with advice to others about giving or receiving advice. Proofread for spelling.

Writing Assignment 3: *Post a notice.* You are a member of a community action committee. For this year's project, the committee will collect clothing for the homeless, hold a bake sale to earn money to fix up a local park, or be involved in some other worthwhile cause. Write a notice that first describes the project and then asks people to participate. Try to be clear, specific, and catchy; your goal is to convince as many people as possible to give clothing, attend your bake sale, or whatever. Your notice will be posted on bulletin boards all over town. Proofread for spelling.

Writing Assignment 4: *Review a movie.* Your college newspaper has asked you to review a movie. Pick a popular film that you especially liked or disliked. Brainstorm, freewrite, or cluster for reasons that you would or would not recommend this film to others. Then in your first sentence, name the film, and state whether or not you recommend it. Explain your evaluation by discussing two or three specific reasons for your reactions to the picture. Describe as much of the film as you need to to make your point, but do not retell the plot. Proofread for spelling.

Writing Assignment 5: *Recall an important experience.* Have you ever had a serious illness or an accident that changed your attitude toward yourself, others, or life in general? Begin by stating what you learned—for example, "When I was sixteen years old, a broken ankle taught me the meaning of friendship." Then explain exactly what happened and why you changed. Proofread for spelling.

UNIT 8

Review

Proofreading We have changed the following composition so that it contains a number of spelling and look-alike/sound-alike errors. First, underline any misspelled words. Then write each correctly spelled word above the line.

Grow Youre Own Houseplants

(1) Every February, I begin turning seeds and pits into lovly houseplants. (2) Buy Easter, I have small citrus, mango, and avocado trees, which I give away too my nieghbors and friends. (3) You two can start plants that will grow beautyfully from seeds, pits, and parts of fruits or vegetables that you normaly throw in the garbage.

(4) To grow a mango tree, for example, first scrub the mango pit. (5) Once the pit is washed and dryed, trim the long hair on it. (6) Than use a small knife to open the pit and remove the seed, which looks like a large bean. (7) Put this seed into to inchs of poting soil, put another half-inch of soil over it, and add water. (8) Let the container drain, put it inside a clear plastic bag, an then close the bag with a twist tie. (9) Finaly, sit the bag in a warm place, but not in direct sunlight.

(10) Wait untill the first leaves begin to show. (11) Then remove the plastic bag, and place the young plant in bright shade or sunlight. (12) When its' about three inches tall, you can start pincheing back the newest leaves. (13) Pinching every branch like this will produce extra branchs, makeing your tree bushy.

429

(14) You will not acheive sucess with garbage seeds and pits 100 percent of the time. (15) Some store-bought fruits and vegetables have been exposed too chemicals to keep them from sprouting, and some are just too old for they're seeds to sprout. (16) If the process dosen't work the first time, just keep tring until it does. (17) You will not be dissappointed as long as you don't quite.

IRIS PROTINICK, STUDENT

Appendix

Parts of Speech Review

A knowledge of basic grammar terms will make your study of English easier. Throughout this book, these key terms are explained as needed and are accompanied by ample practice. For your convenience and reference, below is a short review of the eight parts of speech.

Nouns

Nouns are the names of persons, places, things, animals, activities, and ideas.*

> Persons: Ms. Caulfield, Mike, secretaries
> Places: Puerto Rico, Vermont, gas station
> Things: sandwich, Sears, eyelash
> Animals: whale, ants, Lassie
> Activities: running, discussion, tennis
> Ideas: freedom, intelligence, humor

Pronouns

Pronouns replace or refer to nouns or other pronouns. The word that a pronoun replaces is called its *antecedent*.**

> My partner succeeded; *she* built a better mousetrap!
> These computers are amazing; *they* alphabetize and index.
> Everyone should do *his* or *her* best.
> All students should do *their* best.

---

*For more work on nouns, see Chapter 18.
**For more work on pronouns, see Chapter 19.

Pronouns take different forms, depending on how they are used in a sentence. They can be the subjects of sentences (*I, you, he, she, it, we, they*) or the objects of verbs and prepositions (*me, you, him, her, it, us, them*). They also can show possession (*my, mine, your, yours, his, her, hers, its, our, ours, their, theirs*).

Subject:	*You* had better finish on time.
	Did *someone* leave a red jacket?
Object of verb:	Robert saw *her* on Thursday.
Object of preposition:	That VCR is for *her*.
Possessive:	Did Tom leave *his* sweater on the dresser?

Verbs

Verbs can be either action verbs or linking verbs. Verbs can be single words or groups of words.*

Action verbs show what action the subject of the sentence performs.

> Sonia *bought* a French dictionary.
>
> Jack *has opened* the letter.

Linking verbs link the subject of a sentence with a descriptive word or words. Common linking verbs are *be, act, appear, become, feel, get, look, seem, smell, sound,* and *taste*.

> This report *seems* well organized and complete.
>
> You *have been* quiet this morning.

The *present participle* of a verb is its *-ing* form. The present participle can be combined with some form of the verb *to be* to create the progressive tenses, or it can be used as an adjective or a noun.

Pat *was waiting* for the report.	(*past progressive tense*)
The *waiting* taxis lined up at the curb.	(*adjective*)
Waiting for trains bores me.	(*noun*)

The *past participle* of a verb can be combined with helping verbs to create different tenses, it can be combined with forms of *to be* to create the passive voice, or it can be used as an adjective. Past participles regularly end in *-d* or *-ed*, but irregular verbs take other forms (*seen, known, taken*).

---

*For more work on verbs, see Unit 3.

> He *has edited* many articles for us. (*present perfect tense*)
> This report *was edited* by the committee. (*passive voice*)
> The *edited* report reads well. (*adjective*)

Every verb can be written as an *infinitive: to* plus the *simple form* of the verb.

> She was surprised *to meet* him at the bus stop.

Adjectives

Adjectives describe or modify nouns or pronouns. Adjectives can precede or follow the words they describe.*

> *Several green* chairs arrived today.
> Gordon Lake is *dangerous* and *deep*.

Adverbs

Adverbs describe or modify verbs, adjectives, or other adverbs.**

> Anita reads *carefully*. (*adverb describes verb*)
> She is *extremely* tired. (*adverb describes adjective*)
> He wants a promotion *very* badly. (*adverb describes adverb*)

Prepositions

A preposition begins a *prepositional phrase*. A prepositional phrase contains a preposition (a word such as *at, in, of,* or *with*), its object (a noun or pronoun), and any adjectives modifying the object.†

Preposition	Object
after	*work*
on	the blue *table*
under	the broken *stairs*

---

*For more work on adjectives, see Chapter 20.
**For more work on adverbs, see Chapter 20.
†For more work on prepositions, see Chapter 21.

Conjunctions

Conjunctions are connector words.

Coordinating conjunctions (*and, but, for, nor, or, so, yet*) join two equal words or groups of words.*

> James is quiet *but* sharp.
>
> Ms. Chin *and* Mr. Warburton attended the Ice Capades.
>
> He typed the report, *and* Ms. Helfman mailed it special delivery.
>
> She will go to Norfolk Community College, *but* she will also continue working at the department store.

Subordinating conjunctions (*after, because, if, since, unless,* and so on) join an independent idea with a dependent idea.

> *Whenever* Ken comes to visit, he takes the family out to dinner.
>
> I haven't been sleeping well *because* I've been drinking too much coffee.

Interjections

Interjections are words such as *ouch* and *hooray* that express strong feeling. They are rarely used in formal writing.

If the interjection is the entire sentence, it is followed by an exclamation point. If the interjection is attached to a sentence, it is followed by a comma.**

> *Hey!* You left your wallet in the phone booth.
>
> *Oh,* she forgot to send in her tax return.

REMEMBER: The same word may be used as a different part of speech.

> Harry *thought* about the problem. (*verb*)
>
> Your *thought* is a good one. (*noun*)

---

*For more work on conjunctions, see Chapters 11 and 12.
**For more work on sentences, see Chapter 25.

UNIT 9

Reading Selections and Quotation Bank

Unit 9 contains three parts:

- *Effective Reading: Strategies for the Writer*
  This introduction to the readings section gives tips on how to get the most out of your reading.

- *The Readings*
  Here you will find eighteen readings on a range of interesting subjects. Discussion questions and writing assignments follow each reading.

- *Quotation Bank*
  This section contains seventy-five brief quotations for you to read and enjoy, be inspired by, and use in your writing.

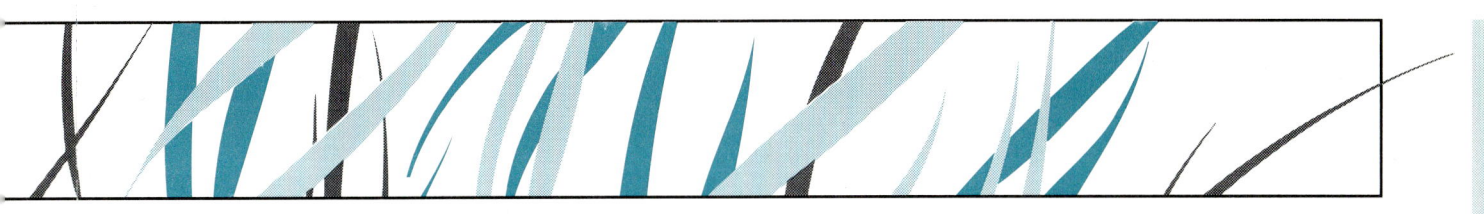

Reading Selections

Effective Reading: Strategies for the Writer

We hope that the reading selections that follow will interest you and make you think. Many deal with issues you face at college, at work, or at home. Your instructor may ask you to read a selection and be prepared to discuss it in class or to write a composition or journal entry about it. The more carefully you read these selections, the better you will be able to think, talk, and write about them. Below are seven strategies that can help you become a more careful and effective reader.

1. **Underline important ideas.** It is easy to forget what you have read, even though you have recently read it. Underlining or highlighting what you consider the main ideas will help you later—when you review the essay—to remember what you have read. Some students number the main points in order to understand the development of the author's ideas.

2. **Write your reactions in the margins.** If you strongly agree or disagree with an idea, write "yes" or "no" next to it. Record other questions and comments also, as if you were having a conversation with the author. Writing assignments will often ask you to respond to a particular idea or situation in a selection. Having already noted your reactions in the margins will help you focus your thinking and your writing.

3. **Prepare questions.** You will occasionally come across material that you cannot follow. Reread the passage. If rereading and further thinking do not help, place a question mark in the margin to remind you to ask a classmate or the instructor for an explanation.

4. **Circle unfamiliar words.** If you come across an unfamiliar word that makes it difficult to follow the sense of what the author is saying, look up the word immediately, write the definition in the margin, and continue reading. If, however, you are able to get a general sense of what the word means from

context—how it fits into the meaning of the sentence—do not break your reading "stride" to consult a dictionary. Circle it, and look it up when you have finished reading the entire selection.

5. **Note effective or powerful writing.** If a particular line strikes you as especially important or moving, underline or highlight it. You may wish later to quote it in your written assignment. Be selective, however, in what you mark. *Too much* annotation can turn a selection into a mass—or mess—of underlinings, circles, and highlighting. An overly annotated essay can make it hard to focus on what is important when the selection is discussed in class or when you write about it.

6. **Vary your pace.** Some selections can be read quickly because you already know a great deal about the subject or because you find the material simple and direct. Other selections may require you to read slowly, practically pausing between each sentence. Guard against the tendency to skim when the going gets tough; more difficult material will usually reward your extra time and attention.

7. **Reread.** If you expect to discuss or write about a particular selection, one reading is usually not enough. Budget your time so you will be able to give it a second or third reading. You will be amazed at how much more you can get from the selection as you reread. You may understand ideas that were unclear the first time around. In addition, you may notice significant new points and details; perhaps you will change your mind concerning ideas you originally agreed or disagreed with. These benefits of rereading will help you to discuss and write about the selection more intelligently. They will also increase your reading enjoyment.

The following essay has been marked by a student. Your own responses to this essay would, of course, be different. Examining how this essay was annotated may help you to annotate other selections in this book and to read more effectively in your other courses.

Women Are Missing from Newspaper Pages

Ellen Goodman

Take last week's papers out of the pile in the corner of the kitchen. Check the (bylines) Check the photos. How many boys, how many girls?

[Annotation: Why does Goodman use the terms "boys" and "girls" here?]

[Annotation: bylines = a line identifying author of an article]

Now put the papers back in the recycle bin, or in the bird cage, or in the kindling box. Wherever. Compare your tabulation with the fourth annual report just released by the Women, Men and Media Project at the University of Southern California.

The folks there surveyed the front page and the local front page of 20 newspapers for the month of February. They came to the unsurprising and unhappy conclusion that women—52 percent of the population—show up just 13 percent of the time in the prime news spots. Lest you think that this is just a reflection of reality, even the stories about breast implants quoted men more often than women.

The names in the stories

Women's names appear *on* the stories more often than *in* the stories. Even so, two-thirds of the bylines on front pages were male and three-quarters of the opinions on op-ed pages were by men. To complete this, uh, picture, less than a third of the photographs on front pages feature women.

This small statistical reminder comes just in time for the American Society of Newspaper Editors' [ASNE] annual convention. In Washington this week, editors will be talking about America and the World, economics and politics, readers and nonreaders. Which brings them back to gender.

One of the less heralded facts of declining newspaper readership in the 1990s is the emergence of a gender gap among people under 35 years old. Young women are seven to nine points less likely to be daily newspaper readers than men.

It would be nice to blame this on the infamous time crunch in young women's lives. Nice to find yet another reason for men to lift the double burden: Share housework, save a newspaper. But full-time working women are more loyal newspaper readers than women who are part-time workers or homemakers.

It turns out that women across the board are more likely than men to feel that the paper doesn't speak to them. Or about them. As Nancy Woodhull, a founding editor of *USA Today* who now runs her own consulting firm, says, "Women around the country really notice when the press doesn't report their existence. It's like walking into a room where nobody knows you're there. If you have choices, you don't go into that room anymore."

The search for a welcome sign to hang on the newspaper door has brought up the question of "women's pages." Back in the 1960s, these pages were the ghetto to which women, children, food, home, and family were restricted. In the crest of the women's movement, many of us in the business embarked on a movement to integrate the whole paper.

What happened was a kind of premature equality. The old women's pages became more or less "unisex." Lifestyle sections wrote about and to women and men. But the rest of the paper remained nearly as lopsided as ever (see Page One [of your newspaper]). The result has been a net loss in the news about women.

Going backward or back to the future

Now there is a lively debate about whether to bring back women's pages. Is that going backward or back to the future? Is that admitting defeat in the struggle to get women's concerns into the rest of the paper or is it some unabashed recognition that women retain separate interests?

Experiments abound and so do opinions. Some women worry that a marketing move to target female readers will inevitably "dumb down" and talk down to them. Others believe that these pages can create a strong forum for a woman's different voice. And still others wonder if you can win the women who are drifting away without offending the loyal female readers who write in to ask, Why is the story about Hillary Clinton in the Lifestyle section?

As someone who has been around this argument for a couple of decades, I have no problem with experiments in re-creating a woman's "place" in the paper IF—here comes the big if— the place doesn't become a ghetto again. And IF it doesn't take the pressure off changing the rest of the paper.

Men and women are more alike in their news interests than they are different. Moreover, the surveys on "difference" that I have seen suggest that what women really want are stories that go deep, that focus on matters close to their lives, that are less about institutional politics than about how institutions affect people. They want to read about families, relationships, health, safety, jobs, learning, the environment. That's a pretty good guide for any gender and any editor's story list.

News decisions rest with the editors and the number of women editors is even smaller than the number of women on the front pages (see masthead). The female membership of ASNE is at an all-time high: 9.7 percent.

masthead = place in a newspaper or mag. where staff is listed

So, if newspapers want to make women feel welcome, begin the way a reader begins. Start with Page One. And keep counting.

A Homemade Education

Malcolm X

Sometimes a book can change a person's life. In this selection, Malcolm X, the influential and controversial black leader who was assassinated in 1965, describes how, while he was in prison, a dictionary set him free.

It was because of my letters that I happened to stumble upon starting to acquire some kind of a homemade education.

I became increasingly frustrated at not being able to express what I wanted to convey in letters that I wrote, especially those to Mr. Elijah Muhammad.[1] In the street, I had been the most articulate hustler out there—I had commanded attention when I said something. But now, trying to write simple English, I not only wasn't articulate, I wasn't even functional. How would I sound writing in slang, the way I would *say* it, something such as, "Look, daddy, let me pull your coat about a cat. Elijah Muhammad—"

Many who today hear me somewhere in person, or on television, or those who read something I've said, will think I went to school far beyond the eighth grade. This impression is due entirely to my prison studies.

It had really begun back in the Charlestown Prison, when Bimbi first made me feel envy of his stock of knowledge. Bimbi had always taken charge of any conversation he was in, and I had tried to emulate[2] him. But every book I picked up had few sentences which

---

1. Elijah Muhammed: founder of the Muslim sect Nation of Islam
2. emulate: copy

didn't contain anywhere from one to nearly all of the words that might as well have been in Chinese. When I just skipped those words, of course, I really ended up with little idea of what the book said. So I had come to the Norfolk Prison Colony still going through only book-reading motions. Pretty soon, I would have quit even these motions, unless I had received the motivation that I did.

I saw that the best thing I could do was get hold of a dictionary—to study, to learn some words. I was lucky enough to reason also that I should try to improve my penmanship. It was sad. I couldn't even write in a straight line. It was both ideas together that moved me to request a dictionary along with some tablets and pencils from the Norfolk Prison Colony school.

> "I saw that the best thing I could do was get hold of a dictionary—to study, to learn some words."

I spent two days just riffling[3] uncertainly through the dictionary's pages. I'd never realized so many words existed! I didn't know *which*

---
3. riffling: thumbing through

words I needed to learn. Finally, just to start some kind of action, I began copying.

In my slow, painstaking, ragged handwriting, I copied into my tablet everything printed on that first page, down to the punctuation marks.

I believe it took me a day. Then, aloud, I read back, to myself, everything I'd written on the tablet. Over and over, aloud, to myself, I read my own handwriting.

I woke up the next morning, thinking about those words— immensely proud to realize that not only had I written so much at one time, but I'd written words that I never knew were in the world. Moreover, with a little effort, I also could remember what many of these words meant. I reviewed the words whose meanings I didn't remember. Funny thing, from the dictionary first page right now, that "aardvark" springs to my mind. The dictionary had a picture of it, a long-tailed, long-eared burrowing African mammal, which lives off termites caught by sticking out its tongue as an anteater does for ants.

I was so fascinated that I went on—I copied the dictionary's next page. And the same experience came when I studied that. With every succeeding page, I also learned of people and places and events from history. Actually the dictionary is like a miniature encyclopedia. Finally, the dictionary's A section had filled a whole tablet—and I went on into the B's. That was the way I started copying what eventually became the entire dictionary. It went a lot faster after so much practice helped me pick up handwriting speed. Between what I wrote in my tablet, and writing letters, during the rest of my time in prison I would guess I wrote a million words.

I suppose it was inevitable that as my word-base broadened, I could for the first time pick up a book and read and now begin to understand what the book was saying. Anyone who has read a great deal can imagine the new world that opened. Let me tell you something: from then until I left that prison, in every free moment I had, if I was not reading in the library, I was reading on my bunk. You couldn't have gotten me out of books with a wedge. Between Mr. Muhammad's teachings, my correspondence, my visitors—usually Ella and Reginald—and my reading of books, months passed without my even thinking about being imprisoned. In fact, up to then, I never had been so truly free in my life.

Discussion and Writing Questions

1. Malcolm X says that in the streets he had been the "most articulate hustler" of all, but that in writing English he "not only wasn't articulate, [he] wasn't even functional" (paragraph 2). What does he mean?

2. What motivated Malcolm X to start copying the dictionary? What benefits did he gain from doing this?

3. What does Malcolm X mean when he says that until he went to prison, he "never had been so truly free in [his] life" (paragraph 11)?

4. Have you seen the 1992 film *Malcolm X*? Do you think the film's prison scenes show how strongly Malcolm X was changed by improving his writing skills?

Writing Assignments

1. Did you ever notice a difference between your speaking skills and your writing skills? Write about a time when you needed or wanted to write something important but felt that your writing skills were not up to the task. What happened?

2. Malcolm X's inner life changed completely because of the dictionary he copied. Write about a time when a book, a story, a person, or an experience changed your life.

3. Choose three entries on a dictionary page and copy them. Then describe your experience. What did you learn? Can you imagine copying the entire dictionary? How do you feel about what Malcolm X accomplished? Where do you think he got the motivation to finish the task?

Mrs. Flowers

Maya Angelou

Maya Angelou (born Marguerite Johnson) is widely known today as the poet who read her work at President Clinton's inauguration and as the author of *I Know Why the Caged Bird Sings.* In this book, her life story, she tells of being raped when she was eight years old. Her response to the traumatic experience was to stop speaking. In this selection Angelou describes the woman who eventually "threw her a life line."

For nearly a year, I sopped around the house, the Store, the school and the church, like an old biscuit, dirty and inedible. Then I met, or rather got to know, the lady who threw me my first life line.

Mrs. Bertha Flowers was the aristocrat of Black Stamps. She had the grace of control to appear warm in the coldest weather, and on the Arkansas summer days it seemed she had a private breeze which swirled around, cooling her. She was thin without the taut[1] look of wiry people, and her printed voile[2] dresses and flowered hats were as right for her as denim overalls for a farmer. She was our side's answer to the richest white woman in town.

---

1. taut: tight, tense
2. voile: a light, semi-sheer fabric

3 Her skin was a rich black that would have peeled like a plum if snagged, but then no one would have thought of getting close enough to Mrs. Flowers to ruffle her dress, let along snag her skin. She didn't encourage familiarity. She wore gloves too.

4 I don't think I ever saw Mrs. Flowers laugh, but she smiled often. A slow widening of her thin black lips to show even, small white teeth, then the slow effortless closing. When she chose to smile on me, I always wanted to thank her. The action was so graceful and inclusively benign.[3]

5 She was one of the few gentlewomen I have ever known, and has remained throughout my life the measure of what a human being can be. . . .

6 One summer afternoon, sweet-milk fresh in my memory, she stopped at the Store to buy provisions. Another Negro woman of her health and age would have been expected to carry the paper sacks home in one hand but Momma said, "Sister Flowers, I'll send Bailey up to your house with these things."

7 She smiled that slow dragging smile, "Thank you, Mrs. Henderson. I'd prefer Marguerite, though." My name was beautiful when she said it. "I've been meaning to talk to her, anyway." They gave each other age-group looks.

8 Momma said, "Well, that's all right then. Sister, go and change your dress. You going to Sister Flowers's." . . .

9 There was a little path beside the rocky road, and Mrs. Flowers walked in front swinging her arms and picking her way over the stones.

10 She said, without turning her head, to me, "I hear you're doing very good school work, Marguerite, but that it's all written. The teachers report that they have trouble getting you to talk in class." We passed the triangular farm on our left and the path widened to allow us to walk together. I hung back in the separate unasked and unanswerable questions.

11 "Come and walk along with me, Marguerite." I couldn't have refused even if I wanted to. She pronounced my name so nicely. Or more correctly, she spoke each word with such clarity that I was certain a foreigner who didn't understand English could have understood her.

12 "Now no one is going to make you talk—possibly no one can. But bear in mind, language is man's way of communicating with his fellow man and it is language alone which separates him from the lower animals." That was a totally new idea to me, and I would need time to think about it.

13 "Your grandmother says you read a lot. Every chance you get. That's good, but not good enough. Words mean more than what is set down on paper. It takes the human voice to infuse[4] them with the shades of deeper meaning."

14 I memorized the part about the human voice infusing words. It seemed so valid and poetic.

15 She said she was going to give me some books and that I not only must read them, I must read them aloud. She suggested that I try to make a sentence sound in as many different ways as possible.

---

3. benign: kind, gentle
4. infuse: to fill or penetrate

"I'll accept no excuse if you return a book to me that has been badly handled." My imagination boggled at the punishment I would deserve if in fact I did abuse a book of Mrs. Flowers's. Death would be too kind and brief.

The odors in the house surprised me. Somehow I had never connected Mrs. Flowers with food or eating or any other common experience of common people. There must have been an outhouse, too, but my mind never recorded it.

The sweet scent of vanilla had met us as she opened the door.

"I made tea cookies this morning. You see, I had planned to invite you for cookies and lemonade so we could have this little chat. The lemonade is in the icebox."

It followed that Mrs. Flowers would have ice on an ordinary day, when most families in our town bought ice late on Saturdays only a few times during the summer to be used in the wooden ice-cream freezers.

She took the bags from me and disappeared through the kitchen door. I looked around the room that I had never in my wildest fantasies imagined I would see. Browned photographs leered or threatened from the walls and the white, freshly done curtains pushed against themselves and against the wind. I wanted to gobble up the room entire and take it to Bailey, who would help me analyze and enjoy it.

"Have a seat, Marguerite. Over there by the table." She carried a platter covered with a tea towel. Although she warned that she hadn't tried her hand at baking sweets for some time, I was certain that like everything else about her the cookies would be perfect.

They were flat round wafers, slightly browned on the edges and butter-yellow in the center. With the cold lemonade they were sufficient for childhood's lifelong diet. Remembering my manners, I took nice little lady-like bites off the edges. She said she had made them expressly for me and that she had a few in the kitchen that I could take home to my brother. So I jammed one whole cake in my mouth and the rough crumbs scratched the insides of my jaws, and if I hadn't had to swallow, it would have been a dream come true.

As I ate she began the first of what we later called "my lessons in living." She said that I must always be intolerant of ignorance but understanding of illiteracy. That some people, unable to go to school, were more educated and even more intelligent than college professors. She encouraged me to listen carefully to what country people called mother wit. That in those homely sayings was couched the collective[5] wisdom of generations.

When I finished the cookies she brushed off the table and brought a thick, small book from the bookcase. I had read *A Tale of Two Cities* and found it up to my standards as a romantic novel. She opened the first page and I heard poetry for the first time in my life.

> "I was liked, and what a difference it made. I was respected not as Mrs. Henderson's grandchild or Bailey's sister but for just being Marguerite Johnson."

---

5. collective: gathered from a group

"It was the best of times and the worst of times . . ." Her voice slid in and curved down through and over the words. She was nearly singing. I wanted to look at the pages. Were they the same that I had read? Or were there notes, music, lined on the pages, as in a hymn book? Her sounds began cascading[6] gently. I knew from listening to a thousand preachers that she was nearing the end of her reading, and I hadn't really heard, heard to understand, a single word.

"How do you like that?"

It occurred to me that she expected a response. The sweet vanilla flavor was still on my tongue and her reading was a wonder in my ears. I had to speak.

I said, "Yes, ma'am." It was the least I could do, but it was the most also.

"There's one more thing. Take this book of poems and memorize one for me. Next time you pay me a visit, I want you to recite."

I have tried often to search behind the sophistication of years for the enchantment I so easily found in those gifts. The essence escapes but its aura[7] remains. To be allowed, no, invited, into the private lives of strangers, and to share their joys and fears, was a chance to exchange the Southern bitter wormwood[8] for . . . a hot cup of tea and milk with Oliver Twist.[9]

I was liked, and what a difference it made. I was respected not as Mrs. Henderson's grandchild or Bailey's sister but for just being Marguerite Johnson.

Childhood's logic never asks to be proved (all conclusions are absolute). I didn't question why Mrs. Flowers had singled me out for attention, nor did it occur to me that Momma might have asked her to give me a little talking to. All I cared about was that she had made tea cookies for *me* and read to *me* from her favorite book. It was enough to prove that she liked me.

Discussion and Writing Questions

1. Angelou vividly describes Mrs. Flowers' appearance and style (paragraphs 2–5). What kind of woman is Mrs. Flowers? What words and details convey this impression?

2. What strategies does Mrs. Flowers use to reach out to Marguerite?

3. What does Marguerite's first "lesson in living" include (paragraph 24)? Do you think such a lesson could really help a young person live better or differently?

4. In paragraph 31, the author speaks of her enchantment at receiving gifts from Mrs. Flowers. Just what gifts did Mrs. Flowers give her? Which do you consider the most important gift?

---

6. cascading: falling like a waterfall
7. aura: a special quality or air around something or someone
8. wormwood: something harsh or embittering
9. Oliver Twist: a character from a novel by Charles Dickens

Writing Assignments

1. Has anyone ever "thrown you a life line" when you were in trouble? Describe the problem or hurt facing you and just what this person did to reach out. What "gifts" did he or she offer you (attention, advice, and so forth)? Were you able to receive them?

    If you prefer, write about a time when you helped someone else. What seemed to be weighing this person down? How were you able to help?

2. Mrs. Flowers read aloud so musically that Marguerite "heard poetry for the first time in my life." Has someone ever shared a love—of music, gardening, or history, for example—so strongly that you were changed? What happened and how were you changed?

3. Many people have trouble speaking up—in class, at social gatherings, even to one other person. Can you express your thoughts and feelings as freely as you would like in most situations? What opens you up, and what shuts you up?

Papa, the Teacher

Leo Buscaglia

Leo Buscaglia was the youngest of four children of Italian immigrants. In this selection, he describes how a father with only a fifth-grade education taught his children to respect—and even love—learning.

Papa had natural wisdom. He wasn't educated in the formal sense. When he was growing up at the turn of the century in a very small village in rural northern Italy, education was for the rich. Papa was the son of a dirt-poor farmer. He used to tell us that he never remembered a single day of his life when he wasn't working. The concept of doing nothing was never a part of his life. In fact, he couldn't fathom[1] it. How could one do nothing?

He was taken from school when he was in the fifth grade, over the protestations[2] of his teacher and the village priest, both of whom saw him as a young person with great potential for formal learning. Papa went to work in a factory in a nearby village, the very same village where, years later, he met Mama.

For Papa, the world became his school. He was interested in everything. He read all the books, magazines, and newspapers he could lay his hands on. He loved to gather with people and listen to the town elders and learn about "the world beyond" this tiny,

---

1. fathom: understand; get to the bottom of
2. protestations: objections

insular[3] region that was home to generations of Buscaglias before him. Papa's great respect for learning and his sense of wonder about the outside world were carried across the sea with him and later passed on to his family. He was determined that none of his children would be denied an education if he could help it.

Papa believed that the greatest sin of which we were capable was to go to bed at night as ignorant as we had been when we awakened that day. This credo[4] was repeated so often that none of us could fail to be affected by it. "There is so much to learn," he'd remind us. "Though we're born stupid, only the stupid remain that way." To ensure that none of his children ever fell into the trap of complacency,[5] he insisted that we learn at least one new thing each day. He felt that there could be no fact too insignificant, that each bit of learning made us more of a person and insured us against boredom and stagnation.

> "The greatest sin . . . was to go to bed at night as ignorant as we had been when we awakened that day."

So Papa devised a ritual. Since dinnertime was family time and everyone came to dinner unless they were dying of malaria, it seemed the perfect forum for sharing what new things we had learned that day. Of course, as children we thought this was perfectly crazy. There was no doubt, when we compared such paternal[6] concerns with other children's fathers, Papa was weird.

It would never have occurred to us to deny Papa a request. So when my brother and sisters and I congregated in the bathroom to clean up for dinner, the inevitable question was, "What did *you* learn today?" If the answer was "Nothing," we didn't dare sit at the table without first finding a fact in our much-used encyclopedia. "The population of Nepal is . . . ," etc.

Now, thoroughly clean and armed with our fact for the day, we were ready for dinner. I can still see the table piled high with mountains of food. So large were the mounds of pasta that as a boy I was often unable to see my sister sitting across from me. (The pungent[7] aromas were such that, over a half century later, even in memory they cause me to salivate.)

Dinner was a noisy time of clattering dishes and endless activity. It was also a time to review the activities of the day. Our animated conversations were always conducted in Piedmontese dialect[8] since Mama didn't speak English. The events we recounted, no matter how insignificant, were never taken lightly. Mama and Papa always listened carefully and were ready with some comment, often profound and analytical, always right to the point.

---

3. insular: like an island; isolated
4. credo: a statement of belief
5. complacency: a feeling of satisfaction or smugness
6. paternal: having to do with fathers
7. pungent: sharp, spicy
8. Piedmontese dialect: the language spoken in the Piedmont region of northwestern Italy

"That was the smart thing to do." "*Stupido*, how could you be so dumb?" "*Così sia*,[9] you deserved it." "*E allora*,[10] no one is perfect." "*Testa dura* ('hardhead'), you should have known better. Didn't we teach you anything?" "Oh, that's nice." One dialogue ended and immediately another began. Silent moments were rare at our table.

Then came the grand finale to every meal, the moment we dreaded most—the time to share the day's new learning. The mental imprint of those sessions still runs before me like a familiar film clip, vital and vivid.

Papa, at the head of the table, would push his chair back slightly, a gesture that signified the end of the eating and suggested that there would be a new activity. He would pour a small glass of red wine, light up a thin, potent Italian cigar, inhale deeply, exhale, then take stock of his family.

For some reason this always had a slightly unsettling effect on us as we stared back at Papa, waiting for him to say something. Every so often he would explain why he did this. He told us that if he didn't take time to look at us, we would soon be grown and he would have missed us. So he'd stare at us, one after the other.

Finally, his attention would settle upon one of us. "*Felice*,"[11] he would say to me, "tell me what you learned today."

"I learned that the population of Nepal is . . ."

Silence.

It always amazed me, and reinforced my belief that Papa was a little crazy, that nothing I ever said was considered too trivial for him. First, he'd think about what was said as if the salvation of the world depended upon it.

"The population of Nepal. Hmmm. Well."

He would then look down the table at Mama, who would be ritualistically fixing her favorite fruit in a bit of leftover wine. "Mama, did you know that?"

Mama's responses were always astonishing and seemed to lighten the otherwise reverential atmosphere. "Nepal," she'd say. "Nepal? Not only don't I know the population of Nepal, I don't know where in God's world it is!" Of course, this was only playing into Papa's hands.

"*Felice*," he'd say. "Get the atlas so we can show Mama where Nepal is." And the search began. The whole family went on a search for Nepal. This same experience was repeated until each family member had a turn. No dinner at our house ever ended without our having been enlightened by at least a half dozen such facts.

As children, we thought very little about these educational wonders and even less about how we were being enriched. We couldn't have cared less. We were too impatient to have dinner end so we could join our less-educated friends in a rip-roaring game of kick the can.

---

9. *Così sia*: Italian for "so be it"
10. *E allora*: Italian for "oh, well"
11. *Felice*: *Felice* is Buscaglia's real first name. The name *Leo* was taken from Buscaglia's middle name, *Leonardo*.

In retrospect, after years of studying how people learn, I realize what a dynamic educational technique Papa was offering us, reinforcing the value of continual learning. Without being aware of it, our family was growing together, sharing experiences, and participating in one another's education. Papa was, without knowing it, giving us an education in the most real sense.

By looking at us, listening to us, hearing us, respecting our opinions, affirming our value, giving us a sense of dignity, he was unquestionably our most influential teacher.

Discussion and Writing Questions

1. What does Buscaglia mean when he says that his father "wasn't educated in the formal sense" (paragraph 1)? In what way *was* his father educated?

2. How did Buscaglia's father and mother react to information that the children reported at dinnertime? How did their reaction affect Buscaglia as a child? As an adult?

3. Years later, Buscaglia realized that his father had offered the family "a dynamic educational technique" (paragraph 22). What does he mean?

4. What point does the author make by using the population of Nepal as an example in paragraph 14? Is it useful to know the population of Nepal? Why or why not?

Writing Assignments

1. Describe a typical dinnertime in your family as you were growing up. Was dinnertime a time for sharing? Fighting? Eating alone? What effect did this have on you? If you now live away from your birth family, are dinnertimes different?

2. Discuss your attitude toward education. Who or what shaped your point of view? Has your attitude changed since childhood? Why is education important?

3. Did you learn anything new today? If so, describe what you learned. If not, what got in the way of your learning?

Homeless

Anna Quindlen

A columnist for *The New York Times,* **Anna Quindlen often writes about such issues as the changing family, men's and women's roles, the workplace, and sexual harassment. Here she examines one of our society's most difficult problems: homelessness.**

Her name was Ann, and we met in the Port Authority Bus Terminal several Januarys ago. I was doing a story on homeless people. She said I was wasting my time talking to her; she was just passing through, although she'd been passing through for more than two weeks. To prove to me that this was true, she rummaged through a tote bag and a manila envelope and finally unfolded a sheet of typing paper and brought out her photographs.

They were not pictures of family, or friends, or even a dog or cat, its eyes brown-red in the flashbulb's light. They were pictures of a house. It was like a thousand houses in a hundred towns, not suburb, not city, but somewhere in between, with aluminum siding and a chain-link fence, a narrow driveway running up to a one-car garage and a patch of backyard. The house was yellow. I looked on the back for a date or a name, but neither was there. There was no need for discussion. I knew what she was trying to tell me, for it was something I had often felt. She was not adrift, alone, anonymous,[1] although her bags and her raincoat with the grime shadowing its creases had made me believe she was. She had a house, or at least once upon a time had had one. Inside were curtains, a couch, a stove, potholders. You are where you live. She was somebody.

I've never been very good at looking at the big picture, taking the global view, and I've always been a person with an overactive sense of place, the legacy[2] of an Irish grandfather. So it is natural that the thing that seems most wrong with the world to me right now is that there are so many people with no homes. I'm not simply talking about shelter from the elements, or three square meals a day or a mailing address to which the welfare people can send the check—although I know that all these are important for survival. I'm talking about a home, about precisely those kinds of feelings that have wound up in cross-stitch and French knots[3] on samplers[4] over the years.

---

1. anonymous: nameless, lacking identity
2. legacy: something from the past handed down or passed on
3. cross-stitch, French knots: types of stitching in needlepoint
4. samplers: pieces of embroidered cloth

Home is where the heart is. There's no place like it. I love my home with a ferocity[5] totally out of proportion to its appearance or location. I love dumb things about it: the hot-water heater, the plastic rack you drain dishes in, the roof over my head, which occasionally leaks. And yet it is precisely those dumb things that make it what it is—a place of certainty, stability, predictability, privacy, for me and for my family. It is where I live. What more can you say about a place than that? That is everything.

Yet it is something that we have been edging away from gradually during my lifetime and the lifetimes of my parents and grandparents. There was a time when where you lived often was where you worked and where you grew the food you ate and even where you were buried. When that era passed, where you lived at least was where your parents had lived and where you would live with your children when you became enfeebled. Then, suddenly, where you lived was where you lived for three years, until you could move on to something else and something else again.

> "They are not the homeless. They are people who have no homes."

And so we have come to something else again, to children who do not understand what it means to go to their rooms because they have never had a room, to men and women whose fantasy is a wall they can paint a color of their own choosing, to old people reduced to sitting on molded plastic chairs, their skin blue-white in the lights of a bus station, who pull pictures of houses out of their bags. Homes have stopped being homes. Now they are real estate.

People find it curious that those without homes would rather sleep sitting up on benches or huddled in doorways than go to shelters. Certainly some prefer to do so because they are emotionally ill, because they have been locked in before and they are damned if they will be locked in again. Others are afraid of the violence and trouble they may find there. But some seem to want something that is not available in shelters, and they will not compromise, not for a cot, or oatmeal, or a shower with special soap that kills the bugs. "One room," a woman with a baby who was sleeping on her sister's floor, once told me, "painted blue." That was the crux[6] of it; not size or location, but pride of ownership. Painted blue.

This is a difficult problem, and some wise and compassionate people are working hard at it. But in the main[7] I think we work around it, just as we walk around it when it is lying on the sidewalk or sitting in the bus terminal—the problem, that is. It has been customary to take people's pain and lessen our own participation in it by turning it into an issue, not a collection of human beings. We turn an adjective into a noun: the poor, not poor people; the homeless, not Ann or the man who lives in the box or the woman who sleeps on the subway grate.

---

5. ferocity: fierce energy
6. crux: the most important part of an issue
7. in the main: mainly

Sometimes I think we would be better off if we forgot about the broad strokes and concentrated on the details. Here is a woman without a bureau. There is a man with no mirror, no wall to hang it on. They are not the homeless. They are people who have no homes. No drawer that holds the spoons. No window to look out upon the world. My God. That is everything.

Discussion and Writing Questions

1. What does the author mean when she says, "You are where you live" (paragraph 2)?

2. Why does she say, "Homes have stopped being homes. Now they are real estate" (paragraph 6)?

3. Why do some people refuse to live in public shelters?

4. The author states in paragraph 9 that she believes it is important to concentrate on details when we talk about homelessness. Why? What does she believe we gain by concentrating on details?

Writing Assignments

1. What is (or is not) being done in your community about homelessness? As you write, follow Quindlen's example and use vivid details and examples.

2. Describe what you mean by "home." What little details, comforts, colors do you love about your home? In paragraph 4, Quindlen says home is "dumb things." Do you agree?

3. It has been said that America is becoming further divided into two nations: those who "have" and those who "have not." Do you believe America is divided this way? Explain why you feel the way you do.

Say Yes to Yourself

Joseph T. Martorano and John P. Kildahl

Do you believe your thoughts can change your life? If you can change the way you think, say therapists Martorano and Kildahl, you will change the way you feel—and act.

It's the classic story with a twist: a traveling salesman gets a flat tire on a dark, lonely road and then discovers he has no jack. He sees a light in a farmhouse. As he walks toward it, his mind churns:

"Suppose no one comes to the door." "Suppose they don't have a jack." "Suppose the guy won't lend me his jack even if he has one." The harder his mind works, the more agitated he becomes, and when the door opens, he punches the farmer and yells, "*Keep* your lousy jack!"

That story brings a smile, because it pokes fun at a common type of self-defeatist thinking. How often have you heard yourself say: "Nothing *ever* goes the way I planned." "I'll *never* make that deadline." "I *always* screw up."

Such inner speech shapes your life more than any other single force. Like it or not, you travel through life with your thoughts as navigator. If those thoughts spell gloom and doom, that's where you're headed, because put-down words sabotage confidence instead of offering support and encouragement.

Simply put, to *feel* better, you need to *think* better. Here's how:

1. Tune in to your thoughts. The first thing Sue said to her new therapist was, "I know you can't help me, Doctor. I'm a total mess. I keep lousing up at work, and I'm sure I'm going to be canned. Just yesterday my boss told me I was being transferred. He called it a promotion. But if I was doing a good job, why transfer me?"

Then, gradually, Sue's story moved past the put-downs. She had received her M.B.A. two years before and was making an excellent salary. That didn't sound like failure.

At the end of their first meeting, Sue's therapist told her to jot down her thoughts, particularly at night if she was having trouble falling asleep. At her next appointment Sue's list included: "I'm not really smart. I got ahead by a bunch of flukes."[1] "Tomorrow will be a disaster. I've never chaired a meeting before." "My boss looked furious this morning. What did I do?"

She admitted, "In one day alone, I listed 26 negative thoughts. No wonder I'm always tired and depressed."

Hearing her fears and forebodings[2] read out loud made Sue realize how much energy she was squandering[3] on imagined catastrophes. If you've been feeling down, it could be you're sending yourself negative messages too. Listen to the words churning inside your head. Repeat them aloud or write them down, if that will help capture them.

With practice, tuning in will become automatic. As you're walking or driving down the street, you can hear your silent broadcast. Soon your thoughts will do your bidding, rather than the other way around. And when that happens, your feelings and actions will change too.

2. Isolate destructive words and phrases. Fran's inner voice kept telling her she was "only a secretary." Mark's reminded him he was "just a salesman." With the word *only* or *just*, they were downgrading their jobs and, by extension, themselves. By isolating negative words and phrases, you can pinpoint the damage you're doing to yourself. . . .

3. Stop the thought. Short-circuit negative messages as soon as they start by using the one-word command *stop!*

"What will I do if . . . ?" *Stop!*

---

1. flukes: accidents
2. forebodings: feelings that something bad is going to happen
3. squandering: wasting

14 In theory, stopping is a simple technique. In practice, it's not as easy as it sounds. To be effective at stopping, you have to be forceful and tenacious.[4] Raise your voice when you give the command. Picture yourself drowning out the inner voice of fear.

15 Vincent, a hard-working bachelor in his 20s, was an executive in a large company. . . . Although attracted to a woman in his department, he never asked her for a date. His worries immobilized[5] him: "It's not a good idea to date a co-worker," or, "If she says no, it'll be embarrassing."

> "Listen to the words churning inside your head. . . . Short-circuit negative messages as soon as they start."

16 When Vincent stopped his inner voice and asked the woman out, she said, "Vincent, what took you so long?"

17 4. *Accentuate the positive.* There's a story about a man who went to a psychiatrist. "What's the trouble?" asked the doctor.

18 "Two months ago my grandfather died and left me $75,000. Last month, a cousin passed away and left me $100,000."

19 "Then why are you depressed?"

20 "This month, *nothing!*"

21 When a person is in a depressed mood, everything can seem depressing. So once you've exorcised[6] the demons by calling a stop, replace them with good thoughts. . . . Be ready with a thought you've prepared in advance. Think about the promotion you got or a pleasant hike in the woods. In the words of the Bible: ". . . whatever is honorable . . . whatever is lovely, whatever is gracious . . . think about these things."

22 5. *Reorient yourself.* Have you ever been feeling down late in the day, when someone suddenly said, "Let's go out"? Remember how your spirits picked up? You changed the direction of your thinking, and your mood brightened. . . . Practice this technique of going from painful anxiety to an active, problem-solving framework. . . .

23 By reorienting, you can learn to see yourself and the world around you differently. If you think you can do something, you increase your chances of doing it. Optimism gets you moving. Depressing thoughts bog you down, because you are thinking, "What's the use?"

24 Make it a habit to remember your best self, the you that you want to be. In particular, remember things for which you have been complimented. That's the real you. Make this the frame of reference for your life—a picture of you at your best.

25 You'll find that reorienting works like a magnet. Imagine yourself reaching your goals, and you will feel the tug of the magnet pulling you toward them.

26 Over the years we've discovered that when people *think* differently, they *feel*—and *act*—differently. It's all in controlling your thoughts. As the poet John Milton wrote: "The mind . . . can make a heaven of hell, a hell of heaven."

27 The choice is yours.

---

4. tenacious: holding on; stubborn
5. immobilized: kept from moving
6. exorcised: gotten rid of evil spirits

Discussion and Writing Questions

1. What is the point of the story of the traveling salesman and the jack (paragraph 1)?

2. Martorano and Kildahl say that negative inner speech "shapes your life more than any other single force" (paragraph 3). Do you think this statement is true? Why or why not?

3. The authors offer five suggestions for changing negative thinking to positive thinking. Which suggestion do you think would be most useful for you? Why?

4. What is the meaning of John Milton's line "the mind . . . can make a heaven of hell, a hell of heaven" (paragraph 26)? Give examples from experience.

Writing Assignments

1. Describe a person you know who always makes you feel good about yourself. What does he or she say or do that makes you feel this way? Describe a time when you acted in a positive way because of that person's influence.

2. Most of us have negative mental "tapes" that influence the way we feel or act. These might concern our physical appearance, our abilities as a student or worker, or our relationships with other people. In your first sentence, describe a negative thought you have had about yourself. How could you change it and think more positively? How might your feelings and actions change if you did?

3. For a day or two, try using one or more of Martorano and Kildahl's suggestions for changing negative thoughts. Then write about your experience. What negative thoughts did you notice? Were you able to stop those thoughts? If so, did you feel better? Did you act in a more positive way? If the experiment didn't work, do you think it might work if you had more time or practice?

Yolanda

Julia Alvarez

Living in a new country and learning a new language are challenges for anyone. For a young child, whose experience of the world is limited, the challenges may be even greater. This fictional selection by a writer from the Dominican Republic captures one child's fear and wonder in a new country.

Our first year in New York we rented a small apartment with a Catholic school nearby, taught by the Sisters of Charity, hefty[1] women in long black gowns and bonnets that made them look peculiar, like dolls in mourning. I liked them a lot, especially my grandmotherly fourth grade teacher, Sister Zoe. I had a lovely name, she said, and she had me teach the whole class how to pronounce it. *Yo-lan-da.* As the only immigrant in my class, I was put in a special seat in the first row by the window, apart from the other children so that Sister Zoe could tutor me without disturbing them. Slowly, she enunciated the new words I was to repeat: *laundromat, corn flakes, subway, snow.*

> "Slowly, she enunciated the new words I was to repeat: **laundromat, corn flakes, subway, snow.**"

Soon I picked up enough English to understand holocaust[2] was in the air. Sister Zoe explained to a wide-eyed classroom what was happening in Cuba.[3] Russian missiles were being assembled, trained supposedly on New York City. President Kennedy, looking worried too, was on the television at home, explaining we might have to go to war against the Communists. At school, we had air-raid drills: an ominous[4] bell would go off and we'd file into the hall, fall to the floor, cover our heads with our coats, and imagine our hair falling out, the bones in our arms going soft. At home, Mami and my sisters and I said a rosary for world peace. I heard new vocabulary: *nuclear bomb, radioactive fallout, bomb shelter.* Sister Zoe explained how it would happen. She drew a picture of a mushroom on the blackboard and dotted a flurry of chalkmarks for the dusty fallout that would kill us all.

---

1. hefty: heavy
2. holocaust: total destruction
3. what was happening in Cuba: During the Cuban missile crisis of 1962, the United States discovered that the Soviet Union was building nuclear missile launch sites on Cuba. After several weeks of great tension and the threat of nuclear war, the Soviet Union withdrew. In return, President Kennedy agreed not to try again to overthrow the Castro government in Cuba.
4. ominous: threatening

The months grew cold, November, December. It was dark when I got up in the morning, frosty when I followed my breath to school. One morning as I sat at my desk daydreaming out the window, I saw dots in the air like the ones Sister Zoe had drawn—random at first, then lots and lots. I shrieked, "Bomb! Bomb!" Sister Zoe jerked around, her full black skirt ballooning as she hurried to my side. A few girls began to cry.

But then Sister Zoe's shocked look faded. "Why, Yolanda dear, that's snow!" She laughed. "Snow."

"Snow," I repeated. I looked out the window warily. All my life I had heard about the white crystals that fell out of American skies in the winter. From my desk I watched the fine powder dust the sidewalk and parked cars below. Each flake was different, Sister Zoe had said, like a person, irreplaceable and beautiful.

Discussion and Writing Questions

1. Yolanda tells us that the word *snow* is among the words she is supposed to learn (paragraph 1). What other words does she learn that she does not yet have the experience to understand?

2. In paragraph 3, Yolanda describes the scene outside her school window: "I saw dots in the air like the ones Sister Zoe had drawn—random at first, then lots and lots." What did she think she was seeing, and what was she actually seeing? When did you realize what was really happening outside her window that day?

3. Does Yolanda's mistake indicate that she pays attention in school and is a very bright child, or just the opposite? Explain your answer.

4. Yolanda likes her teacher, Sister Zoe, from the start. Is Sister Zoe a good teacher? How can you tell?

Writing Assignments

1. Did you (or anyone you know) ever leave home to live in a new country? What was it like to adjust to a new culture? Choose one or two incidents to write about that capture one aspect of the experience—wonder or frustration, for example.

2. Did you ever have a teacher who was especially important in your life? What was that teacher like? What influence did he or she have on you?

3. Children and people learning languages sometimes draw wrong conclusions based on limited experience. A child, for example, might think that he has to learn to fly like a bird in order "to fly to Grandma's next week." Did you ever draw a mistaken conclusion because you misunderstood a word or words? How did you find out the correct (or generally accepted) meaning?

People and Their Machines and Vice Versa

Peter Gzowski

Which is better for the writer—working on a typewriter or a word processor? Some writers work easily with either machine, whereas others, like Canadian writer and editor Peter Gzowski, have a strong preference.

If I have remembered my own history correctly, it is exactly thirty years ago this week that I arrived in Timmins, Ontario, to begin my life as a newspaperman. Almost every day for those thirty years, I have opened my working procedures the same way. I have cranked a piece of paper into my typewriter, banged out what newspapermen call a slug[1] at the top of the page, usually followed, for reasons I don't know but by a habit I can't break, by the page number typed four or five times, and started pounding away with as many fingers as seemed to fit. Like most old newspapermen, I am as fast as a Gatling gun[2] at my machine, and almost as noisy. I make mistakes—which is like saying Wayne Gretzky gets scoring points—but I strike them out: xxxxxxx or, if I'm really flying, mnmnmnmnmnmn, *m* with the right forefinger, *n* with the left. Afterward, I go over what I've done with the heaviest pencil I can find, changing a word here, a phrase there. I cross out some more, with a bold, black stroke and a flourishing delete sign. I add. Sometimes I make what one of my editors called chicken tracks from the place I had the first thought out into the margin. Out there, I create anew. I scribble up into the bare space at the top, up by the stammering page numbers, and on good days, when my juices are flowing and the ghost of Maxwell Perkins[3] is looking over my shoulder, I carry on from there, turning the page under my pencil, down the outer edges, filling the bottom and off, off into virgin territories, leaving my inky spoor[4] behind me. When I am pleased with what I have done, or when the chicken tracks get too dense to follow, I put a new page in the typewriter and start again. This is not the way anyone taught me to work. But it is the way I have done things. It has served me through five books, more magazine articles than you could shake an art director's ruler at and enough newspaper pieces to line the cage of every eagle that ever flew.

But no more. I am a word-processor man now, or trying to become one. I made the change at the end of this summer. The words I am reading to you now first appeared to my eye etched in

---

1. slug: first line on a printed page giving instructions to the typesetter
2. Gatling gun: a type of machine gun
3. Maxwell Perkins: an editor who helped develop the work of writers Ernest Hemingway and F. Scott Fitzgerald, among others
4. spoor: a wild animal's track or trail

green on a dark screen. Or, rather, some *version* of the words I am reading to you now so appeared. "Green," for instance, was "gereen," or perhaps "jereen," until I danced my cursor around the screen (the "scereen?") and obliterated[5] the extra *e*. "Etched," too, is probably the wrong word. The process by which these words appear is too sophisticated for my manually operated mind, and I no more understand it than I understand what really happens when I turn on the ignition of my car. All I know, in fact, are two things: one, I can do it. If I take my time, and think my way through such delicate differences as that between the "control" key and the shift lock, and resist the urge to hit the space bar (which makes sense to me) and instead hit a simultaneous "control" and *d* (which doesn't) when I want to move my little cursor over one notch, I can, however painstakingly, make the words come out in prose. That's one. Two is that I hate doing it. Over the years, the relationship I have built up with my various manuals[6] is an emotional one. I pound them and they respond, as the Steinway responded to Glenn Gould.[7] I knew I was working because I could hear it, and the measure of what I had accomplished in a working day was often the pile of out-takes that grew in my wastepaper basket, like tailings[8] at a mine. Now, I work silently. I wrote what you are hearing now while my daughter slept in the next room. This was convenient for Alison, but it did not seem to me to be what I have always done for a living. It neither sounded nor felt like *writing*. God, it seems to me, no more meant words to appear in fluorescent electronic letters than he meant pool tables to be pink, or golf balls orange.

> "I am a word-processor man now, or trying to become one."

Discussion and Writing Questions

1. What is meant by the title of this essay, "People and Their Machines and Vice Versa"?

2. In paragraph 1, the author describes writing as a messy, disorganized business. How does he use language to convey this messiness and disorganization to the reader?

3. The author says he had an "emotional" relationship with his typewriters. Why do you suppose he changed to working on a word processor?

4. Why does the author dislike so much being a "word-processor man"? Do you think his feelings will change over time?

---

5. obliterated: wiped out
6. manuals: manual typewriters
7. Glenn Gould: a famous classical pianist
8. tailings: waste material from the mining process

Writing Assignments

1. Describe your own writing process in detail, whether you write with a pen, pencil, typewriter, or computer. Tell your reader step by step what you do, even if some things do not "make good sense." If, for example, you prefer a certain kind or color of pen, describe it. What helps you write well? What gets in the way of good writing?

2. Write about an activity you enjoy that is performed with a simple machine. You could write about riding a bike, working with a piece of lab equipment, or using a particular appliance to cook a favorite meal. Describe your actions and feelings when you use the machine.

3. Many of us now use computers in our day-to-day lives. Describe your first attempts at using a computer or some other machine. Did you adapt easily to the new machine or not? Was your experience humorous, painful, or frustrating? Use details to give your reader a sense of how you felt at the time.

The Gift

Courtland Milloy

Help sometimes comes from unexpected places. This newspaper story describes the generosity of a friend whose gift saved someone's life—and baffled most people who knew him. As you read, ask yourself how you would have acted in his place.

1 When Jermaine Washington entered the barbershop, heads turned and clippers fell silent. Customers waved and nodded out of sheer respect. With his hands in the pockets of his knee-length, black leather coat, Washington acknowledged them with a faint smile and quietly took a seat.

2 "You know who that is?" barber Anthony Clyburn asked in a tone reserved for the most awesome neighborhood characters, such as ball players and ex-cons.

3 A year and a half ago, Washington did something that still amazes those who know him. He became a kidney donor, giving a vital organ to a woman he described as "just a friend."

4 "They had a platonic[1] relationship," said Clyburn, who works at Jake's Barber Shop in Northeast Washington. "I could see maybe giving one to my mother, but just a girl I know? I don't think so."

5 Washington, who is 25, met Michelle Stevens six years ago when they worked for the D.C. Department of Employment Services.

---
1. platonic: nonromantic

They used to have lunch together in the department cafeteria and chitchat on the telephone during their breaks.

"It was nothing serious, romance-wise," said Stevens, who is 23. "He was somebody I could talk to. I had been on the kidney donor waiting list for 12 months and I had lost all hope. One day, I just called to cry on his shoulder."

Stevens told Washington how depressing it was to spend three days a week, three hours a day, on a kidney dialysis machine.[2] She said she suffered from chronic fatigue and blackouts and was losing her balance and her sight. He could already see that she had lost her smile.

> "'I had been on the kidney donor waiting list for 12 months and I had lost all hope. One day, I just called to cry on his shoulder.'"

"I saw my friend dying before my eyes," Washington recalled. "What was I supposed to do? Sit back and watch her die?"

Stevens's mother was found to be suffering from hypertension[3] and was ineligible to donate a kidney. Her 14-year-old sister offered to become a donor, but doctors concluded that she was too young.

Stevens's two brothers, 25 and 31, would most likely have made ideal donors because of their relatively young ages and status as family members. But both of them said no.

So did Stevens's boyfriend, who gave her two diamond rings with his apology.

"I understood," Stevens said. "They said they loved me very much, but they were just too afraid."

---

2. kidney dialysis machine: a machine that filters waste material from the blood when the kidneys fail
3. hypertension: high blood pressure

Joyce Washington, Jermaine's mother, was not exactly in favor of the idea, either. But after being convinced that her son was not being coerced,[4] she supported his decision.

The transplant operation took four hours. It occurred in April 1991, and began with a painful X-ray procedure in which doctors inserted a metal rod into Washington's kidney and shot it with red dye. An incision nearly 20 inches long was made from his groin to the back of his shoulder. After the surgery he remained hospitalized for five days.

Today, both Stevens and Washington are fully recovered. Stevens, a graduate of Eastern High School, is studying medicine at the National Educational Center. Washington still works for D.C. Employment Services as a job counselor.

"I jog and work out with weights," Washington said. "Boxing and football are out, but I never played those anyway."

A spokesman for Washington Hospital Center said the Washington-to-Stevens gift was the hospital's first "friend-to-friend" transplant. Usually, it's wife to husband, or parent to child. But there is a shortage of even those kinds of transplants. Today, more than 300 patients are in need of kidneys in the Washington area.

"A woman came up to me in a movie line not long ago and hugged me," Washington said. "She thanked me for doing what I did because no one had come forth when her daughter needed a kidney, and the child died."

About twice a month, Stevens and Washington get together for what they call a gratitude lunch. Since the operation, she has broken up with her boyfriend. Seven months ago, Washington got a girlfriend. Despite occasional pressure by friends, a romantic relationship is not what they want.

"We are thankful for the beautiful relationship that we have," Stevens said. "We don't want to mess up a good thing."

To this day, people wonder why Washington did it. To some of the men gathered at Jake's Barber Shop not long ago, Washington's heroics were cause for questions about his sanity. Surely he could not have been in his right mind, they said.

One customer asked Washington where he had found the courage to give away a kidney. His answer quelled[5] most skeptics[6] and inspired even more awe.

"I prayed for it," Washington replied. "I asked God for guidance and that's what I got."

Discussion and Writing Questions

1. A year and a half after Jermaine Washington donated a kidney to Michelle Stevens, his friends are still amazed by what he did. Why do they find his action so surprising?

---

4. coerced: pressured into doing something
5. quelled: quieted
6. skeptics: people who doubt or question

2. Washington says, "What was I supposed to do? Sit back and watch her die?" (paragraph 8). Yet Stevens' brothers and her boyfriend did not offer to donate a kidney. Do you blame them? Do you understand them?

3. In what ways has Stevens' life changed because of Washington's gift? Consider her physical status, her social life, her choice of profession, her "gratitude lunches" with Washington, and so on.

4. According to Washington, where did he find the courage to donate a kidney? How did his action affect his standing in the community? How did it affect other aspects of his life?

Writing Assignments

1. Have you ever been unusually generous—or do you know someone who was? Describe that act of generosity. Why did you—or the other person—do it? How did your friends or family react?

2. Do you have or does anyone you know have a serious medical condition? Describe the situation. How do or how can friends help? Can strangers help in any way?

3. Stevens and Washington do not have or want a romantic relationship. "We don't want to mess up a good thing," Stevens says (paragraph 20). Does romance "mess things up"? Write about a time when a relationship changed—either for better or for worse—because romance entered the picture.

Salvation

Langston Hughes

Many people have experienced a crisis in their beliefs. Here Langston Hughes, a poet who first became famous in the 1920s, recalls the day his beliefs, and his life, changed.

I was saved from sin when I was going on thirteen. But not really saved. It happened like this. There was a big revival at my Auntie Reed's church. Every night for weeks there had been much preaching, singing, praying, and shouting, and some very hardened sinners had been brought to Christ, and the membership of the church had grown by leaps and bounds. Then just before the revival ended, they held a special meeting for children, "to bring the young lambs to the fold." My aunt spoke of it for days ahead. That night I was escorted to the front row and placed on the mourners' bench with all the other young sinners, who had not yet been brought to Jesus.

My aunt told me that when you were saved you saw a light, and something happened to you inside! And Jesus came into your life! And God was with you from then on! She said you could see and hear and feel Jesus in your soul. I believed her. I had heard a great many old people say the same thing and it seemed to me they ought to know. So I sat there calmly in the hot, crowded church, waiting for Jesus to come to me.

The preacher preached a wonderful rhythmical sermon, all moans and shouts and lonely cries and dire[1] pictures of hell, and then he sang a song about the ninety and nine safe in the fold, but one little lamb was left out in the cold. Then he said: "Won't you come? Won't you come to Jesus? Young lambs, won't you come?" And he held out his arms to all us young sinners there on the mourners' bench. And the little girls cried. And some of them jumped up and went to Jesus right away. But most of us just sat there.

A great many old people came and knelt around us and prayed, old women with jet-black faces and braided hair, old men with work-gnarled hands. And the church sang a song about the lower lights are burning, some poor sinners to be saved. And the whole building rocked with prayer and song.

Still I kept waiting to *see* Jesus.

Finally all the young people had gone to the altar and were saved, but one boy and me. He was a rounder's[2] son named Westley. Westley and I were surrounded by sisters and deacons praying. It was very hot in the church, and getting late now. Finally Westley said to me in a whisper: "God damn! I'm tired o' sitting here. Let's get up and be saved." So he got up and was saved.

> "I wanted something to happen to me, but nothing happened."

Then I was left all alone on the mourners' bench. My aunt came and knelt at my knees and cried, while prayers and songs swirled all around me in the little church. The whole congregation prayed for me alone, in a mighty wail of moans and voices. And I kept waiting serenely for Jesus, waiting, waiting—but he didn't come. I wanted to see him, but nothing happened to me. Nothing! I wanted something to happen to me, but nothing happened.

I heard the songs and the minister saying: "Why don't you come? My dear child, why don't you come to Jesus? Jesus is waiting for you. He wants you. Why don't you come? Sister Reed, what is this child's name?"

"Langston," my aunt sobbed.

"Langston, why don't you come? Why don't you come and be saved? Oh, Lamb of God! Why don't you come?"

Now it was really getting late. I began to be ashamed of myself, holding everything up so long. I began to wonder what God thought about Westley, who certainly hadn't seen Jesus either, but who was now sitting proudly on the platform, swinging his knickerbockered[3]

---

1. dire: terrible, dreadful
2. rounder's: dishonest person's
3. knickerbockered: wearing knickerbockers (trousers that end just below the knee)

legs and grinning down at me, surrounded by deacons and old women on their knees praying. God had not struck Westley dead for taking his name in vain or for lying in the temple. So I decided that maybe to save further trouble, I'd better lie, too, and say that Jesus had come, and get up and be saved.

So I got up. 12

Suddenly the whole room broke into a sea of shouting, as they saw me rise. Waves of rejoicing swept the place. Women leaped in the air. My aunt threw her arms around me. The minister took me by the hand and led me to the platform. 13

When things quieted down, in a hushed silence, punctuated by a few ecstatic "Amens," all the new young lambs were blessed in the name of God. Then joyous singing filled the room. 14

That night, for the last time in my life but one—for I was a big boy twelve years old—I cried. I cried, in bed alone, and couldn't stop. I buried my head under the quilts, but my aunt heard me. She woke up and told my uncle I was crying because the Holy Ghost had come into my life, and because I had seen Jesus. But I was really crying because I couldn't bear to tell her that I had lied, that I had deceived everybody in the church, that I hadn't seen Jesus, and that now I didn't believe there was a Jesus any more, since he didn't come to help me. 15

Discussion and Writing Questions

1. What did Hughes expect to happen to him during the church meeting?

2. Why did he finally stand up? How was he like or unlike Westley, who apparently didn't see Jesus either?

3. Compare paragraph 12 with the paragraphs above and below it. Notice the number of sentences in paragraph 12. Why does Hughes use a different writing style in this paragraph? Why is the sentence so important?

4. Why was Hughes so upset that night? Do you think he would have felt any better if he had not stood up but had endured everyone's discomfort and insisted on being true to himself?

Writing Assignments

1. Hughes describes the tremendous pressure put on him to "be saved." Write about a situation in which pressure was put on you to believe something or to behave in a certain way. How did you handle the pressure? Looking back, do you feel that your actions were courageous or cowardly?

2. What are your own ideas about religion? Are these ideas the same or different from the ideas that your family holds? Did you become less or more religious (or spiritual) as you grew older? Why?

3. Did you ever make a discovery about something that changed your view of the world in an important way—for example, the circumstances of your birth or adoption, new information about a loved one? Write about that experience. How did your view of the world change?

Forever

Francine Klagsbrun

Francine Klagsbrun has written extensively on relationships between women and men. In this selection, she characterizes healthy marriage as a dynamic, ever-changing process between two people, one that begins only when romance wears off.

Probably every couple that ever existed has looked at one another at some point during or after the honeymoon and wondered, "Who are you?" and "What am I doing here?" For every couple there are expectations and dreams that go unfulfilled. Those who remain married and satisfied with their marriages are willing to discard the fantasies and build a richer and deeper life beyond the illusions.

All marriages, not only those that fail, begin with unreal expectations that color much of what happens between partners. Maggie and Robbie are a good example. They have known one another for years. They are not carried away in transports[1] of romantic blindness about one another, nor does either deny the other's faults. But they are so pleased about getting married, so wanting to be adults now, that they happily gloss over[2] those faults. "We're as different as two people can be, and we'll never change," Robbie says, as though his acknowledgment makes the differences unimportant. "We fight all the time," Maggie laughs, shoving aside the anger that must lie behind the constant bickering. "Of course I'll take off from work when we have a baby," Robbie asserts, denying to himself the drive of ambition that makes him spend every evening working at his desk, leaving little time for the two to be together. And Maggie accepts his assertion, pretending to herself and to him that he will be able to put aside his ambitions when the time comes.

There are many kinds of expectations with which people begin their marriages. "I'll change him/her after we marry" is one of the most common of these—trite,[3] actually, because it is so widely known and often laughed at. The "I'll be happy once I'm married" illusion is also widely held, an anticipation that marriage will take care of all one's emotional needs. Then there is the illusion that "if she loved

---

1. transports: ecstasies
2. gloss over: not take seriously; treat superficially
3. trite: too often used

me, she'd know how I feel," which may begin before marriage and continue well into it. This is the expectation that in some fantasy land of love you never have to tell your partner how you feel or what you want.

Underlying all the other expectations is the expectation of perfection. All of us begin marriages with such high hopes, it is hard to believe that anything about our life could be less than perfect. When imperfections appear (as they must), most couples look around at other marriages and wonder what is wrong with them. They are sure that everybody else's sex life is wonderful, while they have had trouble adjusting to one another; everybody else knows how to communicate feelings, while they have had vicious battles; everybody else is adept at handling finances, while theirs are in constant chaos. Since their marriage isn't perfect, as everybody else's is, they conclude that it is probably no good at all.

Marital therapist Carl Whitaker, who has written and lectured a great deal, believes that a real marriage doesn't begin until that time when the illusions wear off, or wear thin. It takes a couple about ten years, says Whitaker, to realize that the expectations with which they began marriage and the assumptions they held about each other are not quite the way they seemed. At this point they see themselves as having "fallen out of love." He no longer thinks he can change her, and she no longer thinks he can understand her. The characteristics that had once seemed endearing—his fear of flying, her fear of failure—now drive them crazy. They have come to see each other as real people, neither saviors nor therapists, saints nor charming rogues.[4] Each knows the other's vulnerabilities, and knows well how to hurt the other. Now their marriage is at a crossroads. They can become locked onto a pattern of fighting and making each other miserable; they can become involved in outside affairs; they can decide that this is not what they bargained for and split; or they can create a true marriage. That is, they can come to accept the frailties and vulnerabilities each has, accept them and respect them, and in doing so, discover a much more profound love for the real person whom they married.

> "A marriage is a process . . . it never stays the same and it never completes itself."

It may not take ten years for Whitaker's "ten-year-syndrome" to occur. It may take three weeks or five months or two decades for the exaggerated expectations and fantasies to fall away and for a couple to find themselves face to face with one another, confronting the realities of their marriage.

If they make the decision to stay together, they will begin the real process of marriage. Marriage is a process because it is always in flux;[5] it never stays the same and it never completes itself. It is a process of changing and accepting change, of settling differences

---

4. rogues: rascals
5. flux: change

and living with differences that will never be settled, of drawing close and pulling apart and drawing close again. Because it is a process that demands discipline and responsibility, it can bring frustration and pain, but it also can plumb[6] the depths of love and provide an arena for self-actualization as nothing else can.

If Maggie and Robbie stay married, their marriage will have a special kind of romance. It will not be only the romance of loving one another, and it will not only be the romance of sexual excitement—although those will be part of their marriage. The romance of a marriage that lasts beyond the illusions comes in its incompleteness, and in the adventure of exploring the unfolding process together.

Discussion and Writing Questions

1. The author says that all marriages begin with unreal expectations (paragraph 2). Give some examples of unreal expectations. What does the author believe must happen to these expectations for a marriage to succeed?

2. What does the author think of the communication between Maggie and Robbie? Why?

3. The author believes that marriage "is a process" (paragraph 7). What does she mean by this? What predictable stages occur in this process?

4. Once the romantic illusions are gone, does the relationship become boring? What, according to Klagsbrun, is exciting about a long-term relationship?

Writing Assignments

1. Write about a relationship you have had or a relationship you are familiar with in which the couple found themselves "at a crossroads." How did they handle this turning point? What happened?

2. Write about a situation that you approached with high hopes. Did those early hopes change over time? Try to give your reader a sense of the events you experienced and feelings you had. Did you come to a more realistic understanding of the situation? Why or why not?

3. Klagsbrun describes the "real process of marriage" as one that "demands discipline and responsibility" (paragraph 7). What else do you think marriage, or any healthy relationship, demands? Describe the characteristics of a successful relationship, as you see them.

---

6. plumb: examine deeply

Sports Nuts

Dave Barry

Dave Barry is a Pulitzer Prize–winning humorist who writes a column for *The Miami Herald*. This essay, on men who are fanatic about sports, is written in Barry's usual tongue-in-cheek style.

Today, in our continuing series on How Guys Think, we explore the question: How come guys care so much about sports?

This is a tough one, because caring about sports is, let's face it, silly. I mean, suppose you have a friend who, for no apparent reason, suddenly becomes obsessed with the Amtrak Corporation. He babbles about Amtrak constantly, citing[1] obscure railroad statistics from 1978; he puts Amtrak bumper stickers on his car; and when something bad happens to Amtrak, such as a train crashes and investigators find that the engineer was drinking and wearing a bunny suit, your friend becomes depressed for weeks. You'd think he was crazy, right? "Bob," you'd say to him, as a loving and caring friend, "you're a moron. The Amtrak Corporation has *nothing to do with you*."

But if Bob is behaving exactly the same deranged[2] way about, say, the Pittsburgh Penguins, it's considered normal guy behavior. He could name his child "Pittsburgh Penguin Johnson" and be considered only mildly eccentric. There is something wrong with this. And before you accuse me of being some kind of sherry-sipping ascot[3]-wearing ballet-attending MacNeil-Lehrer Report–watching wussy, please note that I am a sports guy myself, having had a legendary athletic career consisting of nearly a third of the 1965 season on the track team at Pleasantville High School ("Where The Leaders Of Tomorrow Are Leaving Wads Of Gum On The Auditorium Seats Of Today"). I competed in the long jump, because it seemed to be the only event where afterward you didn't fall down and throw up. I probably would have become an Olympic-caliber long-jumper except that, through one of those "bad breaks" so common in sports, I turned out to have the raw leaping ability of a convenience store. I'd race down the runway and attempt to soar into the air, but instead of going up I'd be seized by powerful gravity rays and yanked *downward* and wind up with just my head sticking out of the dirt, serving as a convenient marker for the other jumpers to take off from.

So, OK, I was not Jim Thorpe,[4] but I care as much about sports as the next guy. If you were to put me in the middle of a room, and in one corner was Albert Einstein, in another corner was Abraham

---

1. citing: offering examples of
2. deranged: crazed, insane
3. ascot: an English necktie
4. Jim Thorpe: famous Native American football and track star

Lincoln, in another corner was Plato, in another corner was William Shakespeare, and in another corner (this room is a pentagon) was a TV set showing a football game between teams that have no connection whatsoever with my life, such as the Green Bay Packers and the Indianapolis Colts, I would ignore the greatest minds in Western thought, gravitate toward the TV, and become far more concerned about the game than I am about my child's education. And *so would the other guys.* I guarantee it. Within minutes Plato would be pounding Lincoln on the shoulder and shouting in ancient Greek that the receiver did *not* have both feet in bounds.

Obviously, sports connect with something deeply rooted in the male psyche,[5] dating back to prehistoric times, when guys survived by hunting and fighting, and they needed many of the skills exhibited by modern athletes—running, throwing, spitting, renegotiating their contracts, adjusting their private parts on nationwide television, etc. So that would explain how come guys like to *participate* in sports. But how come they care so much about games played by *other* guys? Does this also date back to prehistoric times? When the hunters were out hurling spears into mastodons,[6] were there also prehistoric guys watching from the hills, drinking prehistoric beer, eating really bad prehistoric hot dogs, and shouting "We're No. 1!" but not understanding what it meant because this was before the development of mathematics?

> "... I turned out to have the raw leaping ability of a convenience store.... but I care as much about sports as the next guy."

There must have been, because there is no other explanation for such bizarre phenomena as:

- Sports-talk radio, where guys who have never sent get-well cards to their own mothers will express heartfelt, near-suicidal anguish over the hamstring problems of strangers.

- My editor, Gene, who can remember the complete starting line-ups for the New York Yankee teams from 1960 through 1964, but who routinely makes telephone calls wherein, after he dials the phone, he forgets who he's calling, so when somebody answers, Gene has to ask (a) who it is, and (b) does this person happen to know the purpose of the call.

- Another guy in my office, John, who appears to be a normal middle-aged husband and father until you realize that he spends most of his waking hours managing a *pretend baseball team.* This is true. He and some other guys have formed a league where they pay actual money to "draft" major-league players, and then they have their pretend teams play a whole pretend season, complete with trades, legalistic memorandums,

---

5. psyche: the mind
6. mastodons: prehistoric animals resembling elephants

and heated disputes over the rules. This is crazy, right? If these guys said they were managing herds of pretend caribou,[7] the authorities would be squirting lithium[8] down their throats with turkey basters, right? And yet we all act like it's *perfectly normal.* In fact, eavesdropping from my office, I find myself getting involved in John's discussions. That's how pathetic I am: I'm capable of caring about a pretend sports team that's not even my own pretend sports team.

So I don't know about the rest of you guys, but I'm thinking it's time I got some perspective in my life. First thing after the Super Bowl, I'm going to start paying more attention to the things that should matter to me, like my work, my friends, and above all my family, especially my little boy, Philadelphia Phillies Barry. 10

Discussion and Writing Questions

1. Barry often humorously exaggerates to make a point. Find several examples of exaggeration in his essay.

2. What details or points of the essay do you find particularly funny?

3. Why do you suppose Barry talks about Einstein, Lincoln, Plato, and Shakespeare in paragraph 4? Could he have chosen other famous men to make his point?

4. Do you think that "sports connect with something deeply rooted in the male psyche," as Barry states in paragraph 5? What is that "something"? What about the female psyche?

Writing Assignments

1. Fill in the blank in the following line, "Today, in our continuing series on How Gals Think, we explore the question:

   _____?"
   Then write a paragraph exploring your topic. Be as humorous or as serious as you wish.

2. Reread Barry's description of his attempts at the long jump in paragraph 3. Then describe your own efforts in a sport you thought you might be good at but weren't.

3. Is there a sport you really like—either watching or playing? Describe your love of this sport, giving at least two reasons why the sport appeals to you.

---

7. caribou: a kind of Arctic deer
8. lithium: a drug used to treat mental illness

I Hope the Redskins Lose

Tim Giago

Would you like it if your favorite football team was named the "Palefaces"? How about the "Blackskins"? "Yellowskins"? Tim Giago, an Oglala Lakota from the Sioux Nation, asks these questions as he considers the image of the Native American in sports.

The bad news is the Washington Redskins beat the Detroit Lions. The good news is the national media have finally caught on to the complaints American Indians have been voicing for many years. The media will gather in Minneapolis for Super Bowl Sunday on January 26 [1992] with note pads, camera lenses and microphones at the ready to cover what will be the largest protest by American Indians against a professional football team in the history of this country. Our complaint: very simply, Indians are people, not mascots.[1]

We have just entered the year when American history will be scrutinized, analyzed, eulogized,[2] criticized and sterilized. It is the year of Christopher Columbus. More accurately, it is the year of the indigenous[3] people of the Western Hemisphere, of those with red skin. It is the year the non-Indian should form a new awareness of the Indian, a new awareness based on mutual respect. That respect will never be honest until we, as American Indians, are included in the race of human beings.

---

1. mascots: symbols or "pets" of a team
2. eulogized: praised highly
3. indigenous: native

As an Oglala Lakota (Sioux), born and raised on the Pine Ridge Reservation of South Dakota, I find it very hard to understand why non-Indians find it hard to understand why we consider it insulting to be treated as mascots. If white and black America is so inconsiderate of its indigenous people that it can name a football team the Redskins and see nothing wrong in this, where has our education system gone wrong?

When you, as black, yellow, white or brown Americans, watch the Super Bowl this year, do what I did while watching Washington beat Detroit. During the first quarter, I had John Madden substitute "Yellowskins" for "Redskins." In the second quarter I substituted "Brownskins." I started the second half by having Mr. Madden call Washington the "Whiteskins." And finally, in the fourth quarter, I replaced "Redskins" with "Blackskins." Try it and you will see how demeaning,[4] degrading and insulting it is to the people of different colored skin.

> "The American Indian has lost so much to the white man since 1492. Must we also be used as mascots?"

This is not a new issue to the Indian people. I have been writing about "Indians as mascots" for nearly 15 years. Recently, Senator Paul Simon has been outspoken in attempting to rid the University of Illinois of its dreadful mascot, Chief Illiniwek. Last month he read my editorial on Indians as mascots into the Congressional Record hoping he would be able to educate the rest of that august[5] body to be more sensitive to the First Americans. But for the most part, the American government and the media have paid little or no attention to our complaints.

At the recent national convention of the National Congress of American Indians in San Francisco, workshops were set up to help plan the Super Bowl protest. Charlene Teters—a graduate of the University of Illinois who has long fought the Chief Illiniwek mascot there—showed a roll of toilet paper she bought near the school. The figure of Illiniwek was imprinted on each tissue. "Mascots disgrace Indian people," she said. "When a static[6] symbol is used to represent a group of people, it gives off a one-dimensional image and devalues the living individuals." Some might wonder why Indians are so offended by being used as mascots and namesakes when there are so many other things wrong in Indian country. William Means, director of the International Indian Treaty Council, has an answer: "If we can't get white America to understand the basic issue of human respect, how can we get them to understand more substantive[7] issues like sovereignty,[8] treaty rights and water rights?"

During a radio talk show I was on, at the time of the Atlanta Braves brouhaha,[9] a lady named Diane called to say she had

---

4. demeaning: damaging to dignity
5. august: stately, honorable
6. static: unchanging
7. substantive: having substance, important
8. sovereignty: self-rule
9. brouhaha: commotion, conflict

attended a high school with a team nicknamed "Indians." She said she was proud to paint her face, stick feathers in her hair and make Hollywood war whoops as part of her cheerleading duties. "I felt we were honoring the Indian people," she said. Suppose your team was called the "African-Americans," I asked her. Would you paint your face black, wear an Afro wig and prance around the football field trying to imitate your perceptions of black people? She responded, "Of course not! That would be insulting to blacks." My point is made, I responded.

Never mind that there are certain Indian individuals, tribes or groups who profit by selling plastic tomahawks, turkey-feather ceremonial bonnets and other trinkets to the rabid[10] sports fans who would use this paraphernalia[11] to denigrate Indians. As history has recorded, there have always been sellouts who rode with the cavalry against their own.

We saw the Atlanta Braves fall in the World Series and the Florida State Seminoles get their tail feathers clipped after flying high most of 1991, and Indian people across America cheered. We also heard sports announcers attempting to make light of racist antics. We witnessed insensitive television directors focus their cameras on the wild, painted and feathered fans swinging their plastic tomahawks while the band played its version of the Hollywood-created version of Indian music. Hey yah! hey yah!

I'll close with a facetious[12] prediction: that Jack Kent Cooke, the owner of the Washington Redskins, will be seized with remorse for having insulted the Indian people all of these years. He will change the name of his team to the "Palefaces," after his own race and that of one of his favorite singers, Madonna. The team song will be changed from "Hail to the Redskins" to "Like a Virgin." What an honor it will be for the white race.

And furthermore, I predict the Buffalo Bills will skin the Redskins in Super Bowl XXVI. It will be the first time in history a Buffalo ever skinned a Redskin.

The American Indian has lost so much to the white man since 1492. Must we also be used as mascots? If we cannot get back the land, will you at least give us back our dignity?

Discussion and Writing Questions

1. Why does the author think it is "bad news" that the Redskins won the game against the Lions (paragraph 1)? Why do you suppose he begins his essay by saying this?

2. What is the point of the story about the radio talk show that the author tells in paragraph 7?

3. Why do you think so many sports teams have been named after Native Americans?

---

10. rabid: crazed, extreme
11. paraphernalia: gear, stuff
12. facetious: not serious, sarcastic

4. Do you agree with the author that this practice demeans Native Americans? Why do you agree or disagree?

Writing Assignments

1. Shakespeare once asked, "What's in a name?" What *is* in a name? Are names really so important? Write about an experience in which a name someone was called had an important effect on him or her, or on others. What was the name and what power did it have to hurt or encourage?

2. Write a letter to Tim Giago describing your thoughts about this mascot issue. If you disagree with him, try to write your letter so that you resolve your differences rather than highlight them.

3. Giago notes that he has written about "Indians as mascots" for fifteen years. Do you feel so strongly about any issue that you could write about it for that long? Describe that issue so that your readers see its importance as you do.

Desert Kin

Edward Abbey

Edward Abbey was a park ranger, environmentalist, and nature writer. Here he describes his encounters with animals in the desert that lead him to examine his own behavior and the connectedness of all living things.

I share the housetrailer with a number of mice. I don't know how many but apparently only a few, perhaps a single family. They don't disturb me and are welcome to my crumbs and leavings. Where they came from, how they got into the trailer, how they survived before my arrival (for the trailer had been locked up for six months), these are puzzling matters I am not prepared to resolve. My only reservation concerning the mice is that they do attract rattlesnakes.

I'm sitting on my doorstep early one morning, facing the sun as usual, drinking coffee, when I happen to look down and see almost between my bare feet, only a couple of inches to the rear of my heels, the very thing I had in mind. No mistaking that wedgelike head, that tip of horny segmented[1] tail peeping out of the coils. He's under the doorstep and in the shade where the ground and air remain very cold. In his sluggish condition he's not likely to strike unless I rouse him by some careless move of my own.

---
1. segmented: divided in sections

There's a revolver inside the trailer, a huge British Webley .45, loaded, but it's out of reach. Even if I had it in my hands I'd hesitate to blast a fellow creature at such close range, shooting between my own legs at a living target flat on solid rock thirty inches away. It would be like murder; and where would I set my coffee? My cherry-wood walking stick leans against the trailerhouse wall only a few feet away, but I'm afraid that in leaning over for it I might stir up the rattler or spill some hot coffee on his scales.

Other considerations come to mind. Arches National Monument[2] is meant to be among other things a sanctuary[3] for wildlife—for all forms of wildlife. It is my duty as a park ranger to protect, preserve and defend all living things within the park boundaries, making no exceptions. Even if this were not the case I have personal convictions to uphold. Ideals, you might say. I prefer not to kill animals. . . .

I finish my coffee, lean back and swing my feet up and inside the doorway of the trailer. At once there is a buzzing sound from below and the rattler lifts his head from his coils, eyes brightening, and extends his narrow black tongue to test the air.

After thawing out my boots over the gas flame I pull them on and come back to the doorway. My visitor is still waiting beneath the doorstep, basking in the sun, fully alert. The trailerhouse has two doors. I leave by the other and get a long-handled spade out of the bed of the government pickup. With this tool I scoop the snake into the open. He strikes, I can hear the click of the fangs against steel, see the stain of venom. He wants to stand and fight, but I am impatient; I insist on herding him well away from the trailer. On guard, head aloft—that evil slit-eyed weaving head shaped like the ace of spades—tail whirring, the rattler slithers sideways, retreating slowly before me until he reaches the shelter of a sandstone slab. He backs under it.

You better stay there, cousin, I warn him; if I catch you around the trailer again I'll chop your head off.

A week later he comes back. If not him his twin brother. I spot him one morning under the trailer near the kitchen drain, waiting for a mouse. I have to keep my promise.

This won't do. If there are midget rattlers in the area there may be diamondbacks too—five, six or seven feet long, thick as a man's wrist, dangerous. I don't want them camping under my home. It looks as though I'll have to trap the mice.

However, before being forced to take that step I am lucky enough to capture a gopher snake. Burning garbage one morning at the park dump, I see a long slender yellow-brown snake emerge from a mound of old tin cans and plastic picnic plates and take off down the sandy bed of a gulch. . . . The gopher snake, *Drymarchon corais couperi*, or bull snake, has a reputation as the enemy of rattlesnakes, destroying or driving them away whenever encountered.

Hoping to domestic this sleek, handsome and docile[4] reptile, I release him inside the trailerhouse and keep him there for several

---

2. Arches National Monument: a park near Moab, Utah
3. sanctuary: an area where wildlife is protected
4. docile: obedient

days. Should I attempt to feed him? I decide against it—let him eat mice. What little water he may need can also be extracted from the flesh of his prey.

The gopher snake and I get along nicely. During the day he curls up like a cat in the warm corner behind the heater and at night he goes about his business. The mice, singularly quiet for a change, make themselves scarce. The snake is passive, apparently contented, and makes no resistance when I pick him up with my hands and drape him over an arm or around my neck. When I take him outside into the wind and sunshine his favorite place seems to be inside my shirt, where he wraps himself around my waist and rests on my belt. In this position he sometimes sticks his head out between shirt buttons for a survey of the weather, astonishing and delighting any tourists who may happen to be with me at the time. The scales of a snake are dry and smooth, quite pleasant to the touch. Being a cold blooded creature, of course, he takes his temperature from that of the immediate environment—in this case my body.

> "The two snakes come straight toward me, . . . the forked tongues flickering, their intense wild yellow eyes staring directly into my eyes."

We are compatible.[5] From my point of view, friends. After a week of close association I turn him loose on the warm sandstone at my doorstep and leave for a patrol of the park. At noon when I return he is gone. I search everywhere beneath, nearby and inside the trailer-house, but my companion has disappeared. Has he left the area entirely or is he hiding somewhere close by? At any rate I am troubled no more by rattlesnakes under the door.

The snake story is not yet ended.

In the middle of May, about a month after the gopher snake's disappearance, in the evening of a very hot day, with all the rosy desert cooling like a griddle with the fire turned off, he reappears. This time with a mate.

I'm in the stifling heat of the trailer opening a can of beer, barefooted, about to go outside and relax after a hard day watching cloud formations. I happen to glance out the little window near the refrigerator and see two gopher snakes on my verandah[6] engaged in what seems to be a kind of ritual dance. . . . A shameless *voyeur*,[7] I stare at the lovers, and then to get a closer view run outside and around the trailer to the back. There I get down on hands and knees and creep toward the dancing snakes, not wanting to frighten or disturb them. I crawl to within six feet of them and stop, flat on my belly, watching from the snake's eye level. Obsessed with their ballet, the serpents seem unaware of my presence. . . .

They intertwine and separate, glide side by side, . . . turn like mirror images of each other and glide back again, wind and unwind

---

5. compatible: able to get along well together
6. verandah: porch
7. *voyeur*: someone who finds excitement in watching others

again. This is the basic pattern but there is a variation: at regular intervals the snakes elevate their heads, facing one another, as high as they can go, as if trying to outreach or overawe the other. . . .

18 I crawl after them, determined to see the whole thing. Suddenly and simultaneously they discover me, prone[8] on my belly a few feet away. The dance stops. After a moment's pause the two snakes come straight toward me, still in flawless unison, straight toward my face, the forked tongues flickering, their intense wild yellow eyes staring directly into my eyes. For an instant I am paralyzed by wonder; then, stung by a fear too ancient and powerful to overcome I scramble back, rising, to my knees. The snakes veer and turn away from me in parallel motion, their lean elegant bodies making a soft hissing noise as they slide over the sand and stone. I follow them for a short distance, still plagued by curiosity, before remembering my place and the requirements of common courtesy. For godsake let them go in peace, I tell myself. Wish them luck and (if lovers) innumerable offspring, a life of happily ever after. Not for their sake alone but for your own.

19 In the long hot day and cool evenings to come I will not see the gopher snakes again. Nevertheless I will feel their presence watching over me like . . . deities,[9] keeping the rattlesnakes far back in the brush where I like them best, cropping off the surplus mouse population, maintaining useful connections with the primeval.[10] Sympathy, mutual aid, symbiosis,[11] continuity. . . .

20 We are obliged, therefore, to spread the news, painful and bitter though it may be for some to hear, that all living things on hand are kindred.[12]

Discussion and Writing Questions

1. The first animals that the author mentions are mice. How does he feel about them (paragraph 1)?

2. Abbey has more than one reason for not killing the rattlesnake when he first sees it. What are they (paragraphs 3–4)? Does he later kill it (paragraphs 7–8)? Why?

3. Abbey's relationship with the gopher snake is simple in the beginning and then becomes more complicated. What are his feelings at first? What different emotions does he have as he watches the mating pair (paragraphs 16–18)? Did your feelings about snakes change as you read this essay?

4. What does Abbey mean when he says that "all living things on hand are kindred" (paragraph 20)? How does the whole selection lead up to this conclusion? Why does he say that this news may be "painful and bitter" for some to hear?

---

8. prone: lying down
9. deities: gods and goddesses
10. primeval: ancient
11. symbiosis: a relationship between participants who depend on each other
12. kindred: related to one another; relatives

Writing Assignments

1. Have you ever felt especially connected to the natural world? Did a special place or experience make you feel that way? If so, describe the experience, including the setting.

2. Do you now have or did you ever have a pet? How do you (or did you) feel toward it? Describe an incident that shows one aspect of your relationship with your pet.

3. Observe an insect, a bird, or an animal very closely for a period of time. Take notes on its appearance, its activities, its relationships, if any. Is it a creature that many people dislike or want to kill—a roach, for instance? Describe this creature in detail, explaining whether your feelings changed as you watched it.

Perfume

Barbara Garson

Some people work year after year at dull, repetitious jobs. Why do they do it? How do they stand it? To find out, journalist Barbara Garson interviewed hundreds of workers for her book *All the Livelong Day*. Here, she visits a factory that makes beauty products.

1   Helena Rubenstein makes over two hundred products (if you count different colors). Here in F&F—filling and finishing—there are usually about two dozen lines working at once. Each line is tended by ten to twenty women in blue smocks who perform a single repeated operation on each powder compact, deodorant bottle or perfume spray as it goes past. . . .

2   There are about 250 blue-smocked women in filling and finishing. They are mostly white, mostly middle-aged, and mostly earning "second" incomes. But there's a peppering of black and Latin women in the room, one or two unmarried girls on each line, and an increasing number of young mothers who are the main support of their families. . . .

3   Herbescence is a relatively simple line. The lead lady takes the filled bottles of spray mist out of cartons and places one on each black dot marked on the moving belt. The next two women put little silver tags around the bottle necks. Each one tags every other bottle. The next nine women each fold a protective corrugated cardboard, unfold a silver box, pick up every ninth spray-mist bottle, slip it into the corrugation, insert a leaflet, put the whole thing into the box and close the top. The next seven ladies wrap the silver Herbescence boxes in colored tissue paper. The women don't actually have to count every seventh box because, as a rule, when you finish the twists and folds of your tissue paper, your next box is just coming

along with perhaps a half second to relax before you reach for it. The tissue-papered boxes are put into cartons which in turn are lifted onto skids[1] which, when filled with several thousand spray colognes, will be wheeled out by general factory help or skid boys.

4 Since the line doesn't involve any filling machines, it was a bit quieter at Herbescence. The women didn't have to shout. They could just talk loudly to each other and to me.

5 "You writing a book about cosmetics?" . . . "About Helena's?" . . . And then with greater disbelief: "About these jobs?". . . "About *us?*"

6 Then I got my instructions.

7 "Write down how hard we work."

8 "How boring."

9 "You ought to come back here on a nice hot summer day. They got air conditioning upstairs in lipsticks but it's not for the women. Don't let 'em hand you a line. It's just 'cause the lipsticks might melt."

> *"After four minutes, or about two hundred bottles, the effects of the break seemed to be wearing off."*

10 "Write about how fast the lines are now. It used to be a pleasure to work here. Now you can't keep up. They keep getting faster."

11 "Write about the new supervisors. Why should they treat you like dirt just because you work in a factory?"

12 "Be sure to say how boring."

13 Some twenty years ago, before all the talk about job enrichment, Local 8–149 fought for the right to rotate positions on the assembly line. Now the women change places every two hours. In addition the entire crew of certain particularly unpleasant lines is rotated every three days.

14 "Not that one job is so much different from another," said Dick McManus, local union president, "but at least the women get to move around. They sit next to different women. They get to have different conversations."

15 Maxine Claybourne, a fortyish, flourishing, light yellow black woman, was the new leading lady of the Herbescence line. Since the break she had been putting the bottles out one on each black line. After four minutes, or about two hundred bottles, the effects of the break seemed to be wearing off. Eyes were hypnotized, hands reached heavily for the boxes, bottles, wrapping paper and tags.

16 "Here's a gift, girls," Maxine announced. She took a comb out of her pocket and, between every self-confident stroke, set a bottle down on the belt. They came out neatly on every *other* black dot.

17 Gradually the gift was carried down the line. "This is beautiful," said the boxers as the farther-spaced bottles arrived. "Thanks, Max." Then after a minute it reached the wrappers. "This is how it should always be." And finally: "It used to be this way when I first started here," said the woman filling cartons at the end.

---

1. skids: platforms for stacking and moving heavy items

And then, without any noticeable shift, Maxine began putting the bottles on every dot again.

"I can do things like that," she told me, "when the supervisor moves away. When he comes back . . . [and she cast her eyes in the direction of the man I had not seen approaching] well, at least the girls get to enjoy a little break. One way or another, you got to get through the day."

The line settled down to its old pace again. I left Maxine and headed down to the other end.

"I started here," a woman said, answering my question, "to send my kids to college, but they're all grown up now."

"That's what I did," said the woman next to her. "First you put your kids through school, then you start to pay for a car, then it's new rugs, and before you know it — I'm here fifteen years."

The women nodded. That seemed to be the story for the second-income workers.

A young black woman who hadn't said a word till then muttered sullenly, "Some of us are here to pay for the rent, not buy rugs."

The older women went on. Perhaps they didn't hear her.

"And then you stay because of the other girls."

"Yeah, you stay to keep up with the gossip."

"And there's self-improvement here. You come to work every day, you get more conscious of your clothes, your hair."

"Real self-improvement," a woman objected, "You should hear the language I pick up. My husband says, 'The language you use, you sound like you work in a factory.'"

The most important benefit from the past struggles in this factory, and from the impartial rotation systems, has no official recognition. There is no clause in the contract that says that the workers shall have the right to laugh, talk and be helpful to one another. Nor is there a formal guarantee that the workers can shrug, sneer or otherwise indicate what they think of the supervisors.

But most of the women at Helena Rubenstein are helpful to each other and they present a solid front to the supervisors.

The right to respond like a person, even while your hands are operating like a machine, is something that has been fought for in this factory. And this is defended daily, formally through the grievance process and informally through militant kidding around.

I spent my last hour at Helena Rubenstein back at the Herbescence line, watching hands reach for piece after piece until my own eyes grew glazed and my head throbbed with each bottle that jerked past. And yet, when I looked up it was only four minutes later. I forced myself to stay for a full twenty minutes; then I finally blurted out, "How do you do it seven hours a day?"

"You don't do it seven hours a day," was the answer. "You just do it one piece at a time."

Discussion and Writing Questions

1. Describe the process by which a perfume bottle is packaged on the Herbescence perfume spray assembly line.

2. What reasons do the workers give for working on the line? Why do some of them stay so long if they do not enjoy their work?

3. What "gift" does Maxine Claybourne give her coworkers?

4. Which would you prefer: a boring, high-paying job or an interesting low-paying job? Why?

Writing Assignments

1. Have you ever worked at a dull, repetitive job? Describe step by step what the job involved and your reaction to it, so that the reader can experience it as you did. Did you do anything to make the job more pleasant or interesting? What?

2. "Most of us, like the assembly line worker, have jobs that are too small for our spirit," says Nora Watson in Studs Terkel's book *Working*. What do you think she means by this? Do you agree? Describe a job that would be "big enough for your spirit."

3. Some people believe that a positive attitude can make even the most boring job interesting. Agree or disagree, using examples from your own or others' experience.

Friends of Dirt, Unite!

Ann Lovejoy

How important to you is a neat and clean house or apartment? In this short essay, written for the *Seattle Weekly*, Ann Lovejoy sets forth her views on dirt, and tells why, in her house anyway, it's there to stay.

Friends of dirt, unite! I want to start a consciousness-raising group about dirt—household dirt, inside dirt, dirt in intimate environments. You see, unlike so many superwomen one reads about, I refuse to be a slave to household perfection. I am often asked how I manage to "do it all." Enter my house, and you'll see how. I don't. Compared to me, many bachelors might be considered house-proud. Not that I have no pride. In my house, there are heaps, mounds, veritable[1] mountains of laundry; my pride lies in the fact that they are clean mountains.

---
1. veritable: true or real

When it comes right down to it, life is short. Sometimes very short. If I have only five or ten years to live, do I want to spend them playing sock lotto? If I really look deep into my soul, I have to say no. If my kids were to lose their mom suddenly, would they be better off remembering that the laundry was always put away or that Mom always had time to read, to sing, to listen, to go for aimless rambles? If my husband were to be lost to us, would we miss him most for his winning ways with a dust mop or a hedge clippers? Think about it.

This is not to say I have no standards at all. The operative parts of the bathroom get cleaned almost daily. This is not from principle, really—two small boys with indifferent[2] aim make it a necessity. The dishes get done at least once a day, and put away, too—in fact, all of the real work areas are comparatively tidy. Comparatively. This ability to keep certain areas tidy mystifies some of our near and dear. "If you can do it *there*," they query[3] plaintively, "why not everywhere?" Hey, I'm a New Woman. If I have learned anything from my years of parenting, from various liberation groups, from hospital nursing and working in a hospice,[4] it is to do the important things first, the others later, if at all.

> "If my husband were to be lost to us, would we miss him most for his winning ways with a dust mop or a hedge clippers?"

This isn't a militant stand; we too enjoy the house best when it is clean and tidy. Getting there is not, however, half the fun. So why don't we just give in and hire help? It's a combination of things, really: lack of money, deep convictions about not hiring other people to do what we won't do for ourselves, and an inability to get geared up for pre-cleaning for the cleaning service.

I know that I'm not alone in putting my life's work, our family play, ahead of repetitive household chores. True, only a handful of my acquaintances are similarly slovenly,[5] but how many soulmates can one expect to have in this imperfect world?

Discussion and Writing Questions

1. Why do you suppose the author wants to "start a consciousness-raising group about dirt" (paragraph 1)?

2. What is the main reason that the author gives for not wanting to "be a slave to household perfection" (paragraph 1)?

3. Why doesn't the author want to hire someone to help her clean? In your opinion, are her reasons sensible or not?

4. What things does the author consider more important than a tidy house?

---

2. indifferent: not careful
3. query: ask
4. hospice: a place or program that cares for the needs of dying patients
5. slovenly: messy, untidy

Writing Assignments

1. The author says she has learned to "do the important things first, the others later, if at all" (paragraph 3). What are the important things in your life? Are you able to do them first, or do they sometimes get lost among the unimportant things that take your time?

2. Married women currently do more housework than their husbands, even when both have outside jobs or careers. Is this fair? Give your views on whether household chores should be equally shared.

3. Write a lighthearted description of how you can "do" a task by "not doing" it. Describe the specific task, the results of your inaction, and how others respond.

Discovery of a Father

Sherwood Anderson

Children sometimes find it hard to understand and accept a parent's behavior. In this selection, classic American author Sherwood Anderson recalls the night he stopped blaming his father and discovered the bond between them.

1 You hear it said that fathers want their sons to be what they feel they cannot themselves be, but I tell you it also works the other way. A boy wants something very special from his father. I know that as a small boy I wanted my father to be a certain thing he was not. I wanted him to be a proud, silent, dignified father. When I was with the other boys and he passed along the street, I wanted to feel a flow of pride. "There he is. That is my father."

2 But he wasn't such a one. He couldn't be. It seemed to me then that he was always showing off. Let's say someone in our town had got up a show. They were always doing it. The druggist would be in it, the shoe-store clerk, the horse doctor, and a lot of women and girls. My father would manage to get the chief comedy part. It was, let's say, a Civil War play and he was a comic Irish soldier. He had to do the most absurd things. They thought he was funny, but I didn't.

3 I thought he was terrible. I didn't see how mother could stand it. She even laughed with the others. Maybe I would have laughed if it hadn't been my father.

4 Or there was a parade, the Fourth of July or Decoration Day. He'd be in that, too, right at the front of it, as Grand Marshal or something, on a white horse hired from a livery stable.

5 He couldn't ride for shucks. He fell off the horse and everyone hooted with laughter, but he didn't care. He even seemed to like it. I remember once when he had done something ridiculous, and right

out on Main Street, too. I was with some other boys and they were laughing and shouting at him and he was shouting back and having as good a time as they were. I ran down an alley back of some stores and there in the Presbyterian Church sheds I had a good long cry.

Or I would be in bed at night and father would come home a little lit up and bring some men with him. He was a man who was never alone. Before he went broke, running a harness shop, there were always a lot of men loafing in the shop. He went broke, of course, because he gave too much credit. He couldn't refuse it and I thought he was a fool. I had got to hating him.

There'd be men I didn't think would want to be fooling around with him. There might even be the superintendent of our schools and a quiet man who ran the hardware store. Once I remember there was a white-haired man who was a cashier of the bank. It was a wonder to me they'd want to be seen with such a windbag. That's what I thought he was. I know now what it was that attracted them. It was because life in our town, as in all small towns, was at times pretty dull and he livened it up. He made them laugh. He could tell stories. He'd even get them to singing.

If they didn't come to our house they'd go off, say at night, to where there was a grassy place by a creek. They'd cook food there and drink beer and sit about listening to his stories.

He was always telling stories about himself. He'd say this or that wonderful thing had happened to him. It might be something that made him look like a fool. He didn't care.

If an Irishman came to our house, right away father would say he was Irish. He'd tell what county in Ireland he was born in. He'd tell things that happened there when he was a boy. He'd make it seem so real that, if I hadn't known he was born in southern Ohio, I'd have believed him myself.

If it was a Scotchman the same thing happened. He'd get a burr[1] into his speech. Or he was a German or a Swede. He'd be anything the other man was. I think they all knew he was lying, but they seemed to like him just the same. As a boy that was what I couldn't understand.

And there was mother. How could she stand it? I wanted to ask but never did. She was not the kind you asked such questions.

I'd be upstairs in my bed, in my room above the porch, and father would be telling some of his tales. A lot of father's stories were about the Civil War. To hear him tell it he'd been in about every battle. He'd known Grant, Sherman, Sheridan[2] and I don't know how many others. He'd been particularly intimate with General Grant so that when Grant went East to take charge of all the armies, he took father along.

"I was an orderly at headquarters and Sim Grant said to me, 'Irve,' he said, 'I'm going to take you along with me.'"

It seems he and Grant used to slip off sometimes and have a quiet drink together. That's what my father said. He'd tell about the day Lee surrendered and how, when the great moment came, they couldn't find Grant.

"You know," my father said, "about General Grant's book, his memoirs. You've read of how he said he had a headache and how,

---

1. burr: sound of a Scottish accent
2. Grant, Sherman, Sheridan: great Civil War generals

when he got word that Lee was ready to call it quits, he was suddenly and miraculously cured.

"Huh," said father. "He was in the woods with me.

"I was in there with my back against a tree. I was pretty well corned.³ I had got hold of a bottle of pretty good stuff.

"They were looking for Grant. He had got off his horse and come into the woods. He found me. He was covered with mud.

> "Life in our town . . . was at times pretty dull and he livened it up. He made them laugh. He could tell stories."

"I had the bottle in my hand. What'd I care? The war was over. I knew we had them licked."

My father said that he was the one who told Grant about Lee. An orderly riding by had told him, because the orderly knew how thick he was with Grant. Grant was embarrassed.

"But, Irve, look at me. I'm all covered with mud," he said to father.

And then, my father said, he and Grant decided to have a drink together. They took a couple of shots and then, because he didn't want Grant to show up potted before the immaculate Lee, he smashed the bottle against the tree.

"Sim Grant's dead now and I wouldn't want it to get out on him," my father said.

That's just one of the kind of things he'd tell. Of course the men knew he was lying, but they seemed to like it just the same.

When we got broke, down and out, do you think he ever brought anything home? Not he. If there wasn't anything to eat in the house, he'd go off visiting around at farmhouses. They all wanted him. Sometimes he'd stay away for weeks, mother working to keep us fed; and then home he'd come bringing, let's say, a ham. He'd got it from some farmer friend. He'd slap it on the table in the kitchen. "You bet I'm going to see that my kids have something to eat," he'd say, and mother would just stand smiling at him. She'd never say a word about all the weeks and months he'd been away, not leaving us a cent for food. Once I heard her speaking to a woman in our street. Maybe the woman had dared to sympathize with her. "Oh," she said, "it's all right. He isn't ever dull like most of the men in this street. Life is never dull when my man is about."

But often I was filled with bitterness, and sometimes I wished he wasn't my father. I'd even invent another man as my father. To protect my mother I'd make up stories of a secret marriage that for some strange reason never got known. As though some man, say the president of a railroad company or maybe a Congressman, had married my mother, thinking his wife was dead and then it turned out she wasn't.

So they had to hush it up but I got born just the same. I wasn't really the son of my father. Somewhere in the world there was a very dignified, quite wonderful man who was really my father. I even made myself half believe these fancies.

---

3. corned: drunk on corn whiskey

29 And then there came a certain night. He'd been off somewhere for two or three weeks. He found me alone in the house, reading by the kitchen table.

30 It had been raining and he was very wet. He sat and looked at me for a long time, not saying a word. I was startled, for there was on his face the saddest look I had ever seen. He sat for a time, his clothes dripping. Then he got up.

31 "Come on with me," he said.

32 I got up and went with him out of the house. I was filled with wonder but I wasn't afraid. We went along a dirt road that led down into a valley, about a mile out of town, where there was a pond. We walked in silence. The man who was always talking had stopped his talking.

33 I didn't know what was up and had the queer feeling that I was with a stranger. I don't know whether my father intended it so. I don't think he did.

34 The pond was quite large. It was still raining hard and there were flashes of lightning followed by thunder. We were on a grassy bank at the pond's edge when my father spoke, and in the darkness and rain his voice sounded strange.

35 "Take off your clothes," he said. Still filled with wonder, I began to undress. There was a flash of lightning and I saw that he was already naked.

36 Naked, we went into the pond. Taking my hand he pulled me in. It may be that I was too frightened, too full of a feeling of strangeness, to speak. Before that night my father had never seemed to pay any attention to me.

37 "And what is he up to now?" I kept asking myself. I did not swim very well, but he put my hand on his shoulder and struck out into the darkness.

38 He was a man with big shoulders, a powerful swimmer. In the darkness I could feel the movement of his muscles. We swam to the far edge of the pond and then back to where we had left our clothes. The rain continued and the wind blew. Sometimes my father swam on his back and when he did he took my hand in his large powerful one and moved it over so that it rested always on his shoulder. Sometimes there would be a flash of lightning and I could see his face quite clearly.

39 It was as it was earlier, in the kitchen, a face filled with sadness. There would be the momentary glimpse of his face and then again the darkness, the wind and the rain. In me there was a feeling I had never known before.

40 It was a feeling of closeness. It was something strange. It was as though there were only we two in the world. It was as though I had been jerked suddenly out of myself, out of my world of the schoolboy, out of a world in which I was ashamed of my father.

41 He had become blood of my blood; he the strong swimmer and I the boy clinging to him in the darkness. We swam in silence and in silence we dressed in our wet clothes, and went home.

42 There was a lamp lighted in the kitchen and when we came in, the water dripping from us, there was my mother. She smiled at us. I remember that she called us "boys."

"What have you boys been up to," she asked, but my father did not answer. As he had begun the evening's experience with me in silence, so he ended it. He turned and looked at me. Then he went, I thought, with a new and strange dignity out of the room. 43

I climbed the stairs to my own room, undressed in the darkness and got into bed. I couldn't sleep and did not want to sleep. For the first time I knew that I was the son of my father. He was a story teller as I was to be. It may be that I even laughed a little softly there in the darkness. If I did, I laughed knowing that I would never again be wanting another father. 44

Discussion and Writing Questions

1. In what ways was Anderson's father a disappointing or even a bad father and husband? What role do you think his drinking played in his behavior?

2. Anderson says that one night he saw on his father's face "the saddest look I had ever seen" (paragraph 30). Why do you think Anderson's father looked—and felt—so sad?

3. Why did the swimming incident change the relationship between the author and his father? How did their relationship change?

4. At the end of this selection, Anderson recognizes his similarities to his father (paragraph 44). What are these similarities?

Writing Assignments

1. Anderson says that "a boy wants something very special from his father" (paragraph 1). Is this true? What did you, as a boy or as a girl, want from your father? Did you get it?

2. Have you ever been embarrassed by the behavior of your parent (or guardian)? How did that person act? Why did you feel embarrassed? Perhaps choose one incident that reveals his or her behavior and your response. Did you ever discuss the incident with the person involved?

3. Have you ever come to see a person differently? What changed your mind—or your heart? Describe your impressions of this person before and after the change. In what ways did your relationship with that person also change as a result?

Four Directions

Amy Tan

Have you ever possessed a certain skill or strength, and then, as you grew, lost it? Amy Tan, a Chinese-American novelist who lives in San Francisco, writes about a young chess player who seemed unbeatable—at age ten.

I was ten years old. Even though I was young, I knew my ability to play chess was a gift. It was effortless, so easy. I could see things on the chessboard that other people could not. I could create barriers to protect myself that were invisible to my opponents. And this gift gave me supreme confidence. I knew what my opponents would do, move for move. I knew at exactly what point their faces would fall when my seemingly simple and childlike strategy would reveal itself as a devastating and irrevocable[1] course. I loved to win.

And my mother loved to show me off, like one of my many trophies she polished. She used to discuss my games as if she had devised the strategies.

"I told my daughter, Use your horses to run over the enemy," she informed one shopkeeper. "She won very quickly this way." And of course, she had said this before the game—that and a hundred other useless things that had nothing to do with my winning.

To our family friends who visited she would confide, "You don't have to be so smart to win chess. It is just tricks. You blow from the North, South, East, and West. The other person becomes confused. They don't know which way to run."

I hated the way she tried to take all the credit. And one day I told her so, shouting at her on Stockton Street, in the middle of a crowd of people. I told her she didn't know anything, so she shouldn't show off. She should shut up. Words to that effect.

That evening and the next day she wouldn't speak to me. She would say stiff words to my father and brothers, as if I had become invisible and she was talking about a rotten fish she had thrown away but which had left behind its bad smell.

I knew this strategy, the sneaky way to get someone to pounce back in anger and fall into a trap. So I ignored her. I refused to speak and waited for her to come to me.

After many days had gone by in silence, I sat in my room, staring at the sixty-four squares of my chessboard, trying to think of another way. And that's when I decided to quit playing chess.

Of course I didn't mean to quit forever. At most, just for a few days. And I made a show of it. Instead of practicing in my room every night, as I always did, I marched into the living room and sat down in front of the television set with my brothers, who stared at me, an unwelcome intruder. I used my brothers to further my plan; I cracked my knuckles to annoy them.

---

1. irrevocable: impossible to cancel or halt

"Ma!" they shouted. "Make her stop. Make her go away." 10

But my mother did not say anything. 11

Still I was not worried. But I could see I would have to make a stronger move. I decided to sacrifice a tournament that was coming up in one week. I would refuse to play in it. And my mother would certainly have to speak to me about this. Because the sponsors and the benevolent associations[2] would start calling her, asking, shouting, pleading to make me play again. 12

> "I could no longer see the secret weapons of each piece, the magic within the intersection of each square."

And then the tournament came and went. And she did not come to me, crying, "Why are you not playing chess?" But I was crying inside, because I learned that a boy whom I had easily defeated on two other occasions had won. 13

I realized my mother knew more tricks than I had thought. But now I was tired of her game. I wanted to start practicing for the next tournament. So I decided to pretend to let her win. I would be the one to speak first. 14

"I am ready to play chess again," I announced to her. I had imagined she would smile and then ask me what special thing I wanted to eat. 15

But instead, she gathered her face into a frown and stared into my eyes, as if she could force some kind of truth out of me. 16

"Why do you tell me this?" she finally said in sharp tones. "You think it is so easy. One day quit, next day play. Everything for you is this way. So smart, so easy, so fast." 17

"I said I'll play," I whined. 18

"No!" she shouted, and I almost jumped out of my scalp. "It is not so easy anymore." 19

I was quivering, stunned by what she said, in not knowing what she meant. And then I went back to my room. I stared at my chessboard, its sixty-four squares, to figure out how to undo this terrible mess. And after staring like this for many hours, I actually believed that I had made the white squares black and the black squares white, and everything would be all right. 20

And sure enough, I won her back. That night I developed a high fever, and she sat next to my bed, scolding me for going to school without my sweater. In the morning she was there as well, feeding me rice porridge flavored with chicken broth she had strained herself. She said she was feeding me this because I had the chicken pox and one chicken knew how to fight another. And in the afternoon, she sat in a chair in my room, knitting me a pink sweater while telling me about a sweater that Auntie Suyuan had knit for her daughter June, and how it was most unattractive and of the worst yarn. I was so happy that she had become her usual self. 21

But after I got well, I discovered that, really, my mother had changed. She no longer hovered over[3] me as I practiced different 22

---

2. benevolent associations: charities
3. hovered over: paid close attention to

chess games. She did not polish my trophies every day. She did not cut out the small newspaper item that mentioned my name. It was as if she had erected[4] an invisible wall and I was secretly groping each day to see how high and how wide it was.

23 At my next tournament, while I had done well overall, in the end the points were not enough. I lost. And what was worse, my mother said nothing. She seemed to walk around with this satisfied look, as if it had happened because she had devised this strategy.

24 I was horrified. I spent many hours every day going over in my mind what I had lost. I knew it was not just the last tournament. I examined every move, every piece, every square. And I could no longer see the secret weapons of each piece, the magic within the intersection of each square. I could see only my mistakes, my weaknesses. It was as though I had lost my magic armor. And everybody could see this, where it was easy to attack me.

25 Over the next few weeks and later months and years, I continued to play, but never with that same feeling of supreme confidence. I fought hard, with fear and desperation. When I won, I was grateful, relieved. And when I lost, I was filled with growing dread, and then terror that I was no longer a prodigy,[5] that I had lost the gift and had turned into someone quite ordinary.

26 When I lost twice to the boy whom I had defeated so easily a few years before, I stopped playing chess altogether. And nobody protested. I was fourteen.

Discussion and Writing Questions

1. Why did the child and her mother fight? Do you think the mother really wanted "all the credit" for herself (paragraph 5)? Why did she refuse to speak to the child after their argument?

2. The mother and daughter almost seem locked in a chess match of their own after their argument. What do you think is happening between them? Does the daughter's age—adolescence—have anything to do with it?

3. Why do you suppose the author says she had lost more than the last tournament, she had lost her "magic armor" (paragraph 24)?

4. The author says that "nobody protested" when she gave up chess permanently at age fourteen (paragraph 26). Do you think people might have protested if she were a boy? Why or why not?

Writing Assignments

1. Did you possess a talent or strength as a young person that you later lost? What happened? What caused you to change?

---

4. erected: built
5. prodigy: a person with enormous talents in a particular area

2. Adolescence is for most people a time of enormous change, and change often produces great anxiety. Was there an incident in your adolescence that caused you such anxiety—because you or your surroundings were somehow changing? Describe this incident.

3. Research suggests that once they reach adolescence, many girls give up asserting themselves—in sports, in class, and in student government, for example—because they feel pressure to be "feminine." Do you think this is true? Discuss why or why not, using yourself or a young woman you know as an example.

For a Parent, There's No Language Dilemma

Ana Veciana-Suarez

The issue of bilingual education—the teaching of two languages in the public schools—has become an increasingly sensitive one in recent years. Some argue for the practice; others oppose it. In a recent issue of the *Miami Herald*, a concerned parent argues that two languages are better than one.

My son Christopher cannot roll his R's.[1]

I realize that on the seismic[2] chart of development this does not rate as high as a diagnosis of dyslexia,[3] but in my book of milestones it falls squarely between not being able to tie your shoelaces and repeated fighting with classmates.

In increasingly Latin Miami, rolling R's is a survival skill. In Christopher's future world, it will mean more money and better opportunities. It will allow him to communicate with his many older relatives, to connect with the culture of his heritage.

Having lived most of his life in Palm Beach County, Christopher can barely speak Spanish. He understands most everything especially if the conversation has to do with food or play. But ask him to complete a sentence or answer a question and his eyes grow wide and blank. He hesitates. His tongue proves to be as stubborn as a pack mule at the foot of a hill.

This causes him much stress, and it mortifies[4] me. I'm the one to blame. From the beginning, when he babbled his first words, I should have insisted on Spanish because eventually he would have learned, and preferred, English.

---
1. roll his R's: pronounce the letter R like a native speaker of Spanish
2. seismic: like an earthquake
3. dyslexia: a reading disorder
4. mortifies: badly embarrasses

As a daughter of Cuban exiles, I grew up speaking Spanish at home. I learned to read and write it. At one time, the rules of where to place the accents were second nature when I put pen to paper. No more. I make my living in English, and English is the language that comes more easily. This saddens me. I am losing an important and valuable part of my personal history.

Not everyone feels this way. In fact, language is a volatile[5] issue in South Florida. It is the red flag that separates the "us" from "them," the rallying cry for those who feel that immigrants must melt in, not stay apart.

I know both sides of the language argument. I've heard those complaints from strangers as well as from those close and dear to my heart. A childhood friend, who moved north when she felt she could not compete in a job market that often required Spanish as well as English, confided that she wasn't sure people like me, people not willing to give up that part of their identity, would ever be American enough. These were not words of hate; they were of love and concern.

---

5. volatile: explosive

As a kid, I knew a few children in the neighborhood who spoke broken Spanish, accented and irregular. They were teased and labeled "cubanos arrepentidos," which loosely translates into regretful Cubans.

> "From the beginning, when he babbled his first words, I should have insisted on Spanish."

My children, I vowed, would not grow up to be like them. They would speak both languages fluently and, because I'm such a stickler for grammar, they would also learn them correctly.

But I have failed, and now the urgency of making up for lost years has become as important for cultural reasons as economic and emotional ones. I want them to be able to speak to their grandparents as freely as they do with their neighbors. I want them to have an edge in what is quickly becoming a global village.

The two older ones, exposed to Spanish for a longer period, speak it well enough to be acceptable. Their trouble lies in pronunciation and verb tenses.

But until our return to Miami, Christopher had spent more than half of his seven years in a place where no one spoke Spanish. His exposure was limited to periodic visits with grandparents, when the communication between them was an odd amalgam[6] of sign language and Spanglish.[7]

Not so long ago in school a teacher read a story with a few words in Spanish. He was the only child able to translate those words for the rest of the class. He came home triumphant and demanding. He wanted to know more.

So now almost every night before bed, we sit together to make our way through an ancient reader his father's grandmother mailed page by page from Cuba in the early 1960s.

"Va, ve, vi, vo, vu," he repeats after me. "Una uva. Una uva en la mesa."

After the first lessons, the oldest two asked to read, too. "But not from a baby book," insisted the 10-year-old. "A real book." We got a real book.

Together we have begun a lifelong journey into a place whose doors open only when the R's are rolling. This is where history takes on a face and a name, where lilt[8] and inflection[9] suggest identity, culture, an unusual past that enriches and assures a hopeful future.

We are learning to double our L's and squiggle the top of our N's. We are learning from where we have come and where we are going, and, perhaps more importantly, why the two cannot be separated.

I know that their lives, like mine, will sometimes appear fractured. "What do you dream in?" a boss once asked me. "Depends," I answered.

---

6. amalgam: mixture

7. Spanglish: a mixture of Spanish and English

8. lilt: lightness in the voice

9. inflection: change in pitch or tone when speaking

Their lives, like mine, will grow into a duality[10] of more than language, and they will be better for it. Rest assured, it will not make them any less American.

Discussion and Writing Questions

1. What reasons does Veciana-Suarez offer for wanting her boys to speak Spanish as well as English?

2. The author speaks of "us" and "them" (paragraph 7). What does she mean by these terms?

3. Why does the author discuss her own experiences with two languages (paragraphs 6 and 9)?

4. Why did Christopher suddenly want to learn more Spanish after he translated Spanish words for his class at school (paragraphs 14–15)? What changed his attitude?

Writing Assignments

1. Write about an aspect of your own cultural, racial, ethnic, or religious background that makes you proud, that you don't want to lose. Do you feel, like the author, that you can hold on to this identity and still be American?

2. Do you speak a language other than English at home? If so, describe where and how you learned, or are learning, English. If English is your first language, have you tried to learn a second? If you have, describe your experience.

3. Can the United States continue to be called the "melting pot" if people speak a language other than English at school or at work? Why or why not? Argue for one side of this issue or the other, or, if you prefer, discuss both sides.

---

10. duality: having two parts or sides

Quotation Bank

This collection of wise and humorous statements has been assembled for you to read, enjoy, and use in a variety of ways as you write. You might choose ones that you particularly agree or disagree with and use them as the basis of journal entries and writing assignments. Sometimes when writing a paragraph or essay, you may find it useful to include a quotation to support a point you are making. Or you may simply want to read through these quotations for ideas and for fun. As you come across other intriguing statements by writers, add them to the list—or write some of your own.

Writing

Writing, like life itself, is a voyage of discovery.
—Henry Miller

Writing is the hardest work in the world not involving heavy lifting.
—Pete Hamill

I think best with a pencil in my hand.
—Anne Morrow Lindbergh

I write to discover what I think.
—Daniel J. Boorstin

I see but one rule: to be clear. If I am not clear, all my world crumbles to nothing.
—Marie Henri Beyle Stendhal

To me, the greatest pleasure of writing is not what it's about, but the inner music that words make.
—Truman Capote

Writing is the only thing that when I do it, I don't feel I should be doing something else.
—Gloria Steinem

7

I never travel without my diary. One should always have something sensational to read on the train.
—Oscar Wilde

8

Nothing quite new is perfect.
—Cicero

9

A professional writer is an amateur who didn't quit.
—Richard Bach

10

Learning

I could walk twenty miles to listen to my worst enemy if I could learn something.
—Gottfried Wilhelm von Leibnitz

11

The mind is a mansion, but most of the time we are content to live in the lobby.
—Dr. William Michaels

12

Education is . . . hanging around until you've caught on.
—Robert Frost

13

Prejudices, it is well known, are most difficult to eradicate [remove] from the heart whose soil has never been loosened or fertilized by education; they grown there, firm as weeds among stones.
—Charlotte Brontë

14

Many receive advice; few profit from it.
—Publius

15

Pay attention to what they tell you to forget.
—Muriel Rukeyser

16

Education is what you have left over after you have forgotten everything you have learned.
—Anonymous

17

Only the educated are free.
—Epictetus

18

The basic purpose of a liberal arts education is to liberate the human being to exercise his or her potential to the fullest.
—Barbara M. White

19

All things are possible to him [or her] who believes.
—Brother Lawrence

20

Love

Love consists in this: that two solitudes protect and touch and greet each other.
—Rainer Maria Rilke   21

It is not easy to find happiness in ourselves, and it is not possible to find it elsewhere.
—Agnes Repplier   22

To love and to be loved is to feel the sun from both sides.
—David Viscott   23

So often when we say "I love you," we say it with a huge "I" and a small "you."
—Archbishop Antony   24

Choose your life's mate carefully. From this one decision will come ninety percent of all your happiness or misery.
—H. Jackson Browne, Jr.   25

Marriage is our last, best chance to grow up.
—Joseph Barth   26

A divorce is like an amputation; you survive, but there's less of you.
—Margaret Atwood   27

No partner in a love relationship should feel that she [or he] has to give up an essential part of herself [or himself] to make it viable [workable].
—May Sarton   28

I can't mate in captivity.
—Gloria Steinem   29

Gold and love affairs are difficult to hide.
—Spanish proverb   30

Love doesn't just sit there, like a stone; it has to be made, like bread, remade all the time, made new.
—Ursala K. Le Guin   31

To be loved, be lovable.
—Ovid   32

Work and Success

The best career advice to give the young is, find out what you like doing best and get someone to pay you for doing it.
—Katherine Whilehaen   33

Can anybody remember when times were not hard and money not scarce?
—*Ralph Waldo Emerson* 34

Eighty percent of success is showing up.
—*Woody Allen* 35

Nothing great was ever achieved without enthusiasm.
—*Ralph Waldo Emerson* 36

There are two things to aim at in life: first, to get what you want and, after that, to enjoy it. Only the wisest . . . achieve the second.
—*Logan Pearsall Smith* 37

Money is like manure. If you spread it around, it does a lot of good, but if you pile it up in one place, it stinks like hell.
—*Clint W. Murchison* 38

If you have built castles in the air, your work need not be lost; that is where they should be. Now put foundations under them.
—*Henry David Thoreau* 39

It is never too late to be what you might have been.
—*George Eliot* 40

A celebrity is a person who works hard all his [or her] life to become well known, then wears dark glasses to avoid being recognized.
—*Fred Allen* 41

I think most of us are looking for a calling, not a job. Most of us, like the assembly line worker, have had jobs that are too small for our spirit.
—*Nora Watson* 42

The secret of joy in work is contained in one word—excellence. To know how to do something well is to enjoy it.
—*Pearl Buck* 43

A good reputation is more valuable than money.
—*Publius* 44

Very little is needed to make a happy life.
—*Marcus Aurelius Antoninus* 45

When you reach for the stars, you may not quite get one, but you won't come up with a handful of mud.
—*Leo Burnett* 46

Family and Friendship

Making the decision to have a child—it's momentous. It is to decide forever to have your heart go walking around outside your body.
—Elizabeth Stone
47

Any mother could perform the jobs of several air-traffic controllers with ease.
—Lisa Alther
48

Familiarity breeds contempt.—*Aesop;*
49

—and children.—*Mark Twain*
50

It takes a village to raise a child.
—African proverb
51

Nobody who has not been in the interior of a family can say what the difficulties of any individual of that family may be.
—Jane Austen
52

If there is anything that we wish to change in the child, we should first examine it and see whether it is not something that could better be changed in ourselves.
—Carl Jung
53

Insanity is hereditary—you get it from your children.
—Sam Levenson
54

Govern a family as you would fry small fish—gently.
—Chinese proverb
55

Everything that irritates us about others can lead us to an understanding of ourselves.
—Morton Hunt
56

The meeting of two personalities is like the contact of two chemical substances: if there is any reaction, both are transformed.
—Carl Jung
57

The only way to have a friend is to be one.
—Ralph Waldo Emerson
58

Wisdom for Living

Seize the day; put no trust in the morrow.
—Horace
59

Don't be afraid your life will end; be afraid that it will never begin.
—Grace Hansen
60

My life, my *real* life, was in danger, and not from anything other people might do but from the hatred I carried in my own heart.
—*James Baldwin* 61

No one can make you feel inferior without your consent.
—*Eleanor Roosevelt* 62

Life is under no obligation to give us what we expect.
—*Margaret Mitchell* 63

What we anticipate seldom occurs; what we least expect generally happens.
—*Benjamin Disraeli* 64

Take your life in your own hands and what happens? A terrible thing: no one to blame.
—*Erica Jong* 65

Regret is an appalling waste of energy: you can't build on it; it is good only for wallowing in.
—*Katherine Mansfield* 66

Grief dares us to love once more.
—*Terry Tempest Williams* 67

Flowers grow out of dark moments.
—*Corita Kent* 68

Lying is done with words and also with silence.
—*Adrienne Rich* 69

Pick battles big enough to matter, small enough to win.
—*Jonathan Kozol* 70

You can't hold a man [woman] down without staying down with him [her].
—*Booker T. Washington* 71

A fanatic is one who can't change his [her] mind and won't change the subject.
—*Winston Churchill* 72

To me, old age is always fifteen years older than I am.
—*Bernard Baruch* 73

Time wounds all heels.
—*Jane Ace* 74

When you come to a fork in the road, take it.
—*Yogi Berra* 75

ACKNOWLEDGMENTS

Text Credits

Page 45—*Cosmic Quest: Searching for Intelligent Life Among the Stars* by Margaret Poynter and Mitchell J. Klein. Copyright © 1984 by Atheneum. Reprinted by permission of the author.

Pages 438–441—"Women Are Missing from Newspaper Pages" by Ellen Goodman. Copyright © 1985 by The Washington Post Company. Reprinted by permission of Summit Books, a division of Simon & Schuster, Inc.

Pages 441–443—"A Homemade Education" from *The Autobiography of Malcolm X* by Malcolm X, with Alex Haley. Copyright © 1964 by Malcolm X and Alex Haley. Copyright © 1965 by Alex Haley and Malcolm X. Reprinted by permission of Random House, Inc.

Pages 444–447—"Mrs. Flowers" from *I Know Why the Caged Bird Sings* by Maya Angelou. Copyright © 1969 by Maya Angelou. Reprinted by permission of Random House, Inc.

Pages 448–451—"Papa, the Teacher" from *Papa, My Father* by Leo F. Buscaglia, Ph.D. Copyright © 1989, by Leo F. Buscaglia, Inc. Published by Slack, Inc.

Pages 452–454—"Homeless" from *Living Out Loud* by Anna Quindlen. Copyright © 1987 by Anna Quindlen. Reprinted by permission of Random House, Inc.

Pages 454–456—"Say Yes to Yourself" from Joseph T. Martorano and Joseph P. Kildahl, *Beyond Negative Thinking*. Copyright © 1989 by Plenum Publishing Corporation. Reprinted with permission.

Pages 458–459—"Yolanda" from *How the Garcia Girls Lost Their Accents* by Julia Alvarez. Copyright © Julia Alvarez 1991. Published by Plume, an imprint of New American Library, a division of Penguin Books USA Inc. First published in hardcover by Algonquin Books of Chapel Hill. Reprinted by permission of Susan Bergholz Literary Services, New York.

Pages 460–461—Peter Gzowski, "People and Their Machines and Vice Versa" from *The Morningside Papers* by Peter Gzowski. Used by permission of The Canadian Publishers, McClelland & Stewart, Toronto.

Pages 462–464—"The Gift" by Courtland Milloy. Copyright © 1992, *The Washington Post*. Reprinted with permission.

Pages 465–468—"Salvation" from *The Big Sea* by Langston Hughes. Copyright © 1940 by Langston Hughes. Copyright renewed 1968 by Arna Bontemps and George Houston Bass. Reprinted by permission of Hill and Wang, a division of Farrar, Straus & Giroux, Inc.

Pages 468–470—"Forever" from *Married People: Staying Together in the Age of Divorce* by Francine Klagsbrun. Copyright © 1985 by Francine Klagsbrun. Used by permission of Bantam Books, a division of Bantam Doubleday Dell Publishing Group, Inc.

Pages 471–473—"Sports Nuts" from *Dave Barry Talks Back* by Dave Barry. Copyright © 1991 by Dave Barry. Reprinted by permission of Crown Publishers, Inc.

Pages 474–476—"I Hope the Redskins Lose" by Tim Giago. Reprinted by permission of Tim Giago.

Pages 477–480—"Desert Kin" by Edward Abbey. Reprinted by permission of Don Congdon Associates, Inc. Copyright © 1968 by Edward Abbey.

Pages 481–483—Barbara Garson, "Perfume" from *All the Livelong Day* by Barbara Garson. Copyright © 1972, 1973, 1974, 1975 by Barbara Garson. Used by permission of Doubleday, a division of Bantam Doubleday Dell Publishing Group, Inc.

Pages 484–485—"Friends of Dirt, Unite!" by Ann Lovejoy. Reprinted by permission of the author. Ann Lovejoy is the author of numerous books and articles on gardening and cooking.

Pages 486–490—"Discovery of a Father" by Sherwood Anderson. Reprinted by permission of Harold Ober Associates Incorporated. Copyright © 1939 by *The Reader's Digest*. Copyright renewed 1966 by Eleanor Copenhaver Anderson.

Pages 491–493—"Four Directions" by Amy Tan. Reprinted by permission of The Putnam Publishing Group from *The Joy Luck Club* by Amy Tan. Copyright © 1989 by Amy Tan.

Pages 494–497—"For a Parent, There's No Language Dilemma" by Ana Veciana-Suarez. Reprinted by permission of *The Miami Herald*. Copyright © 1992.

Photo Credits

Page 442—UPI/Bettmann; Page 463— © Beverly Rezneck; Page 474—Copyright © Mark E. Gibson; Page 495—Rob Tringali/Sportschrome.

Index

A/an/and, 392–394
Accept/except, 394–395
Action verbs, 58–59, 432
Active voice, 140–141
Address (persons), commas used for direct, 343–344
Addresses (location), commas used in, 347–349
Adjectives
  bad/worse/worst, 285–286
  comparatives with, 280–283, 285–286
  defining and writing, 275–279, 433
  demonstrative, 286–287
  good/better/best, 285–286
  good or *well*, 279–280
  past participles used as, 144–149
  superlatives with, 283–286
Adverbs
  comparatives with, 280–283, 285–286
  conjunctive, 211–217
  defining and writing, 275–279, 433
  superlatives with, 283–286
  using *good* or *well*, 279–280
Agreement. *See also* Present tense
  defining, 83–86, 108
  with irregular verbs, 86–92
  in past tense, 112
  practice in, 95–99
  in present progressive tense, 153
  with pronoun subjects, 93–95
  in questions, 104–105
  with singular subjects, 101–102
  with *there is/there are*, 102–104
  with *who/which/that*, 105–107
And, pronouns joined by, 266–268
Antecedents
  defining, 250–251, 431
  pronouns clearly referring to, 261–263
  singular, 253–254
Apostrophes
  used for contractions, 353–355
  used to show possession, 355–360
Appositives, commas to set off, 344–345

Bad/badly, 285–286
Bad/worse/worst, 285–286
Been/being, 395–396
Body of paragraph. *See also* Paragraphs
  developing ideas for, 18–20
  topic sentence and, 12–14
  using examples in, 33–36
Brainstorming
  examples of, 6–7
  explanation of, 6
  paragraph bodies, 19
  paragraph topics, 15
Buy/by, 396–397

Can/could, 164–165
Capitalization
  in quotations, 363–366
  rules of, 332–334
Clauses
  nonrestrictive relative, 222–224
  restrictive relative, 221–222
Clustering
  explanation of, 7–9
  paragraph topics, 15
Coherence, in paragraphs, 36–40
Collective nouns, 256–258
Comma splice, 197–202
Commas
  for addresses (location), 347–349
  for appositives, 344–345
  for coordination and subordination, 181, 182, 349–350
  for dates, 346–347
  for direct address, 343–344
  with introductory phrases, 341–342
  with items in series, 340–341
  for parenthetical expressions, 345–346
  in quotations, 363–366
Comparatives
  of adjectives and adverbs, 280–283, 285–286
  bad/badly, 285–286
  good/well, 285–286
Comparisons, pronouns in, 268–270
Complete verbs
  spotting, 61–64
  writing sentences with, 68–71

Concise writing, 26–28
Conjunctions
  coordinating, 181–185
  defining, 181, 434
  subordinating, 187–195
Conjunctive adverbs
  defining and using, 211–213, 217
  list of common, 212
  punctuating, 214–216
Consistency
  in person, 312–315
  in tense, 307–311
Consonants
  defining, 376
  doubling final, 377–380
  identifying vowels and, 376–377
  before suffixes, 381
Contractions
  apostrophes used for, 353–355
  and look-alikes/sound-alikes, 398–400, 410–411, 420–424
  negative verb forms as, 91–92, 119–120, 170–172
Coordinating conjunctions
  commas for, 181, 182, 349–350
  defined, 181
  use of, 181–185, 434
Coordination
  with conjunctive adverbs, 211–217
  with coordinating conjunctions, 181–185. *See also* Coordinating conjunctions
  with semicolons, 206–209

-d/-ed verb endings, 112–113, 115, 125, 432
Dates, commas for, 346–347
Demonstrative adjectives, 286–287
Descriptive words
  adjectives as, 144–149, 275–287, 433
  adverbs as, 211–217, 275–286, 433
  appositives as, 344–345
  linking verbs as, 60–61, 144–148
Direct address, commas for, 343–344
Direct quotations
  defining, 362–363
  ending direct, 366–368

506

Index 507

punctuating simple direct, 363–364
punctuating split, 364–366
Double negatives, 170–172
Draft writing
final, 28–31
first, 23, 29

-e, dropping or keeping final, 381–382
-ed/-d verb endings, 112–113, 115, 125
ei/ie spelling, 385–387
-es
added to nouns and verbs, 384–385
added to singular subjects, 84
Exact language, 25–26
Examples, used in paragraph writing, 33–36
Except/accept, 394–395
Exclamation points
at end of sentences, 330
in quotations, 366

Final drafts, 28–31
Fine/find, 397–398
First drafts, 23, 29
Fixed-form helping verbs
can and could, 164–165
defining and spotting, 161–162
list of, 162
revising double negatives and, 170–172
using, 162–163
will and would, 166–167
writing infinitives and, 167–169
Focused freewriting, 5–6
Fragments. See Sentence fragments
Freewriting
explanation of, 4
focused, 5–6
guidelines for, 4–5
paragraph topics, 15

Good/better/best, 285–286
Good/well, 279–280

Helping verbs
explanation of, 62
fixed-form, 161–172
with passive voice, 140–144
with past participles, 69, 125, 128
with present participles, 69
with progressive tense, 153, 154, 158
Hyphenated nouns, 243

ie/ei spelling, 385–387
In/on, 292–293
Incomplete verbs, 68
Indefinite pronouns, 253–256
Indirect quotations, 362–363
Infinitives, 167–169, 433
-ing modifiers, 226–229
-ng verb form. See Present participles
explanation of, 69
with irregular verbs, 115
in progressive tenses, 151–159
Intensive pronouns, 271–272
Interjections, 434
Introductory phrases, 341–342

Irregular verbs
list of, 114–115, 128–130
past participles of, 128–135, 432
past tense of, 114–117, 128–130
present tense of, 86–92
It/its, 398–400

Journal keeping, 9–10

Know/knew/no/new, 400–401

Like, 294
Linking verbs
defining and spotting, 60–61, 432
list of common, 60
with past participles, 144–145, 148
Look-alikes/sound-alikes. See also Spelling
Look-alikes/sound-alikes
a/an/and, 392–394
accept/except, 394–395
been/being, 395–396
buy/by, 396–397
fine/find, 397–398
it/its, 398–400
know/knew/no/new, 400–401
lose/loose, 402–403
mine/mind, 403–404
past/passed, 404–405
quiet/quit/quite, 405–406
rise/raise, 406–407
sit/set, 408–409
suppose/supposed, 409–410
their/there/they're, 410–411
then/than, 412–413
thought/taught, 413–414
threw/through, 414–415
to/too/two, 415–417
use/used, 417–419
weather/whether, 419–420
where/were/we're, 420–421
whose/who's, 422
your/you're, 423–424
Lose/loose, 402–403
-ly, adverbs ending with, 276, 277

Mapping. See Clustering
Mine/mind, 403–404
Modifiers
-ing, 226–229
parenthetical expressions as, 345–346

Negatives, revising double, 170–172
New/no/know/knew, 400–401
Nonrestrictive relative clauses, 222–224
Not
to be with, 119–120
to do with, 91–92
Nouns
capitalization of, 332–334
collective, 256–258
defining, 241, 431
hyphenated, 243
plural, 241–246
as sentence subjects, 93
signal words to identify, 244–245
signal words with of, 246–247
singular, 241–245

Objective case, 264, 266, 268
Objects
of prepositions, 56, 291
pronouns as, 263, 264, 268
Of, signal words with, 246–247
On/in, 292–293
Or, pronouns joined by, 266–268
Order of importance, in paragraphs, 39–40

Paragraphs
body of, 12–14, 18–20, 33–36
brainstorming ideas for, 19
explanation of, 11–12
grouping ideas in, 22–23, 36–40
limiting topic for, 14–15
proofreading, 30–31
selecting and dropping ideas for, 21–22, 45–46
topic sentence for, 12–18, 45
turning assignments into, 41–43
writing and revising, 23–28, 31
writing final draft for, 28–31
Parallelism
defining and writing, 316–321
used for special writing effects, 321–322
Parenthetical expressions, 345–346
Passive voice, 140–144
Past participles
defining, 69, 124–125, 432
of irregular verbs, 115, 128–135
in passive voice, 140–144
in past perfect tense, 138–140
in present perfect tense, 136–138
of regular verbs, 125–127
used as adjectives, 144–149
Past/passed, 404–405
Past perfect tense, 138–140
Past progressive tense
avoiding incomplete, 158–159
defining and writing, 154–156
using, 156–158
Past tense
of to be, 118–120
compared to present progressive tense, 154
irregular verbs in, 114–117
regular verbs in, 110–113
Perfect tenses
past, 138–140
present, 136–138
Periods
at end of sentences, 329
in quotations, 363–366
Person, consistency in, 312–315
Phrases
introductory, 341–342
prepositional, 56–57, 100–101, 291
Plural nouns
defining, 241–244
following one of the or each of the, 246
signal words to identify, 244–245
Plural subjects
explanation of, 54
pronouns as, 84–95
Possession
apostrophes to show, 355–360

defining, 355
pronouns in, 265–266
pronouns that show, 263, 265–266
shown in look-alikes/sound-alikes, 399, 403, 410, 422, 423
Prepositional phrases
explanation of, 56–57, 291, 433
finding subject of sentences that contain, 100–101
Prepositions
defining, 56, 290–292, 433
in/on for place, 293
in/on for time, 292–293
like, 294
list of common, 57, 290
object of, 56, 291
words requiring certain, 294–297
Present participles
explanation of, 69, 432
of irregular verbs, 115
Present perfect tense, 136–138
Present progressive tense
avoiding incomplete, 158–159
defining and writing, 151–153
using, 156–158
Present tense
of *to be*, 86–88
changing subjects to pronouns in, 93–95
compared to present progressive tense, 152
defining agreement in, 83–86
of *to do*, 90–92
of *to have*, 88–90
practice in agreement in, 95–99
special problems in agreement in, 99–107
Progressive tenses
avoiding incomplete, 158–159
past, 154–156
present, 151–153
using, 156–158
Pronouns
changing subjects to, 93–95
and collective nouns, 256–258
in comparisons, 268–270
and consistence in person, 312–315
defining, 250–253, 431–432
indefinite, 253–256
intensive, 271–272
joined by *and* or *or*, 266–268
referring to special singular constructions, 259–261
reflexive, 271–272
relative, 105–107, 218–224
with *-self* and *-selves*, 271–272
as subjects, objects, and possessives, 263–266, 268, 432
using *who*, *which*, or *that* as relative, 105–107, 219, 221–224
vague and repetitious, 261–263
Proofreading, 30–31
Punctuation. *See also specific forms of punctuation*
at beginning and ending of sentences, 329–331
of quotations, 363–368
of relative pronouns, 221–224
of subordinating conjunctions, 191–195

Question marks
at end of sentences, 329
in quotations, 366, 367
Questions
choosing correct verb in, 104–105
in quotations, 366, 367
Quiet/quit/quite, 405–406
Quotation marks, 363–368
Quotations
defining direct and indirect, 362–363
ending direct, 366–368
punctuating simple direct, 363–364
punctuating split, 364–366

Raise/rise, 406–407
Reflexive pronouns, 271–272
Regular verbs
past participles of, 125–127
in past tense, 110–113
Relative clauses
nonrestrictive, 222–224
restrictive, 221–222
Relative pronouns. *See also* Pronouns
defining and using, 218–221
using *who*, *which*, or *that* as, 105–107, 219, 221–224
Restrictive relative clauses, 221–222
Revising paragraphs
for concise language, 26–28
for exact language, 25–26
need for, 23
for unity, 23–24
Rise/raise, 406–407
Run-ons, 197–202

-s
added to nouns and verbs, 384–385
added to singular subjects, 84
apostrophes to show possession in words that don't end in, 355–357
apostrophes to show possession in words that end in, 357–360
-self/-selves, 271–272
Semicolons
defining and using, 207–209
used with conjunctive adverbs, 214–217
Sentence fragments
completing thoughts to avoid, 72–76
writing sentences with complete verbs to avoid, 68–71
writing sentences with subjects and verbs to avoid, 66–68
Sentences
with complete verbs, 68–71
completing thoughts in, 72–75
defining, 51
parallelism in, 316–323
punctuation beginning and ending, 329–331
subjects in, 51–54
written with subjects and verbs, 66–68
Series, commas after items in, 340–341
Set/sit, 408–409
Signal words, 244–247
Singular nouns
defining, 241–244

signal words to identify, 244–245
Singular subjects. *See also* Subjects
adding *-s* or *-es* to, 84
explanation of, 54
spotting special, 101–102
Sit/set, 408–409
Space order, in paragraphs, 38–39
Spelling. *See also* Look-alikes/sound-alikes
adding *-s* or *-es*, 384–385
changing or keeping final *-y*, 382–384
choosing *ie* or *ei*, 385–387
doubling final consonant, 377–380
dropping or keeping final *e*, 381–382
identifying vowels and consonants, 376–377
improving your, 375–376
Subjective case, 263, 264, 268
Subjects
adding *-s* or *-es* to singular, 84
changed to pronouns, 93–95
defining and spotting, 51–54
pronouns as, 263, 264
singular and plural, 54–56
spotting special singular, 101–102
verb agreement with, 99–101
writing sentences with, 66–68
Subordinating conjunctions
commas for, 349–350
defining and using, 187–190, 434
list of, 189
punctuating, 191–195
Subordination, 181, 182, 349–350
Suffixes
-s/-es, 384–385
after final *e*, 381–382
after final *y*, 382–384
beginning with consonants, 381–382
beginning with vowels, 377–382
consonants before, 381
to word ending in *-y*, 382–384
Superlatives
with adverbs and adjectives, 283–286
with *bad/badly*, 285–286
with *good/well*, 279–280
with *most*, 283–285
Suppose/supposed, 409–410
Syllables, in spelling, 377–380

Taught/thought, 413–414
Tense. *See also specific tenses*
consistency in, 307–311
past, 110–120, 154
past perfect, 138–140
past progressive, 154–159
present, 86–107, 152
present perfect, 136–138
present progressive, 151–159
That
as demonstrative adjective, 286–287
as relative pronoun, 105–107, 219, 221–224
Their/there/they're, 410–411
Then/than, 412–413
There, to begin sentence, 102–104

These/those, 286–287
This/that, 286–287
Thought/taught, 413–414
Threw/through, 414–415
Time order, in paragraphs, 36–38
To be
    been/being, 395–396
    as helping verb, 69
    with *not*, 119–120
    past participle with forms of, 140, 144–145
    past tense of, 118–120
    present tense of, 86–88, 432
    in progressive tenses, 151–159
To do
    with *not*, 91–92
    present tense of, 90–92
To have
    as helping verb, 69, 124–127, 131, 132
    in past perfect tense, 138–140
    in present perfect tense, 136–138
    in present tense, 88–90
To/too/two, 415–417
Topic sentences
    and body of paragraph, 12–14
    choosing, 45
    explanation of, 11–12
    writing, 15–18
Topics, limiting, 14–15

Transitional expressions, conjunctive adverbs as, 212
Two/to/too, 415–417

Unity, revising paragraphs for, 23–24
Use/used, 417–419

Verbs. *See also* Helping verbs; Irregular verbs; *specific verbs*
    with *-es/-s*, 384–385
    action, 58–59, 432
    with active voice, 140–141
    agreement with subjects, 93–95
    defining and spotting, 58–59
    fixed-form helping, 161–169
    helping, 62, 69, 125, 128, 153, 154, 158, 161–172
    incomplete, 68
    infinitives of, 167–169, 433
    irregular, 114–117, 128–135
    linking, 60–61, 144–145, 148, 432
    of more than one word, 61–64
    negative forms of, 91–92, 119–120, 170–172
    objects of, 264
    overview of, 432–433
    with passive voice, 140–144
    past participles of, 125–135
    past perfect tense of, 138–140
    past tense of, 114–117
    in questions, 104–105
    regular, 110–113, 125–127
    and sentence fragments, 66–76
    and tense consistency, 307–309
    writing sentences with, 66–68, 68–71
Voice, active and passive, 140–144
Vowels
    defining, 376–377
    suffixes beginning with, 377–382

Weather/whether, 419–420
Were/where/we're, 420–421
Which, as relative pronoun, 105–107, 219, 221–224
Who, as relative pronoun, 105–107, 219, 221–224
Whose/who's, 422
Will/would, 166–167
Writing
    avoidance of, 3
    concise, 26–28
    techniques to improve, 43
    techniques used to start, 10. *See also* Brainstorming; Clustering; Freewriting; Journal keeping

-y, changing or keeping final, 382–384
Your/you're, 423–424

Index to the Readings

Abbey, Edward, 477–481
Alvarez, Julia, 458–459
Anderson, Sherwood, 486–490
Angelou, Maya, 444–448

Barry, Dave, 471–473
Buscaglia, Leo, 448–451

Desert Kin (Abbey), 477–481
Discovery of a Father (Anderson), 486–490

For a Parent, There's No Language Dilemma (Veciana-Suarez), 494–497
Forever (Klagsbrun), 468–470
Four Directions (Tan), 491–494
Friends of Dirt, Unite! (Lovejoy), 484–486

Garson, Barbara, 481–484
Giago, Tim, 474–477
The Gift (Milloy), 462–465

Goodman, Ellen, 438–441
Gzowski, Peter, 460–462

Homeless (Quindlen), 452–454
A Homemade Education (Malcolm X), 441–444
Hughes, Langston, 465–468

I Hope the Redskins Lose (Giago), 474–477

Kildahl, John P., 454–457
Klagsbrun, Francine, 468–470

Lovejoy, Ann, 484–486

Malcolm X, 441–444
Martorano, Joseph T., 454–457
Milloy, Courtland, 462–465
Mrs. Flowers (Angelou), 444–448

Papa, the Teacher (Buscaglia), 448–451

People and Their Machines and Vice Versa (Gzowski), 460–462
Perfume (Garson), 481–484

Quindlen, Anna, 452–454

Salvation (Hughes), 465–468
Say Yes to Yourself (Martorano & Kildahl), 454–457
Sports Nuts (Barry), 471–473

Tan, Amy, 491–494

Veciana-Suarez, Ana, 494–497

Women Are Missing from Newspaper Pages (Goodman), 438–441

Yolanda (Alvarez), 458–459

Commonly Misspelled Words

1. across
2. address
3. answer
4. argument
5. athlete
6. beginning
7. behavior
8. calendar
9. career
10. conscience
11. crowded
12. definite
13. describe
14. desperate
15. different
16. disappoint
17. disapprove
18. doesn't
19. eighth
20. embarrass
21. environment
22. exaggerate
23. familiar
24. finally
25. government
26. grammar
27. height
28. illegal
29. immediately
30. important
31. integration
32. intelligent
33. interest
34. interfere
35. jewelry
36. judgment
37. knowledge
38. maintain
39. mathematics
40. meant
41. necessary
42. nervous
43. occasion
44. opinion
45. optimist
46. particular
47. perform
48. perhaps
49. personnel
50. possess
51. possible
53. prefer
53. prejudice
54. privilege
55. probably
56. psychology
57. pursue
58. reference
59. rhythm
60. ridiculous
61. separate
62. similar
63. since
64. speech
65. strength
66. success
67. surprise
68. taught
69. temperature
70. thorough
71. thought
72. tired
73. until
74. weight
75. written